The Great White Brotherhood in the Culture, History, and Religion of America reveals the little-known role of the masters of wisdom who work together with their chelas to fulfill the cosmic destiny of the millions of souls evolving on the planet earth.

This book is the record of a special event: a four-day conference held at the base of Mount Shasta, an ancient focus of the Great White Brotherhood. Over twenty-three hundred devotees journeyed to "Shasta 1975 — A Conference for Spiritual Freedom" to partake of the light of the Brotherhood in dictations, lectures, mantras, and meditations. For many it was *the* event of the decade.

In reading these pages, may you experience soul communion with the ascended masters and discover the path to your immortal destiny.

The culture, the history, and the religion of America is a phenomenon of the Great White Brotherhood. For by the unseen hand and the very specific guidance of the ascended masters, America—the heart, the mind, the soul of a world—was born. America is the place of the rise of the feminine potential of man and woman. It is the place of creativity—aspiration and inspiration engendering the rise of the God consciousness in all. It is the place where freedom of religion, freedom of speech, freedom of the press, and freedom to assemble provide the foundation for the individual pursuit of cosmic consciousness.

RAINBOW BRIDGE
636 Blossom Hill Rd.
San Jose, CA 95123
[408] 972-8290

THE GREAT WHITE BROTHERHOOD

BROTHERHOOD

in the Culture, History and Religion of America

Teachings of the Ascended Masters given to

ELIZABETH CLARE PROPHET

SUMMIT UNIVERSITY 🌀 PRESS®

The Great White Brotherhood
in the Culture, History and Religion of America
Teachings of the Ascended Masters
given to Elizabeth Clare Prophet

Library of Congress Catalog Card Number: 76-7635
International Standard Book Number: 0-916766-16-0

This book is set in 11 point Garamond with 1 point lead.
Printed in the United States of America
First Printing 1976. Second Printing 1978. Third Printing 1983
Fourth Printing 1985. Fifth Printing 1987

Acknowledgment: To the Philosophical Research Society, Inc.
for permission to reprint chapter 14 of *The Secret Destiny of America*
by Manly Palmer Hall.

For information on the magnificent art of Nicholas Roerich, write
Nicholas Roerich Museum, 319 West 107th St., New York, NY 10025.

Cover: *Star of the Hero,* a painting by Nicholas Roerich.

SUMMIT UNIVERSITY 🌑 PRESS®

In the name of Mary the Mother

and her son, Jesus the Christ,

we dedicate this book to Saint Germain,

the Great Teacher of the Aquarian age.

The flame of the Christ consciousness is the one flame that rises as a fountain of light, a tribute to all peoples and all nations who have come to this soil and this continent for the great gathering of the elect—for that time in history when, by the power of the spoken Word, ascended masters, hierarchies of light, should talk with mankind again and walk with mankind and prepare the way for the Second Coming of the Christed One in the hearts of all mankind. This is the destiny of America: to set forth that City Foursquare that is the foundation of the new order of the ages, the order of freedom, the order of the Aquarian age. And from that square the pyramid of life does rise. It remains for a people fervent in devotion to the flame to place the capstone on the pyramid of this civilization wrought by man in God and God in man.

—Godfre

INTRODUCTION

From its discovery in 1492, America—her culture, her history, and her religion—has been carved out of the lines of a cosmic destiny. Not that any man or any nation can be considered the center of a universe—but that the purpose to which that man and that nation are called may affect the destiny of millions of souls in this and other systems of worlds.

As Jesus the Christ was ordained to demonstrate the example of the Christ consciousness which all must bear and as Gautama the Buddha was called to illustrate the path of the Buddha which all must one day become, so America was chosen by the hierarchy of the cosmos known as the Great White Brotherhood* to be that nation where the blueprint of the divine mandala of each and every nation would be fulfilled.

America's place in the destiny of the cosmos comes to the fore under the influence of the hierarchy of Aquarius. It is the place where the Cosmic Virgin enshrines the flame of freedom not in temples made with hands, but upon the altar of the hearts of a people. Drawn from every nation, from every lifewave and evolution, the American people are chosen as the standard-bearers of an age—not by the favoritism of an anthropomorphic God, but

*The Great White Brotherhood is a spiritual order of hierarchy, an organization of ascended masters united for the highest purposes of God in man as set forth by Jesus the Christ, Gautama Buddha, and other World Teachers. The word "white" refers not to race, but to the white light of the Christ that surrounds the saints and sages of all ages who have risen from every nation to be counted among the immortals.

by the choice of a free will God-ordained. The elect of the Lord are those who elect to be the instruments of the Lord.

And so America is the Motherland come again. Founded by the Brotherhood on the matrix of the original thirteen of Christ and his apostles, it is the fulfillment of the destinies of the peoples of Lemuria and Atlantis, of ancient Greece and Rome, of the golden ages of China and India, of Egypt and Europe. To America the pilgrims of freedom have marched. Over four centuries they have journeyed to the place prepared in the wilderness for the coming of the Woman clothed with the Sun and the birth of her Divine Manchild.

Jesus and Gautama set the pattern for the mastery of the light of God within the heart and the mind; and they both said, "What I have done you can also do."[1] Following in the way of the Christ and the Buddha, we come to the place where the soul of man and woman is reborn. We come to the birth of a nation conceived in liberty. The conception of America is truly a cosmic conception, for it is the place where the souls of a "peculiar people"[2] will not rest until they have attained the cosmic consciousness that is the essence of Mother.

The culture, the history, and the religion of America is a phenomenon of the Great White Brotherhood. For by the unseen hand and the very specific guidance of the ascended masters, America—the heart, the mind, the soul of a world—was born. America is the place of the rise of the feminine potential of man and woman. It is the place of creativity—aspiration and inspiration engendering the rise of the God consciousness in all. It is the place where freedom of religion, freedom of speech, freedom of the press, and freedom to assemble provide the foundation for the individual pursuit of cosmic consciousness.

Because that consciousness can be attained only through the disciplines and the initiations of the Christ and the Buddha, because it can be attained only when the soul is truly free to follow the course of its inner destiny, America was founded by the ascended masters as a place secure, protected—a land of abundant resources and opportunity, a land where the forum of the greatest souls of the ages would one day produce the greatest science and the greatest religion of all time and space.

In order for the soul to attain cosmic consciousness, it must become the Mother. Where there is life, where there is joy, where there is self-discipline in creativity, where there is love and freedom, there is the Mother ray activating the soul to self-awareness. There is the Mother ray giving birth to the Christ and the Buddha that is the real identity of every man, woman, and child.

America is an experiment of the Great White Brotherhood. No psychological or astrological predictions determine her fate. There is nothing automatic about the fulfillment of a cosmic destiny. America is simply opportunity, the gift of freedom, like the gift of free will, in the hands and the hearts of a peculiar people. If indeed there is to be a cosmic destiny forged and won on this continent, it will be because this people have made the work of the ages their own.

Hard work has brought us to this moment in our history and hard work will bring us to the sealing of the capstone in the pyramid of our life. Jesus our Master said, "The Father worketh hitherto, and I work";[3] and John Kennedy, who caught the vision of a people free to outpicture their God-identity in every walk of life, said, "Here on earth God's work must truly be our own."

The masters of the Great White Brotherhood are people like you and me who have lived and worked among us and who, by congruency with the inner blueprint of life, have become one with the Great Spirit whom the first Americans knew well, whom the Israelites identified as the sacred fire of the I AM THAT I AM and experienced as "a pillar of fire by night and a pillar of a cloud by day."[4] The ascended masters are the graduates cum laude of every culture and every history and every religion. They are Americans in the cosmic sense, for they have consecrated consciousness to Christ, to Buddha, and to Mother. They live and move among us; yet to know them, we must become like them.

These masters from the near and distant past are the saints and the sages whose lives are marked by self-sacrifice on behalf of humanity, humility before the inner Presence, obedience to the cosmic code, and an overwhelming love for all life. They have inspired every aspect of achievement in our culture, in the arts and sciences, in our government and our economy, in education, and in that indomitable spirit of freedom that yet holds the courage to dream the dream of love, of truth, and of liberty for all mankind.

The ascended masters are the sponsors of a new race, a new lifewave, and a new age of self-discovery, of self-transformation which can be born only in the hearts of those who yet believe in the miracle of life unfolding life. Americans are a unique people who have the courage to walk the path of perfecting the self while yet looking at their imperfections squarely with balance and maturity. This ability to sustain the vision in the midst of the battle of life is the gift of opportunity and freedom which America gives to the world and to the cosmos.

If America can prove the law that is the foundation of her life, it will mean that every nation and every world and every system of worlds can do the same. Thus by individual effort do men and nations carve a cosmic destiny.

ELIZABETH CLARE PROPHET
Messenger for
the Great White Brotherhood

Retreat of the Resurrection Spiral
Colorado Springs, Colorado

CONTENTS

Cave of Symbols
Gemini 1975

To All Who Love Freedom, Hail!

A conference for spiritual freedom is truly the need of the hour. For while the defenses of material freedom are wasting away on the boundaries of a planet, in the souls of a people a true spiritual freedom must be wrought.

I come as the Hierarch of the Aquarian Age and I come as the humble servant of the light of freedom within you. To all who would preserve that freedom, both spiritually and materially, I say, Welcome to Shasta 1975! I am your host for four days of communion in the Lord's Spirit, and I am also the host of many masterful beings who have ascended into the light of freedom who are gathering for this communion of devotees.

The program includes dictations from the heavenly hosts to be given through the messenger of the Great White Brotherhood, Elizabeth Clare Prophet, whom I sponsored long ago to be the mouthpiece of hierarchy in this period of transition from Pisces to Aquarius. Lectures by the messenger will set forth the principles of cosmic law which must be practiced and protected if this nation and any nation are to endure in the flame of freedom. Masters and cosmic beings will speak to humanity to define universal truth and its immediate application to world dilemma.

To all who cherish liberty and the dream of freedom at home and in the world community, to all who would defend cosmic consciousness as the right of every man, woman, and child, again I say, Welcome to Shasta 1975! I shall see you there. May you also be blessed with the vision of the Lord's hosts.

In the flame I remain

Saint Germain

1

SONGS AND MANTRAS OF FREEDOM
Freedom in the Heart, the Mind, the Soul

A Lecture by Elizabeth Clare Prophet

The heavens declare the glory of God; and the firmament
sheweth his handywork. Day unto day uttereth speech, and night
unto night sheweth knowledge. There is no speech nor language,
where their voice is not heard. Their line is gone out through all
the earth, and their words to the end of the world. In them hath he
set a tabernacle for the sun. . . .[1]

The Great White Brotherhood Saluteth Thee

The Great White Brotherhood saluteth thee, and we welcome
you to Shasta 1975. Thank you for coming at this hour of the Holy
Spirit to join with us in mantras of freedom—freedom in the
heart, the mind, and the soul.

We come together in the Word. We come together in the
power, the wisdom, the love of the Logos. Our hearts are filled
with rejoicing in the oneness of our flame. As we commune in the
oneness of that flame, may we intone together the sacred Word
that came from the beginning, that fulfills unto the ending, the
Word that intones consciousness, being, wholeness. Let us give
together the sacred AUM. [Audience chants "AUM" three times.]

O eternal God within the heart of all life, O flame, living fire,
breathing awareness of all that we are, of all that thou art, we
salute life! We salute wholeness! And we come together in thy
flame, in thy name, to be thy flame. Make us one, even as we are

one. So let our oneness flow as the crystal-clear waters of life and the water of the living Word. Let our oneness be the rejoicing of the atoms of God coalescing to immortal destiny. Our prayer is joy. Our prayer is communion. Our prayer is love, O God!

We Are One

The rejoicing in the heart of the flame of oneness can also be intoned by a mantra that we love to give, the simple statement of the law of being, "We are one." As we share the oneness of the flame, we realize that all separation, all that has kept us apart, comes to naught as we commune in the living flame, in the presence of nature, in the presence of the Great White Brotherhood.

The sacred word AUM releases the frequency of the Word, the same Word that went forth as the origin of creation. The ancients knew the power of the Word. Civilizations have risen and fallen in the power of the spoken Word. The mantras of the East, sacred intonations, have come down for hundreds of thousands of years from priests and priestesses of Lemuria. And all that comes forth comes out of the sacred AUM.

We follow the ray of the sun back to the fiery core. We follow the light within the heart back to the sun of the Presence. When we affirm the word AUM, we affirm true being. To affirm that being is to become that being. To declare that being is to know who I AM. The sacred AUM that we give is the indestructible sound. It is the immensity. Out of the AUM comes our oneness.

May we unite in the power of the spoken Word to give the affirmation "We are one," as though tracing a sunbeam back to the sun of the AUM. Let us simply say together, "We are one." [Audience repeats "We are one" eight times.] May we give this chant as a song of affirmation of oneness. [Audience sings: "We are one, we are one, we are one! We are one, we are one, we are one!" ten times and chants "AUM" three times.]

AUM

The sound of the Word—the Word of the sound. It is a Sanskrit word. It means "I bow, I agree, I accept." AUM! I accept my immortal destiny. I accept my reason for being. I accept my responsibility to be. AUM. I accept the components of my reality. I accept the flame as God within me.

AUM is the most abstract and yet the most concrete symbol of divinity. It is an instrument of self-realization. It is yours to keep. It is released from your heart by the breath of God. No mechanical instrument, no machine, not the might of civilization can equal the AUM. Only you can intone the AUM, because you are God in manifestation. Out of this one eternal syllable all that exists comes forth. All that comes forth returns to the AUM.

The AUM is spelled *A-U-M,* and each of the letters stands for a component of our divinity. And each letter is intended to be sounded separately. [Messenger chants "AUM."] When we blend the trinity, we intone simply the AUM. Past, present, and future form the Trinity. We are all that we are as past, as present, as future realization of the AUM. In the East the Hindus refer to the Trinity as Brahma, Vishnu, and Siva; and in the West—Father, Son, and Holy Spirit. The concept is the same.

The *A* comes forth from Alpha as the initiator, the creator, the origin of spirals of consciousness, the origin of being. It is the thrust of power. The *M* is the *Om* of Omega, the conclusion, the integrator and the disintegrator of form and formlessness. The positive and negative polarities of being are spoken. From the *A* to the *Om,* all of the vastness of creation is contained. And the *U* in the center is you, the Real Self, the Anointed One, the Christed One, the Buddha of the light—you in universal manifestation, in particular manifestation, the Trinity. This is the power of preservation, of concentration, of cohesion as identity. From the origin of the Father to the ultimate of the Mother, we are embraced as the identity of their love. Let us intone the AUM once again. [Audience chants "AUM" three times.]

Throughout this conference we will use the AUM at various points for the raising of all energies into the center of God-awareness. The AUM is used for going into the fiery core of being. The fiery core that is symbolized in the T'ai chi, that S symbol of the white and the black—that white fiery core is in your heart as the Father-Mother God. Each time we intone the AUM, we are sending energy back from the periphery of creation to the center. We are sending signals unto God that we are coming Home. And our Home is the AUM.

This path of moving toward the center of the cosmos is a path that all of creation is taking as we cycle back to the origin, back to the source. All of life, all of cosmos, stars and galaxies are cycling to the center, into the inbreath of the white-fire core. For thousands of years, the path of going back to the center has been outlined by teachers of the Far East. Systems complex and simple have been set forth and followed, taught by teachers to their disciples. This has been the path of the East. In the West we are taught how to go forth from the center, and so the West is given a religion and a teaching whereby the fiery core of being can burst forth and be released to fulfill the cycle of the inbreath and the outbreath.

I AM THAT I AM

Thousands of years ago, the initiation of this action of the law in the East was given unto Moses, and we still hold that fire and that legacy as when Moses saw the fire of the core of his own being objectified in the bush that was aflame that was not consumed.[2] And the voice out of the bush declared Self-awareness, being that proceeded from the fiery core and declared our God-identity, "I AM WHO I AM." In the Egyptian, "NUK PA NUK." "And Moses said unto God, Behold, when I come unto the children of Israel, and shall say unto them, The God of your fathers hath sent me unto you; and they shall say to me, What is his name? what shall I say unto them? And God said unto Moses, I AM THAT I AM: and he said, Thus shalt thou say unto the children of Israel, I AM hath sent me unto you."[3]

So I say to you this day, "I AM hath sent me unto you." And you can say to me, "I AM hath sent me unto you." The glory, the rejoicing of being sent by the Lord, sent out from the fiery core, thrust from the nest of creation, sent forth to be the I AM THAT I AM! May we repeat the words together as a mantra which the Lord God gave to Moses. This is a mantra of the children of Israel: "I AM hath sent me unto you." [Audience repeats, "I AM hath sent me unto you" three times.]

When we speak our mantras from the heart and we feel the flow of the intensity of the fire of the heart and we commune one to another in the response of love, we feel the swelling and the swirling of the flame that is our common light, our one light. The ascended masters of the Great White Brotherhood teach their chelas to go within to the fiery core, to dip into the fountain of light with the sacred AUM, to tarry there as Jesus did when he withdrew from the multitudes and went to a place set apart. And they teach us to come forth in the name of God—by that name "I AM THAT I AM."

Therefore, the cycle of the AUM and the I AM THAT I AM which we chant gives the alternating current of going within to the Father, coming out with the Mother. So the law that is written in the inward parts of man is the name of God written in the heart.[4] In living fire, *A-U-M* is written in your heart. It is written in the Sanskrit; it is written in the English; it is written in the tongues of angels. It is a kernel of light that speaks in every language.

For the Word goes forth and "the heavens declare the glory of God; and the firmament sheweth his handywork. Day unto day uttereth speech, and night unto night sheweth knowledge. There is no speech nor language, where their voice is not heard." This is the voice of the One from the inner heart speaking in the wilderness of the human consciousness, "Prepare ye the way of the Lord, make his paths straight."[5]

Out of Being We Go Forth: Unto Being We Return

We come together in this communion of light to prepare the way, the channels of being, to prepare the chakras, to prepare the vessels of consciousness, the vehicles of our four lower bodies, for the flow of the AUM and the flow of the I AM THAT I AM. And all else proceeds from that fiery core. And all that we speak and all that we say and all of our mantras and all of the dictations and the lectures—all comes forth from the AUM and the I AM THAT I AM. Out of being we go forth: unto being we return.

Let us think of ourselves in that barren country where Moses was. In the name of the I AM THAT I AM, let us travel back in *akasha*, in the records of time and space written upon the ethers; and let us stand at that point in time and space where Moses stood. Let us hear with the hearing of the ear the eternal sound of the Creator: I AM THAT I AM. Let each one commune within the heart, in the chamber of the heart, to hear the voice of God speaking. [Pause.] And now let us give answer unto the Lord of creation, the law of creation within our hearts: I AM THAT I AM. [Audience chants "I AM THAT I AM" six times.]

This fiat of being is the name of God. And more than a name, it contains the energy of creation. The first I AM stands for the letter *A* in the AUM. It is God as Alpha declaring, I AM. The THAT stands for the *U,* the transition, the passing of energy unto Omega in the second I AM—the trinity again expressed. It is God on high declaring, "I AM THAT I AM. I AM that manifestation below which I declare to be I AM." It is God above as a flame affirming that God is the flame within our hearts.

When we say, "I AM THAT I AM," we are not saying, "I AM THAT I AM." God within us is saying, "I AM THAT I AM." For who but God within has the authority to declare being, consciousness, Self-awareness? Can the clay speak? Can the vessel perform without the flame? Can the leopard change his spots?[6] Can the outer form be anything but subject unto the inner flame? Let us let God speak through us, "I AM THAT I AM." [Audience chants "I AM THAT I AM" three times.]

I and My Father Are One: I and My Mother Are One

The Father-Mother God is the center of all life—this plus-minus factor, this energy field, this core of consciousness that we call God. God is energy. God is the Alpha-to-Omega, the atom of selfhood. God is the fiery core of the atom, the seed, the idea of man, of planets, of stars and suns. The Father-Mother God is the nucleus of energy systems. You are an energy system. I am an energy system. We are born to conquer that energy. Wherever God is, life springs forth from the perfect union of Spirit (Alpha, Father) and Matter (Omega, Mother).

Declaring the oneness when we say, "We are one," we are saying that we are one with Father, with Mother, with the masculine-feminine principle of life which is the total center and circumference of being. Won't you rejoice with me to sing the mantra "I and my Father are one, I and my Mother are one"? There is the movement of consciousness into the fiery core, into the masculine polarity, into the feminine polarity.

You find as you sing that there coalesces around you the white sphere, the sphere out of which you were born, into which you return. It is the forcefield of the Great White Brotherhood. As you sing the mantra and give it the intonation of the Word, all of the energies of your being realign in the positive-negative polarity and you find yourself an electrode, a magnet for all energies of being that have strayed out of alignment to come into the polarity that is God. When we attain that perfect polarity, we become masters of life. This is the goal of the path that is set before us. [Audience sings: "I and my Father are one, I and my Mother are one! I and my Father are one, I and my Mother are one!" ten times.]

The Core of Consciousness

We come to establish and to reestablish the true nature of being. We find that being within as the fiery core that we have defined as the AUM and the I AM THAT I AM. Yet who can define—which means to circumscribe—consciousness that is God? We have touched upon the sacred Word that God has given of himself whereby, tracing the intonation of the sound and the joyous rays within our hearts, we might find the core of consciousness. When we touch the name of God, we touch the flame. When we touch the flame, we touch fohat—energy, light that will go forth in response to the spoken Word.

I would like to sing with you a fiat of freedom, song number 208, "Light, Set Me Free!" [7]

When we say, "Light, set me free!" we are speaking to that fiery core that is the AUM, that is the I AM THAT I AM, that is the masculine-feminine polarity of being, the Father-Mother God. And we are giving a fiat: Light, set me free! Light, set me free! Light, set me free! Now, light command, command, command my being to be free! Light, demand my being free! Light, expand within my being! Because this light I AM, I declare that I AM that light! I declare that I AM a being of violet fire! The violet fire proceeds out of the white-fire core. It is the flame of freedom which we will seize and run with in this class. And finally we sing, "I AM the purity God desires!"

In the AUM, in the I AM THAT I AM is God as being, as life desiring to be more being, life, consciousness. As we flow with that, as we impose our fiats of creation upon it, that fire expands from within. There is a certain expansion that takes place in meditation; but the mounting of the crescendo and the anchoring of the light in Matter, in molecules, in substance, in Terra, in earth must come forth through the power of the spoken Word. This is why man, the co-creator with God, is given the power to utter speech even as the Lord God utters speech. This is the sacred gift that enables us to make the spark of our divinity act in this plane. By the spoken Word we obey the fiat of the Lord "Take dominion over the earth! Take dominion over the earth!" Let us take dominion with this mantra of freedom, "Light, set me free!" [Audience sings song three times.]

Light, Set Me Free!

Light, set me free!
Light, set me free!
Light, set me free!
Light command, light command,
        light command, command, command!
Light demand, light demand, light demand, demand, demand!
Light expand, light expand, light expand, expand, expand!
Light I AM, light I AM, light I AM, I AM, I AM!
I AM a being of violet fire,
I AM the purity God desires.

Please rise. Place your attention upon your heart and let the fire of creation go forth from your heart to the heart of God. [Audience chants "AUM" three times and "I AM THAT I AM" three times.] Thank you and good morning.

July 3, 1975
9:00-10:00 A.M. P D T

2

WELCOME TO SHASTA 1975

A Lecture by Elizabeth Clare Prophet

Welcome to Shasta 1975! Welcome in the name of the entire Spirit of the Great White Brotherhood. Welcome in the name of your own Real Self. Welcome in the name of the angels who have escorted you here. Welcome in the name of the archangels and the Elohim who have brought together, by the fiat of creation, the mountains and the valleys and this focus of Shasta prepared in the mind of God aeons ago for the coming of the anointed ones to this place here below to celebrate the birth of the living flame. Welcome in the name of Saint Germain, master of the Aquarian cycle. Welcome in the name of Jesus the Christ and Gautama Buddha. Welcome in the name of all who have walked the path of overcoming and who have been victorious.

A Mandala in the Heart of the Holy Spirit

Shasta 1975 is a mandala in the heart of the Holy Spirit. Nineteen seventy-five is the year of the Holy Spirit marking the final quarter of the century in which the flame of the Holy Spirit is released to mankind. We will be talking about the quadrants of the centuries and how man realizes the flame within as aspects of the Creator's consciousness as the decades unfold cycles on the cosmic clock.

We come together at the midpoint of the year of the Holy Spirit to celebrate the converging of God in man, of the

Brotherhood ascended with the Brotherhood unascended. We come to this point already consecrated by God, by Elohim, by self-realized beings already consecrated to light and to the flame of the Mother to consecrate again, to reconsecrate by taking the flame from our hearts, thrusting that flame into the center of Shasta and saying, "I confirm, I accept, I AM that light that God has anchored here!"

How fortunate we are to be together in the tent of the Lord! How many people have gathered in tents through the ages! The children of Israel gathered in tents, and our forefathers and those in the deserts. In the tent we come, and we sit beneath the canopy of the Lord's hosts.

We feel the movement of the wind of the Holy Spirit. We feel the breath of angels. We feel the hovering and the brooding of the Brotherhood of Mount Shasta. We feel the brooding of our own Real Self making contact, making contact. The light below, the light above flowing together—this is our reason for coming.

We Come to Experience God

We come not to talk about God, but to experience God—not to talk about love, but to be love, to be truth. We come to experience flow. Too long have we talked about it. We come to be. And the test of knowledge, the test of our understanding, the test of the law, is our be-ness of that knowledge, that understanding, and that law. So we come together for four days to be in the flame, to be in the consciousness of the One. If you do not experience a new phase, a new awareness of selfhood, then make it known; for I would touch every heart.

The Brotherhood has sent me. As we said in our morning meeting, "I AM hath sent me unto you." The Brotherhood hath sent me to you. The Brotherhood hath sent you to me. We are sent to be one, because in our oneness is a great conflagration of the Spirit, of the energies of creation, of what we really are—that stuff that dreams and destinies are made of.[1] We come together because we are facets of the one flame. By blending our facets we know more of Infinity, more of Eternity, more of God.

The Quarterly Cycles of the Years

This is why the ascended masters, founding The Summit

Lighthouse, ordaining the messengers, set the cycle of quarterly conferences. So according to the cycles of the year, the flame of hierarchy, the torch of hierarchy, could be passed quarter by quarter according to the cycles of the release of that energy from the white-fire core of a cosmos which we call the Great Central Sun.

At winter solstice the impetus of the flame of fire goes forth. And it marks the highest aspect of mankind's consciousness as hierarchy comes in the New Year's class to anchor the pattern and the blueprint of life in what is called the etheric plane of the planet and also in what is referred to as the etheric body of mankind.

We carry that torch for that three-month cycle, and we come to the altar of the forces of spring and of the resurrection and of the rebirth when all that is in the blueprint in the etheric plane, at the white-fire core, must be stepped down to what is called the mental plane and the mental bodies of mankind. We lay the torch of winter solstice before the hierarchies of the resurrection and we take up the flame of vernal equinox. That is our Easter convocation in the new birth, renewing cells, renewing consciousness.

Now we come before the altar of hierarchy to lay down that torch in sacred ritual and to take up the torch of summer solstice. As we have carried in the winter the flame of the Father and in the spring the flame of the Son, so in summer we take the torch of the Divine Mother. This is the purpose of Shasta 1975—that in the year of the Holy Spirit, we blend our energies with the flow of that Spirit and we come to know the self as the feminine counterpart of God. We come to know the soul that is the negative polarity of the Godhead within us. We flow with the releases of the energies of the sun. Which sun? The Great Central Sun, the sun that is the white-fire core of being, the sun that we call the I AM Presence, the fire that was the I AM THAT I AM revealed to Moses.

As the cycles of the year turn again, we will take this torch that has become a fire infolding itself in our hearts, and we will lay it at the altar of solar hierarchies at the autumn equinox at our fall conference. We will then take up the final dispensation of the year—the action of the lowering into the physical plane of all of the energies that we have been given through the year.

The torch that we receive at Shasta during the summer is for the control of the waters of being, waters that flow as feeling, waters of the mind, water as *energy-in-motion*, emotion. We come in the name of all who have conquered water. We come to say with the Prince of Peace: "Peace, be still! Peace, be still! Peace, be still!"[2]

Four Days to Experience God in the Four Lower Bodies

The four days of the conference are planned after these cycles of the seasons and the turning of the energies and their release. And therefore, this day we celebrate the birth of the soul in the etheric body. This day is for the release of fire—fire that is a flame. The release comes forth through our mantras, through our lectures, through our dictations, through our communion. It is for the clearing of the channels of the etheric body, the clearing of the channels of the chakras, the rededication of the fiery blueprint of the soul.

When this pattern is set at the conclusion of this day, we will take that flame anchored in our hearts, we will place our bodies in the place of rest and be taken to the Retreat of the Brotherhood of Mount Shasta. This is a sacred experience accorded to those who will make the call. When you go to rest this night, if you will say to your own Real Self, to the I AM THAT I AM within: "Take me, Father-Mother God, into the arms of the Holy Spirit; transport my soul according to thy will into the Retreat of Mount Shasta," the guardian angels will accompany your soul to that focus and the cycle of training and initiation will continue through the night. Thus the twenty-four-hour cycle from nine this morning to nine tomorrow morning will be the fulfillment of the pattern of the mandala of the class and the renewing of your own divine plan.

Tomorrow morning, then, we take up the torch of renewing the energies in the mental plane, the mental body. All of the day's lectures and dictations will be dedicated to the anchoring of the mind of the Buddha, the mind of the Christ, the real mind that is the flame of the Creator within you. It will be for the purging of the mind of all unwanted debris, all knowledge that is useless, all that has been garnered even at subconscious levels that blocks the flow of the natural creative intelligence that flows for the liberation of the soul. At the conclusion of tomorrow's events, you can make the call again to be taken to the inner retreat; and the initiations will continue through the night for the clearing and the mastery of the mental body.

The third day of the class is consecrated to the victory of your control and mastery of the flow of energy-in-motion, of the water element, of feelings—control line by line as measured cadence of the Creator's harmony as released into this expanding cup. The feeling body is also called the desire body. It is a very powerful body; it blends with the ocean of the Mother's consciousness. When you contemplate the movement of the sea, you feel what the power of the emotional body can be when brought under the control of the Real Self, the real mind of the Creator within you. So the third day of the conference and the third conference of the year, which is Shasta 1975, are for the control of that flow.

The fourth day, the culmination of our communion, will be for the anchoring of all of this in the physical body and for the alignment of the four lower bodies with the flame within the heart. As we continue our lectures and our communion together, the pattern of the class will unfold and become more and more real to you. This is the pattern that I would give to you this morning so that you can understand that the hierarchies of light have a cosmic purpose in mind when they convoke chelas to a place, to a time, to a point where Infinity merges with the finite plane and we find ourselves in the oneness of life.

The Purpose to Which We Are Called

You have come in response to the call of hierarchy. You have responded because you have the inner contact. You have responded because your master has called you, whether it be Saint Germain or Jesus or Lord Buddha or the Master of Mount Shasta. You have come by the response of your soul and the yearning to be whole by God's grace. Hierarchy above and below, hierarchy which *you* are, will accomplish that purpose to which we are called.

We are forcefields of a living flame. Individually we represent the unique snowflake, the unique grid, a crisscrossing of fields of energy—energy flowing from starry bodies and suns beyond and galaxies we have never seen. We are, in truth, energy fields. We have come together and our auras blend; and all of the blending of these energy fields below as the body of God on earth, above as the body of ascended hosts, merges to fill in the pattern, the mandala that is the unique manifestation of hierarchy for this class, for this four-day spiral.

Morya says the mandala of the class "is like a snowflake— unique in its design, never seen before, never to appear again. . . . Each lecture that is scheduled and each dictation that is given fills in a portion of the mandala, and the application of the students intensifies the action of the sacred fire that can be released to the planet"[3]—not only to the planet, but to the solar system, to all lifewaves evolving therein, to the stars in our sector of the galaxy, to the entire galaxy and beyond.

You Are a Unique Point in the Mandala of Shasta 1975

You are a grid of light. You are a unique point in the mandala of Shasta 1975. Through your presence, through your flame, God will work miracles through this conference because God will anchor through you a portion of himself that he cannot anchor through anyone else in the entire cosmos. *You* are an individualization of the God flame. You are a crystallization of that flame. You are a snowflake. You are the wonder of wonders. You are the miracle of life. You are the creation, you are the Creator all in one. You are the most important of all creation. We must not allow any philosophy, any power whatsoever, to take from us this understanding of the uniqueness of the flame which we bring.

The ascended master Lanello—who walked with us until only a few short years ago as the first messenger in The Summit Lighthouse for the Great White Brotherhood as Mark L. Prophet, who made his ascension on February 26, 1973—has spoken to us of Shasta 1975. He has said:

I remain with you and with the Mother for a victorious 1975! And I place my focus at the peak of Mount
Shasta, and I place that electrode for the drawing of all
who are tied to my heart for the victory of the age. And
that mandala is set and it is secure. So now let us see what
the eager ones can accomplish for the conference of
Freedom 1975 in the heart of Shasta.[4]

You are the eager ones. You are the souls yearning to be free. You are the ones who sense the majesty of the mountain. And as you approached the mountain, your heart burst as a flame and you felt the response of the Brotherhood as you came. Closer and closer you made your way, and you knew there was something unique about Shasta, something special—*something.* "Something" is the Great White Brotherhood. "Something" is evolutions of sons and daughters of God who have consecrated the flame of life in this place.

Be the Mountain!

Are there inhabitants of Shasta? Are there retreats? Are there pathways into the earth connecting all retreats of the Great White Brotherhood? To all of these questions I must give a resounding Yes! Yes, Shasta is filled with souls of light. Yes, Shasta is the focal point of ancient Lemurians and priests and priestesses of the sacred fire. Yes, I say. Confirm it by your own attunement. Confirm it by your communion. Go within to the mountain and, as Hercules says, "be the mountain!...Let all rush, then, to meet the mountain!"[5] This is the word of Hercules, an Elohim of God.

Hercules is God's self-awareness as power, as the will of the flame. The Elohim are the Lords of Creation who formed the planets and the starry bodies in answer to the fiat of the Lord. Hercules, the Elohim of the First Ray, declares, "Let all rush, then, to meet the mountain!" This means, let your energies rush to the heart of the mountain. Feel them flow to the center! Feel them blend with the heart of a planet and a people who have been keeping the flame for us for thousands of years, waiting—waiting for the awakening. He says:

> Rush, then, to meet the mountain, the circular base rising to the center as the single peak—ancient volcano, Shasta, glistening in the morning light! So let the mountain you scale now be the mountain that rises from your own consciousness...a mountain not of karma, but of light, of God-momentum that you build cycle by cycle, raising up the energies of being and knowing "I AM the holy mountain of God....I AM the magic mountain of being."[6]

What does it profit us to come to the mountain that another has created? We must create our own mountain, our own mountain of light that begins in the fiery core of the AUM of the heart, of the I AM THAT I AM. We must be mountain builders.

Priests and priestesses of Mu raised Shasta as a tribute to the flame
of the Divine Mother even as we sit in meditation on the Mother
ray. And as the yogis of the East sit to raise the Goddess Kundalini,
so by raising that fire they raise the mountain of white-fire light.
Let us raise our mountain. Let us be the holy mountain of God. Let
us be that holy mountain. So Hercules says:

> Now be that mountain! Be Shasta!...Feel the
> pulsations of a mountain built upon the attainment of
> priests and priestesses of ancient Mu who raised that
> mountain as a tribute to the Mother flame.
>   ...O magic mountain of the Mother, be then the
> forcefield of our love that magnetizes mankind to that
> conference of spiritual freedom, Shasta 1975, marking
> the place where the Holy Spirit and Mother light
> born again draw the victors bold into the Aquarian spiral. [7]

Let us now meditate on being the mountain. Place your attention upon your heart; go into your heart as we meditate together.

Flow, O Fires of Our Hearts

Flow, O fires of our hearts! O my heart, flow unto the holy
mountain of love! Flow, O sacred fire! Gabriel Archangel, let flow
the fire of purity! We raise up within being and consciousness a
tribute unto the Creator of all life, unto the Father-Mother God,
unto the heart of a mountain and of the Brotherhood of that
mountain.

Flow, O fires of my heart! Flow unto Shasta! Flow, O my soul!
Flow into the crystal-clear water of life! Flow over the river of my
heart into the fountain of Shasta! O light of the I AM THAT I AM,
come forth in response to the fire of our hearts and return now that
flow of our hearts multiplied by the fiat of the Word, I AM THAT
I AM! We would be receptors of the mountain and the holy fire of
the mountain. We would be reflectors of the mountain and the
fire of the Mother within. We salute the Brotherhood. We salute
the eternal Spirit of Life. I AM THAT I AM!

July 3, 1975
10:36-11:14 A.M. P D T

The alchemy of freedom that begins within the soul of man and woman is a flame that burns on—a flame that will not be quenched. Inaugurating an Aquarian age of freedom is Saint Germain, master of the flame of freedom. He is the key figure in the history of the planet and in the founding of America as a nation where all mankind have the opportunity to be free. Freedom is not only a flame, but it is an identity—a consciousness. We will explore the fires of freedom as God's awareness of self-hood. We will talk about what it really means to be free and how to pursue freedom from karma, from the rounds of rebirth, from the limitations of time and space. We will discuss the illusions and confusions of a false freedom purveyed by the fallen ones as political, social, economic, and religious freedom.

FREEDOM IS A FLAME

A Lecture by Elizabeth Clare Prophet

What Is Spiritual Freedom?

We come to celebrate spiritual freedom. What is spiritual freedom? To define it we must know what freedom itself is. Then we will know what is spiritual freedom, what is material freedom, what is soul freedom, what is God freedom. What does it mean to be free? This is a question totally misunderstood by some, uncomprehended by others. A unique people upon the planet Terra have come to define freedom, to enshrine it here upon this land, to celebrate that flame. We come together for the cosmic purpose not only of defining freedom, not only of communing with freedom, but of becoming that flame of freedom. Each day of the four we will dedicate the flame of freedom to burst forth in another level of consciousness, in one of the four lower bodies of a planet and a people. We come then to the meaning of freedom as a flame at the etheric level.

Freedom begins within the soul of man, of woman. What is the soul? The soul is the living potential of God that demanded and therefore was accorded by Life the opportunity to go forth, to come out from the fiery core, to manifest an identity and an individuality. And therefore the soul was sent forth into the planes of Mater with the gift of free will. That is where the flame of freedom begins. It could not exist except as the gift from the Creator to the creation.

The gift of free will is not understood; for mankind have various reasons for determining that their fate is preordained,

whether by the stars or by a doctrine or a dogma or by their karma
or by their dharma. They do not recognize that energy fields are
the instrument of the Real Self. Whether these energy fields are
formed of our stars or of our karma or of our past or whatever, the
key factor in free will is that the soul is ordained to take the reins of
energy, of control of energy, to determine the fate of that energy
field.

The Responsibilities of Free Will

You are an energy field. Your soul was given the authority to
"take dominion over the earth."[1] (The "earth" means the
densification, the materialization, of the energies of God.) That is
our assignment. We pursue spiritual freedom as the means of
tracing back to our origin the whys and the wherefores of the
descent of the soul. To accept the premise of free will means to
accept the responsibilities of free will. To accept the responsibilities of free will, we must be able to look at cause and effect.
What are the causes that we have allowed by free will to cycle forth
from this energy field which is our identity? And as we behold the
march of time, the movement of the spirals of space, what are the
effects of those causes we have set in motion?

Have you ever looked upon some devastating manifestation in
your life, in your home, among your friends, and realized that by
the spoken Word you created havoc, you perhaps created sorrow,
perhaps the crumbling of another's identity or the withering of a
soul? Did you realize in that moment that you were a creator, that
you sent forth a cause, an energy spiral that resulted in an effect?
You have known, then, that you had free will. You have also
known that God made you a co-creator with him and that in that
moment you exercised the faculty to create and that was the result.
Have you also seen how you have brought joy and hope and smiles
and happiness to people by releasing a cause that resulted in an
effect? This is free will. This is responsibility.

Now as we contemplate our power in the flame of freedom, in
freedom itself, we come upon that awesome responsibility and we
ask the question: If I am a flame and the name of that flame is
freedom and I have free will and I can create with God, what are
the far-reaching consequences of my creating, of my freedom? Do
my energies reach the stars? Do they reach the central sun or are

they confined to this room or do they not even leave the forcefield of my consciousness? What is the forcefield of my consciousness? What is the extension of being, the circumference of selfhood? Those who rebel against the law of life and of being do not easily admit the far-reaching consequences of free will, of the use of the flame of freedom.

Immanuel Kant, the eighteenth-century philosopher, gave the categorical imperative, "Act as though your actions should be taken up and imitated by the whole world." Determine your actions by asking yourself, "Would I have all mankind do that which I am doing?" He had very good reason for stating thus; for it is a law of life that whatever we do resounds as the sound of the Word, as the sound of the AUM, upon life. Whatever we do has impact upon every living soul.

We come into the responsibility of the flame of freedom and we hear the voice of God. The only true freedom that man can have and know and be is the freedom that God has ordained. This freedom can be known only when man masterfully employs the gift of free will to direct the energies of his life in the fulfillment of his divine blueprint. For only when man can control his life can he control his destiny, and his destiny is his true and only freedom. When we pursue spiritual freedom, we are pursuing our right to fulfill our cosmic destiny, our manifest destiny.

The Choice Is to Be

We have the freedom to choose to be or not to be—to be the soul patterning the inner blueprint or to be the soul not patterning the inner blueprint. It is a choice. It is a choice to be—to be aligned with the inner blueprint of our own Real Self, to come into conformity with the law of that Self, or to remain outside reality. In the very core of being, you know that you are real. You know that you have a connection to an ultimate Source beyond, a source that was before the breath of life was infused into the clay vessel, a source that will continue beyond the putting-aside of that clay vessel.

"Before Abraham was, I AM!"[2] That is the fiat of the Real Self within you, the Anointed One. That Anointed One is a permanent part of life, of reality; but the soul is not. The soul is not yet made permanent, because the soul elected to go forth from that fiery core to carve out a destiny, to have free will, to be free for a while in time and space. Therefore, we come together as living souls, as potentials of the Godhead desiring to merge with the Real Self, desiring to discover that Real Self. For our souls have already determined that we do not want to remain in outer darkness, in the field of effect. We want to go to the Cause.

Clearing the Channels of Being

This conference is dedicated to the clearing of the channels in your being that you may walk over the highway of a cosmos back to the Source that is the sacred fire of life within you. We will pursue that freedom to be our Real Self with a passion, a passion not yet known upon the planet; for we will add the passion of the fervor of our heart's desire to be free to all others who have walked to the fiery core of being. And by the momentum of that entire manifestation of souls ascended known as the entire Spirit of the Great White Brotherhood, we will reinforce our freedom, our right to be free here below.

When we contact that flame, when we clear the highway of our God for the soul to rise to that central fire, that fire of freedom on the altar of being, then all of life, nature, the governments of the nations, all mankind must come into conformity with that flame. Then we will know how to solve the problems of war and peace, of the economy, of the government, of all of the crisscrosses and all of the discord and dissonance that we find in the four lower bodies of a planet and a people as we mark the anniversary of the Declaration of Independence.

So as we mark that anniversary, we come together to declare the independence of the soul, of the right of the soul to be free in the flame. And when we ratify and put our names to that declaration and come together in the white-fire core of being, we will find ourselves a mandala—a mandala of Christed ones, of the center flame and the twelve marking the thirteen disciples. And again and again as this mandala spirals through this communion, we lay the foundation, we lay the setting of what is called the magnet, the Great Central Sun magnet.

The Great Central Sun magnet is the magnet of your heart's fire. It is a magnet that is set as a diamond in the consciousness of God that draws mankind from every walk of life to some new hope of freedom, some new spark, some new realization. Every man, woman, and child upon the planet will know a new air and a new breath of freedom because we mark the destiny of our souls. What we consecrate here, what we dedicate here, is indeed for the building of the new order of the ages.

Mankind Forgot the Source of Freedom

There was a time when all mankind forgot the Source, forgot that flame of freedom, forgot that freedom was a flame. And the flame went out. It was following the fall of Lemuria; and the descent of mankind's consciousness in that fall was to the most primitive state ever known on earth—to that point where man became almost like a beast, almost walking on all fours, not even being able to stand erect, not even having the sense of respect for the flame that burns in the heart. At that moment cosmic councils determined: "There is not one, no, not one soul on Terra who acknowledges and adores the fire of freedom, the flame of freedom. There is no further reason for being for Terra."

Cosmic councils determined that Terra should go the way of many other stars, many other homes of evolutions whose entire lifewaves elected not to be. Can you imagine an entire lifewave electing not to be? It is not too hard. We only have to go out into civilization today and see what mankind are electing to be to say to ourselves, "By the grace of God have we even recognized there is an alternative to the outer man." So cosmic councils decreed Terra should be no more, because cosmic councils were obliged to ratify what the free will of mankind had already decreed: Not to be.

Sanat Kumara:
The First Keeper of the Flame

In that moment, in that supreme moment that was the judgment of a planet and a people, a flame of freedom leaped. It was the flame of Sanat Kumara, known as the Ancient of Days, the memory of whom is so great it is even recorded in the Old Testament in the Book of Daniel.[3] The Ancient of Days, Sanat Kumara, was the hierarch of Venus, sister star to Terra in this solar system. Sanat Kumara came before those councils. He stood. He thrust his hand and he said:

"Wait! Do not snuff out Terra. I will go! I will be the soul on Terra who elects to keep the flame of freedom for all life. I will keep that flame until some respond, until one responds and then the few and then the many come to acknowledge the fire of the heart. I will go." By free will a hierarch who did not have to come to Terra came to Terra. He was already free. He elected to come to set the captives free, to liberate the souls, prisoners bound by their own animal, carnal consciousness.

So came Sanat Kumara. He came from Venus. He came with Lords of Flame. He came with many souls from other planets in this system who volunteered to keep the flame with him. And they, too, raised their hands and said: "Sanat Kumara, O Lord of Flame, we will not let thee go alone to Terra. We will come also! We will come to minister unto our brothers and sisters who have forgotten the flame, who have forgotten the force of freedom within the soul." And so the volunteers came. They came with Sanat Kumara; they came to Shamballa.

Shamballa, city of light, so named by the Ancient of Days, was the place where he enshrined upon the altar of the temple that was built there the flame of life that is called the threefold flame. It is the flame of your Real Self, of the Anointed One. It is also called the Christ flame. It is called the tripartite light, because it is the focus of power, wisdom, and love—the blue, the yellow, the pink. It is the focus of the Trinity of the aspects of creation: Brahma, Vishnu, and Siva—Father, Son, and Holy Spirit. It is the focus of the AUM, the trinity of Alpha becoming Omega through the individualization of the flame—you.

So the flame was enshrined, the retreat was built, and Sanat Kumara became the first Keeper of the Flame after the fall of man and woman on Terra. The story of Sanat Kumara is told in the Keepers of the Flame brochure, and also the story of other souls and other ascended masters who came because he came to keep the flame—the story of Saint Germain carrying the flame of the Aquarian age and coming in this time and in this space to found an order called the Keepers of the Flame Fraternity dedicated to keeping the flame of freedom on behalf of mankind in memory of the Ancient of Days.[4]

Not only in memory, for the Keepers of the Flame Fraternity is composed of souls who also came with that original band, souls who have also been here for aeons teaching mankind, showing mankind the way. And in their teaching and in their showing, sometimes forgetting and thereby making karma and becoming tied to the evolutions of mankind, they finally come to the place where, with a mighty fiat of God-determination, they are determining: "This is the life! This is the embodiment! This is the time and place where I will be free, where I will make my calling and election sure, where I will ratify the flame of freedom, of Shamballa, and of my soul!"

This freedom to bring forth the flame is something that must come from within. Because we have free will, the desire must be our own. We must desire to be free. As soon as we have the desire, we tie into the great momentum of the desire of God to be free, which reinforces our desire, and we have the movement of the waters and of the fires of freedom within us—the desiring of the soul confirming the desiring of the Spirit. (The term "Spirit" refers to the I AM Presence, the individualization of your own God flame.) The initiation must come from here below. Then it is ratified and expanded by all above, by the entire hierarchy of the Great White Brotherhood, by the ascended masters.

Prince Siddhartha and Lord Maitreya: The First to Respond

Prince Siddhartha was the first to respond to the flame of Shamballa kept by Sanat Kumara. He left his castle. He left the opportunity for worldly power and dominion. He left his wife and child in the prime of life, and he went forth to find that flame. And when he found that flame, he became the Buddha of all the world. The first to respond, he was the initiate of Sanat Kumara.

And the second to respond was Lord Maitreya. By their response to the flame of freedom, by their mastery of the use of the gift of free will, these souls confirmed the reality of the flame— these souls rose to the light that burns in the heart. The soul of each one became one in the living flame of the heart. By becoming one with the fire, the threefold flame, the soul attained its immortal reunion with the I AM Presence, with God, with the central Source, through the ritual that is known as the ascension in the light. By the election of the soul, by the determination to be free, these beings proved their immortality. They proved themselves to be permanent atoms in the body of God and they carved a pathway for us to follow. Following them, we define the flame of freedom.

An ascended master, then, is one who, like Gautama and Maitreya, Jesus or Confucius or any master you can name, has chosen at a certain moment to be free. In making that decision, that one does not turn back, does not heed any other call, any other voice, any other lure from the Path. The soul that has chosen to be free moves over the spirals of God's consciousness and over the spirals of its own karma, step-by-step, on that path back to the Source.

The purpose of the incarnation of the soul is discovered. It is the mastery of the energy fields of time and space. When these are mastered, karma is balanced; dharma—or reason for being, or duty to life—is satisfied. Then the soul receives the invitation of the I AM Presence to rise up and be the Anointed One, the Christ Self, the Christ flame. And the Christ flame, in the ritual of the ascension, merges with the I AM THAT I AM, and behold, the star of your divinity is born and forevermore you are one! You have transcended the cycles of rebirth. You are freed from the wheel and the rounds of karma. You are an ascended master.

All who have ever overcome time and space and proven the victory over sin, disease, and death on Terra are the ascended masters who comprise the Great White Brotherhood. The Great White Brotherhood is the body of the elect. It is the fraternity of souls who have ascended and become one with the white light. It does not refer to race or color of skin; for souls have risen from every race, every religion, every nation, every walk of life, and every age to master time and space. For the flame of freedom is no respecter of persons, places, conditions, or things. It can be invoked at any time.

You Can Decide to Be Free

Anywhere you are, you can decide to be free. Have you ever consciously made that decision? Have you ever firmly set your feet upon the path of freedom, dedicated your entire life to be free, been willing to set aside all that interferes with your freedom in the light?

In the Christian faith, there is that moment of conversion and coming forth to the altar and declaring Christ as Saviour. So there is also a moment in your life when you must declare the intent of your life, when by free will you must say: "In my hand God has placed a spiral of energy. It is the incarnation of my soul. It is my right to be free. It is my opportunity to prove my freedom. Now I will take that precious gift of threescore and ten. I will dedicate it to the freedom of my soul; for I know that in proving that freedom for my soul, I will prove that freedom for every man, woman, and child upon the planet. And every precept that I prove will be a marker for all who come after me."

That is a moment. And it is a moment like the moment of declaring Christ as Saviour. The Christ who is your saviour is your Real Self, your fiery core, your identity. That same identity which was in Jesus which he proved to be the Christ, that same identity which was in Gautama and Maitreya which they proved to be the Buddhic light, is in you. They could never have proved that identity had they not made a decision. You are free to make that decision now.

What have we but the now? Do we have our yesterdays? Do we have our tomorrows? Our yesterdays are the thrust of Alpha. Our tomorrows will be the fulfillment of that thrust in the return to Omega. Our now is the *U* of the AUM. It is Universal Being proving itself where we are now.

Won't You Be Free?

Saint Germain spoke of the moment of his freedom in a dictation. He said:

> Will you understand the beauty of divine freedom that can be your own, that is your own, that is the lot of every man—once he realizes that the passion that he feels for freedom is in itself the seed of freedom?...
>
> I recall how long ago when first my own mentor, my spiritual teacher, and the internal realm of light within me spoke out of the living flame and said, "Won't you be free?" And I first contemplated the idea "Won't you be free?"[5]

Think of that! The master of the Aquarian age, the age of freedom, the two-thousand-year dispensation of the release of freedom from the Great Central Sun—this master Saint Germain tells us that there was a moment long, long ago, hundreds of thousands of years ago, when his soul on Terra first contemplated the bidding of the Lord within to his soul, "Won't you be free?" And he tells us his response. His soul said unto the Lord and the law within, "Why not?" Why not? "And so," he says, "I took a forward step in spiritual consciousness."

My heart friends, you who are so one with me in the fire of being at this moment, I come before you with an invitation from the entire Spirit of the Great White Brotherhood, from your own Real Self, from the flame and the voice that speaks out of the living flame. I come with that invitation from the Brotherhood of Mount Shasta, from all who have ever responded to the call of Sanat Kumara, from all lifewaves and evolutions of a cosmos. I come and I say, too, Won't you be free? Won't you come into the flame of freedom?

The Fiat of Freedom

Before mankind could understand the meaning of a fiat of freedom, before the cycles were ready for the West to accept the mantras of the East or even the mantras of the teachers of the West, Saint Germain fed into the etheric belt, the mental belt, the emotional belt, and the physical belt of the earth the momentum of the violet flame through the Strauss waltzes, presaging the Aquarian age. In this music we flow with the movement of the music of the violet flame.

The music of the flame of freedom was released by Saint Germain a century ago while he was busy at work as the Wonderman of Europe, moving as an ascended being among the courts of Europe, coming forth from his retreat in Transylvania, where the flame of freedom is anchored in the Rakoczy mansion. Saint Germain inspired in that era the waltzes of Johann Strauss. The three-quarter time of the waltz has the rhythm of the threefold flame of power, wisdom, and love. It is the beat of your heart; it is the actual rhythm of the fire within. And now we come a century later to confirm by the power of the spoken Word the living flame of freedom within us.

In the name of Saint Germain, hierarch of the Aquarian age, let us declare our freedom in the simple mantra of the violet flame, which is the seventh-ray aspect of the sacred fire and the ray of the Aquarian age. Let us affirm that fire within us. Let us affirm that seventh ray by saying, "I AM a being of violet fire—I AM the purity God desires!" That simple mantra can take the suspended energies of your soul and lock them into a fiat of freedom as you make your decision in the eternal Now to be free. Why not?

When we use the name of God "I AM," as we spoke of the name I AM THAT I AM given unto Moses out of the flaming fire of the bush that burned but was not consumed, when we take that I AM, we are saying the name of God and affirming, "God in me is." Remember, every time you use I AM in the first person, you are declaring, "God in me is." It is an affirmation of your Real Self. It releases the fire of your heart to fulfill the destiny to which you send it forth. If you say, "I am well, I am happy, I am whole," the fire leaps and makes a cycle through your four lower bodies to ratify that fiat. And when you say the reverse, you create the consequences; and by free will you sit in the spiral, in the energy field of your own creation. This is law. We know it to be law.

Therefore, when we say, "I AM a being of violet fire—I AM the purity God desires!" we are saying, "God in me is a being of violet fire—God in me is the purity God desires!" What a wonderful thought! When the soul decides to be free, instantly the flame leaps within the heart and ratifies that covenant that the soul makes with the Creator. And our Maker ratifies the covenant and speaks through us, by the power of the spoken Word (that eternal Logos), this mantra of being.

When you say this mantra, believe it or not—this is not Ripley's, this is the ascended-master law of cosmos—believe it or not, the flow of the Word goes forth from the throat chakra, from the heart chakra, in a clockwise spiral around your being as a coil. And you, as a pillar of energy, become a coil of the fire of freedom surrounding your being. And every being in cosmos who is one with the fire of freedom is flowing in that coil! This is cosmic law. Things equal to the same thing are equal to each other.

When you declare that God in you is a being of violet fire, God in you is the purity God desires, Saint Germain, Lord Zadkiel, the Archangel of the Seventh Ray, Holy Amethyst, the Archeia (twin flame of an archangel), the Elohim Arcturus and Victoria who also serve the flame of freedom, Omri-Tas, the ruler of the violet planet, and 144,000 priests of the sacred fire from the violet planet all converge through the power of your spoken Word to release the fiat of freedom through you. This is alchemy! This is alchemy! This is the rejoicing of the flame! This is the gift of free will that God has given us!

The Flame of Freedom Is Within

Can you imagine that we have lived in darkness so long, that we have lived without this truth and this law that is the foundation of our reason for being? Can we even think that a moment ago we did not exercise that flow and that law? Can we even think that there are evolutions and lifewaves who do not learn this law as the fundamental premise of being? And does not all of nature teach us that the flame of freedom is within?

As we look at the stars in the heavens and the multiplication of the seeds in all of nature, over and over again God is saying: "I AM the flame of freedom in the heart of the seed that becomes the tree, that becomes the flower, that becomes a star. I AM the flame of freedom within you." This is the essential message of the Great White Brotherhood restoring to us our lost divinity, our lost inheritance. We have found it again. We have come to the flame. Let us declare our freedom in this mantra. [Audience gives the mantra "I AM a being of violet fire—I AM the purity God desires!" fifty-six times and concludes by chanting "AUM" three times.]

In the flow of the mantra, the stepping-up of the tempo corresponds to the stepping-up of the vibration of the light flowing through you. When you let the Logos release the Word, when you let the Real Self speak the Word through you, the natural flow of light intensifies the giving of the mantra. This is an example of how the white-fire core receives all back unto itself and how all of the words of the mantras become the sacred AUM. And all of the colors, the rainbow rays of the prism of God's consciousness, return to the white-fire core; and the violet flame becomes the white light as the mantra converges in the AUM.

As God controls the speaking of the mantra through you, God controls the flow of the electrons in the orbits around the atoms. Scientists are recognizing that each individual has his own cosmic clock. They are telling us what we always have known—that we each have a unique vibration, that vibration consists of the frequencies of all of our atoms and molecules, and the combination of all put together makes the tone of identity which we recognize when we greet our friends, when we have affinities for one another and perhaps repulsions for other parts of life which are out of harmony with the whole. That vibration, that frequency, has to do with how the Word is flowing through the atoms and what the cycles of the electrons are.

You Become the Flame

When the flame of freedom comes into being, takes over being, and you become that flame, you have a new pitch, a new sound, "a new name which no man knoweth saveth he that receiveth it."[6] The name is the sacred name I AM THAT I AM. You control your own vibration by free will, by your determination of what you do with your energy and your forces. As you increase the merging with your Real Self by increasing the tempo of a mantra, you are controlling a whole cosmos of atoms and molecules and energy fields.

So don't be concerned when we step up the mantra and it goes faster than you can pronounce it, because it is moving toward the center of the AUM. By and by, you will master speaking those words individually so quickly that they are no more but dissolve in the AUM. Remember that when you feel that resistance to the stepping-up of the mantra, it is the resistance of the former self, of a former frequency that doesn't want to quite keep up with the decision of the soul to be free. So there's that part of being that lags behind, that is comfortable—that movement or that motionlessness of inertia.

And so it is free will tying into the fire of the heart that must penetrate every aspect of self once the decision is made to be free. Once we make that decision, we take the mantras of the teachers, the true teachers, because they are in the mantras. We follow their guidance and their teaching. It might be a bit uncomfortable. It might get a little warm, because in transmutation there is chemicalization and you can actually feel physical heat as the violet flame consumes the dross that impedes the flow of the electron.

The Science of the Spoken Word

I would like us to give this mantra once again in the understanding that there is a very definite science to it. We begin slowly, controlling each word as we control each electron. Then we step up and we find that we can maintain control at an increased vibration—just as man has conquered movement in time and space, securing inventions for greater and greater speed, finally breaking the barrier of sound. This we do in our chakras by the control of the Word and the science of the Word.

I would like to ask everyone to experiment with the mantra. If you do not exercise the power of the spoken Word, you will be an island in the midst of a sea of flame. For by free will, which the supreme law of cosmos respects in you, that flame cannot coalesce and form that spiral if you do not give the fiat. This is the law of the throat chakra, of free will, and of the science of the spoken Word.

We usually consider ourselves to be rational. We consider ourselves to have learned the scientific method of proving a hypothesis to see whether or not it concludes in a manifestation that is empirically valid in time and space. If we would be scientists to prove a new science, a new dispensation, we must be bold, fearless to experiment with the unknown.

The flame is unknown until you make it your own. You hear me talk about it. You see me giving the mantra. If you don't try, you will not know, you will never know. You will stand in the bleachers making life, as Morya says, a spectator sport, watching while others walk before you on the path of initiation. Trying a mantra has with it no obligation. You can try it and leave it or you can try it and take it.

This is a conference for spiritual freedom. To have spiritual freedom, you must be willing to experiment freely, to take the formulas of the master alchemist, Saint Germain, to try them out. If they don't fit, you are no worse for the experiment; you have learned something. You have worked in the laboratory of the Spirit with the true alchemists, the ascended masters.

So let's try this mantra. Let's see what it will do! Let us put God and the law and the teaching and the whole Great White Brotherhood to the test. Let's say: "Okay, Great White Brotherhood, prove the law! I will make myself a willing instrument. You prove it to me. You show it to me. I'm from Missouri; I want to see proof! I want to know that that flame of freedom really works." Okay, we'll prove it. [Audience gives the mantra "I AM a being of violet fire—I AM the purity God desires!" fifty-two times and concludes by chanting "AUM" three times.]

In the name of the entire Spirit of the Great White Brotherhood, in the name of your own Real Self, and by the authority of your own free will, we seal you in the flame of freedom. In the name of the Father and of the Mother, of the Son and of the Holy Spirit, it is finished!

July 3, 1975
11:14-12:18 P.M. PDT

Fiats of Freedom is an exercise of the spoken Word affirming the flame of freedom enshrined in the heart. To swim in the cosmic ocean, to merge with the waves of his will, to become the wave and the will and then with a mighty thrust to inundate all life with the consciousness of the movement of God's mind—this is to impose your will that has melted into the mountain of his will upon the cosmos of being. Fiats of freedom are fiats of free will to be the will of the Source. Energy in motion, a cosmic ocean: this is God.

4

FIATS OF FREEDOM
Your Will Imposed upon the Cosmos of Being
Are You a Co-Creator with Life?

A Lecture by Elizabeth Clare Prophet

The Fiery Core of Being

This morning we spoke about the white-fire core of being and the definition of being as the I AM THAT I AM, the name of God which when spoken contains the power of the Word that releases the fohat of creation. We spoke of the AUM as being the three letters of the sacred Word that stand for the trinity and that focalize the going-within to the fiery core.

We understand that in the fiery core of each individual being there is the polarity of Alpha and Omega. In every star, in every sun, in you as a soul, in you as a God flame, that polarity is. We see that being which comes forth from the Great Central Sun to be whole always manifests the polarity of the masculine and feminine rays. We call those who are one in the fiery core of being twin flames. Twin flames are the coordinates of the sacred fire in their own single mandala, created out of the same blueprint, the same fiery core.

When we study the hierarchies of ascended masters and of the Great White Brotherhood, we notice that the higher we proceed in consciousness—to the level of the archangels, the Elohim, and cosmic beings—the more we come in contact with components of life that have balanced this aspect and are one in the flame. We can invoke the momentum of twin flames throughout the cosmos to amplify the wholeness of our own white-fire core, to create within us and intensify the Great Central Sun magnet which magnetizes the counterpart of our identity.

Each one of us has a twin flame somewhere, whether in time and space or in eternity, that is unique. There is only one twin flame, not many. There is one identity in the entire cosmos that shares your blueprint, the coordinate of your individuality. And that coordinate could be an ascended master; it could be the very ascended master that drew you to this class; it could be a child in arms; it could be someone in the etheric retreats or the person sitting next to you.

We are not as concerned to find the twin flame as we are to find the fiery core of being, because in the fiery core of being is the totality of selfhood. I say this because it is important that we see that every system of worlds has a set of twin flames that is governing its destiny and that receives the impetus from the Solar Logos of the perfect polarity of Alpha and Omega. In our solar system, focusing the Sun behind the sun, which is the spiritual manifestation behind the physical, are the twin flames who are called Helios and Vesta. They control the flow of life, the flow of energy, to this entire system of worlds. When we tie into their heart flame, we feel the magnification of our own.

May we sing to beloved Helios and Vesta a song entitled "The New Day." These words were given in a dictation by Vesta, the mother of our solar system. Whenever you give this wherever you are, you make contact with the sun; and when you develop a momentum on this mantra, you will find, as I have found invariably, that if it is a cloudy day, the sun will come peeping through.

It's an amazing realization to think that a consciousness ninety-three million miles away in time and space can receive the pulsation of your heart chakra and respond with the speed of light. Won't you make your attunement with your heart and send your love to the sun. The worship of the sun, of course, is an ancient custom on the planet—the contacting of Aton, being *at one* with Aton. [Audience sings song three times.]

The New Day
by Vesta

Helios and Vesta,
Helios and Vesta,
Helios and Vesta,

Let the light flow into my being,
Let the light expand in the center of my heart,
Let the light expand in the center of the earth,
And let the earth be transformed into the new day!

The Misuse of Free Will

Won't you turn the page as we become a sun to "Keep My Flame Blazing." Keepers of the Flame have a commission from Sanat Kumara to nourish the flame of life blazing on the altar, the heart's altar, of all mankind. The point of the fall of man and woman that is actually recorded in Genesis is that period before the flood of Noah when the intention of men's hearts was continually to do evil.[1] We have the recording in Genesis of the life span of mankind being nine hundred years, and then the life span becomes threescore and ten.[2] What happened? The edict went forth from the cosmic councils that mankind were misusing the gift of fire, the gift of the sacred fire, through the misuse of free will. They were taking that fire and using it not to the glory of God, but to the glory of the lesser self. So came the fiat which commanded the reduction in the size of the flame of the heart.

When mankind walked the earth as Methuselah did, they walked the earth standing in the threefold flame; and the crystal cord, the lifeline to the center of the Godhead, was like a mighty cylinder of light comparable to what is known as the tube of light. All that energy God gave freely to mankind as long as mankind used the gift of free will to God's glory.

Then came the abuse of power, the abuse of wisdom, the abuse of love. So the cosmic edict went forth, and the threefold flame was reduced to one-sixteenth of an inch in height and the crystal cord was reduced to a thread. This was done so that the Godhead would be releasing to mankind only that amount of energy sufficient to sustain life in the four lower bodies until mankind, by their own free will and their own fiat, would determine to expand that flame to the glory of God in manifestation in man and in woman. This is the size the threefold flame remains today—one-sixteenth of an inch in height in average mankind.

When individuals set their feet upon the path of initiation and begin to invoke the flame from on high, the flame in the heart expands. And so it begins to increase. A very slight increase in that flame results in tremendous illumination, a much greater power. In fact, the expansion of that threefold flame is the definition of the Christed One, the Anointed One—one who is anointed by fire. The great avatars of the ages were avatars because they increased the size of the flame by their devotion, by nourishing it, by giving it attention, by adoring it, by communing with it, by visualizing it. Let's give this invocation, "Keep My Flame Blazing"—its purpose, to increase your self-awareness as a living flame, as a living potential. [Audience sings song three times.]

Keep My Flame Blazing

In the name of the beloved mighty victorious Presence of God, I AM in me, my very own beloved Holy Christ Self, beloved Mother Mary, beloved Kwan Yin, beloved Ascended Lady Master Nada, beloved Lanello, the entire Spirit of the Great White Brotherhood and the World Mother, I decree:

> Keep my flame blazing,
> By God's love raising,
> Direct and keep me in my rightful place!

> I AM Presence ever near me,
> Keep me mindful of thy grace;
> Flame of Christ, ever cheer me,
> In me show thy smiling face!

The I AM Presence

The Chart of Your Divine Self (see illustration facing p. 48) is in our book *Climb the Highest Mountain,* together with a description of the chart in detail, the components of which I would like to go over with you. May I read briefly from *Climb the Highest Mountain.* We are here setting about to define the white-fire core of being which we have talked about as the I AM THAT I AM, the sacred AUM. It is your center of God-awareness. What exactly is the I AM Presence?

When God said, "Let there be light," and there was light, He implemented the expansion of the light by giving birth to individual Spirit-sparks. These drops of his cosmic identity were scattered throughout the universes as billions of seeds of light, each one with a unique destiny, yet each one an exact replica of the original Unity that was and is God. Separated in the time-space configuration yet forever one with the central sun, or centrosome of the Eternal, these sparks of the Divine Image were created that each soul might express an aspect of the individuality of the Godhead. Thus in the upper figure [in the chart] we see the design of a personalized fragment of the Deity, the very Presence of God himself, the individual Spirit-spark that is known as the I AM Presence.

Because the Presence of God is one with the essence and being of God, we acknowledge that "our God is one Lord." We understand that although his Electronic Presence be multiplied billions of times for the purpose of his individualization in form, God is still one—one individed Whole. Just as one times one times one will always equal one, so God times God times God still equals God. Although not all have understood this mystery, we have seen that it is most assuredly within the capacity of the Great Geometer to sustain an infinite number of focuses of himself and still maintain his oneness.[3]

This is the most amazing concept and gift of the ascended masters in this age. The knowledge of the I AM Presence was first revealed in the 1920s and 30s by Godfre, who will speak to us in a dictation this afternoon. He delivered to America and to all mankind the message of Saint Germain, the master of the Aquarian age, that you and you and you have an individualized God Presence. This God Presence that you see diagramed is a point of Infinity; it is the origin of your soul. Your soul came forth from this white-fire core.

Some call the Presence the Divine Monad. It is a tangible, pulsating sphere of white light that is above you. "Draw nigh to me and I will draw nigh to you"[4] is the word of your own I AM Presence. God individualized is the means whereby God personifies the flame. This sphere of light is very close to those who meditate upon the law of being, on cosmic consciousness. It transcends time and space; and yet because we are in time and space, it appears that in moments of darkness, despair, and discord we are far, far from the I AM Presence. In moments of harmony we

feel the flow, the currents, and the compassion—the frequencies
of that Presence which we call God, which Jesus called "our Father
which art in heaven." [5]

Therefore, even though the Presence is not in time and space,
the relationship of your soul to the Presence changes according to
consciousness. We say then, for want of better words, that in time
and space at times this sphere of light is very close, hovering just
above the head of the devotee. In those who totally ignore God, it
may be a thousand feet away. There is a drawing nigh and receding
of the Presence according to frequency. This follows the law of
correspondence, which states, "Things equal to the same thing are
equal to each other." When in your heart you personify the flame
and you adore the flame, the flame becomes the magnet which is
the same magnet that is in the heart of your Presence. And so the
two become one, and you become the living awareness of God.

Now let us further consider what God is. What is this
"flaming flame that shall not be quenched"? [6] What is this voice
that spoke and said, "Our God is a consuming fire"? [7] Ezekiel saw
the I AM Presence in the fire infolding itself. [8] The Presence has
been seen by devotees, followers of God, throughout the ages; and
so it has been recorded in sacred literature. There is hardly one
group of scripture anywhere in the world that does not somewhere
mention fire as the origin and the ultimate of consciousness. The
I AM Presence is the sacred fire. The I AM Presence is cosmic
consciousness. The I AM Presence is, at this moment, the permanent aspect of being.

Remember, the soul is not yet permanent; the soul can be
lost. "The soul that sinneth, it shall die," Ezekiel, the prophet of
the Lord, said. [9] The soul is that portion of being which we ratify
by conforming it to the law of the I AM Presence through the
correct exercise of free will. The soul that went forth into Matter
entered into a consciousness of relativity, of time and space.

The I AM Presence in the plane of Spirit does not dwell in
temples made with hands; [10] it does not dwell in time and space. It
is the absolute. "Behold, I AM of purer eyes than to behold
iniquity." [11] The I AM Presence is the aspect of being that simply is
being, is consciousness, is God aware of itself. It is the very center
of creation which the Hindus describe as that being without attribute, without putting on personality. It is being before it
becomes the Trinity, before it becomes Brahma, Vishnu, and Siva.

The I AM Presence is your lodestone of perfection. Without the point of perfection, we could not hope to attain perfection. Some have questioned whether or not perfection is a legitimate goal. It would not be legitimate if there did not exist perfection already somewhere within being. The perfection that exists is the I AM Presence.

If you want to conclude this by induction, you can just look at the fact that we always strive to improve, to do better, to perfect something we are working on, to become better at this or that. It is that movement of being towards perfection, the same movement of being that inspired the writing of *Jonathan Livingston Seagull,* the story of a seagull that is striving for perfection. That is the soul. The bird is the symbol of the soul taking flight, soaring to the center of the I AM Presence. Transcending the planes, it goes into the octaves of light.

The Real Self

Because we dwell in relativity, because that which we desire to attain is the Absolute, there is required the Mediator, that point of consciousness which can be aware of the Absolute simultaneously as it is aware of the relative—aware of the soul passing through experience, passing through initiation, while also aware of the I AM Presence as the blazing fire, the sun of cosmic consciousness. That mediator is your own blessed Real Self, the Anointed One.

Once the avatars proved their own cosmic identity as the Real Self, they were called by the name of the Real Self. Hence, Gautama was called Gautama the Buddha because he realized his Real Self as the Buddhic light. And Jesus came to be known as Jesus the Christ because he personified the Real Self. We call him Jesus the one who became the Christ, the one who attained to the Real Self, to the Mediator. The central figure depicted in the chart of the Presence, then, we call your Real Self or your Christ Self.

The very first premise in the teaching of the Great White Brotherhood and of all the masters who have ever walked the earth is that this Christ Self, this Real Self, is not unique to the avatars who have proven that Self, but it is the potential of every man, woman, and child created by God.

It is written that it is the Word that was made flesh, the only begotten Son of God.[12] We have discussed how God can be one times one times one—an individualized I AM Presence—and still be one. The great mystery of the oneness of Christ and yet that Christ being in all is in the statement of Jesus "This is my body, which is broken for you." [13]

The body consciousness of the Christ, the Second Person of the Trinity, becomes the fragments individualized as the individualized Christ Self just as the individualized I AM Presence is God—the one God individualized—and is always one, even though we all can pray to that independent point of identity which is our own God Source.

Understanding this necessitates that we transcend time and space, because time and space make everything appear separate and everything appear in numbers. We eliminate time and space and we're all in a tiny ball of white fire. Scientists talk about this— about Matter going in together and compressing. They see this happening in stars and suns. And this Matter that presses into itself is without electrons and the heavy neutrons become a tremendous weight.

To identify oneness in God and to translate it in time and space, we come back to this relative understanding. And so the ascended masters teach that you have an individual Christ Self, that you have an individualized I AM Presence. We set the pattern of this teaching before you in order to build the concept of fiats of freedom. It is because we have that Source and that Source is our true identity that we have the authority to utter the fiats of the Lord.

The Authority for Creation

The concept of fiats and the science of the spoken Word is explained in the paperback *The Science of the Spoken Word*.[14] It is very interesting that we take our authority for giving forth the commands of God from sacred scripture itself. But had that portion of scripture been lost, we would still have the confirmation of the authority by the flame itself which blazes within our hearts. It's always interesting to me, however, to find that the teachings of the ascended masters can be derived from the sacred scriptures of the world.

Isaiah saw this concept and translated it for the children of Israel. "Thus saith the Lord, the Holy One of Israel and his Maker,

Ask me of things to come concerning my sons, and concerning the work of my hands command ye me."[15] This is the Word of the Lord received by Isaiah. It is the teaching of his I AM Presence, just as the I AM Presence of Moses taught Moses out of the flame and the I AM Presence of Jesus taught Jesus out of the flame.

When we accept the responsibility of free will to enter the planes of Matter, we enter that level of consciousness where God, or the I AM Presence, has given into our hands the complete authority for creation. When you think about life and all of the miseries and the suffering attendant upon life on this planet and the war, you cannot justify a Creator that is loving and wise and good who would allow this to happen unless you understand that he has turned over to all of us the gift of free will. He has made clear in his covenants and in his laws that unless we ask, unless we give back to him the free will that he has given to us, he does not interfere with our affairs.

You should try this in your own life. Try doing something without God; then try asking God to help you. See what a difference it makes. I met a woman not long ago, a very devout Christian, who told me of an experience she had as a child which illustrates this very well. She said to me, "You know, everything I do, I do in the name of the Father, the Son, and the Holy Spirit. My friends think I'm a bit queer, but I do it anyway." And she said, "I'm going to tell you why."

"When I was a little girl, I was living in England and I had to get up very early in the morning to light the fire. It just seemed that the more I tried to light that fire, the more it wouldn't burn. And I would struggle with the matches and struggle with the matches and it just wouldn't ignite.

"So one day, after watching me struggle for some time, my grandmother said to me, 'If you would simply say, "In the name of the Father, the Son, and the Holy Spirit, let the fire be lit," you would not have the struggle.'"

So the woman said it. And lo and behold, the fire came forth without a struggle! She said sometimes she would forget to say that and the same old struggle and the same old problem would occur. Then she would remember she had omitted calling God into the midst of her effort and she would do so and the fire would light. So it became a lesson and a momentum for a lifetime.

This is the basic law of the plane of Matter where we live. Not a single ascended master, not an angel, not an Elohim, is allowed to interfere in your life unless you invite that one to come in by free will. If you say, "In the name of my I AM Presence, in the name of my Real Self, the Christed One within me, I call forth the seven mighty Elohim," by cosmic law they must instantaneously come forth and release the light of their consciousness.

A lawyer is one who stands before the bar in defense of his clients. He must know the law in order to win his case for his clients. What has happened to mankind is that they have lost the knowledge of cosmic law, so they don't know what laws to invoke on their own behalf. The Real Self of all of us is the advocate with the Father—the lawyer who stands and intercedes before the I AM Presence. When we know the law, we can give forth the fiats of that Real Self.

And we know that the law, like a mathematical formula, always works. Two plus two always equals four—not just sometimes, not at the whim of a precarious Creator, not at the whim of one who answers today but not tomorrow. The law is both exact and exacting. It demands that we fulfill it in order to enjoy its bounty.

The Causal Body

What we have then in the concept of fiats of freedom is that there is a giant sphere of pulsating light above each individual in this tent and above all mankind. It is scintillating with the unlimited potential of the Godhead. It is waiting to be opened up and to be released as blessing, as bounty, as wisdom, as light, as love, as direction. There is that I AM Presence surrounded by the spheres of light which you see in the chart. They are called the rings of the causal body.

The causal body is your body of First Cause—the divine blueprint; all of the good, all of the energy you have ever properly used in the correct exercise of free will, is garnered there. It is your mansion. In my Father's house are many mansions.[16] It is your dwelling place; it is the place out of which you came, to which you will return. It is your Father's house, the biding place of your I AM Presence. It is where you store up the treasures of energies that you consecrate to God.

That causal body is distinct and individual for every soul. One

star differeth from another in glory.[17] Your I AM Presence is the
star of your being. The star that appeared over Bethlehem was the
causal body of Jesus. Many times people do not think to look, but
where children of light are born, where avatars are born, there is
usually an unusual manifestation of brilliance in the heavens. It is
the causal body marking the place of the descent of the soul into
time and space.

The rings of the causal body are the frequencies of the rays of
the prism of God's mind, and these rings denote different
vibrations of energy. For instance, the white-fire core is the center
of purity. Surrounding it is the yellow sphere, which contains all of
the wisdom of the mind of God ever outpictured by your soul in all
of its incarnations. Then comes the pink sphere of love. Each of
these spheres denotes a different aspect of cosmic consciousness
which you have dwelled upon and become, somewhere, sometime,
in your evolution. So we all have a unique causal body, and that's
where our talents come from; that's where genius comes from.
These are the energies we are given to develop lifetime after
lifetime.

The Mediator Screens the Call

When we give forth fiats of freedom, the energy that is ours—
our bank account, our own reservoir of light in our causal body—
can be released in time and space. The Mediator is the consciousness which screens the call. "Ye ask and receive not, because
ye ask amiss," Jesus taught about prayer.[18] Other World Teachers
have taught about prayer. The prayer that conforms to the inner
blueprint of life is the prayer that is answered. All prayer is answered; silence is an answer from God. It may be an indication that
our prayer requires illumination, requires rewording, that we need
to tune into the inner matrix and understand what to pray for.

Since the soul does not know completely its divine destiny, it
appeals to the Mediator who can perceive that destiny locked in the
I AM Presence and who can also perceive its point of evolution.
The greatest single blessing from the teachings of the ascended
masters after the I AM Presence is the knowledge of the Christ Self,
which some have called the Higher Mental Body.

When we make a call in the name of the Christ Self and in the
name of the I AM Presence, we can be assured that the Christ Self
will screen the call and will give back the answer according to the

will of the Creator. That way we are not calling for things that are
not in conformity with the whole scheme of the law of cosmos.

The Heart, Connecting Point for All Being

Some of you know of the Tibetan Master, Djwal Kul. Djwal
Kul has recently released *Intermediate Studies of the Human
Aura.* He says:

> In the heart there is a pulsation of life becoming life
> that is the established rhythm of the cosmos reflected from
> the heart of God to the heart of the Great Central Sun,
> through the heart of the Elohim, thence to all lifewaves
> evolving in time and space. The heart is the focal point for
> the flow of life individualized as the I AM Presence, the
> Divine Monad of individuality, and the Christ Self that is
> the personification of the reality of being for every soul.
> The heart is the connecting point for all being, for all self-
> consciousness. Through the heart all mankind are one;
> and through the heart the Christ of the One, the only
> begotten son of the Father-Mother God, becomes the
> Christ of all lifewaves unfolding God's life throughout the
> cosmos.[19]

You'll notice in the I AM Presence the rays of light
proceeding from the Divine Monad. These rays of light connect all
other parts of hierarchy. This means that when through meditation
we enter into communion with the I AM Presence, at that point of
contact with the I AM Presence, we are also one with all other parts
of God, of Life, throughout cosmoses we know not of, who have
ever become one with that I AM Presence. When we sing, "We are
one, we are one, we are one," we also have that contact.

The threefold flame blazes in the heart of the I AM Presence.
It pulsates to the heartbeat of God. It releases the energy we
require for daily existence over that cord called the crystal cord.
The crystal cord very much resembles the umbilical cord that ties
the child to the mother. This is the umbilical cord that ties an
infant humanity to the Godhead, providing us with the nourish-
ment of energy sufficient unto our daily needs. So the energy
pulsates, extending then to the level of the Christ consciousness
that is the Real Self. There the threefold flame is anchored again
and the cord continues, and the energy continues to flow and is

anchored in the heart of man and woman evolving in time and space.

We see then a new aspect of the Trinity. We see God the Father as the I AM Presence, God the Son as the Christ Self, God the Holy Spirit as the flame that is in the temple of our being. "Know ye not that your body is the temple of the Holy Ghost?" [20] And the living God is that flame, that fire.

Fiats of Free Will

When we feel this action of the Trinity and establish the flow in meditation, then we have contacted the Source whence came all the creation. We have our connection to the energy flow. And the fiats we give forth by the power of the spoken Word can transform an entire cosmos—a cosmos that is the microcosm of your soul and your four lower bodies, a cosmos that is the Macrocosm of worlds beyond this solar system. All of life in Matter must conform to the fiats of freedom by law. When we understand the law, then truly we enter into that joint heirship; we all share that heirship with the Real Self, the Christ.

The greatest fear Gautama had was that his disciples would not understand that they, too, must become the Buddha. The greatest fear Jesus had was that his disciples would worship Jesus and fail to become the Christed ones themselves. So we have today the remnants of the teachers. We must follow the remnants back to the Source—follow the light ray, follow the thread of the teaching, and let the Holy Spirit reveal to us these mysteries.

The ascended masters give to us the fact that the light of an entire cosmos, of the Great Central Sun, of the individualized I AM Presence, can be released here and now to transform the world through the science of the spoken Word. Each time you give a fiat of freedom, you are calling on God to qualify the flame within the heart with a certain qualification or aspect of that virtue.

Now before proceeding any further with theory, I would like to give with you "The Flame of Freedom Speaks," Decree 7.26. This is the fiat of freedom which Saint Germain released to be waiting for you when you heard the flame speaking within the heart, "Won't you be free?" and you responded, "Why not?" In the moment when you decide to make your declaration of independence from all outer bondage and to enter again the flame of the heart, this is the fiat of freedom that is waiting from the heart of the Master of Freedom. In honor of Saint Germain, won't you stand to give this fiat of your soul's liberation? [Audience gives Decree 7.26 three times.]

The Flame of Freedom Speaks

The flame of freedom speaks—the flame of freedom within each heart. The flame of freedom saith unto all: Come apart now and be a separate and chosen people, elect unto God—men who have chosen their election well, who have determined to cast their lot in with the immortals. These are they who have set their teeth with determination, who have said:

I will never give up
I will never turn back
I will never submit
I will bear the flame of freedom unto my victory
I will bear this flame in honor
I will sustain the glory of life within my nation
I will sustain the glory of life within my being
I will win my ascension
I will forsake all idols and
I will forsake the idol of my outer self
I will have the glory of my immaculate divinely
    conceived Self manifesting within me
I AM freedom and
I AM determined to be freedom
I AM the flame of freedom and
I AM determined to bear it to all
I AM God's freedom and he is indeed free
I AM freed by his power and his power is supreme
I AM fulfilling the purposes of God's kingdom

And in full faith I consciously accept this manifest, manifest, manifest (3x) right here and now with full power, eternally sustained, all-powerfully active, ever expanding, and world enfolding until all are wholly ascended in the light and free! Beloved I AM, beloved I AM, beloved I AM!

Fiats of freedom is an exercise of the spoken Word, affirming the flame of freedom enshrined in the heart. To swim in the cosmic ocean, to merge with the waves of his will, to become the wave and the will, and then with a mighty thrust to inundate all life with the consciousness of the movement of God's mind—this is to impose your will that has melted into the mountain of his will upon the cosmos of being! Fiats of freedom are fiats of free will to be the will of the Source, energy in motion, a cosmic ocean. This is God.

When we think about obeying a God who is a God like Jehovah—a figure, an identity, punishing, putting forth laws, rebuking mankind, even allowing the devil to tempt mankind and then punishing mankind for responding—we build up, as mankind most assuredly has, a rebellion against that Creator, a rebellion against authority. We want our freedom; we want our freedom to be what we want to be. The idea of anyone outside of ourselves telling us we can't do this, we can't do that, we have to do this, we have to do that, you don't do this and you don't do that, you'll go to hell and you'll die and you'll be there forever in fires of perdition is not only repugnant: it is an insult to the creative mind.

The Correct Use of Free Will

Let us approach this subject with reason. "Come now, and let us reason together, saith the Lord." [21] First of all, God never imposes his will upon you. Did you know that? God never interferes with free will. He has bestowed that free will and he will not take it back—not so long as you have opportunity, as the cycles of his appointing go, to work out your own destiny in time and space. It is only at the end of that opportunity of many, many incarnations when the original impulse of light, the sphere of energy, has been exhausted, that the accounting comes.

If the energy has been used through free will to increase the awareness of God, then the soul becomes immortal and permanent. If the soul has not used free will to do this, the soul goes through what is known as the second death; it ceases to be. That second death and that judgment, which is spoken of in the Book of Revelation, is the source of all of the fear of hellfire and damnation. [22]

Now this is the understanding. Obedience to God simply

means entering into the oneness of the flame that we already are. It means following the lines of individuality back to the Source of identity. It means conforming to the law of our own being. Now who in his right mind would ever rebel against his own being? Who in his right mind would take that course of suicide to deny his own Self, his own flame, his own reality? It seems to me we have a lot of people on this planet who are not in their right minds.

This is the deception of the archdeceivers of mankind. They have created a fierce God that is not the real God; then they have incited rebellion against that God. They have gotten the souls of mankind, by the twist of the teaching and the twist of the law, to actually take a stand in defiance of their own I AM Presence, their own lifeline to eternity, their own Source of energy and power, their own Real Self, to the death of the soul. How do you like that?

Godfre is known as God Obedience because he discovered the key. When you flow with the law of your own cells, your own atoms, you move with the cosmos—just as Jesus discovered it and became it. The ultimate of becoming one with that law of your own being is expressed in this fantastic statement: "All power is given unto me in heaven and in earth." [23] All life flows to you because you are one with the core of life everywhere. Things equal to the same thing are equal to each other.

Why is cancer taking so many people upon the planet today? It is the rebellion of the cells. They are following the rebellion of mankind's consciousness, which is a rebellion against the law of harmony, of our own flow. We see this cancer not only in the physical bodies, but as a mass energy moving to the body politic, to the economy, to the nation. It is the substance of the rebellion which has occurred because mankind have not understood who I AM.

The losing of the name of God, I AM THAT I AM, that was secured through Moses, is the great loss of identity which must be regained in this century if we are to forge and win a freedom for mankind. It is not only a name: it is the light of the Godhead. It bursts when it is spoken. The only reason we do not see it burst forth, that we do not see it the moment we say its name, is that we have the encrustations of centuries of misuse of that flame. We have become so dense that we cannot see the fire in our hearts.

Lord Lanto, a Chinese mystic who worked with Confucius,

determined that the one legacy he would leave his disciples was the vision of the fire in the heart. He meditated on the flame within his heart until it could be seen through the skin, through his chest. It glowed, and all of his disciples had the revelation of that fire. Even today in India, when testing whether or not a disciple is truly in meditation, the teacher checks the chest to see if there is a roseate glow around the heart. This is the indication of the fire flowing.

It does not take long if you develop a momentum in fiats of freedom to release the energy of the Word and the Logos. What is the will of that God that we call energy? There's a great definition of God that is explained in *Climb the Highest Mountain*. It is really a liberation from orthodoxy and doctrine that encases this God in an image that is not the real God.

G-O-D is the code word for geometry of divinity. [24] The geometry of your divinity is what is locked in that Monad of the I AM Presence. The whole geometrization of fire that will extend your destiny worlds beyond this world aeons after you have overcome time and space—this geometry, this blueprint, this formula of your cosmic identity—is already locked in that Monad. So it is called God—geometry of divinity. It's your potential, the total potential of what you can become.

Now if you blend with the law of your inner being, nothing is impossible to you. If you fight it, rebel against it, you are just spinning your wheels, wasting your soul's opportunity for incarnation. In other words, you are "blowing" a whole lifetime. So we discover the Real Self. We realize rebellion is folly. Would we rebel against the law of mathematics, or against the law of the nucleus of the atom and its components, or the law of energy in motion as electrons, or the chemistry of molecules that makes up the whole being we call man?

We are not in rebellion against these laws, because they are scientific. That's the whole key. The law of our inner identity is also scientific; we can prove every aspect of that law. We can surrender to that law and know we will not lose any part of identity or being by coming into conformity with it—but we will gain an entire cosmos.

Fiats of freedom, then, are based upon the great mantra that Jesus gave us in the hour of his greatest suffering, his greatest proving of the law: "Not my will, but thine be done." [25] Who is the "thine"? The "thine" is your Real Self; the "thine" is the inner lodestone of reality; the "thine" is the law that makes up your identity. Not my will, but thine be done! Not my will, but thine be done! It becomes a mantra that sings within the very atoms. Will you try it with me? "Not my will, not my will, not my will, but thine be done." [Audience gives mantra twelve times.]

The Law of Karma and the Gift of the Violet Flame

We are living in an age when we are at the stage of the harvest. We are seeing manifest in the world at large, and in our own lives, a vast accumulation of effects that are the product of causes we have set in motion since the fall of man and woman, the fall of the Lemurian continent, and the subsequent fall of Atlantis recorded as the flood of Noah. We are living in a time when the law of cosmos requires that before the turn of the century many causes set in motion through thousands of incarnations must be balanced. The energy comes full circle; this is the law of karma.

Karma is simply cause in manifestation. Cause, as we send forth, returns. It's like the law of the boomerang: "Whatsoever a man soweth, that shall he also reap." [26] Do you wonder why you have misfortune, why you have problems, why you have joy, why you have bliss? It is the return of that which you have sent forth; this is the law of energy. Energy cycles out from your chakras and it must return. It has your stamp, your identity, your spiral on it. It goes forth, it covers the earth, and it returns. And the conclusion of the spiral coalesces in your four lower bodies for better or for worse. We can't change the past; we can only change the future by changing the present.

Saint Germain, the hierarch of the Aquarian age, which is the age of freedom, came forth to deliver to mankind the gift of violet fire. Violet fire is the energy of the Holy Spirit that is for the forgiveness of sin and for transmutation. The release of the violet flame, which is the flame of freedom, into our four lower bodies consumes by the action of the Holy Spirit the causes we have set in motion that are not of the light before they can become effects in our lives not to our liking.

You see, what mankind has become, through the misuse of free will, is the sorcerer and the sorcerer's apprentice. The sorcerer's apprentice learns the formula of the magician and gets carried away with it and doesn't know how to stop it. There is nothing more clear, nothing more concrete, than watching, as I have watched in recent months, individuals passing from this world through the death of cancer and other diseases. We see coming into physical manifestation in the body temple the effects of causes set in motion sometimes fifty to one hundred thousand years ago.

Saint Germain knew that we would be required before the turn of the century to meet those energies and meet that substance, that misqualified energy. So he went before the Lords of Karma and he asked to be given the dispensation to give mankind the violet flame. In his *Pearls of Wisdom* entitled "The Chela and the Path," [27] Morya explains how Saint Germain received that dispensation and at what cost—the assuming of the responsibility for mankind's misuse of the violet flame.

So the violet flame has been given and I have seen it in action. And I know of the recordings, over and over again, of individuals who averted disease and all types of personal misfortune by the invocation of that aspect of the Holy Spirit called the violet flame. It meets the spiral at the level of the etheric body, the mental body, and emotional body before it becomes physical.

A spiral is a coil of energy that, through our fiats, comes out from the chakras in a clockwise direction. As it cycles through consciousness and being, it first goes through the etheric or memory body, coalescing as a pattern and a blueprint in the subconscious. We all know that all the impressions of life are recorded there; they also become components of that which we become. Then this spiral cycles through the mind as concept, as idea, then through the feeling body as emotions, as desire, as feeling. When it has gone all that way, it finally manifests physically.

For example, if I should hold resentment or hatred in my heart for another part of life and this energy should go forth from me, it's not going to immediately manifest as a boil upon my arm. It will go forth as hatred; it will be a burden to the soul I am sending it to. It will cycle through his being and it will gain momentum by all the other forcefields of hatred in the world. Finally it will cycle back to me and return to my doorstep. It may come back three embodiments later as some accident that occurs to me. There are no accidents. Accidents precipitate the flow of energy from the inner bodies to the physical.

How can we avoid the head-on collision with karma? The Hindus call it the car of juggernaut. It's the concept of a car on a roller coaster that just keeps going. It's karma coming in; it's the spiral turning the wheel of the law. And it keeps going unless something arrests it.

What can arrest the spiral except God, except the Holy Spirit, except our free will aligned with that Spirit and saying, "God, help me! God, come into my life and take command over this substance of disease, this substance of imperfection, over this bad temper, or this impurity, or this imperfection. I want to stop being in bondage to my karma. Make me free! Make me free!" God hears that call and answers with the violet flame even before you know the violet flame exists. When you make a call for freedom, God sends his violet-flame angels, because that's what freedom personified is.

Now you know the teaching of karma that is given in the East. It is the law that we balance karma; and there are many paths of yoga that lead to the balancing of karma, that lead to the overcoming of the round of rebirth. But chiefly it's the paying back, step by step, one by one, of all those persons we have ever contacted when there has been a flow of energy that is less than the flow of light from the Real Self. This means all human interchange of any kind whatsoever.

Can you imagine in the next twenty-five years having to meet everyone you have ever known in the last two hundred fifty thousand years of incarnation? It would be like a stepped-up movie where everyone is running around and frantically trying to balance all this karma before the day of reckoning.

Well, Saint Germain anticipated this eventuality hundreds of thousands of years ago. While we were still misqualifying energy, he was conceiving of a plan whereby at the time we finally woke up, there would be hope, there would be intercession, there would be dispensations, there would be a way out. That's the violet flame. The gift of Saint Germain, after the gift of the I AM Presence and the Christ Self, is this supreme dedication of the flame of freedom upon the altar of your heart.

The Ritual and the Requirements of the Ascension

Saint Germain comes. He comes as real and even more real

and more tangible than I am, standing before you. He knocks at the door of your heart; he presents to you this gift of freedom. He has said that if you invoke this flame of freedom diligently in this lifetime, you have the opportunity to be free from the round of rebirth and to return to the heart of your I AM Presence in the ritual of the ascension. This is unheard of! For thousands and thousands of years we have not had this open door, this opportunity. We are living in a cosmic moment.

The requirement for the ascension is the balancing of 51 percent of your karma. This is a dispensation of this century. The requirement was formerly 100 percent, so very few of mankind ever got through the portals to eternity. Fifty-one percent of all energy you have ever used must be drawn into alignment with your Source, your I AM Presence, with the inner law of your being.

When this happens, you automatically become a candidate for the ascension. You are contacted by the Brotherhood. A master announces to you that you have earned your ascension. Will you take it or will you remain on earth to serve the evolutions here? he asks. You make your decision in consultation with your Christ Self.

A requirement in addition to the balancing of 51 percent of your karma is the fulfillment of your divine plan. You came forth from the I AM Presence as a soul to perfect a certain work that no one else can perform in Matter. You must perform that work before you can return. You may balance 51 percent of your karma, but if your divine plan is not fulfilled, you will remain. This often happens. Saints become very devoted to the flame; yet they do not have the contact with humanity whereby they complete the building of the pyramid of life—the culmination of what is called the sacred labor, the very special work, the handiwork that is yours to consecrate upon the altar of humanity.

The violet flame, then, is the means whereby we can avoid the coming-down upon us of that karma that is so intense that the body cannot withstand the energy spiral and therefore passes through death and we are required to incarnate again. I have seen this happen again and again and again. Individuals have come to the point of reckoning, a specific point in time and space where, according to what is called their cosmic clock, a certain portion of energy misqualified twenty-five thousand years ago is plunked upon their doorstep by the angels of karma.

They come and they do that; they plunk it. It's a little bundle

of energy. They put it on your doorstep—here it is. And all of a
sudden you're deathly ill; you're in bed. One minute you're
healthy; the next minute you're sick. If you have enough fire
flowing through you, youth and vitality, you overcome the spiral.
It becomes transmuted by passing through your four lower bodies.

That's like the process of slow oxidation, of rusting. That's
another way of transmuting karma. The suffering of the saints is
transmutation. The bearing of the sins of the world in the body of
Christ through suffering is transmutation. It's the painful method.
The Aquarian dispensation gives us the opportunity to balance
karma through spontaneous combustion. The flame within your
heart can pass through the four lower bodies and consume the
cause and core of spirals of karma before they ever manifest as
disease or problems or burdens or catastrophe in our lives.

I'd like us to give together Decree 70.11. The names of the
beings listed in the preamble of the decree are all God-free
beings—ascended masters or cosmic beings. Some have been free
of the round of rebirth for millions of years. When we speak their
name, instantaneously they are one with the heart chakra. They
intensify the action of the violet flame. This is hierarchy; this is the
chain of cosmic consciousness. This is the reason why we have
gurus; this is why we have ascended-master teachers. When we
pray, they reinforce our prayer. So these masters always reinforce
the action of freedom and of the violet flame. When we give the
call, we give it by the authority of the I AM Presence, by the
authority of the Christ Self, so we know we are operating in
conformity with cosmic law in even making the call. [Audience
gives Decree 70.11 three times.]

I AM the Violet Flame

In the name of the beloved mighty victorious
Presence of God, I AM in me, and my very own beloved
Holy Christ Self, I call to beloved Alpha and Omega in
the heart of God in our Great Central Sun, beloved Saint
Germain, beloved Portia, beloved Archangel Zadkiel,
beloved Holy Amethyst, beloved mighty Arcturus and
Victoria, beloved Kwan Yin, Goddess of Mercy, beloved
Oromasis and Diana, beloved Mother Mary, beloved
Jesus, beloved Omri-Tas, ruler of the violet planet,

beloved Great Karmic Board, beloved Lanello, the entire Spirit of the Great White Brotherhood and the World Mother to expand the violet flame within my heart, purify my four lower bodies, transmute all misqualified energy I have ever imposed upon life, and blaze mercy's healing ray throughout the earth, the elementals, and all mankind and answer this my call infinitely, presently, and forever:

> I AM the violet flame
> In action in me now
> I AM the violet flame
> To light alone I bow
> I AM the violet flame
> In mighty cosmic power
> I AM the light of God
> Shining every hour
> I AM the violet flame
> Blazing like a sun
> I AM God's sacred power
> Freeing every one

And in full faith I consciously accept this manifest, manifest, manifest (3x) right here and now with full power, eternally sustained, all-powerfully active, ever expanding, and world enfolding until all are wholly ascended in the light and free! Beloved I AM, beloved I AM, beloved I AM!

Can you feel that flame really wanting to go ahead and charge, wanting to make you step up the momentum of your mantra? It's almost like holding back a team of wild horses. You can feel that flame and that power of God wanting to give this. When you feel the freedom of the suns which are your chakras and you feel the fire moving around them, it is that compulsion to move with the vibration of the fire. And as we said this morning, each one has his own cosmic clock; each one has the timing of his frequency. A good way to get in tune with the violet flame is to make it the violet singing flame which Zadkiel called it. So let us sing this mantra and visualize a sea of violet flame into which we plunge for the clearing of our four lower bodies. [Audience sings Decree 70.11 four times.]

How many of you have never made an invocation to the violet flame in this life? Can you raise your hands? [Approximately nine hundred people raise their hands.] I would like to mention to you that you probably have not made an invocation to the violet flame for ten thousand years or more. The reason is that this teaching of the Great White Brotherhood has not been released outside the retreats of the masters until the dispensation in this century, which means that at this particular moment when we began this morning with our fiat "I AM a being of violet fire," that was the first time in ten thousand years or more that your etheric body, your subconscious, has had the experience of the baptism of the Holy Ghost of which John the Baptist spoke when he said: "One cometh after me whose shoes I am not worthy to unlatch. He will baptize you with the Holy Ghost and with fire."[28] This is the power of the Christed One. This is what Jesus imparted in his healings, in his forgiveness of sin. It was the conveyance of fire and specifically, many times, the violet fire, so that sins were forgiven, karma was dissolved. Thereby the lame could walk, the deaf could hear, the blind could see. This is necessary.

All who have walked the path of the ascension have come into the awareness of the violet flame. Many saints along the path, kneeling before the altars of the mosques, the cathedrals of the world, the temple in their meditation upon the law of being, have had the revelation, the private revelation, of the violet flame. And through that revelation they have earned their ascension.

Now we are living in a time when this knowledge is for all who will take it and run with it. It is the flame that we keep, the flame that we give, the flame that we become. Concluding, then, this portion of our afternoon session, may I commend you to the science of the Master Alchemist, Saint Germain. May I commend you to the laboratory of your own soul where you can prove, by the authority of your I AM Presence and your Real Self, that God is a consuming fire. Thank you.

July 3, 1975
2:30-3:40 P.M. PDT

5

AN INTRODUCTION TO THE ASCENDED MASTERS, THE MESSENGERS, AND GODFRE

A Lecture by Elizabeth Clare Prophet

Ascended Masters

You've come to Shasta to hear the ascended masters. Saint Germain has bid you welcome. We have defined *ascended masters* today as those who've mastered time and space, passed their initiations, balanced at least 51 percent of their karma, and ascended into the Presence of the I AM THAT I AM to become immortal God-free beings. We have said that these masters comprise the Spirit of the Great White Brotherhood—the fraternity of the saints who have pledged to serve mankind until all mankind are free in the ritual of the ascension. The Great White Brotherhood is the company of saints, the hosts of the Lord who have said: "We are free, but we are not going to desert our unascended brothers and sisters who remain in bondage."

You know the story that is given in Buddhist scriptures about these three men who approached the wall. And there's something fantastic going on inside this wall. And one boosts the other up, and he looks inside and he goes into bliss. He's in ecstasy! He climbs over and hops down, and the other two don't know what's inside and they sit there dumbfounded. What's over on the other side of that wall? So the next one gets boosted up and he looks inside and he climbs over, and he's never heard of again. So the third one says, "Well, I'm going to find out what's going on, on the other side of that wall!" So he climbs up and looks over, and he beholds the souls of beings who are liberated. But he forgoes his liberation. He doesn't hop over the wall. He comes back to tell mankind what's on the other side of the wall.

The Great White Brotherhood

The Great White Brotherhood is the company of ascended masters who have said: "We are not going on in the cosmos beyond and leaving Terra behind. We will stay; we will tarry." At this moment in cosmic history, the door is wide open. The Great White Brotherhood is sponsoring the release of the spoken Word through conferences, through writings, through books, through weekly *Pearls of Wisdom* and the Keepers of the Flame Lessons. They are releasing the full teaching that the dispensations of cosmic law allow at the conclusion of the two-thousand-year cycle of Pisces.

At the end of each two thousand years, there is an impetus of light whereby the door opens and cosmic law is presented for the next dispensation. The time of Jesus was the last time that there was this intensity. And before that, in the Mosaic dispensation, again we had new revelations of the law, of the I AM. We're living in a bountiful time, a time of cosmic abundance—a time when we can reap a harvest of spiritual fruit from our causal bodies, strike a blow for the Lord, win our victory, climb over that wall, and help mankind over, too. All that can happen in this twenty-five-year cycle.

The Founding of The Summit Lighthouse

So, to fulfill this plan, the ascended masters—namely El Morya, who is the Chief of the Darjeeling Council of the Great White Brotherhood—contacted Mark L. Prophet in 1958 and told him to found The Summit Lighthouse in Washington, D.C. He had been trained by Morya since childhood and also prior to this life. His assignment, then, was to go to Washington, which he did, to found The Summit Lighthouse.

Three years later I was contacted by El Morya in Boston, where I was in college, and also called to be trained as a messenger. I was introduced to Mark Prophet. He became the instrument of my training under El Morya and Saint Germain. The purpose of the training: to release the sacred scriptures for the Aquarian age—the two-thousand-year dispensation of the writing of the law of the flame of freedom which had already been begun through the messengers Godfre Ray King and Lotus Ray King in the I AM movement in the late twenties and thirties.[1]

That was an endeavor and a movement begun by Saint Germain. What Saint Germain went through, the dispensations necessary, the calling-together of a body of devotees, and what happened and transpired in their response to the flame of freedom, is a saga of souls—souls of freedom who have written an immortal page in the history of a planet.

The Messenger as the Witness

We are coming together today to hear a dictation by an ascended being, the ascended master Godfre, who also walked the earth as a messenger. A messenger is not a channel, not a spiritualistic medium. A messenger comes under the dispensation of the prophets.

In every age, the Brotherhood has had those who are called the witnesses—those who write down the law, who give the warning, and who give the prophecy to the people who are chosen. Those who are chosen are those who choose to listen and to identify with the flame of that which is real. God has never left mankind without messengers, without prophets. They have gone unrecognized, unheeded, and civilization and karma have taken their course. But they have always been present—some known, some unknown.

The training to be a messenger takes place over thousands of years. It is not something you can get by psychic studies; it's not something you can get by your own effort. For all of the training, the conclusion of the training is the *gift* of prophecy; it is the gift of the spoken Word. It is an assignment and an ordination. I was ordained by the master Saint Germain to represent him and to complete the mission of beloved Godfre Ray King (Guy Ballard).

I recall coming into incarnation in the year of his ascension, standing before the Lords of Karma, and agreeing to continue the work of releasing the knowledge of the I AM Presence, the Real Self, and the violet flame. I made that vow before the Lords of Karma, who are the ascended masters who govern the cycles of the release of karma on behalf of mankind in this system of worlds. I made that vow to Godfre; and from the moment I knew of the teachings of the masters, I pursued that calling.

The ascended masters function at the plane of our I AM Presence. When we are one with the I AM Presence, we are one with the ascended masters. The messenger stands at the level of the Christ Self, or the Real Self, of mankind. The messenger is the one who assists the soul to make contact with the Christ Self so that the Christ Self can release to the soul and to the outer consciousness the teachings of the I AM Presence and the ascended masters. Hence the messenger stands representing the Christ Self until there is no longer any need for the messenger and all mankind behold the I AM Presence and the ascended masters face to face.

So the dispensation of prophets and messengers is an intermediary dispensation. It is for that period when mankind cannot hear the voice of God. When they do, each man, each woman, sits under his own vine and fig tree.[2] The vine is the crystal cord; the fig tree is your causal body—your own Tree of Life.[3] And you, in meditation under your own vine and fig tree, commune with the Spirit of the Great White Brotherhood.

The Meeting of the Master
through the Power of the Spoken Word

As you see your I AM Presence in the chart of the Presence, visualize, then, the master who will be speaking at the particular time scheduled in the class as one with your Presence, releasing the power of the spoken Word, the consciousness of God, through your own I AM Presence, through your Christ Self, into your heart chakra. I stand before you focalizing the spoken Word, coalescing for all to hear, for all to feel the vibration which the master anchors through me as contact.

Some have come to conferences and have seen the master standing where I stand or where Mark has stood. First you feel the Brotherhood as a sense of direction pushing you to do this, pulling you away from that. Then you feel the presence of the masters perhaps as pulsations of light, as a burning within the heart. You feel radiation and you can hear it as the rushing of a mighty wind.[4] You can hear it as the sound of a waterfall as it descends upon you. You can feel it as a tingling through your body. All these are the signs of the presence of the masters and of your I AM Presence coming into greater and greater proximity to your consciousness here below.

You hear the voice of God speaking in your heart. You hear it with the inner ear. You hear the voice of conscience. You may also then meet the master face to face as the disciples did on the road to Emmaus,[5] as Peter did when he was fleeing Rome on the Appian Way. He saw Jesus standing there, already an ascended being. And Peter said to Jesus, *"Quō vādis?"* "Where are you going, Lord?"

It's interesting. I don't think Peter even digested the fact that he was talking to an ascended being. Impetuous Peter—he sees his Lord and asks, "Where are you going, Lord?" And his Lord says, "I am going to Rome to be crucified again." Peter knew then he must turn back and go to Rome and bear the sins of the world as his master had done. And he was crucified, and he chose to be crucified upside down because he said he was not worthy to be crucified in the same manner as his Lord.

So the meeting of the master on the road of life is an experience you may very well have. And this conference is like the Appian Way. On the road of life we have come. We have tarried here in our tent, and the masters are coming. And they are here! And you can very well expect to see them, but not physically. You will see them because they exalt your consciousness, your third-eye vision. This chakra puts you in tune with your soul faculties.

We have five physical senses; we have soul faculties also. These soul faculties penetrate beyond the physical. If your I AM Presence and Christ Self choose to step up the vibrations and open the window of the third eye, you may very well see the master who in the moment of the dictation is lowering his frequency as we are raising our frequency. So the meeting ground, as the masters descend and we ascend, is the plane of the Christ Self, which is outpictured in the messenger representing the Christ Self of all.

I trust you will understand what our attunement is and that the only way to get God or to get any portion of God as hierarchy is through the flame in your heart. I can't do it for you; even the masters can't do it for you. They come to help you do it yourself. The ascended masters' teachings in this age are a do-it-yourself kit. They give us the instruction, the formula; but nothing happens until *we* do it.

When you meditate for the dictation, we ask that you place your feet flat on the floor and keep your hands separated. This is for your attunement; this is for the flow of energy through your chakras. And we ask that you meditate upon your Presence and upon the master who is speaking and receive in your heart the radiation, the light, and the impression, as you hear the spoken Word.

Godfre Embodied as George Washington

Now I'd like to talk to you about Godfre and his embodiment as George Washington. For many reasons, it is altogether fitting that at Shasta 1975 Godfre should be coming to deliver the first dictation. As many of you know, Shasta has been the meeting ground of masters and their disciples. Specifically, Godfre first met Saint Germain on the mountain, we hear, at the place called Panther Meadow—the very first contact with the master that inaugurated his mission and the writing of *Unveiled Mysteries, The Magic Presence,* and *The "I AM" Discourses.* Here is where it took place. It was an appropriate forcefield. It *is* a meeting ground. There are places on the planet that are more conducive than others to the meeting of the masters and their chelas, because in the ethers and in the earth, there are these grids of light, focal points, where energy of an extraordinary vibration can be released. Mount Shasta is such a place.

Godfre, in his final incarnation, was fulfilling the spiral begun as George Washington. As George Washington, he released the thrust of the flame of Alpha for the founding of our nation. Saint Germain, who sponsored America as the place where all mankind should come to learn of the teaching of the Real Self, the Christ Self, sponsored Washington and placed within his heart the mandala of freedom that was to be fulfilled in this century.

I know you have heard many stories about George Washington, and most of you know something of his life and of the history surrounding his life. I have selected for our reading this afternoon a chapter from the work of Manly Palmer Hall, *The Secret Destiny of America.* It concerns a subject—the prophecy of William Hope—that I feel few of you have heard about and it gives us a very interesting insight. It gives us insight into the fact that every soul has a cosmic destiny that can be deciphered, can be known, can be determined, if it is the will of God to release it. From this reading we can see that as Godfre had a destiny in America, so we also have a destiny that can be known, that each soul here is unique in the destiny of the freedom of a world crying out on its knees to be free.

The Prophecy of Sir William Hope

George Washington had just been born when the governor of Edinburg Castle wrote a prophecy that this infant born overseas was starred by fate to lead the colonies to freedom; this prediction also named, four decades in advance, the year of the Declaration of Independence.

In the Congressional Library at Washington, D.C., is a curious little book entitled, *Vindication of the True Art of Self Defense.* It is a work on fencing and dueling, published in 1724 by Sir William Hope, Bart., a deputy governor of Edinburg Castle. In this copy and facing the title page an engraving has been inserted of the badge of the Royal Society of Swordsmen; underneath it is written, "Private Library of Sir William Hope." The Library of Congress has had this book since 1879.

The text of this curious little book is of no special interest, but on the blank flyleaves is written in the hand of Sir William Hope an extraordinary prediction concerning the destiny of the United States of America. It was written, signed and dated forty-four years before the beginning of the Revolutionary War.

At the time the thirteen American colonies semingly [*sic*] had no dream of independence. George Washington had just been born, in Virginia. Twenty of the fifty-six men who were to sign the Declaration of Independence were then small boys, and eighteen others were yet unborn.

Little information is available concerning Sir William Hope; but from the text of his prediction it appears that he was devoted to the study of astrology, and based his strange prophetic poem upon an interpretation of the starry influences. There is also a hint of the Cabala in the manner used by Hope to indicate the men referred to in his prediction.

The prophecy of Sir William Hope begins with these lines:

> 'Tis Chaldee says his fate is great
> Whose stars do bear him fortunate.

Of thy near fate, Amerika, [*sic*]
I read in stars a prophecy:

Fourteen divided, twelve the same,
Sixteen in halfs—each holds a name;
Four, eight, seven, six—added ten—
The life line's mark of Four gt. men.

From the text, the prophecy covers the period from 1732 to 1901. From the history of our country during this period of time, Hope selected four men, and the numbers which he used to indicate them are shown as the prophecy unfolds. He summarizes the lives of these four men by totaling the number of years that each lived. He does this in the line, *Four, eight, seven, six—added ten—"* [*sic*] Four plus eight, plus seven, plus six, equal 25, the added ten is the cipher making a total of 250. At the time of his death George Washington was 68, Abraham Lincoln 56, Benjamin Harrison 68, and William McKinley 58. The total of these years is 250.

The next twelve lines are devoted to a description of George Washington and the struggle of the American colonies for independence.

This day is cradled, far beyond the sea,
One starred by fate to rule both
bond and free.

The prophecy is dated 1732, and in that year George Washington was born beyond the sea, in Virginia. The reference to bond and free is believed to indicate that slavery would exist during Washington's time in the colony of Virginia.

Add double four, thus fix the destined day
When servile knees unbend 'neath
freedom's sway.

By double four we can read 44, which if added to the date, 1732, gives 1776, the year of the American Declaration of Independence.

> Place six 'fore ten, then read the patriot's
>   name
> Whose deeds shall link him to a deathless
>   fame.
> Add double four, thus fix the destined day

There are six letters in the name George, and ten in Washington, and this Cabala when added to the previous and subsequent descriptions, can leave no doubt as to the man intended in the prophecy.

> Whose growing love and ceaseless trust
>   wrong none
> And catch truth's colors from its glowing sun!
> Death's door shall clang while yet his
>   century waits,
> His planets point the way to other's pending
>   fates.

These lines contain not only a glowing tribute but an exact bit of prophesy. Washington died on December 14, 1799, just 17 days before his century passed into history.

> Till all the names on freedom's scroll shall fade,
> Two tombs be built, his lofty cenotaph be made—

Freedom's scroll is the Declaration of Independence, which is now carefully preserved under yellow cellophane because the signatures have begun to fade. The body of George Washington has rested in two tombs; and his lofty cenotaph, the Washington Monument, is 555 feet high, the tallest memorial ever constructed to the memory of a man.

> Full six times ten the years must
>   onward glide,
> Nature their potent help, a constant,
>   prudent guide.

If six times ten years, or sixty years, be added to the date of the death of Washington the result is 1859, when John Brown raided Harper's Ferry and was hanged for attempting to incite a slave revolt, a circumstance leading directly to the United States of America engaging in the great Civil War to preserve the freedom of all of its people.

> Then fateful seven 'fore seven shall sign
>   heroic son
> Whom Mars and Jupiter strike down
>   before his work is done.
> When cruel fate shall pierce, though
>   artless of its sword;
> Who leaves life's gloomy stage
>   without one farewell word.
> A softly beaming star, half veiled
>   by Mars' red cloud
> Virtue, his noblest cloak, shall form
>   a fitting shroud.

There are seven letters in Abraham, and seven letters in Lincoln. He is the "heroic son" elected to the Presidency in 1860, re-elected in 1864, and assassinated April 14, 1865. He was indeed struck down before his work was done, for slavery was not abolished by constitutional amendment until the end of that year, and the Civil War was not proclaimed to be at an end until August 20, 1866.

The reference to life's gloomy stage is the more extraordinary because Lincoln was assassinated at Ford's Theater while watching a play; and he never spoke again after the assassin's bullet struck him although he lived for several hours.

References to President Benjamin Harrison are contained in the two following lines:

> Then eight 'fore eight a later generation rules,
> With light undimmed and shed in progress'
>   school.

There are eight letters in Benjamin, and eight in Harrison. He ruled in a later generation, 1889 to 1893. His administration was justly climaxed by the great

Columbian Exposition at Chicago in 1893. Here, invention, transportation, industry, art, science, and agriculture exhibited the progress which they had made in the first century of American national existence. This is probably the 'progress school' referred to in the prediction. Harrison's administration was not dimmed by war or by any scandals in high office.

> Then six again, with added six shall rise,
> Resplendent ruler—good, and great—
> and wise.
> Four sixes hold a glittering star that on
> his way shall shine;
> And twice four sixes mark his years
> from birth to manhood's prime.

While the verses accurately describe President McKinley, this is the only instance in which the numbers do not appear to fit the name. Research, however, indicates that the original form of the family name would permit it to be divided, thus, Will-Mc Kinley, which means, Will, the son of Kinley. In this form, each of the combinations would contain six letters. Four sixes, or 24, agrees with President McKinley being the 24th man to hold the presidential office. And twice four sixes, or 48, was the age of McKinley at the time he was elected Governor of his native state, which might be said to be his 'manhood's prime'. There is no reference to McKinley's second term or his assassination. But the prophecy definitely states that it goes no farther than the end of the 19th Century. It does indicate earlier however, that McKinley's life was to be 58 years, which was correct.

The prophecy ends with four more lines:

> These truths prophetic shall completion see
> Ere time's deep grave receives the
> Nineteenth Century!
> All planets, stars, twelve signs and
> horoscope
> Attest these certain truths foretold
> by William Hope.

Following this, is the statement that the prophecy was 'Writ at Cornhill, London, 1732.' At the bottom of the page are four other lines written by some later member of the Hope family as a tribute to the memory of Sir William Hope:

> The learned hand that writ these lines
>   no more shall pen for me,
> Yet voice shall speak and pulses beat
>   for long posterity.
> This soul refined through love of kind
>   bewailed life's labors spent,
> Then found this truth, his search from youth,
>   Greatness is God's accident.—

James Hope

As is usual with material of this kind, efforts have been made to prove the Hope Prophecy to be a forgery; but up to the present time no tangible evidence has been advanced to disprove the prediction. Always in these matters, the critic takes the attitude that such predictions can not be made, and if a writing appears to be authentic then it must be imposture. The book has been in the Library of Congress for more than 60 years. The prediction about both Harrison and McKinley relate to incidents taking place after the book was placed in the Congressional Library.[6]

The Spiritual Destiny of America

America has a secret destiny. America is the place prepared for the coming of the Divine Woman, for the raising-up of the feminine ray, for the liberation of woman, and for her delivery of the Divine Manchild unto the age. This means that here, in fertile soil prepared by patriots, prepared by lovers of freedom, by the men and women of the centuries, is the place where the grid and forcefield of the Great White Brotherhood is placed for the teachings of the I AM Presence, the Christ Self, and the alchemy of the violet flame to be released and received. To this land have been brought souls who can receive the teachings, who have been trained at inner levels in the retreats of the Great White

Brotherhood. This is indeed the virgin soil prepared for the Cosmic Virgin.

In our forthcoming lectures in this conference in celebration of our independence and our flame of freedom, we will look at the spiritual destiny of America and the spiritual destiny of all mankind. And by pursuing the cycles of the cosmic clock—which is the ascended masters' astrology for the golden age—and many other means that the masters have given to us, we will see how, line by line, this destiny was secured even aeons before the birth of a nation.

This prophecy is true. I have examined the record with Saint Germain. Had I not done so, I would not have read it to you. And its merit lies in the fact that we see that the working-out of cosmic destiny is the movement of spirals that have their origin so far beyond our realization of that destiny as to make us simply sit in wonder of the stars. "O Lord our Lord, how excellent is thy name in all the earth! . . . When I consider thy heavens, the work of thy fingers, the moon and the stars, which thou hast ordained; what is man, that thou art mindful of him? and the son of man, that thou visitest him?" [7]

With all of the vastness of creation and the plan contained in the seed of the atom, what are *we* to receive the gift of immortality? The very special creation, the potential for godhood—this is the gift of the flame that we are.

July 3, 1975
4:20-5:05 P.M. PDT

Godfre is a being freed by God for the grand ritual of the return to the fiery core of life. This core of being we address as the I AM Presence. All of the masters speaking at this conference have won their spiritual freedom and their permanent individuality through reunion with the Presence in the ritual of the ascension. The ascension is the goal of life not only for the few, but for the many. The ascension is the cosmic moment of soul freedom. Godfre, who won his freedom through obedience to the law of being, teaches us to ascend moment by moment by raising our thoughts and feelings, our energies and actions.

6

FREEDOM THROUGH OBEDIENCE
TO THE LAW OF BEING

A Dictation by the Ascended Master Godfre

To Souls Overcoming Bondage

In the stillness of each heart, I enshrine the flame of freedom!

I come in answer to the call of light-bearers of the centuries. I come in answer to the call of souls evolving on Terra desiring to be free. And the desiring of those who are not born free, but who are in bondage, is greater than those who know the flame of freedom and have received the fanning of the fires of freedom within the heart. Therefore, I respond to souls throughout the planetary body overcoming bondage in whatever form and the tyranny of the carnal mind in whatever form.

I come as a patriot of light unto all nations, enshrining the flame of freedom in the hearts of patriots everywhere attuned to the fires of freedom. I greet the morning sun as the light which God has placed within your hearts. I come to consecrate that which has been consecrated already. I come to pour the oil, the sacred oil of gladness, as an unguent of healing, as a medium of initiation, as the anointing of the body of God upon earth for the trials and the triumphs which are to come.

A Vision of America

I come with a vision of America. I come holding in my heart that vision that has been placed there by Saint Germain, the God

of Freedom to the earth and her evolutions. As that great patriot
came of old to me, came then to inspire freedom and the Constitution of the United States, so I come also, passing the torch of
freedom which has been mine to carry, summoning the light-
bearers, calling all to the circle of harmony and the law of the One,
the One out of many.

So is the flame of the Christ consciousness the one flame that
rises as a fountain of light, a tribute to all peoples and all nations
who have come to this soil and this continent for the great
gathering of the elect[1]—for that time in history when, by the
power of the spoken Word, ascended masters, hierarchies of light,
should talk with mankind again and walk with mankind and
prepare the way for the Second Coming of the Christed One in the
hearts of all mankind. This is the destiny of America: to set forth
that City Foursquare that is the foundation of the new order of the
ages, the order of freedom, the order of the Aquarian age.[2] And
from that square the pyramid of life does rise. It remains for a
people fervent in devotion to the flame to place the capstone on
the pyramid of this civilization wrought by man in God and God
in man.

The Lord's Hosts Encompassed Round About

I send forth the flame of God-free beings who assemble with
me, who were with me even at Valley Forge and in many battles
that have been won for the cause of light in many centuries. The
Lord's hosts are encompassed round about as this is the holy tent of
the congregation of the righteous who have understood in part the
meaning of freedom. Hail, sons and daughters of Liberty! I salute
the flame within you! And I AM one in that flame. And my fervor
for America is a fervor for the race of God-conscious beings who
know the name of God and who will carry that flame to the four
winds, to the uttermost parts of the sea, to all nations, kindreds,
peoples, and tongues. The torch has already been passed in the
inception of this nation of a flame of freedom that must be
conveyed to all peoples.

And now as the centuries have rolled and we come to that
point of the celebration of twice the hundred, we see many
changes, many ways of the flowing of the cycles of life. We behold
a new consciousness and attitudes as the Piscean age has given way

to the Aquarian age. America is a nation consecrated for Aquarius and for that flame of freedom. To the efforts of all who have given their lives, their fortunes, and their sacred honor to this cause, I add my own flame and my ascended consciousness and my causal body. And I give to you this day that momentum which can be yours for the fray, that momentum of light to carry as a burden of victory, as a burden of responsibility, as a burden before the Fourteen Ascended Masters who focus the mandala of God-government to this nation.

The Inscribing of Cosmic Law in the Body of God upon Earth

Let it be known, then, that the law which is written in the inner parts of man and woman this day is written by angels who stand clothed upon with garments of living fire, having the golden pen within their hands.[3] And they write the law of God-government for this nation upon the hearts and the minds and the conscience of a people that those who are ordained to be the forerunners of the government of the golden age might know that standard, might perceive that law, might take that law and run with it as the torch of freedom to the ages.

The inscribing of cosmic law in the body of God upon earth is a further implementation of the incarnation of the Word—the Word itself being the Logos, the reason of God that comes as the individualization of the God flame. This, then, is the dispensation of hierarchy and of Saint Germain: to coalesce in the God-awareness of a mighty people and a mighty nation the foundations of the law that shall be unto a planet as the Ten Commandments that were given to the children of Israel and as the new commandment given by Christ unto the disciples and as the law of the unfoldment of the cycles of Aquarius.[4] So let it be written not on tablets of stone, but on the sacred altar of the heart where no man can desecrate the sacred Word that comes from on high as fingers of living flame carve out the sacred destiny of a soul, of a nation, of a planet and a people.

Students of the I AM
Receive the Dispensation of the Divine Mother

I AM Godfre! I reveal myself to the faithful! I amplify the

momentum of all who have served the cause of the teachings of the I AM. I extend to all students of the I AM throughout the world the call to come into the home, the place of the Divine Mother, and receive from her hand the teachings that I give, carrying forth the earlier dispensations of this century unto the next century that are written even for your victory and for your ascension.

Fear not, for I AM here! And I stand at Shasta where I stood before the master Saint Germain to consecrate each soul to the receiving of that cup and that elixir, that living flame, to the receiving of that initiation and that oneness with the hosts of the Lord. I come to consecrate and to initiate those who are willing to have their vibration brought into the dispensation of the Divine Mother and of the Holy Spirit.

I AM Godfre! I surely am that frequency and that life and that love which you have known! Behold then the continuity of hierarchy! Behold the message to the new student and to the student of long standing that it is the teaching of the I AM Presence and the chart of the I AM Presence that is the *key* to your immortality! It is the *key* to your ascension! Take that as the law and let it be the legacy which you give to mankind—that you make your life count for Saint Germain, for all that has been given of the forces of freedom and the lives that have been sacrificed to this cause, lives you know not of around the world who have suc-cumbed to the dragon, even the dragon of World Communism.

Give Me Liberty or Give Me Death

Understand that many patriots in many nations have given their lives for that Mother flame and for that contact with light which they felt within their souls, which they would not surrender. And they declared even within their souls with that patriot Patrick Henry, "Give me liberty or give me death!" This is a liberty of soul. This is a liberty whereby you have the right to pursue your ascension, to pursue the calling and the election which is yours ordained. This is that liberty to invoke God as you see fit. It is that liberty to come together, to assemble, to speak freely, to worship, to have the Trinity of God within your heart.

The Proclamation of Freedom Signed by the Saints

Understand, then, that the four sacred freedoms are ever

being challenged by the forces of tyranny and that I am on guard in the cosmic honor flame to defend the souls of all mankind. I come with a scroll then. It is the proclamation of freedom signed by the saints, by the righteous who are robed in white, waiting for their turn, for their ascension—saints who have walked the earth, some who are in the retreats of hierarchy, some who are in the retreats of the Brotherhood who are working with this company of unascended devotees in incarnation, working hand in hand in a noble effort to enshrine freedom in the hearts of all mankind.

Aleksandr Solzhenitsyn, Spokesman for Freedom

Understand, then, that the spokesman for freedom in this hour of America's destiny and America's crisis comes not as a patriot of this soil, but a patriot out of the Soviet Union. The one Aleksandr Solzhenitsyn comes forth in this hour of the celebration of freedom to warn the American people! As a prophet of freedom he comes forth, sponsored then to point the way of the Liar and his lie and the way of victory. Understand, then, that America would not heed her own, and therefore the Lord God has seen fit to send another to prove the oneness of the flame of freedom in the hearts of all mankind and the devotees who are waiting daily upon the Lord as the only hope of their salvation to retain life in embodiment in this age.

I tell you, precious ones, the only way to defeat the forces of hatred, of greed, and of war in whatever form they manifest in whatever society is by the flame of freedom. It is the flame and only the flame that will turn back greed in a capitalistic economy as well as in a communistic economy. Do you understand that these conditions are not white and black and all is not glory here and all is not infamy there; but hearts of freedom burn in every continent, on every soil. And these are one in the flame of hierarchy; these are one with your invocations and calls this day as you have communed in the heart of freedom and in the holy mountain of God.

Conquer the Self

I plead for sanity before you! I plead that you put aside all vanity! I plead, then, that you concern yourselves with the concerns of the hour and not with trivia and not with selfishness and the pursuit of vain pleasure. Many before you have sacrificed more for a lesser cause. What greater cause is there, I say, than the cause of freedom to a planet? That cause is threatened as never before, and that cause must be won as a spiritual victory first, and then all life will come into conformity and bow before the victors of the Spirit.

Therefore, conquer the self! Conquer the tyranny of the self! Conquer the flow of life! Learn the art of alchemy, not the art of war. Learn the art of freedom. Learn the art of flow of sacred fire. Be a patriot who enshrines the sacred fire in every heart, in every nation. Be one who accepts the calling of God to send forth light daily to all peoples everywhere yearning to be free.

Light-Bearers of the World Unite for the Victory

Mankind are truly one in the flame. And it is the fallen ones and the archdeceivers in every nation, in every society, who are the spoilers, who are the ones who misuse those sacred institutions which have been ordained by God for God-government across the face of the earth. Let us then consume the cause and core of all difference, of all separation! Let it be consumed by the sacred fire! And let the light-bearers of the world unite for the victory of the Holy Spirit.

Let it be, then, a conflagration of sacred fire that proclaims the victory and the independence as the fireworks on the Fourth of July! Let it be the soaring of fire from the hearts of devotees around the world! And as they send forth those signals in the sky, let those lights meet, then, as sons and daughters of God in China, in Russia, in Africa and Europe, on every continent, in North and South America. Release then the fire of the heart for the victory— not as bombs bursting in air, but as spheres of light bursting, proclaiming: "I am free! I am free! I am free! I will have my victory! I will have my ascension! I will have that freedom for every man, woman, and child upon this planet!"

Be a Chalice for Hierarchy and for Humanity

This is where the line is drawn! This is the line. Therefore I say, come to the line! And be ready to seize that flame and take that calling and take that flame from the Elohim who are even now quickening the four lower bodies and the chakras for the subsequent releases in this class which shall be for a step-up of your four lower bodies which must serve as a living chalice of freedom to contain that fire and that flame! Therefore, be a chalice for hierarchy and for humanity! Recognize responsibility! Take that cape now which I wore as George Washington! Feel the weight of that cape sufficient to keep a general warm on a cold winter's night. Take that cape and feel what capability, what responsibility is when a people depend upon you because you have the flame of freedom.

Understand that many desiring to be free look to you and you and you because you have the fire in the heart vouchsafed to you by Saint Germain. Understand that you can never again live alone unto yourself, but you must live all one for God and man and for the victory. This is the responsibility for bringing in a golden age! This is the responsibility for transition into Aquarius! We played our part on the stage of life. Now you must play your role!

Staying Power, Staying Wisdom, Staying Love

Play it well! For I say, in centuries to come as light-bearers gather, they will extol the name of God, I AM THAT I AM, which has been enshrined in the hearts of you who have determined not to forsake the battlefield, not to turn your back on the Mother, not to turn your back on the cause of the Great White Brotherhood. In this moment in cosmic history, it is the staying power of sons and daughters of light which will make all the difference. Therefore, let us see what your staying power is, what your staying wisdom and staying love shall be! Let us see what you are willing to lay down as sacrifice for the cause in order to come into conformity with the law of being, that conformity which is called obedience.

Obedience, the Byword of Honor

Obedience is the byword of honor. Let us have, then, peace with honor within the souls of mankind! And if we cannot have it in all mankind, then at least let us show forth to cosmic councils and to the Ancient of Days that on this freedom celebration, July Fourth, 1975, the few and the many gathered at Shasta to have and to hold peace with honor in the soul. Let us show forth to hierarchy and to all who have gone before that there is a body upon earth of those who will not compromise the flame of freedom, who will not surrender that flame, who will give the precision of the intonation of the Word, who will prove that flame by the science of the Word, and who will prove it not for self alone or for selfish purpose, but for all mankind!

Enter into the Fraternity of the Great White Brotherhood

Enter, then, into the fraternity of the Great White Brotherhood! For many here who have not heard our word before yet have been called and have been already initiated by masters of the Great White Brotherhood in preparation for a cosmic mission upon Terra, I say, welcome! Welcome to the forcefield of Saint Germain! Welcome to the battlefield! This is where the line is drawn!

I thank you and bid you good afternoon.

July 3, 1975
5:25-5:47 P.M. P D T

Man is a carrier of light and energy. He also carries love and the wisdom of the ages. The torch that is passed is the fire of illumination handed down from life to life, from the central sun of cosmos to stars and planets and people. The torchbearers of all ages comprise the cosmic hierarchy of masterful beings known collectively as the Great White Brotherhood. They are Elohim and archangels, Lords of Flame and masters of the seven rays. They are elementals and nature spirits. In this age of Aquarius, the torch is passed to any and all among mankind who will accept it.

7

THE TORCH IS PASSED
Carrying the Light into the New Age

A Lecture by Elizabeth Clare Prophet

Godfre made quite clear today our responsibility of carrying the light into the new age, playing our role on the stage of life, and playing it well. He released to us the fervor of his devotion to freedom; and that fervor is the flame of love—love that follows the torch unto the victory, love that seizes the torch and carries it.

Man is a carrier of light and energy. He also carries love and the wisdom of the ages. The torch that is passed is the fire of illumination handed down from life to life, from the central sun of cosmos to stars and planets and people. The torchbearers of all ages comprise the cosmic hierarchies of masterful beings known collectively as the Great White Brotherhood. They are Elohim and archangels, Lords of Flame and masters of the seven rays. They are elementals and nature spirits. In this age of Aquarius, the torch is passed to any and all among mankind who will accept it.

An Outline of Hierarchy

In this lecture we will give an outline of hierarchy and of the Great White Brotherhood, because it is important that we understand the order that is heaven's first law and how that order manifests in the release of light from the central sun all the way down from the coordinates of hierarchy to our point in time and space.

Beginning in the heart of the Great Central Sun, hierarchy

manifests as the stepping-down of the energies of Alpha and
Omega, of the sacred AUM, of the I AM THAT I AM that is the
fiery focal point for the whole of creation, the whole of the cosmos.
The Elohim and cosmic beings carry the greatest concentration, the
highest vibration of light that we can comprehend in our state of
evolution. Alpha and Omega are beings ascended who represent
and focus the Father-Mother God in the Great Central Sun. They
are the highest expression of twin flames that we know of, and we
refer to them as our Father-Mother God. John the Beloved heard
them called "the beginning and the ending." In fact, it was the
Lord who spoke, "I AM Alpha and Omega, the beginning and the
ending." [1]

Proceeding out from the Great Central Sun, beings who have
earned the right through concentration of energy, of consciousness, of awareness of God, step down this release of sacred
fire for lesser evolutions who have not passed the initiations
required for them to contain such a concentrated manifestation of
light. The term "cosmic being" is a title, not only a description.
One newly ascended from the planes of earth with 51 percent of
his karma balanced would not be termed a "cosmic being." A
cosmic being is one who is aware of self as cosmos, who can ensoul
a cosmos and be aware of energy fields and the control of energy
fields that are vast, beyond our ability to even comprehend.

Cosmic Beings and the Twelve Solar Hierarchies

There are certain cosmic beings who came forth when Saint
Germain volunteered earlier in this century to help mankind and
to give the dispensation of the violet flame. One was his teacher,
the Great Divine Director; another is mighty Cosmos, who releases
the secret rays. Victory from Venus is also termed a cosmic being. It
simply means their awareness of the God flame is able to ap-
proximate measures of cosmic consciousness, the highest that can
be contained.

Surrounding Alpha and Omega, then, are cosmic beings and
the twelve solar hierarchies.* These hierarchies of light act as step-
down transformers. We refer to the twelve hierarchies surrounding
the central altar by the names of the signs of the zodiac, for want of
any other name. We speak, then, of a hierarchy of Capricorn, a
hierarchy of Cancer, a hierarchy of Aries and of Libra. These
*See Diagrams of the Cosmic Clock, figures 1-16.

hierarchies are mandalas of cosmic beings. For instance, the hierarchy of Capricorn could contain as its nucleus 144,000 cosmic beings acting as step-down transformers for the flame that is released from the heart of Alpha and Omega in the Great Central Sun which we call God-power. It is the energy that initiates cycles. Each of these twelve solar hierarchies has an appointment by God to release a certain aspect of the creative light.

We find that the stepping-down of energies is individed over and over again. As the twelve hierarchies take the twelve parts, other hierarchies break these down. As frequency is stepped down, so other virtues are borne by separate lifestreams, by separate ascended masters, angels, archangels, and so forth. In the hierarchy of heaven, all have their place; all have their function.

The angels are beings who have not left the purity of God's consciousness, except in some cases where they volunteered to incarnate in bodies like ours to help mankind. Angels that are called the seraphim and the cherubim who have never touched human creation, have never incarnated and been subject to the fall and the density of imperfection, maintain the highest purity of the consciousness of God. There are ministering seraphim and cherubim who make their way twenty-four hours a day standing before the altar of God and singing "Holy, holy, holy, Lord God Almighty!"[2] They hold the frequency of purity which they radiate to the lifewaves and evolutions that continue in the vastness of cosmos.

Scientists consider there are billions of galaxies. Billions of galaxies! When we think of the vastness of the galaxy we live in and then try to comprehend billions of these revolving around a Great Central Sun, it almost defies our ability to equate with the cosmos in which we live. And all of this controlled by hierarchy, cosmic consciousness, beings aware of self as God, as cosmos. And yet all of this which scientists have observed is still only the physical spectrum of the cosmos—a very thin line, a frequency. What is above and below this frequency is yet another vastness of cosmos, of infinity, and also of planes that still are part of time and space. We see that in examining hierarchy, we do need to expand consciousness even to contain a concept of what Morya calls *com-measurement*—the ability of the individual soul to measure itself against the Infinite, which is quite a task in itself.

The key hierarchies, then, are the twelve hierarchies that form the cosmic clock around the central sun, which we will be studying further on in this conference. Then come the cosmic beings. We see a trinity, an order of manifestation where there are three kingdoms of servants, each serving as one of the aspects of the threefold flame.

Elohim and Elementals: The Power Ray

The Elohim, the most powerful aspect of the consciousness of God, include in their hierarchy elemental builders of form. Elementals are the sylphs that control the air, the gnomes that control the earth, the undines that control the water, and the salamanders that control the fire element. These four aspects also govern man's four lower bodies. Serving directly under the Elohim are the beings of nature—the four beings of the elements, who are the twin flames who have dominion over all of the evolutions of the gnomes, salamanders, sylphs, and undines.

Oromasis and Diana are the twin flames of the fiery element. Their salamanders may stand before you nine to twenty feet tall. When you see them, they are a moving rainbow fire with an identity in the fire. They are a white light—a white flame merging into the colors of the rainbow. They are a spectacular sight! They concentrate the energies of sacred fire. They are servants of man, servants of the ascended masters. They serve to keep the physical, mental, and emotional bodies clean by the action of fire. Oromasis and Diana have given dictations. They are ascended beings. But their salamanders are not ascended; they are serving in the planes of Matter. When the dictations have come forth from Oromasis and Diana, there has been an intensity of heat greater than the chelas ever imagined or dreamed they could experience.

Then there are Aries and Thor, twin flames of the air element, who also govern mental action. Under them serve the mighty sylphs who control the air currents, air pressure, and the purification of the air. And they are fighting the pollution of the air and bearing the burden of mankind's pollution. We have the ascended beings Neptune and Luara, who control the beings of water—the undines—and the flow of energy in the feeling body of mankind. Virgo and Pelleur control the earth element and the gnomes. All of these, then, serve under the Elohim.

The seven mighty Elohim and their divine complements,

their feminine counterparts, are the builders of creation. It was they who responded to the fiat of the Lord God "Let there be light: and there was light" and the fiat of creation to create the worlds.[3] The term "Elohim" is a sacred sound. It is an intonation. Even the repetition of the name releases a tremendous power, and so we give it as a chant: Elohim!

We find that throughout the Bible there are hundreds of references to God as the Divine Us, as Elohim, which is a plural noun, showing that man's awareness of God was as a plural being, as a dual being of the polarity of the masculine and feminine. The Elohim are the Spirits of God, the morning stars which sang together in the beginning.[4] They represent the power of creation— the blue ray, the blue flame in your heart. They represent, in the Trinity of Father, Son, and Holy Spirit, the Father aspect; or, in Brahma, Vishnu, and Siva, the aspect of Brahma—the thrust of creation that comes forth from the masculine aspect of the Godhead.

Christed Ones, Sons and Daughters of God: The Wisdom Ray

The second kingdom in the hierarchy, corresponding to the Second Person of the Trinity, is the kingdom of the Christed ones—the sons and daughters of God, including the seven chohans of the rays and their embodied chelas. These are the ascended masters, and this is *you* in the state of becoming an ascended master. Because you are evolving in time and space, your evolution will culminate in the kingdom that falls on the second ray, the yellow aspect of the threefold flame. It is the mission of the beings who serve in this order to anchor the mind of God, the intelligence of God, the directives of the Creator's consciousness. And as we focus that intelligence, the beings of the elements become the servants to implement that intelligence, that intelling of the mind of God.

Therefore, serving in this aspect in this kingdom of hierarchy, we are given tests and initiations in the correct use of mental faculties, in the correct use of free will, in the reason of the Logos. And this is the action of the Word that is made flesh.[5] It is the Word incarnate that is that Second Person of the Trinity. That is this kingdom. So ascended masters and their chelas moving upward in the spiral of God consciousness comprise that order God has created to be the directors of creation and of the flow.

Archangels and Angelic Hosts: The Love Ray

Finally, the third kingdom, functioning in the pink flame of divine love: the angelic hosts—the seven mighty archangels and their divine complements and all of the different types of angels that serve mankind. They serve us at the level of the feeling body. They bring to us hope and joy and laughter, constancy, and a quickening. They sustain the mental concepts that we receive that are ours to hold in our kingdom, the second aspect. Without the angelic hosts, the concepts which we give forth would not put on the feeling body, the desire body that draws the tremendous momentum of the Creator for precipitation in the physical plane. There is very little that we can bring forth as alchemists unless we have the feeling of the creation, the intense love of the creation, the love of that which we are bringing forth.

The angelic hosts silently stand by the children of the light and the sons and daughters of God. They stand guard as sentinels, as pillars of fire, guarding our creation, guarding our consciousness, giving us that quickening in moments of doubt and despair when the mission must go on, when we must conquer. They infuse us with that energy which is the feeling of God, which is that momentum.

Balance of the Three Kingdoms
of the Servants of God

These three kingdoms working in balance, in harmony, are assigned to outpicture the trinity of the threefold flame of life on a cosmic scale. The very flame that burns at Shamballa, that is within our hearts—the blue, the yellow, and the pink—has all of this as ramification in the cosmic hierarchy. Studying these kingdoms of hierarchy, we also learn something about how we apply the flame that is in our hearts. We learn, then, that it is the energy of the blue ray, the thrust of power, that gives impetus to the idea that is contained within the mind of God. Without that thrust of energy, the idea has no momentum. It is like the arrow that is shot from the bow. It is the energy of the pulling back that gives the momentum to the arrow that is the idea of God going into manifestation.

It is the action of the pink flame of love that sustains the creation. This is the action of the Holy Spirit. The angelic hosts are instruments of the Holy Spirit. When we have received the thrust of power, the law, the blueprint of what has to be created, when we have set the mental matrix of the idea, when we have brought forth the creation through love, there is then the necessity to sustain and nourish the creation. That sustaining, that staying power, that staying energy, is always supplied by the angelic hosts. And it is supplied in ourselves by the development of love and the virtues, the qualities, and the feelings that are necessary.

We spoke of the balanced threefold flame as being the mark of the Christed One, the mark of attainment in the new age. We also see that on a cosmic scale in the Macrocosm, it is necessary for these three kingdoms to function in harmony so that in a planet, in a solar system, the threefold flame, as ensouled by hierarchies, is also in balance. If mankind evolving toward becoming masters of life do not even know that that is the path they are on, do not even understand initiation or the laws governing initiation, do not understand hierarchy as a chain of being, how can they pursue even their own way, even their own kingdom of becoming Christed ones? They know not that to become the Real Self is the goal of life. Since that purpose and that goal have not been set for mankind, they cannot even begin to understand the fusion with the other two kingdoms—the beings of the elements and the angelic hosts.

Denial of Hierarchy and Its Purposes

Of course, I am very well aware, as you are aware, of the fact that we are living in an age when science is king. And scientists tell us there are no beings of nature, no elementals, that all things run by themselves in this cosmos. Fantastically, things run by themselves! There are no angelic beings, there are no elementals, and really, there are no Christed ones because the scientists declare that the kingdom of the Christed ones is merely an advanced form of the animal kingdom—*Homo sapiens,* a species.

We find, then, that through a perversion of that science which is truly the flame of the Mother, there is a total denial of hierarchy and its purposes. We find that mankind are not easily taught the nature of individuality, the special nature of the flame. I often feel surprise going through an audience when I talk about the uniqueness and importance of the individual. Today, people don't think they count; they don't think they matter. They're just part of the sea of the mass consciousness, the lowest common denominator—mediocrity. And it doesn't really matter, people think, if I'm alive or I'm not alive. So there is that denial of the flame, that denial of the Real Self, that denial of purpose.

To talk to the world today about a hierarchy of ascended beings and about the order of hierarchy is to introduce something that perhaps has not been talked about since early Christian times when Origen of Alexandria described these orders of celestial beings. It is simply something too great to imagine. I think that the burden of responsibility when one accepts hierarchy is so great that it is one of the aspects that turns people aside.

The Antahkarana of Life

When we understand hierarchy, we see the importance of the flame that we carry as a link in a tremendous chain—not just a single chain, but, as it were, a golden chain mail—interconnecting links that span a whole cosmos in what is called the *antahkarana* of life. It is the web of life. It is like a vast knitting of the Cosmic Virgin, and each stitch is a point of the individualization of the God flame. Each point is necessary. At each point there is the converging of the spirals of Alpha and Omega that forms the fiery cross of life. And where this cross, this focal point, is manifest, there identity springs forth as cosmic beings, as Elohim, elementals, angels, archangels, and Christed man and woman.

The awareness of God is what infuses the material cosmos with the flame, the Spirit of Life. Without the awareness of the flame, the entire cosmos becomes a mechanical, physical, chemical manifestation devoid of meaning. When we realize that all of hierarchy that has gone before us in this chain, holding the frequencies above us which are greater than that which we are able to bear, and that all of hierarchy beneath us, all beings who hold lesser frequencies than our own, for whom we hold a key and a frequency—that all of this above and below pivots on our individualization of the God flame, we are seized with the enormity of the responsibility that we bear.

To fail to take the torch that is passed from the hierarchies beyond means that all kinds of lifewaves below will not receive the torch. And the neglect of our responsibility is a dropped stitch in the knitting of the Cosmic Virgin—like black holes in outer space. We see that our striving to be, to be free, to carry the flame of freedom at all costs, is done not for ourselves alone; it is done because of the millions of cosmic beings who stand above us and who are counting on us to carry the torch for the millions of life-waves who have yet to evolve to the place where we stand.

You Are Hierarchy

The message of the Great White Brotherhood is simply this: You are hierarchy; you count. You count as the supreme manifestation of God. Your counting as this manifestation means that you must count yourself—your self-worth—not as a human being, but as a flame. It is the flame in you that doeth the work. It is the flame in you that is essential. It is the individualization of that flame through your soul that makes you unique, that makes you the mandala. When I say "not as a human being," I mean not "human" in the sense of being limited, being mortal, or having misqualified energy—but you in the sense of the Real Self.

The purpose of creation, the purpose of the creative fiat which brought forth your soul, was to adorn a spiritual-material cosmos with a unique aspect of the Godhead focused in the Great Central Sun. If you fail to be that flame, cosmos will be without the focalization of that facet of the diamond shining mind of God. Now this should not cause us to give vent to pride, to an egocentrism; but it should lead us to thinking of the wonder of that flame and the glory that God has placed as a portion of himself within. On the contrary, it should make us vastly humble—and yet not subservient, not self-deprecating, not full of self-condemnation.

The Condemnation of Self

We find, then, that the condemnation of self is the first tool of the fallen ones whereby the entire hierarchy is denied. We find that chelas coming into the teachings of the ascended masters must pass the hurdle of overcoming self-condemnation. Self-condemnation is the denial that you are the potential, the living flame, of God. It is the denial of yourself as the Christed One. It is the denial of your soul's opportunity to be. This condemnation does not even originate in yourself. It is a weight of the mass consciousness which exists at subconscious as well as conscious levels. When you condemn yourself, you are condemning God. When you condemn God, this is black magic. And so you practice against yourself, denying yourself out of existence.

Correct Assessment of Selfhood

To seize the torch that is passed and to run with it, we must have a correct assessment of selfhood. And that always begins with "I of mine own self can do nothing. It is the Father in me that doeth the work. My Father worketh hitherto, and I work."[6] It is the sense of knowing that when you say "I," it is God who is the "I." But it is not making the ego that God. It is not making the carnal mind and all of its misuses of the sacred fire that God. It is taking the line that is drawn by the Mediator, your Real Self, and understanding that on one side of the line falls the reality of your self-awareness as God and on the other side the synthetic image— the product of a synthetic civilization, of a mechanization concept.

In *Climb the Highest Mountain,* the structure of which was outlined by beloved El Morya, the chapters on "Your Synthetic Image" and "Your Real Image" show that it is not altogether a simple process to separate in consciousness the tares from the wheat, to define the reality of the I AM THAT I AM and to understand all that opposes that reality.[7] This is why we have hierarchy. Those who have gone beyond us on the path, the ascended masters, come very close to us; and they help us to discern truth— in ourselves first, and then in the world. They help us to see what is real and what is unreal. Mankind cannot truly progress without these cosmic teachers. Without hierarchy, we would not have the measuring rod to define identity. So hierarchy comes forth. El Morya says:

Look up into the stars and know that there identity has realized selfhood in God. Know that the stars in the firmament of God's being reflect the glory of the "elder

days of Art"⁸—of those forgotten yesteryears when sons
and daughters of God, members of the early root races of
this and other systems of worlds, triumphed in the law of
the Logos, overcame time and space, and ascended to the
plane of God-reality where they sustain the starry body
and the starry consciousness of concentrated fire, leaving a
counterpart in Matter to mark the point of victory. Stars
are markers of those who have overcome. Thus you, too,
can say: "We shall overcome. Earth shall become a star.
The evolutions of Terra shall be free."⁹

A Path of Initiation

The fact that hierarchy exists provides for us a path of
initiation. Initiation is the step-by-step process whereby the being
who is immediately above you in attainment gives you the
teaching and the understanding that enables you to rise a step and
assume that place, that role of the teacher. When you are
prepared, you liberate the teacher. The teacher may also advance
one step. This is also a law of hierarchy: the teacher cannot advance
unless the teacher has chelas coming after him who will keep the
flame at the point which he is vacating. It's like moving forward in
chairs one step at a time.

Guru and Chela

We see that in the teachings of East and West, there have
always been the chelas and the gurus and this correct relationship.
You may find that your teacher is an unascended being. You may
find that in the mastery of science or of music or of art, you apprentice yourself to a great teacher, one who knows more than you.
And when you have learned all that that teacher can impart, you
go on. Perhaps you surpass the teacher. This is always the prayer of
the teacher—that the students will exceed the level of attainment
of the teacher. As John the Baptist said, "He must increase, but I
must decrease."¹⁰

In a previous incarnation, John the Baptist was the guru of
Jesus. Now he comes forth to pave the way for his pupil to be the
Christed One. This is Elijah and Elisha, guru and chela of the Old
Testament, proving the law. Elijah ascends into heaven and his

chela, Elisha, takes up his mantle—which is the momentum, the authority of the teacher—smites the waters of Jordan, is proclaimed a prophet, and works miracles among the people of Israel. Elisha incarnates again and again and finally comes as Jesus, the Christed One. And his teacher, honoring his disciple, is given the dispensation to incarnate, to clear the way for the coming. Now you understand the mystery "He must increase, but I must decrease." This is the order of hierarchy.

"When the Pupil Is Ready, the Teacher Appears"

We find, then, that when we have exhausted all worldly teachers, when we have shown ourselves willing to submit to the teacher on earth whom we still can profit from, when we have shown ourselves humble and patient and willing to take correction, willing to conform to discipline, the ascended masters—who are waiting in the wings of life, waiting for us to be ready to receive an ascended-master teacher—come forth. And you know the saying, "When the pupil is ready, the teacher appears."

What constitutes readiness? Readiness is the path of initiation. Each test that you pass gives you the right to carry a greater concentration of the sacred fire in your heart chakra, in all of your chakras. This greater concentration of energy needs to be guarded by greater discipline, by greater harmony, by fastidious attention to detail. You find yourself gaining mastery. You find yourself coming into the presence of the ascended masters.

They come, and they give initiations in the most unexpected ways. You expect to be received and bowed to by the teacher, but the teacher uses the beggar on the street or the maid or the garbage collector to test the threshold of your mastery. Will you explode because he spills the garbage all over your yard? Or will you stand and say, "Behold, this is a test!"

Morya has a famous quote that has stayed with me all the years of my, shall we say, trials and tribulations as a chela of the ascended masters. He says, "If the messenger be an ant, heed him!" You never know who the master is going to send to see how you will receive his representative. If you pass the test of receiving his representative, the representative will go on his way and you will receive the Lord himself. Jesus said it. He gave the formula for initiation "Inasmuch as ye have done it unto one of the least of these my brethren, ye have done it unto me."[11] So we find the path of karma yoga, balancing karma through service, is won as we recognize the service of God in man, as we recognize that when we receive a prophet in the name of a prophet, we receive a prophet's reward.[12]

Lessons on the Path

There are great lessons to be learned on the path of initiation. Morya is a very stern guru, and he has a very interesting sense of humor. He keeps at the entrance to his retreat in Darjeeling a very gruff chela who has no appearance whatsoever of mastery or of even being worthy to stand at the gate of the master's retreat. This chela speaks gruffly. Perhaps he is not dressed in the best of attire. And those who come to knock at the door—if they come in their finery and have disdain for the gatekeeper, then the master determines that they are not worthy to be received. It's a very interesting thing.

We learned of the gatekeeper of the Royal Teton Retreat. His name is Alphas. Mention was made of him in a dictation, because to him the greatest mission, the greatest calling in life and the highest honor, was to be the gatekeeper of the Royal Teton Retreat. It makes one think of Fishbait, the caller in the Senate who has gained fame over many years.

We see, then, that service to the masters, in whatever office, whatever humble position, is keeping that point in hierarchy, keeping that stitch in the golden chain mail until we are ready to occupy the next position and assume the responsibilities attendant upon that position. We ought to be very content to be in the position that we hold. We ought to see that we do well and master that focal point, whether it be a job in the world or in the household or as father or as mother or as teacher. Whatever your calling, whatever your work, that is where the masters give the tests; that is where the tests take place.

Direct Contact with the Ascended Masters

Life is the guru until we show that nothing in this world is able to deter us from the humility of the flame, from the service of the Real Self of all. We find that having passed certain tests, we come directly into contact with the ascended masters. Their lessons—the Keepers of the Flame Lessons, the books they have written through their various messengers, the *Pearls of Wisdom*— all of these represent an intensification of contact with hierarchy, until you are face to face with a guru as you kneel at the altar of your own heart, the chamber of your heart where the guru appears in your meditation. The masters are guides along the way until we develop the discrimination to understand who and what are the real hierarchies.

The Y in the Path

We must understand that inasmuch as there is a path of initiation and choices to be made and the gift of free will, some have entered the path, misused the gift, and chosen incorrectly. There is the point of choice that is known as the Y in the path; there is the point at which you must elect to take the right-handed path or the left-handed path. The right-handed path is taking the knowledge of the Brotherhood, the initiations, and the energies of the I AM Presence and using these solely to the glory of the flame and to the service of humanity. The left-handed path is taking all of this and using it to the glory of the ego. This path has been outpictured in the way of Satanism, in the way of the inverted five-pointed star whereby the Christ is inverted, the carnal mind is elevated, and all of the energies that God gives are used for the gratification of the senses and the gratification of the ego.

A False Hierarchy

Unfortunately, the right- and the left-handed paths are not so clearly defined when the choices come. But come they will; and if we meet them with determination and humility, relying upon the flame within, we will pass the tests of life. Many have failed, however. Those who have failed through their pride, their ambition, and their ego have not been content to remain in the shadows obscured, unrecognized. And therefore, they have set themselves up as a counterfeit hierarchy, a false hierarchy. Point counterpoint, they misrepresent the ascended masters and their hierarchies. This is why John warned that Antichrist should come.[13]

Antichrist is the personification of the opposition to all who would personify the Christ. Since Jesus became the Christ, he warned of that which would come to oppose that light. We find, then, that there are false teachers and true teachers. Jesus gave us the formula for dividing the way. Can sweet water and bitter come forth from the same fountain?[14] He said, "Wherefore by their fruits ye shall know them."[15] All of the false teachers quote the same spiritual truths as the ascended masters. They quote similar teachings, though there may be variations and perversions. Therefore, it is not to the teaching that we look, but to the fruits in the life of the teacher.

"Try the Spirits"

We examine the vibration of the teacher. We test the frequencies. John said, "Try the spirits to see whether they are of God."[16] When you aren't able to sense vibration, to sense frequency, how can you test the vibration of the teacher? You pray. You pray to the Real Self. You pray to the I AM Presence. You ask for guidance. You ask to be given a sign, and you do not precipitate that sign and force some kind of a manifestation that does not come from God. It is best not to commit yourself until you are sure.

When you are going through the period of anchoring your soul's consciousness in God, you take each precept, each law that is given, and you prove it. When you can have confidence in the teacher, as we can have confidence in the ascended masters, you, as the chela, know then that it is safe to trust the guru. Therefore, we take the word of the guru that is given to us and we act upon it in faith—not always understanding, not always knowing. We follow the teachings of Jesus and Gautama, the true teachers of the ages, in faith, not always knowing where they will lead us.

The reward for faith and faithfulness on the Path is understanding, and this is the order of the Trinity. The blue ray must be provided by the chela—the thrust of faith in the teacher—so that the teacher can deliver the teaching, which is the yellow ray of understanding. And when that yellow ray is delivered unto the chela, then the chela bursts forth in the flame of love; and the love spiral kindles the arc which forms the chain of hierarchy whereby your heart is indissolubly linked to the heart of the teacher.

We see, then, that the Path requires faith, that it also requires testing. It requires the testing of the law that is given, the testing of the flames. The ascended masters want you to challenge every aspect of being and consciousness and of the teaching. When you challenge in humility, in the name of your Real Self, and in the name of the I AM Presence, God will not fail to give you proof of the way.

We must remember that those who impersonate the ascended masters will set themselves up as the mediator in place of your Real Self. They will make you rely on them as the source of information, as the source of some great thing that is coming forth. They will keep you in a pattern of running back and forth till you come to the place where you have to ask this individual permission to do almost anything. You find yourself, then, becoming subservient to the will, perhaps the human will, of a teacher who is displacing your own contact, your own Mediator, the Real Self which God has provided for you.

The One Path

We find that the Path has many aspects. The Path, as it has been given to Mark and me as messengers for the Brotherhood, has been outlined in many of our books. These bear study and consideration as you make your way on the Path. There is really only one Path that leads to the summit of life, your own I AM Presence. There are many lesser paths, but when you come into the one Path, you come under the one law of your own I AM Presence. It is the ladder—like Jacob's ladder with the angels ascending and descending.[17]

There are steps of initiation, thirty-three in number, which every devotee of the flame must pass if he is to make his ascension. There are no alternatives to these initiations. There is no roundabout way of getting around these initiations. Jesus said, "The kingdom of heaven suffereth violence, and the violent take it by force."[18] The violent are those on the left-handed path who want to seize the power of God without the necessary surrender of the human consciousness. They would circumvent hierarchy, circumvent the masters, circumvent initiation, and proclaim themselves as Christed Ones.

When you come into the teachings of the ascended masters,

they provide the way, very sure, very clearly marked. Morya has spoken of the solitary climbers who insist on going it alone. He says that the heights of the Himalayas are strewn with the remains of those who have rejected hierarchy, who have said: "I don't need hierarchy. I don't need those teachers of mankind to pave the way. I will find it on my own."

You know, this really doesn't make sense in any area of human endeavor. When we determine to study mathematics, music, or whatever else, we find the best teacher. We learn all the teacher can impart, and then we forge ahead on our own when we find no other teacher. Why should we spend an entire embodiment discovering for ourselves all of the laws of chemistry or physics which have been discovered over hundreds of years with many lives investing their time and their effort? We take that which comes to us from the hierarchy of science; it is our foundation. We may check, we may challenge, we may disagree. We may attempt to see and prove whether or not all that has been said is true. But we go forward.

The Passing of the Torch

This is the passing of the torch! This is how civilization moves forward! And when you cross the threshold from this life to the next, it will be the carrying of the torch of all that has been gleaned by the souls of humanity and the offering of that fruit upon the altar of God. The torch has indeed been passed—the torch of the teaching of the ages, the teachings of the ascended masters, and the torch of a higher frequency into which this world must merge. The light has been sent forth from the central sun. The planet earth is expected to rise in initiation of planetary dimension. The entire planet is expected to go up a notch. It has to, because the solar system is going up, the galaxy is going up, this sector of the cosmos is going up.

When we are not prepared for initiation, when we cannot take that step because our frequency, the light we carry, is not sufficient, then we find ourselves in that state of outer darkness. Jesus described it in the twenty-fourth chapter of the Book of Matthew. He said, "There shall be weeping and gnashing of teeth."[19] The casting into outer darkness of the soul is what happens when the law demands initiation and the soul rebels against the natural forward movement of its own inner law, its own inner spiral.

What happens in these times when mankind are not prepared? We have seen that in the past, continents have sunk. Cataclysm comes forth; many lives are lost. Nature shrugs. Nature will not hold back. Nature must balance what mankind refuse to balance. The beings of the elements, the beings of nature, and the Elohim take command in that hour of initiation; and they must effect planetary transmutation through cataclysm if mankind fail to make the invocations, to make the concentrated action of the light within themselves that is necessary to hold the balance.

We live in a time when we wonder if the world will survive the pollution. And there is so much chaos, so much grasping and grabbing of territories—the brink of World War what? Solzhenitsyn says, in a recent front-page article in the California papers, that we've lost the Third World War—we can at least try to win the Fourth World War. He speaks about all of the landed areas of the world being lost to the flame of freedom. We are in such a state of turmoil. There is hardly a soul upon the planet who can keep his harmony for twenty-four hours. And yet the light is oncoming from the Great Central Sun; the light demands a step-up in frequency.

Who Will Seize the Torch?

This torch, this light, is passed from the Great White Brotherhood, from the ascended hierarchy, to those who will take it, to those who will seize it. This conference is convoked by the ascended masters to determine who will seize the torch, who will realize that they must carry in their heart the flame of freedom and the light for mankind.

In every age, it is the few who hold the balance whereby transition can be made. There was great furor and turmoil and chaos in the days of Rome. Jesus and the disciples and the group, the mystical community that surrounded them, carried the flame for the Piscean age for all the world. In each age there has been a master and a group of devotees who have carried the balance so that the earth could survive and civilization could continue with continuity.

A Serious Moment in Cosmic History

We stand at the threshold of an age that is somewhat unique in that this is the period when the karma of thousands of years, tens of thousands of years, must be balanced in order to make the transition. It is no longer possible for the few to hold the balance for the many. Therefore, at this moment hierarchy is contacting their chelas to see if the many will respond to hold the balance so that earth can pass into the new dispensation without a total disruption through cataclysm or war or atomic holocaust or mass disease or such a disruption of life through pollution as to effectively destroy millions upon the planetary body. These are the options we face. It is a serious moment in cosmic history.

When we began The Summit Lighthouse and there were just a few devotees surrounding that flame, Morya said that the fate of the planet could well depend on a few dozen chelas, on whether or not they would have the staying power to keep that flame until the many would respond. And he went so far as to say that the fate of a solar system and a sector of the galaxy would also depend upon these few because there is that domino effect. If the earth is lost, it creates an imbalance in the planets of the solar system. If more and more planets go the way of the left-handed path, soon the solar system is cast out of hierarchy, and that affects this sector of the galaxy, and so on.

We find that the light-bearers in every age are like the little boy with the finger in the dike, holding back the water until help comes. This is the meaning of the Path. It has been going on for a long time. We have a sacred opportunity. We have a sacred commitment. Let us consider, then, as we commune together, as the days pass, the meaning of hierarchy and our role in hierarchy.

July 3, 1975
8:16-9:16 P.M. PDT

The Elohim are the seven Spirits of creation, the morning stars which sang together in the origin of being. In the Hebrew, the Bible abounds with this name for God which indicates a plurality in unity. The Elohim are the Divine Us. When God said, "Let us make man in our image, after our likeness," it was the twin flames of the Elohim who fashioned "male and female" out of the divine polarity of Alpha and Omega.

> For we know in part, and we prophesy in part. But when that which is perfect is come, then that which is in part shall be done away....For now we see through a glass, darkly; but then face to face: now I know in part; but then shall I know even as also I am known.

Cyclopea is the Elohim of vision. That means his cosmic consciousness ensouls the vision of the Creator. Creation is an action of the faculty of God's vision. Cyclopea holds the vision for all of life, and thus he is known as the all-seeing eye of God. He teaches mastery of the third eye and lends his momentum of vision for the freedom of lifewaves and planetary homes like Earth and Venus and Mars and countless others beyond our solar system and galaxy.

8

THE PLACEMENT OF THE CAPSTONE
UPON THE PYRAMID OF BEING

A Dictation by the Elohim Cyclopea

Let serenity on the brow of the Divine Mother be the quality of patience that invokes the all-seeing eye, that compels into manifestation within you the vision without which the people will surely perish.[1]

The Vision That Will Make You Whole

Life is incomplete without the vision of the goal. I AM the Elohim Cyclopea come to give you the vision that will make you whole! It is the vision of the victory. And the path that leads to victory is the path over which the flame, as crystal fire, flows from the heart of Mother, enshrining souls in the mandala of perfection.

I AM Cyclopea! I hold within my brow God's awareness of life as the all-seeing, all-knowing manifestation. It is the vision of God that holds the cosmos, the precipitation of Mater and of the planes of Spirit. I hold the destiny of galaxies. I hold the formula of cycles unfolding, of life unfolding and infolding itself. Now let the hearing of the ear and the seeing of the eye be the perception of your own immaculate divinity! Your origin is in purity, not in sin. And you have been told there is no original sin for souls originated in God, conceived in liberty, conceived in the heart of Cosmic Virgin.

Therefore, I raise my hand. It is the hand of an Elohim, and I pass it across the forcefield of your consciousness. And I wipe away the sin that has confined you to duality, to relativity, to relative good and evil whereby you know not the way, for you know not identity. Be cleansed of that momentum of original sin! Be purified by the vision of Virginia, my consort! Now see and behold that fiery destiny locked—and I say locked—within your heart. For your own Christ Self holds the key, and you must take the key and unlock that destiny. Masters ascended or unascended will not take from you the joy and the glory of unlocking that sacred formula of identity. I hold the chemistry of that formula. I hold the plan of the components of identity.

The Etheric Blueprint of the All-Seeing Eye

I AM Cyclopea! I initiate the spiral of the all-seeing eye of God for a people and a planet, for the destiny given unto this nation to hold the vision for all nations of the new order of the ages! Therefore, I come as the instrument of the Godhead to place at the etheric level the capstone of the all-seeing eye upon the pyramid, the four sides of the temple of being in Mater. I place that focal point within each individual here who, by free will now silently within the heart, asks to receive that etheric blueprint of the all-seeing eye which is the key to the proper functioning of that chakra. I place it there for all who will hear or read my word, and I place it upon the pyramid of America.

Now let the etheric matrix come forth from the heart of God! Let it be initiated in this year of the Holy Spirit, in this sign of the Divine Mother, as the vision of the victory for all peoples, all souls and lifewaves and root races evolving upon Terra! Let it be the magnet! Let it be the drawing-up of the energy of all of the lower chakras as Life consecrates life to *be* the wholeness of the immaculate design!

The Beam in the Eye of God

You *are* conceived by God as whole! Enter into the wholeness of the etheric blueprint of life! Claim your wholeness in every level of consciousness! Accept the fiat of the master healer of life *"Be thou made whole!"* Know, then, when you desire, as one who is drowning in the sea of the mass consciousness, to be rescued from that pull of the mass consciousness, that there goes forth from this etheric matrix of the all-seeing eye a coil of light. It is the beam in the eye of God. It is the lifeline! It is hurled to souls desiring to be saved from the downward spiral of the energies of the bottomless pit of astral desire.

Know, then, that by this matrix placed at the etheric level, you have the nearness of that momentum of the eye that is upon the sparrow, the eye that is upon every elemental and every electron, on every movement and pulsation of energy, transformation and transmutation throughout all galaxies in every plane of God Self-awareness. Know that the all-seeing eye of God contains all this—that you cannot even move your little finger that the all-seeing eye of God does not record the vibration and the energy movement that ripples across a cosmos.

Know then that that beam of light, that beacon that comes forth by God seeing perfection of all creation, is a lifeline that you may call forth, that you may use, that you may seize and follow to the center of life! And thereby when you have hold of that light beam of the eye of God, no force, no magnetism, no pull of death, decay, and disintegration, can tear you from the path of initiation.

Follow the spiral of the beam of light back to the vision; and you will find within that eye, standing there, the Cosmic Virgin. For in the eye of Alpha is the vision of Omega, and in the eye of Omega is the vision of Alpha! This also is the flow between twin flames as you reinforce the immaculate image of one another's God-identity. This is the flow of soul mates and of those who walk the path hand in hand. And therefore, beauty is indeed in the eye of the beholder, and you can enter the sphere of the eye of God even as you would enter the chamber of the heart and find there the formula of creation.

Testing the Action of the All-Seeing Eye

I bid you welcome into the plane of all-seeing. And I thrust before you the opportunity of testing, testing the action of the all-seeing eye! Try the mantra of Cyclopea! Let it be the alchemy that magnetizes, by a vortex of emerald fire, all energies of being into the cube of cosmic destiny! The sacred formula of alchemy: Theos equals God; Rule equals Law; You equals Being. Theos plus Rule plus You equals God's Law active as Principle within your Being (TRY). You are the keystone in the arch of the sacred AUM! You are the keystone between the pillars of Alpha and Omega; and the keystone that you are is the all-seeing eye, even in the temple of your body sacred.

Now then, take the mantra and prove, as many students have also proven, that the giving of the mantra can focalize truth on the political scene, in the world at large, in every nation, in the home, until that which is done in secret by the fallen ones is shouted from the housetops and there is the exposure of the lie![2] And when the debris of the lie is cleared—the coming of truth, the crystallization of truth; for mankind shall know the truth in this age and the truth shall make them free! [3]

Guard the Vision, Guard the Victory

Be then the focus of truth; and watch how, as watchmen on the wall of life, by letting the beacon of the all-seeing eye go forth into the night, you clear a path—yea, carve a path—a light ray whereby souls will find the path of initiation and the entering-in to the true cosmic purpose of identity. [Silence] I call thee forth, O light of the eye of God! Come forth within each one! Come forth! Come forth and be the beacon to all souls yearning to be free!

I AM Cyclopea. I have accomplished as I have spoken unto you this night the establishment of certain forcefields within you and certain inner actions and keys. This assignment being accomplished, I take my leave of you. And I leave you with this word: Watch! Watch that ye enter not into temptation.[4] Watch for the initiations of the all-seeing eye. Guard the vision and thereby guard the victory! Watch; and let no man, no woman, take the crown, the capstone of life.[5] I AM Cyclopea!

July 3, 1975
10:31-10:45 P.M. PDT

9

CITIZENS OF A COSMOS
Patriarchs of the Law, Patrons of Life, and Patriots of Liberty

A Lecture by Elizabeth Clare Prophet

Good morning, everyone. And a happy Fourth of July! Shortly after midnight, it dawned on me, "It's the Fourth of July!" and the thrill of the flame of freedom was upon me. Won't you be seated for our lecture, "Citizens of a Cosmos."

Roles of Hierarchy

This is a very exciting subject, one which tells us more about hierarchy, which we studied last evening, and about the assuming of the roles of hierarchy according to the threefold flame of the Cosmic Christ and the individual Christ flame.

We are speaking of patriarchs of the law, patrons of life, and patriots of liberty. I see these three types of individualizations of the God flame as the groups into which humanity generally fall, and I see them as corresponding to the plan of hierarchy. As we contemplate what has made our nation and our planet what it is, for better or for worse, we cannot fail to take into consideration these roles of hierarchy, because until we assume our point in hierarchy, we have not the individualization of the God flame.

Morya says that "every man should realize his essential individuality, his privilege, God-given, of expressing unique qualities of Life that he can use to endow the universe from the fountain of his own life and love. But there are lessons to be learned, understandings to be sought and found, and old senses to be cast aside, transmuted and, in some cases, re-created."[1]

We have a cosmic clock which we will be unfolding during this class that Mother Mary has given to us. It is given for the purpose of determining the cycles of karma, of dharma, of opportunity, of individuality. We will design that clock for you tomorrow at 2:30 and also show you your destiny on that clock, the destiny not of being subject to a worldly astrology, but a fiery destiny of a cosmic astrology determined by the hierarchies of light and your own free will.

When we take this clock, we place upon it these three categories: the patriarchs of the law, the patrons of life, and the patriots of liberty. You can draw on your note pad a circle and divide it into three, trisecting it at the twelve, four, and eight o'clock lines, making a pie of three pieces. This takes the mandala of the soul and shows the trinity of the action of the threefold flame. We place this mandala upon humanity and we see how patriarchs, patrons, and patriots figure.

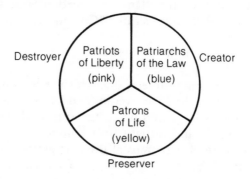

Patriarchs of the Law

First come the patriarchs of the law. They carry the flame of the law, the blueprint of any organization. They have leadership capabilities. They are always able to see the whole and the relationship of the parts to the whole; therefore they are organizers. They can delegate authority. They write the laws; they execute the laws; they administer the laws. And more than this, they are organizers in any phase of a project. If a project does not have a patriarch of the law, it will not succeed.

Blue, Yellow, Pink

Patriarchs of the law have to be understood; they have idiosyncrasies. They carry a tremendous thrust of energy into any project; and their one goal is to see the project through, just as Lincoln's one goal was to see the Union through. Sometimes they use harsh measures and stern measures that override the concerns of the patriots of liberty or the patrons of life and others who are more associated with the detail or the parts of the whole. Therefore, they tend to be unpopular and they also tend to be isolated. They are isolated because the blue ray, like the blue color, is not a ray that attracts. It is a ray of thrust.

When a patriarch of the law can combine with the blue ray the energy of the patriot and the patron, then he becomes a focal point in any age for the drawing of the masses and the magnetization of the flame of the Holy Spirit that can kindle about anything that the person puts his mind to. We will review in our lecture some of these patriarchs who were able to carry the threefold aspect. When the patriarch of the law has the balance of the patriot and the patron, he becomes a man of the centuries like Abraham Lincoln.

Now the concept of the patriot as the one ensouling the pink flame and the concept of the patron being the one who ensouls the yellow flame completes the mandala of our trinity. When we understand these three flames, we understand the work of these three types.

The patrons of life are the sustainers and the interpreters of the law. They have the understanding and the knowledge, and therefore they can educate the people concerning the law that is set forth as the blueprint of life. Patriots, like the angelic hosts, carry the fervor of love, and they infuse the law and the understanding of the law with the energy that carries the project to the finish and precipitates in the physical octave those projects that are foremost in carrying civilization forward.

When we think of that same trinity which we noted yesterday, the AUM being the symbol of Brahma, Vishnu, and Siva (the Creator, the Preserver, and the Destroyer), we see the patriarchs as the creators, the forgers of civilization, the pioneers. We see the preservers as the patrons of life who sustain that which has been carved. We see, then, the aspect of Siva (Destroyer, or Holy Spirit) as those individuals who constantly create and recreate and go through the cycles of energy. In them is the beginning and the ending and the continuation of cycles. That is why Siva is called the Destroyer, because in order to renew we must have endings and beginnings, and this is the work of the Holy Spirit.

The concept of that continual release and the bursting forth of the pink flame involves the birth-death cycle over and over again. Patriots are involved in the release of an enormous amount of energy of the Holy Spirit, which they sustain with fervor; but it's such a release that it's like a candle that is ignited and goes out and then keeps on going. And that is what is also happening when we consider patriotism today in some of its perversions where people get involved in an overbalance of the death cycle, in an extreme right wing or an extreme left wing.

Actually, if the word "left wing" didn't have a negative connotation, the individuals involved would be considered as patriotic as those in the right wing. But the left wing tends to see patriotism and the preservation of human values as sometimes crossing the boundaries of the nations. The fervor of the left wing gets released in plans of socialism and welfare for the common good of all people, whereas right wing fervor tends to want to preserve individuality and a national identity. Both of these have their places in human history; from both of these we can gain.

The Supreme Individualization of the God Flame

Jesus had in his teaching a place for all spectrums of political as well as religious philosophy. The balance which he gave to his apostles: "Heal the sick, cleanse the lepers, raise the dead, cast out devils: freely ye have received, freely give. For I was an hungred, and ye gave me meat: I was thirsty, and ye gave me drink. Inasmuch as ye have done it unto one of the least of these my brethren, ye have done it unto me"[2]—all of this is the giving of the self, the allowing of the body and the blood of the self to be broken and shared. Yet Jesus is the supreme individualization of the God flame. We see the need, then, for all aspects of the minds of the Christed ones in all spectrums.

The Spectrum of Right and Left

Our beloved El Morya has given us an understanding of where

we stand in the spectrum of politics and religion in his *White Paper*. Actually, politics and religion have been used by the fallen ones to create division and schism and to divide the people, to take from them their vision and to cause them to perish and noble ideals to perish. Morya released this *White Paper* for the enlightenment of light-bearers so they could see above and beyond the political and religious spectrum. He said:

> Ours is not to create division, and The Summit Lighthouse, our organization, reflects those goals which are sound and strengthening to the human spirit. May I say in all cosmic honor that there are virtuous causes across the whole range of human endeavor, but there are many that are unvirtuous, unrighteous, deceptive and wrongly motivated. We cannot identify with any; for our purpose is not to be popular, but to be truthful and to embrace those spiritual causes which will enable the soul itself to expand its life.
>
> I have not denied that the poor, as Jesus said, are with you always. I have not denied man's right to fulfill those social needs which to some have become a way of spiritual service. Likewise, we clearly see that among the traditions of men there are many of virtue, albeit sometimes sagging, that ought to be upheld; but where shall we position the timbers? We cannot identify with the right or the left, and we cannot identify with the middle of the road.
>
> As I speak, truth and error slide, and the human jackal of division has man in derision. The powers of darkness laugh as people espouse this cause and that cause in a radical way. Others are at the center of lukewarmness. They would not wax hot and they would not wax cold. So be it. The salvation of the soul is not served by social reform, nor is it served by opposing social reform. The progress of man can best be accented if it is first set in the right direction. May I point out how this can be done and what our perspective is.
>
> It is reasonable to suppose that there are many things of a spiritual nature unknown to men, and divine revelation has not yet closed its mouth of uttering the

great fiat of the Word. There are those who think religious tradition is complete and that man has but to go about the gentle and yet sometimes not so gentle business of attaching labels to various people and to various groups. These labels are intended not to liberate, but to confine. When the man of honor sees clearly, he will realize that both social reform and opposition to social reform have their own way of sapping his total energy. People feel the need to espouse one cause or the other, and those who are of a radical nature find niches of comfortable radicalism in varying degrees to the right or to the left of center. How one radical can condemn the other is difficult to understand in the light of spiritual knowledge.[3]

I think the first great soul-liberation I had in this life was liberation from a comfortable niche of orthodoxy. And when I broke that receptacle and picked through the egg as a chick coming out and felt that I was free and that I could find God anywhere and everywhere, in any church, in any place, in any tradition, I knew the flow with the Infinite.

The second great soul-liberation was to be free of the political niche of right- or left-wing politics. And the same pecking through that shell experienced within my soul gave me the liberty to espouse truth where truth is found; and therefore I can find truth in any political organization, because truth can only be in one place. Truth resides in the heart of man and woman.

Truth resides in the heart of the true patriarch, the patron, and the patriot of liberty. To find our place in this trinity of hierarchy is what we must put our hearts and minds to this Fourth of July as we declare our independence from the niches created, falsified, by those who seek only to have our souls in bondage to their systems which they have evolved through the pride of the lesser self. Throughout the class, what we will see in the dictations is that we will have more and more understanding of the perspective of where the plumb line of truth falls in right- and left-wing politics, religion, and educational policies.

The main thing to realize is that patriots are the people who carry the flame for the patriarchs and the patrons. They carry the energy that makes it happen. They put the body on the skeleton of an idea or a nation. They must rely on the patriarch to clearly define the law and the patron to interpret the law, because they are the ones that are charged with the energy that will carry it through. Many times the patriots are the masses and many times they are people in power.

Indoctrination of the Masses

Since the beginning of time and staging revolutions and mass movements, those who pervert the law or pervert life know that they have to carry the patriots with them in order to be successful in starting a revolution or a new movement. Therefore, they indoctrinate the patriots with the wrong foundation of concepts and platforms. They can start with a set of premises, with facts and so-called proof that can be a complete network of a lie, and because the patriots are not equipped to penetrate the lie, they will empty the cups of their fervor and of their flame into wrong matrices. Thereby whole movements get carried on because these people are not correctly informed.

Remember, these are the people who have heart. They are not always educated. They have love; they have fervor; they have trust. They have the simple faith that those who are the educated, those who write and make the laws, those who are their teachers, know what they are doing. They can be easily incited, because love is expressed through the feeling body; and so they are incited to get into this niche of political fervor or that niche of political or social action. They are confined by the matrices that are set forth by those who do not have the true action of the blue flame or the yellow flame.

Therefore, we must develop the blue plume. We must become students of the law. We must understand government. We must see how the masters have given us a legacy of several hundred years and then of thousands of years prior to that as the foundation for the American dream and the new order of the ages. We must know our Constitution. We must know that behind our Constitution there is the divine document inspired by Saint Germain. We must see how the outer law conforms to the inner law.

We must appeal to the Holy Spirit and to the ascended masters to interpret that law to us rather than assign to others the interpretation of these laws which come from cosmos, which must be released within the heart flame. We must understand and participate in government. We must become patriarchs of the law; and we must see ourselves as patriarchs not only of the law of America, but of the law of the planet—patriarchs of cosmic law.

The Balance of the Threefold Flame

What we must see, then, is that although mankind generally fall into these three categories, it is time for light-bearers to come of age, to take back unto themselves the blue flame of power, the yellow flame of the teacher, and the pink flame of the patriot. We must be all three. We must have the balance of the threefold flame. We must not assign to those of lesser light our cosmic destiny. We must take the reins of power. We must develop the yellow plume by becoming educated, taking our place in the world community, developing a sacred labor, and patronizing that aspect of life which promotes some aspect of cosmic law.

In other words, we must take to ourselves the cycles of the education of the people in the aspects of the law and not turn them over to any group or any association that is niched comfortably in right- or left-wing concepts of education and theories that have no part of cosmic law. We must not turn over to others the assignment which God has given to us in our joint heirship with Christ, with the Real Self.

Therefore, it behooves every Keeper of the Flame, everyone who comes in contact with the ascended masters' teachings, to take the yellow plume and to carry it as a torch in some accomplishment that is immediately practical in the world community as the world community now is, bringing the flame of sponsorship to whatever area of human endeavor our talents may be applied as we search within to find our divine plan.

Finally, we must be patriots with a fervor. If we have the blueprint and the understanding of the blueprint, we are still not complete. We are almost as the newborn child ready to be released from the mother's womb. When the child comes forth, it is not quickened until the Holy Spirit breathes into the child the breath of life. That breath of life is the pink flame. It is the pink flame that breathes into the law and the understanding of the law the life, the vitality, the creativity that surges and gives civilization the swirling action of the flame. Without that love, without that charity, we have not the fire to ignite any cause.

And so let us let the Holy Spirit give birth within this day to a new nation, a new individuality, a nation that is an ion, an atom of selfhood, a microcosm all inside. And when we give birth to this threefold dream, this threefold manifestation within, then we can also give birth in the macrocosm of our planet to the new order of the ages.

Therefore, we must be patriots of life—patriots not only of our state, but of our planet, our solar system, our sector in the galaxy, the entire galaxy, and the entire cosmos. We dare not let our fervor be compartmentalized, sectionalized. We dare not follow the narrowness of any political/religious spectrum or ideology; for we will thereby confine the Holy Spirit, confine cosmic law to our detriment, to our death.

This means championing that place where God has chosen to incarnate the God flame at a certain point in time and space. The cross of Alpha and Omega was formed—a God was born. You are that God in manifestation. To be a patriot means to champion with fervor the God flame where you are. You are the defender of that God flame where I AM THAT I AM. And where I AM is where my consciousness is, and my consciousness extends in succeeding circles of awareness.

First I am aware of myself—I AM. Then I become aware of myself as a member of a family unit. I defend that family, and I use the energy of love to enshrine the mandala of the family. My family increases to my neighborhood, to projects which involve me, to my livelihood, to my community, to my nation, to my planet, and on and on until those cycles know no bounds and cosmic consciousness is the plane of my awareness.

This, then, is what we must contemplate when we consider true spiritual freedom. To be free means not to be confined by anyone, anything, except the inner law of our own being. When is it right to stage revolution and when is it right to remain in conformity with the laws of the land? This must be gauged by the inner law of cosmos. All that is in harmony with cosmic law must be upheld even at the sacrifice of the lesser self. And we must be willing to recognize rebellion within ourselves, rebellion against that law, and understand that selfishness or self-preservation to the exclusion of the whole has no place if we would understand ourselves as patriarchs, patrons, and patriots of life.

George Washington:
Patriarch of the Law

I would review with you now some of the people who I
feel have made the threefold flame balanced in this nation by
personifying one or more aspects of the trinity. First we must
consider George Washington, the first president of the United
States, carrying the flame of the blue ray in our nation's history,
born in Virginia, February 22, 1732. As commander in chief of the
Continental forces, he remained stalwart and stern during the five
years of war; and the victory was fulfilled when Cornwallis
surrendered to Washington at Yorktown, Virginia, in 1781.

I'm certain you remember as a child celebrating Washington's birthday and looking at that picture of sternness and not
quite knowing how to understand, how to identify with the
sternness of the lawgiver. This is as it should be; this is how
patriarchs manifest the law. It is such a discipline because they
hold in their hands the reins that must draw masses of people into
conformity with a blueprint. That blueprint is a stepping-up of
cosmic law for a new age, and therefore the patriarch has to be
willing to whip the people into the discipline of the new order. As
Moses was a patriarch, he was faced with the proposition of taking
the children of Israel and whipping them into shape during forty
years of wandering in the wilderness.

We find, then, that the patriarch is not always popular,
because he comes in a time when the old order is dying, when
people's morals and understanding of spirituality and of basic laws
are sagging, when there is the greatest corruption, as was the
corruption of the laws which were handed down upon us by
England. We find that patriarchs come with a thrust of power.
They place their rod into the earth, and mankind fall to the right
or to the left of that rod. The patriarch must not stop to consider
whether or not his idea is popular. When he receives from
Almighty God the fervor of the law, he must carry it through unto
the end.

It is very interesting, as we see the plan of our nation
unfolding, that the Revolutionary War lasted five years. This
morning we will have a dictation from mighty Cosmos, who
releases the five secret rays to a planet. These secret rays are for the
testing of souls entering into the white-fire core of Alpha and

Omega. That Revolutionary War was the testing of a handful of souls to see whether or not they could make the sacrifices necessary to enter into the fiery core, which was the origin and the beginning of the mandala of the United States of America.

The thirteen colonies marked the seven rays of the Christic light, the five secret rays, and the eighth ray, which is known as the ray of integration. In order to have a balanced mandala of hierarchy and initiation, it is essential to have thirteen as the basic unit of hierarchy.

Washington had the thrust of power from Almighty God. We hear this in his first inaugural address when he said:

> No people can be bound to acknowledge and adore the Invisible Hand which conducts the affairs of men more than the people of the United States. Every step by which they have advanced to the character of an independent nation seems to have been distinguished by some token of providential agency. And, in the important revolution just accomplished, in the system of their united government, the tranquil deliberations and voluntary consent of so many distinct communities, from which the event has resulted, can not be compared with the means by which most governments have been established, without some return of pious gratitude, along with a humble anticipation of the future blessings which the past seems to presage.[4]

Van Dyke spoke of Washington: "He stands in history not as a lonely pinnacle like Mount Shasta, elevated above the plain 'By drastic lift of pent volcanic fires'; but as the central summit of a mountain range, with all his noble fellowship of kindred peaks about him, enhancing his unquestioned supremacy by their glorious neighborhood and their great support."[5]

This is a statement of hierarchy. It shows us that no individual can complete the divine plan without the support of all aspects of hierarchy. It shows us that we ourselves are incomplete without each other, without the blending of our energies, without our assuming our roles in this trinity of action.

In 1770, an Indian chief had this to say of Washington:

I am a chief and the ruler of many tribes. My influence extends to the waters of the great lakes, and to the far blue mountains. I have traveled a long and weary path that I may see the young warrior of the great battle. . . . It was on the day when the white man's blood mixed with the streams of our forest that I first beheld this chief. I called to my young men, and said, "Mark yon tall and daring warrior. He is not of the Red-coat tribe; he has an Indian's wisdom, and his warriors fight as we do; himself, alone, is exposed. Quick, let your aim be certain, and he dies!" Our rifles were leveled, rifles which, but for him, knew not how to miss—'twas all in vain; a power far mightier than we, shielded him from harm; he cannot die in battle.

I am old, and soon shall be gathered to the great council fire of my fathers in the land of shades, but ere I go, there is something bids me speak in the voice of prophecy. Listen! The Great Spirit protects that man, and guides his destinies; he will become the chief of nations, and a people yet unborn will hail him as the founder of a mighty empire.[6]

Washington did have the overshadowing of Almighty God. He did have the preservation of that immortal soul that paved the way for his incarnation as Guy Ballard and his release once again of the law, fulfilling the spiritual destiny of his role as a patriarch under Saint Germain in America.

George Washington's Vision

I cannot allow the Fourth of July to pass without reading to you that supreme moment in the life of George Washington. This is the vision of General Washington. It was originally published by Wesley Bradshaw, copied from a reprint in the *National Tribune* [Vol. 4, No. 12], December 1880:

The last time I ever saw Anthony Sherman was on the fourth of July, 1859, in Independence Square. He was then ninety-nine years old, and becoming very feeble. But though so old, his dimming eyes rekindled as he gazed upon Independence Hall, which he came to visit once more.

"Let us go into the hall," he said. "I want to tell you of an incident of Washington's life—one which no one alive knows of except myself; and, if you live you will before long, see it verified.

"From the opening of the Revolution we experienced all phases of fortune, now good and now ill, one time victorious and another conquered. The darkest period we had, I think, was when Washington after several reverses, retreated to Valley Forge, where he resolved to pass the winter of 1777. Ah! I have often seen the tears coursing down our dear commander's care-worn cheeks, as he would be conversing with a confidential officer about the condition of his poor soldiers. You have doubtless heard the story of Washington's going into the thicket to pray. Well, it was not only true, but he used often to pray in secret for aid and comfort from God, the interposition of whose Divine Providence brought us safely through the darkest days of tribulation.

"One day, I remember it well, the chilly winds whistled through the leafless trees, though the sky was cloudless and the sun shone brightly, he remained in his quarters nearly all the afternoon alone. When he came out I noticed that his face was a shade paler than usual, and there seemed to be something on his mind of more than ordinary importance. Returning just after dusk, he dispatched an orderly to the quarters of the officer I mention who was presently in attendance. After a preliminary conversation of about half an hour, Washington, gazing upon his companion with that strange look of dignity which he alone could command, said to the latter:

"'I do not know whether it is owing to the anxiety of my mind, or what, but this afternoon as I was sitting at this table engaged in preparing a dispatch, something seemed to disturb me. Looking up, I beheld standing opposite me a singularly beautiful female. So astonished was I, for I had given strict orders not to be disturbed that it was some moments before I found language to inquire into the cause of her presence. A second, a third, and even a fourth time did I repeat my question, but received no

answer from my mysterious visitor except a slight raising of
her eyes. By this time I felt strange sensations spreading
through me. I would have risen but the riveted gaze of the
being before me rendered volition impossible. I assayed
once more to address her, but my tongue had become
useless. Even thought itself had become paralyzed. A new
influence, mysterious, potent, irresistible, took possession
of me. All I could do was to gaze steadily, vacantly at my
unknown visitant. Gradually the surrounding atmosphere
seemed as though becoming filled with sensations, and
luminous. Everything about me seemed to rarify, the
mysterious visitor herself becoming more airy and yet
more distinct to my sight than before. I now began to feel
as one dying, or rather to experience the sensations which I
have sometimes imagined accompany dissolution. I did
not think, I did not reason, I did not move; all were alike
impossible. I was only conscious of gazing fixedly,
vacantly at my companion.

   " 'Presently I heard a voice saying, "Son of the
Republic, look and learn," while at the same time my
visitor extended her arm eastwardly. I now beheld a heavy
white vapor at some distance rising fold upon fold. This
gradually dissipated, and I looked upon a strange scene.
Before me lay spread out in one vast plain all the countries
of the world—Europe, Asia, Africa and America. I saw
rolling and tossing between Europe and America the
billows of the Atlantic, and between Asia and America lay
the Pacific. "Son of the Republic," said the same
mysterious voice as before, "look and learn." At that
moment I beheld a dark, shadowy being, like an angel,
standing, or rather floating in mid-air, between Europe
and America, dipping water out of the ocean in the
hollow of each hand, he sprinkled some upon America
with his right hand, while with his left hand he cast some
on Europe. Immediately a cloud raised from these
countries, and joined in mid-ocean. For a while it
remained stationary, and then moved slowly westward,
until it enveloped America in its murky folds. Sharp
flashes of lightning gleamed through it at intervals, and I
heard the smothered groans and cries of the American

people. A second time the angel dipped water from the ocean, and sprinkled it out as before. The dark cloud was then drawn back to the ocean, in whose heaving billows it sank from view. A third time I heard the mysterious voice saying, "Son of the Republic, look and learn," I cast my eyes upon America and beheld villages and towns and cities springing up one after another until the whole land from the Atlantic to the Pacific was dotted with them. Again, I heard the mysterious voice say, "Son of the Republic, the end of the century cometh, look and learn."

"'At this the dark shadowy angel turned his face southward, and from Africa I saw an ill-omened spectre approach our land. It flitted slowly over every town and city of the latter. The inhabitants presently set themselves in battle array against each other. As I continued looking I saw a bright angel, on whose brow rested a crown of light, on which was traced the word "Union," bearing the American flag which he placed between the divided nation, and said, "Remember ye are brethren." Instantly, the inhabitants, casting from them their weapons became friends once more, and united around the National Standard.

"'And again I heard the mysterious voice saying, "Son of the Republic, look and learn." At this the dark, shadowy angel placed a trumpet to his mouth, and blew three distinct blasts; and taking water from the ocean, he sprinkled it upon Europe, Asia and Africa. Then my eyes beheld a fearful scene: from each of these countries arose thick, black clouds that were soon joined into one. And throughout this mass there gleamed a dark red light by which I saw hordes of armed men, who, moving with the cloud, marched by land and sailed by sea to America, which country was enveloped in the volume of cloud. And I dimly saw these vast armies devastate the whole country and burn the villages, towns and cities that I beheld springing up. As my ears listened to the thundering of the cannon, clashing of swords, and the shouts and cries of millions in mortal combat, I heard again the mysterious voice saying, "Son of the Republic, look and learn." When the voice had ceased, the dark shadowy angel placed his trumpet once more to his mouth, and blew a long and fearful blast.

"'Instantly a light as of a thousand suns shone down from above me, and pierced and broke into fragments the dark cloud which enveloped America. At the same moment the angel upon whose head still shone the word Union, and who bore our national flag in one hand and a sword in the other, descended from the heavens attended by legions of white spirits. These immediately joined the inhabitants of America, who I perceived were well-nigh overcome, but who immediately taking courage again, closed up their broken ranks and renewed the battle. Again, amid the fearful noise of the conflict, I heard the mysterious voice saying, "Son of the Republic, look and learn." As the voice ceased, the shadowy angel for the last time dipped water from the ocean and sprinkled it upon America. Instantly the dark cloud rolled back, together with the armies it had brought, leaving the inhabitants of the land victorious.

"'Then once more I beheld the villages, towns and cities springing up where I had seen them before, while the bright angel, planting the azure standard he had brought in the midst of them, cried with a loud voice: "While the stars remain, and the heavens send down dew upon the earth, so long shall the Union last." And taking from his brow the crown on which blazoned the word "Union," he placed it upon the Standard while the people, kneeling down, said, "Amen."

"'The scene instantly began to fade and dissolve, and I at last saw nothing but the rising, curling vapor I at first beheld. This also disappearing, I found myself once more gazing upon the mysterious visitor, who, in the same voice I had heard before, said, "Son of the Republic, what you have seen is thus interpreted: Three great perils will come upon the Republic. The most fearful is the third (The comment on his word 'third' is: "The help against the THIRD peril comes in the shape of Divine Assistance. Apparently the Second Advent)....passing which the whole world united shall not prevail against her. Let every child of the Republic learn to live for his God, his land

and Union." With these words the vision vanished, and I
started from my seat and felt that I had seen a vision
wherein had been shown to me the birth, progress, and
destiny of the United States.'

"Such, my friends," concluded the venerable nar-
rator, "were the words I heard from Washington's own
lips, and America will do well to profit by them."

The Goddess of Liberty and Micah, Angel of Unity

The visitor was the Goddess of Liberty, the spokesman for the
Karmic Board, the "Lady with a Lamp" who Longfellow prophesied would "stand/In the great history of the land,/A noble type
of good/Heroic womanhood."[7] The coming of the feminine ray,
the ensouling of the nation by the feminine ray, had its origin
in that moment when Washington prayed at Valley Forge. And
the vision of the Divine Mother showed us the conflicts: the
Revolutionary War, the War Between the States, and a third world
conflict that was to follow.

And now we stand with Micah, the Angel of Unity, who
figured in this vision—the son of Archangel Michael, the same
angel who led the children of Israel across the Red Sea, parted the
waters, and held for them the concept of the union;[8] the same one
guiding the true Israelites to found a new nation, a New
Jerusalem. The same angel came forth bringing the heritage of the
patriarchs of the law, patrons of life, and patriots of all ages. That
angel, the Spirit of Unity, has kept America a nation of fifty
sovereign states. When we consider that Europe was not able to
unite under the hand of Saint Germain, that no other continent
has forged a mighty union, we must also concede that God is in
our stars and in our destiny.

Abraham Lincoln:
Patriarch of the Law

May I review for you certain others who figure as key
patriarchs. There is Abraham Lincoln, whom we revere, whose
concept of unity came also from Micah the angel. For him the
thrust of the patriarch of the law was to preserve that law, to
preserve the Union. The concept that he held was that the issue

between the North and the South affected more than the future of
the United States. He saw beyond national borders. He saw what
this union, this mandala, would mean to the heart of a planet. He
said: "It presents to the whole family of man, the question
whether a constitutional republic, or a democracy—a government
of the people, by the same people—can, or cannot, maintain its
territorial integrity, against its own domestic foes."[9]

Lincoln held the immaculate concept of a united and restored
Union. He said: " . . . A house divided against itself cannot stand. I
believe this government cannot endure permanently half slave and
half free. I do not expect the Union to be dissolved—I do not
expect the house to fall—but I do expect it will cease to be divided.
It will become all one thing, or all the other. . . ."[10]

The North and South of America represent the polarity of
Alpha and Omega in the white-fire core of the AUM. Every nation
has the aspects of cosmic consciousness, the aspects of the mandala
of hierarchy. Those who do not understand the whole become
polarized to a part of the plan of hierarchy; and instead of being in
polarity, they come into opposition. The division between the
North and the South was carefully contrived by the fallen ones who
continually attempt to split the atom of selfhood by dividing us in
twain. They work at the family unit, the national unit, the
planetary unit—always dividing and conquering on the basis of
dividing male and female, who are one. We see, then, that the
Civil War was attempting to split the very atom of selfhood. What
would we have done without this patriarch of the law?

Other American Patriarchs

There are other patriarchs who have come forth in America's
history, many in America's early days who set forth the law in the
writing of the Declaration of Independence and the Constitution.
We see the great outstanding figures: Thomas Jefferson, Benjamin
Franklin, Alexander Hamilton, and others. We have our concept
of, perhaps, right and wrong in the consciousness of these early
figures, and we try to put them into niches of the political spectrum. We must realize, however, no matter what their political
stand, that first and foremost, these individuals had at heart the
manifestation of the law and the fervor of patriotism. They represented different aspects of the political spectrum.

We must also remember that even early in our history, the tares were sown with the wheat. Ideologies of the fallen ones that are not of the true teachings of the Great White Brotherhood were also present in the founding of our nation. Sometimes these rubbed off as tarnish, as the mud on the boots of the commander in the field. Yet at the heart, at the core, at the nucleus of the founding of our nation, there was a great enough purity for Saint Germain to work through and thrust the action.

There have been great, great women in the history of America who have figured as patriarchs of the law. There are too many to name. One outstanding woman who set the law of a new dispensation of teaching is Mary Baker Eddy, who sat at the feet of Jesus as Mary, the sister of Martha and Lazarus. She set forth in the 1800s a teaching on the science of the immaculate concept, of holding the perfect image, the perfect blueprint for every part of life, knowing that when we see the vision of perfection, all energy must coalesce to outpicture that perfection.

Saint Frances Xavier Cabrini and Maria Montessori: Patrons of Life

As we examine those that upheld the yellow flame as patrons of life, we see many who have been the sustainers of the law. One great love that comes to my heart as an example of a patron sustaining the law of Christ and the law of liberty is Saint Frances Xavier Cabrini, known as Mother Cabrini, holding the Mother flame for Italy. She went forth from that land where she founded the Missionary Sisters of the Sacred Heart and worked with orphanages and hospitals. Mother Cabrini was called to the United States to care for the Italian immigrants. She built hospitals, schools, colleges, day nurseries, orphanages, and free clinics all over the Western Hemisphere. She had a very deep understanding of the balance of commitment to God and nation. She wrote:

> He who is faithful to God is faithful to his country and to his family, and the more fear of God animates the citizens of a country, the greater and the more respected will the nation be. Moreover, as it is said that nations are formed on the knees of the mother, it follows that the more the mother is venerated in the family, and the more she herself conforms her conduct to that sublime model

that we have in Her, who, repairing the faults of Eve, raised the status of humanity, so much the greater will be those future generations who will form the glory and the prosperity of their country. These principles, my dear daughters, you should teach in your schools, because as educators, you must not only form good Christians, but good citizens for the State, which we wish to be great and respected.[11]

Mother Cabrini was canonized. She made her ascension. This is why we sell the book on her life. Her flame is great for the thrust of education, combined with the flame of another saint who comes from Italy, Maria Montessori, who set forth the pattern of education for the golden age according to the teachings of Mother Mary, which Mary gave to her, precept upon precept, as she began her mission teaching in the slums of Rome.

These great women, these lights of history, no matter what their walk of life, no matter what their religious background, belong not to any niche of orthodoxy. They belong to humanity. They belong to a cosmos. They have set the spirals which continue to chart the destiny of America and the destiny of a planet.

Harriet Beecher Stowe:
Patron of Life

We see Harriet Beecher Stowe, who wrote *Uncle Tom's Cabin*. She said:

This is an age of the world when nations are trembling and convulsed. A mighty influence is abroad, surging and heaving the world, as with an earthquake. And is America safe? Every nation that carries in its bosom great and unredressed injustice has in it the elements of this last convulsion.

For what is this mighty influence thus rousing in all nations and languages those groanings that cannot be uttered, for man's freedom and equality?

O, Church of Christ, read the signs of the times! Is not this power the spirit of HIM whose kingdom is yet to come, and whose will to be done on earth as it is in heaven?...

A day of grace is yet held out to us. Both North and South have been guilty before God; and the *Christian church* has a heavy account to answer. Not by combining together, to protect injustice and cruelty, and making a common capital of sin, is this union to be saved—but by repentance, justice and mercy; for, not surer is the eternal law by which the millstone sinks in the ocean, than that stronger law, by which injustice and cruelty shall bring on nations the wrath of Almighty God![12]

When Lincoln met Harriet Beecher Stowe, he said, "So this is the little lady who made the big war." As you know, *Uncle Tom's Cabin* was the exposure of slavery in all of its degradation of the total human spirit. By taking her stand as a patron of life, as a patron of these people, she was the preserver of the law forged by the patriarchs who had gone before.

You see, then, one who carries the illumination of the law must write the books that inspire the patriots to release that pink flame, to set the captives free, to bring justice to the nation. Those who carry the yellow flame must be constant, steadfast, tenacious, continually moving against the bastions of tyranny that have set themselves up in place of the fortification of the true law of life.

The yellow flame is most potent. It has a high frequency, a very high intensity, as it pierces through the night of human ignorance and shows to the people what the meaning of the republic is, what the meaning of government of the people, by the people, for the people (that same trinity) is. In America we have such a fusion of the consciousness of the Christ light that among all nations, its people, its common people, have the greatest sense of individuality, of self-government, of responsibility, of helping one another. They have an inherent understanding of the flame of freedom—not by their own virtue, but by the virtue of those masters who have planted the mandala and the flame of victory in her soil.

George Washington Carver,
Clara Barton, Albert Einstein:
Patrons of Life

Another great patron of life is George Washington Carver. Born of slaves, eager to learn, he showed how the South could be reborn and replenish her economy. He declared that God had showed him the uses which resulted in three hundred products made from peanuts: cheese, milk, peanut butter, coffee, flour, ink, soap, dyes, and many more. By his flame and his fervor, he brought illumination, creativity, and industry to the South.

There was Clara Barton the founder of the American Red Cross. She spoke of the women who had fought in the battles of the Civil War:

> Mothers—wives—and maidens, would there were some testimonials grand enough for you,—some tablet that could show to the world the sacrifice of American womanhood and American motherhood in that war! Sacrifices so nobly and so firmly—but so gently and so beautifully made.
>
> If like the Spartan mother she did not send her son defiantly to the field,—bidding him return only with his shield, or on it,—if like the Roman matron she did not take him by the hand and lead him proudly to the standard of the Republic; like the true Anglo-Saxon,— loyal and loving, tender and brave,—she hid her tears with one hand while with the other wrung her fond farewell, and passed him to the state.[13]

The feminine ray as the patron of life sees beyond the selfishness of preserving her own in the nest and realizes that the preservation of the cause, the union, the cosmos, the solar system, is far more important than self-seeking and self-satisfaction.

A patron whose mind we have observed in the twentieth century, Albert Einstein, was one of the most amazing beings that has walked the earth. He enunciated the special and general theories of relativity and made great contributions to statistical mechanics and the quantum theory. He established the mass-energy equivalent, the photon theory of light, and upheld the unified field theory. These theories furnished powerful guiding principles in the search for the laws of nature.

The dispensation which he was given by the Karmic Board to release that which led to the splitting of the atom, nuclear fission ($E = mc^2$), came through his consciousness as he is an ancient soul. Those discoveries could not have been made had they not been released by the Lords of Karma; and they were released in the hour

of the darkest trial for America, when America was threatened
to be overrun by the Axis powers of Germany and Japan. And
after the attack on Pearl Harbor when America herself was threatened on her own soil, that invention, that discovery, though
used in war, was able to secure and retain freedom in this hemisphere.

The Lords of Karma are not for war. They are not for
destruction. They are not for the taking-away of life. However,
there is a higher law that governs freedom. There is that law which
Jesus stated when he said: "And fear not them who kill the body,
but are not able to kill the soul: but rather fear him who is able to
destroy both soul and body in hell."[14] Sometimes in preserving a
cause of freedom, it is necessary to sacrifice the body that the soul
might be preserved.

In the course of human history, the Lords of Karma have even
had to make decisions based on the relative state of mankind's
consciousness. The knowledge of nuclear physics was released to
mankind for peaceful purposes, and we trust that it can be so used
without harm, without pollution, without the danger of storing or
depositing those wastes where they will result in future cataclysm.

This is a statement from Albert Einstein after all this had
passed. And of course he regretted the use of his discovery. He
said:

> For the rest of my life I want to reflect on what light
> is. . . .[15] The most beautiful thing we can experience is the
> mysterious. It is the source of all true art and science. He
> to whom this emotion is a stranger, who can no longer
> pause to wonder and stand rapt in awe, is as good as dead:
> his eyes are closed. . . . To know that what is impenetrable
> to us really exists, manifesting itself as the highest wisdom
> and the most radiant beauty which our dull faculties can
> comprehend only in their most primitive forms—this
> knowledge, this feeling, is at the center of true reli-
> giousness.[16]

Great Patriots of Liberty

We come to the great patriots who have forged civilization. I
have chosen three for this morning who have been outstanding in

their inspiration to me in my life. There are many times when we stand as light-bearers with the knowledge of the law, with the understanding of the law vouchsafed to us, and somehow we wonder how we will muster the fervor to go on in the face of the weight of the opposition to the victory. It is in those hours that we remember Lincoln's words at Gettysburg "...that these dead shall not have died in vain."

As I walked through Arlington Memorial Cemetery when I began my mission as a messenger, those words rang into my soul; and I thought of Flanders fields, and I thought of those fields which have since been bulldozed over in France and throughout Europe where lives of men and women of every nation have been given, sacrificed to the cause of freedom. And I said to myself: "The mission shall go on. The teachings shall inundate the earth that these dead shall not have died in vain." I thought of those who had died in concentration camps, those who are even this day political prisoners undergoing tortures behind the iron curtain, those who have been sacrificed in Vietnam and in the Far East. And then we think of the warfare and the strife that continues in the Middle East.

Everywhere, people are willing to die for causes; and if they are not willing, they often are taken anyway by the enemy. When we think of all the blood that has been shed (not the least of which was the blood of Christ) for the very purpose for which we come together this day, we feel that fervor mustering within us—the fervor of all the saints, of all the patriots who have gone before, their love great enough that they could lay down their lives.

Joan of Arc:
Patriot of Liberty

As Joan of Arc said at the stake, "I would rather die than revoke what God has made me to do." To turn back on what God has given us to do is hypocrisy. It is cowardice. It is to recede into the shadows of the not-self. Only love can do what Joan of Arc did and what all of the unknown soldiers and unknown patriots have done. Jesus gave the formula of that love: "For whosoever will save his life shall lose it: and whosoever will lose his life for my sake shall find it."[17] He didn't mean we had to die in order to give birth to liberty; he meant we had to put down the lesser self, the hungry self with the mouth constantly open, getting and getting and fattening the self. We have to relish the lean years, the surrender, the period of the fasting of the senses to give birth to a new order of the ages.

"Greater love hath no man than this, that a man lay down his life for his friends."[18] Who are our friends? Our friends are the ascended masters. Our friends are humanity—the man in the street, the children of the world, the people who populate Terra. These are our friends—more than our friends. They're our brothers and our sisters.

Shall we take so noble a cause, so great an enlightenment as we have been given by the Great White Brotherhood, and hide it under a bushel and say: "I will retreat into the mountains and do my own thing. I will meditate and I will live my life and gain my mastery"? Is it mastery to sit in the hills and watch while civilization is burning and dying and crumbling? It is the height of selfishness. If you read the lives of the great avatars, you will find that their retreats to the mountains were always for short periods of regeneration, of infilling of the Holy Spirit. They returned quickly to give unto the masses that gift which God had vouchsafed unto them. We must do likewise. We must forge our sacred labor.

Patrick Henry:
Patriot of Liberty

May I read to you this day the brave words of Patrick Henry as he was advocating the adoption of the "Virginia Resolutions," which opposed the Stamp Act of the British parliament. This case was a forerunner of the American Revolution. Fearlessly, he exclaimed:

> "Caesar had his Brutus, Charles the First his Cromwell, and George the Third—." His words were cut off. Shouts from the audience filled the room: "Treason! Treason!" and the mob was about to descend on him. He held fast; he silenced them with these words: "And George the Third may profit by their example. If this be treason, make the most of it."[19]

How many of us are willing to stand before the angry mob, to be unpopular for our fervor of love for the law that we know and espouse?

In the 1775 session of the Continental Congress, Patrick Henry gave one of the most inspiring orations in our nation's history. It applies directly to us as we commune today. He said:

> Sir, we are not weak if we make a proper use of those means which the God of nature has placed in our power. Three millions of people armed in the holy cause of liberty, and in such a country as that which we possess, are invincible by any force which our enemy can send against us. Besides, sir, we shall not fight our battles alone. There is a just God who presides over the destinies of nations, and who will raise up friends to fight our battles for us. The battle, sir, is not to the strong alone; it is to the vigilant, the active, the brave. Besides, sir, we have no election. If we were base enough to desire it, it is now too late to retire from the contest. There is no retreat but in submission and slavery! Our chains are forged! Their clanking may be heard on the plains of Boston! The war is inevitable—and let it come! I repeat it, sir, let it come!
>
> It is in vain, sir, to extenuate the matter. Gentlemen may cry, Peace, Peace—but there is no peace. The war is actually begun! The next gale that sweeps from the north will bring to our ears the clash of resounding arms! Our brethren are already in the field! Why stand we here idle? What is it that gentlemen wish? What would they have? Is life so dear, or peace so sweet, as to be purchased at the price of chains and slavery? Forbid it, Almighty God! I know not what course others may take; but as for me, give me liberty or give me death! [20]

Can we not take those words and consider the battle of Armageddon betwixt the forces of light and darkness—a battle being waged right on the platform of our own consciousness, where daily we fight the sluggishness, the perversion of our lifeline to the Presence, where we fight all those forces that attempt to take from us our God-harmony and our liberty? Are not the battle lines already drawn? Can we shrink? Can we go back to our beds and hide under the covers and say, "I will not fight the battle this day"? When we stand in the greatest light, we must be ready to raise the sword (which is the *sacred word* of truth) against the greatest darkness.

When you receive the all-seeing eye from Cyclopea, the price of seeing, of seeing God-Good, is to be able to hold the balance while observing also the diametrical opposite of that good. In order to know good, we must be able to defend good. In order to defend good, we must know the enemy. That is why the closer you come to the white-fire core of being, the closer you come also to what is known as the black sun—created by the fallen ones as the false center, the false focal point of life, which center point is the carnal mind, the beast, the Antichrist.

Truly the battle line is drawn. As Godfre said, this is where the line is drawn—here at this point in time and space. Where God has thrust the energy of his consciousness, right where you stand, the battle line has already been drawn. We cannot shrink from it. We must say with that patriot, "Give me liberty or give me death!" We must have the willingness to fight to the death every enemy pitted against the mind and the consciousness of the Christ—as Thomas Jefferson said, swearing "eternal hostility against every form of tyranny over the mind of man."

Daniel Webster:
Patriot of Liberty

Daniel Webster is another patriot. He made a brilliant speech at the time when the right to secede from the Union was being discussed. He said:

> ...We do not impose geographical limits to our patriotic feeling or regard; we do not follow rivers and mountains, and lines of latitude, to find boundaries, beyond which public improvements do not benefit us. We who come here, as agents and representatives of these narrow-minded and selfish men of New England, consider ourselves as bound to regard with an equal eye the good of the whole, in whatever is within our power of legislation. Sir, if a railroad or canal, beginning in South Carolina and ending in South Carolina, appeared to me to be of national importance and national magnitude, believing, as I do, that the power of government extends to the

encouragement of works of that description, if I were to stand up here and ask, What interest has Massachusetts in a railroad in South Carolina? I should not be willing to face my constituents. These same narrow-minded men would tell me, that they had sent me to act for the whole country, and that one who possessed too little comprehension, either of intellect or feeling, one who was not large enough both in mind and in heart, to embrace the whole, was not fit to be entrusted with the interest of any part. [21]

The Constitution of the United States was not a compact entered into by the states, but it was the law of the land as formulated and ratified by the American people. There can only be "Liberty *and* Union, now and forever, one and inseparable!" [22]

An Awareness of the Whole

This profound statement carries to our understanding the concept that he who is not able to see the whole cannot be entrusted with the governing of the part. Patriots of liberty, patriarchs of the law, and patrons of life dare not view mankind or even the earth herself as a part of the whole. But in order to sponsor the flame of liberty, to be entrusted as patriarchs of the law with the legacy of the Logos, and to be the patrons of the art and culture of life in America and in the planet, we must contain within our consciousness an awareness of the whole, even of the ecology of a solar system in a galaxy and a galaxy in a cosmos. Only when we regard the whole as sacred can we regard the parts as sacred.

Just as the Constitution is not a compact, as Webster said, but the law of the land, so cosmic law, the code of a cosmos, is not something that we elect to have or not to have, or to be or not to be. We have to understand that cosmic law, the constitution that governs the covenant between man and his Maker, is already in fact the law of a cosmos. It already governs being and existence in this world and beyond. What we have to do is broaden consciousness to take in the whole so that we can determine how we, as the part, fit into the whole.

The key, then, to being patriarchs of the law, patrons of life, and patriots of liberty is to harmonize ourselves with that which already exists, to flow with the movement of the spheres, to determine what our destiny is, and then by our free will to elect to conform to it. This is our responsibility. This is our opportunity. This is the big wave, the cosmic wave that we crest! If we miss the crest of this wave of cosmic light, patriarchs, patrons, and patriots, let us ask ourselves, will there be another?

July 4, 1975
10:20-11:42 A.M. P D T

"K-17" is the code name for the ascended master who heads the Cosmic Secret Service. Its members are devotees of the all-seeing eye. They use their God-vision to warn the citizens of cosmos of threats to the security of the individualization of the God flame—threats to life and liberty, threats to the governments of the world and to the family as the basic unit of the Aquarian society. K-17 and his legions are the guardians of the destiny of liberty in America and in every nation on earth. Because of the nature of their service, K-17 and his co-workers are very close to the physical octave, often appearing in physical form as the guardians of right action midst chaos and crisis.

10

AMERICA'S DESTINY AMONG THE NATIONS

A Dictation by the Ascended Master K-17

Servants in the Cosmic Secret Service

I come as the representative of the Cosmic Secret Service. I stand before you and I am not alone; for with me stands Lanello, working closely with the brothers and sisters of our focus to bring to mankind a clear vision of that which is seen and that which remains hidden.

With me also I bring legions of the Cosmic Secret Service, those who have walked the earth among mankind as you now do, who have taken their leave from these octaves, and who have the fervor of sacred fire and of the cosmic honor flame, who carry scepters of authority—for they have won their battles of light and they have forged a union in service unknown behind the scenes in the governments of the nations. Also with me are angels of light, angels who guard the secret destiny of every nation, the destiny of America, and the destiny of a soul! These angels carry with them notations in their notebooks of all those forces and forcefields that are pivoted and posited against the raising of the feminine ray in this age.

Those who serve the Cosmic Secret Service protect the outpicturing of the divine plan by guarding the immaculate conception of the Cosmic Virgin. When they are called into action, these beings of light, very close to the destiny of nations and of the Divine Mother and the Divine Manchild, protect the seed and life aborning in the womb, life aborning in the heart of a nation, until that life comes forth standing tall to take its place, secure.

In the Eye of the Cosmic Virgin

Inasmuch as America is that place where God-government is destined to be carved, an archetype of golden-age civilization, inasmuch as the culture of the Mother, culturing, nourishing life in all its forms, is also intended to reach its zenith here, understand then that we are obliged to guard the growth of each shoot of life. Each twig that is bent must be drawn into alignment with the fiery core. We come in a period of America's destiny when the feminine ray must rise within man and woman as the glorying of purity, a purity beyond any purity which you can even imagine in your outer consciousness. Such is the awareness of the Cosmic Virgin. Through her eye we perceive all infamy, all that works against the carving of the state, the nation, and the soul.

We come then in a moment of history when there is the challenging of the delicate emanations of the five secret rays and the going within to discover the identity of the I AM. We come in an age when World Communism looms, challenging the maiden who carries the torch of illumination unto mankind. And all of the might and the armaments and the material power and all of the millions and billions of dollars that have gone into the building-up of the armed forces of the nations of the world—all of this is ultimately pitted against the soul-freedom of mankind.

Wars are always contrived behind the scenes! I tell you I have stood almost in a physical body, so near and so tangible, in those places of secret on the many continents where the fallen ones in their discussions, contacting even their overlords on the astral plane, do plot and plan the overthrow—militant or evolutionary— of every form of government that enshrines the flame of freedom. And they come with a false flame! It is an emanation of tyranny that is not a flame. It is that which puts out the light. And the stench of that momentum can be seen as that dark mist moving across the landed surface of the earth. Will you challenge it? Or will you allow it then to coalesce and to become a physical manifestation?

The Compromise of the Cosmic Honor Flame

You have heard of the great lives that have been lived as spirals of freedom, setting the pace for the oncoming of the divine light and the hosts of the Lord! And in this age you have seen again and again the compromise of the cosmic honor flame. You do not hear of all that transpires on Terra. You do not know of the atrocities that are occurring this day far worse than that which occurred in the concentration camps of World War II. I tell you, the tortures that souls of light must undergo in those countries that are under the dominion of World Communism would chill you to the very core were you to behold them in this moment. Better, then, that you abide within the flame of freedom.

I come, however, to make known to you this day that this is a force that is not physical, that cannot be blamed on this or that people or this or that ethnic group. For the force of World Communism is a force that began beyond Terra, beyond this time and space! And it is brought not by the children of the light, not by the sons and daughters of God, but by the fallen ones who have evolved their ideology to capture the masses who understand not the delicacies and the intricacies of cosmic law.

Understand the oneness of light-bearers everywhere, as you have been told by Godfre. Understand then that to challenge the fallen ones and their ideology is to challenge Antichrist himself! You have read of the beast that cometh up out of the sea and the beast that ascendeth out of the earth.[1] This is the carnal mind of the mass consciousness of humanity that personifies in world tyranny at every level of consciousness.

Penetration of Forcefields by Our Eye

We come forth, then, carrying the weapon of the all-seeing eye of God. The penetration of these forcefields by our eye is a warning. It is a provision of information to those who demand it. To light-bearers who would know that they might be able to call forth the light of God to consume the darkness, we come! We answer! We provide that inside information so that you can determine what really goes on behind the scenes in Washington and who really controls America's destiny from the standpoint of the plane of Matter.

Those who have usurped the power do not show their faces! Those who control, those who are in office, do not make themselves apparent. And so they allow the people to think that all continues as it has been from the beginning of this nation. Yet all is not well with America! And the clouds that overcast this place signify that there is a shadow across the flame of freedom and a shadow across America this day!

To whom can the hosts of the Lord look when the call goes forth? Who will give answer? Who will say: "I am here to defend liberty no matter what the price! I will pay with the flow-essence of the Christ, with the blood of my life! I will pay with the threefold flame of my heart, my diligence, and my application of the law!" Sons and daughters of Liberty, we are so close and so one—our legions with your own. We mingle with you; we walk beside you. You are not alone. We defend the seeing and the vision and the God-control.

The Vision of the Divine Woman

We come to say, then, that without your calls and invocations, the oncoming tide of darkness could well inundate a planetary body. But the vision of the Divine Woman, of the ultimate victory of her seed that was given to George Washington, is a vision which must be preserved and defended intact within your souls. With that vision, with the ratification of that vision by your invocations, you will see the miracle of the ages. For in this hour only by the grace of God, the hosts of the Lord, and the one who comes riding upon the white horse known as the Faithful and True[2]—only by the grace of the intercession of the heavenly hosts—can the light-bearers hope for the sustainment of spiritual freedom and material freedom upon Terra.

Because the threats are greater than you know, because the controls are greater than you know, and the cruelties also—far more than we could delineate in one or ten dictations—I must come with a warning to say to you, I have heard the fallen ones. I know their plots. I know they count nothing as sacred. And they will repeat what they have already done nation after nation. When they come to conquer, they seek out with their lists and with their categories all those who are the servants of the law, and the patriots, and those who defend life as sacred in the freedom flame. And these are removed, and these are murdered on a wholesale scale as they have been even behind the scenes in Vietnam in these very months.

Expose the Lie of the Dragon!

I tell you, the front of the dragon is only a front. You must have the courage to take the sword of truth and pierce that paper dragon! Expose the lie and be willing to challenge that energy which sounds the might of a mechanization civilization, but which crumbles before the flame of the Mother when that flame is raised up within you even as Moses raised up the brazen serpent in the wilderness, signifying that men ought to worship the Real Self and the flow of life that is God![3]

So I raise up to you the sword of living truth and the scepter of authority! And my angels do place the sword and the scepter in your hands, in the hands of all who will take these to go forth to challenge that which seems to be, but is not. Can you understand that the Liar and the lie is a total fabrication of the carnal mind—like the balloon that bursts when you have the courage to prick that forcefield?[4] Mankind must not shrink before awesome responsibility! Mankind must not think that the hosts of the Lord will desert him on the battlefield of life! Mankind must take the forward step and know that hierarchy takes the next step!

The Vision on the Battlefields of Life

Mankind must remember the vision on the battlefields of life that even was seen by the enemy in World War II—those who thought they had won, those who thought they had conquered all of Europe. And as they were marching to take that land of liberty where freedom is enshrined in the heart of France and thought that all was in their hands, these generals of the foreign armies looked up and saw marching toward them the hosts of the Lord, the angelic hosts, the sons and daughters of God riding then on white horses, led by the one, the Faithful and True. And they saw the oncoming light that would not recede. No matter how they tried or what they did, the hosts of the Lord, as the spiritual armies of heaven, moved against the darkness. And the light prevailed!

And the light shall prevail in every nation when good men and women, faithful to the cause, give their energy and invocation and holy prayer and when they conform their lives to the holy ordinances of Almighty God. When your consciousness is in conformity to that inner will, then the entire will of a cosmos will move to uphold you still.

If you have lived a dull and boring life or a life of mediocrity before coming into the teachings of the ascended masters, may I say that from this moment on, your life will never be dull again. May I say, with a twinkle in my eye, that once you set your foot upon the battleground of life, the joy and the rejoicing is to moment by moment prove the excellence of the name of God, I AM THAT I AM, and to prove that excellence as victory by victory by victory swirls into the center of the torch of illumination of the Cosmic Virgin, even the torch of Gautama Buddha entrusted into the hand of the Mother. So victory by victory, the battles won by the children of the light forge a union, a union of gold, a union for the age of gold.

A Spiral of Vigilance and Determination

Be bold then, and see how the lie recedes, how it is exposed by the sword of truth! Be bold and see how the demons tremble when they hear the steps of the son and daughter of God! See how they quake! See how they run to hide in their lairs! Challenge them, I say, in the name of the living God! Let them come out and give accounting this day! And let them be judged at the Court of the Sacred Fire!

For cosmic justice reigns throughout a cosmos! And there is no injustice. And not one jot or tittle of the law shall pass away till all is fulfilled.[5] Prove then this law! Cite the canons of the law! Cite them in defense of truth and see how the power of the Word proclaiming that truth is an action that defies every tyranny over the mind and consciousness of humanity.

I AM K-17. I have come to impart to you a spiral of my vigilance and my determination to defend freedom on every continent and in every soul. I have come with a vision of the goal and I have come with a vision of the darkness that opposes the goal. Let us see now what light-bearers will do for Saint Germain, the God of freedom to the earth! Let us see what you will do with a torch that is passed—the torch of the Cosmic Secret Service—in defense of freedom!

I AM K-17 in the heart of the flame!

July 4, 1975
12:16-12:35 P.M. PDT

Cosmos is a being whose self-awareness in God includes the all of cosmos; hence the name. He is commissioned by the Logos to ensoul the secret rays—energies of the fiery core of being, energies for initiation in the mysteries of the Christos.

11

THE SECRET RAYS AND THE WHITE-FIRE CORE: LET THE SECRET RAYS DESCEND!

A Dictation by Mighty Cosmos

Hail, Alpha! Hail, Omega! Hail, O Great Central Sun! I AM Cosmos! And I descend into the forcefield of Terra! I come into the hearts of devotees everywhere! I come spiraling the secret rays! And they bore through the consciousness and they bore through the atmosphere and the density of the mass hypnosis of the race. So let the secret rays descend! Let them come now reinforced by legions of the Great Central Sun magnet!

I am holding this flame and this focus at Shasta in this position! And I then am magnetizing energies from the Great Central Sun as rays of light of Alpha and Omega, preparing the way for the coming of that dictation of Alpha and preparing the way of the balance of consciousness of the students of light who will be called ere this conference has concluded to enter into the initiations of the Buddhic light according to the secret rays.

So the cycles have turned, and you have come to the midpoint of the year of the Holy Spirit. Now be prepared, for the action of the secret rays is nigh! And that action is as a fine laser beam. It enters into the consciousness. It separates light from darkness. It forces the cells to come into conformity with the inner blueprint of life. And where cells are found in rebellion to that law, there is chaos and confusion and disintegration and death. Thus the secret rays are a catalyst for souls moving through the echelons, then, of the ladder of life, through the stairway of the Christ and the Buddhic light.

The Commeasurement of a Cosmos

I move with the Elohim! I move among the starry bodies!
I AM the commeasurement of a cosmos defined by the action of
the secret rays within you! Receive the secret rays and understand
the conformity of life within the body temple!

Those who would be the witness unto the Holy Spirit, draw
nigh to me now and know that the secret-ray action of the fiery
core must weave, as a basket weave, a protection of consciousness.
As the veil of the Mother, a veil that is placed over the soul, the
secret rays protect mankind from other rays that are not benign,
rays that sift through the cosmos, through the material universe,
sometimes penetrating harmfully the atmosphere of earth as the
ultraviolet rays of the sun and at other times being completely
blocked and shielded by the forcefield of protection of the Elohim.

The secret-ray frequency is an energy that draws mankind into
a light, into a dimension; and the action of the drawing is as the
crochet hook drawing the thread, drawing the stitch. And sometimes it is painful, and sometimes there is that weeping and
gnashing of teeth as souls who are obliged to enter the fiery core of
life resist the action of the secret rays. And then they come into
that sorrow and that suffering; and if they are fortunate, they have
the discipline of the ascended hosts and of the Divine Mother, who
in that hour of testing raises the sword and compels consciousness
to pass through the grid of white fire.

Planetary Initiation

Without vision the people perish![1] Without the teachers of
mankind, the ascended masters, mankind know not the way. They
do not understand the crucifixion of a planetary body and that the
crucifixion is an initiation whereby mankind must surrender that
life that they might take it again, might lay down their lives and
raise up the Christed One. The perspective of the mystical way is
given in the mystery school. This understanding is the necessary
tool that is altogether required by those who would rise in consciousness, who would be stepped up in vibration.

I have but to raise my hands and with the authority of
Almighty God deliver you into a dimension of light where you
would experience not the bliss of creation, but the agony of a soul

not yet found in the likeness of that frequency. Were I to do this then this day, you would find yourselves moaning and groaning as the thundering and the lightning sounding forth sounds the day also that is the death knell of the human consciousness and the birth of the Everlasting One. Understand, then, that you are where you are because the Lord God has determined, given all things, that this is the most comfortable level of consciousness for you to be in.

If you do not approve of the vibrations of Terra, do not condemn them! I say, challenge them! And reeducate souls waiting for the flame of life. There is no worse enemy of the light than the one who is sent from God to elevate a race who instead utters the condemnation of the Luciferians. If you do not like what you see, *unsee it!* Have you not the power of the all-seeing eye of God?

A Catalyst for Peace

I say, *wake up!* Wake up this day and use your divine inheritance! Use the fire that God has placed within your heart! Let it not remain dormant any longer! If you do not like war, then I say, replace it with peace—not protest! But let the flame of peace within your heart transform the minds of the nations. Be a catalyst for peace by being on fire! And let your eyes be pools of fire! And as you look upon mankind, let the penetration of your gaze be as John the Baptist! Let them call you mad! Let them call you the mad prophet! What of it? Your penetration is the penetration of the eye of God.

How can God release his energy except through mankind? God releases his energy to me in this moment! Ye cannot receive it because your chalices are not big enough! Turn your back on trivia and vanity I say! And let the balloon of consciousness be launched this day! Let hierarchy have a place! It is the same old story. I come forth! I AM Cosmos! I desire to come into Terra and there is no place prepared. I must go to the manger. I must be received there in the midst of elemental life, who yet have the spark of the Holy Spirit.

A Place Prepared

See then: Mark you well, for I have come! And that boring

action of the secret rays will surely fulfill the action whereto it has been invoked by Alpha and Omega! And there shall indeed be weeping and gnashing of teeth, and you will witness that. But I say this to light-bearers: Mark you well! I will return ere twelve months have passed. I expect to find a place prepared. I expect to find the setting into which I shall pour the crystal fires of the secret rays. Be prepared then! For you know not the hour of the coming of the Son of God into your midst.[2]

I say, I expect light-bearers to give answer to the thrust of hierarchy! I expect there shall be striving and a pursuing of the fiery destiny of life. I expect that you shall give at least equal fervor to all who have gone before, to that which they have carried as love and wisdom and power. I expect that this generation will justly stand as a witness to all saints waiting in the wings of life for your victory that they, too, might go on in cosmic service to the flame of freedom.

The Chastisement of Love

On this anniversary of the birth of a nation, I have been assigned by God to give the chastisement of love. This is the Fourth of July spanking I give to America. You are not ready for cosmic light! Therefore, grow up! Look up! And take your immortal destiny! This is that release of energy that is the goad to fulfill a spiral unto the two hundredth anniversary of the flame of freedom.

I AM Cosmos! Anytime anywhere you feel the need of a spanking, just call me and call my secret rays and I will come. And you will see how the Lord loves those whom he chastises.[3] For those who have not the chastisement are not worthy of the attention of the eye of God. They are outside the circumference of their own self-awareness. Consider yourself privileged, then, that the hand of Alpha and Omega has sent me to bear witness unto the truth this day!

I AM Cosmos in the heart of the secret rays! I bid you joy, freedom, and the starry body of your causal bodies. Be free! Be whole! Rise up and take your stand! And be prepared, for I shall return!

July 4, 1975
12:36-12:48 P.M. PDT

"And ye shall know the Truth
and the Truth shall make you free."

The oracles of Delphi were messengers of the gods and goddesses who spoke truth and the wisdom of the law to the ancients. Pallas Athena is more than a Grecian goddess of mythology. Her presence in the universe is the exaltation of the flame of living truth. This truth she holds on behalf of the evolutions of earth as a member of the Karmic Board. The Karmic Board is the Supreme Court for this system of worlds. Its seven members adjudicate world and individual karma. They review the actions of mankind lifetime after lifetime. It is they who determine who shall embody, when and where. They assign souls to families and communities, and they measure out the weights of karma that must be balanced as the jot and tittle of the law.

12

A REPORT FROM THE KARMIC BOARD:
VIALS OF VIOLET FLAME
TO THE BEINGS OF THE ELEMENTS

A Dictation by Pallas Athena, Goddess of Truth

Good afternoon, ladies and gentlemen. I AM come in the fullness of the light of truth. I AM come in the light of freedom. I come bearing scrolls to deliver unto you the deliberations of the Lords of Karma concerning the flow of light, of freedom, and of truth to mankind and to show you a progress report for the first cycle of 1975.

Great inroads have been made of light penetration in the souls of mankind by dispensations invoked from the heart of the light-bearers. Side by side, those who have elected to remain a part of the veil of maya have also been victims of inroads made by those who move across the margent of the world sowing yet the seeds of the enemy among the good wheat.[1]

Point, Counterpoint

When one beholds the flow of light in that moment, that cosmic moment, when a planet is impelled into a new socket of cosmic energy, it is as though beholding a giant chessboard to see how point, counterpoint the light is released. And as the sword of truth which I bear is thrust into the planes of Mater, some fall to the right and some to the left and others remain in that state of the not-choice. They would not divide themselves, and yet they are divided by their failure to choose this day whom they will serve. [2]

Just as there is cause for rejoicing, there is cause for vigilance.

Freedom can come to mankind only when mankind know the truth. Most of that which mankind deem to be truth is partial truth or relative truth. Very few have the contact with the I AM Presence and with the eye of God whereby they can perceive what is the truth of the hour. Angelic hosts come forth to reinforce this truth which shall give freedom! Even as the Liberty Bell tolls, tolling the freedom of souls and of nations, so in the hearts of a planet and a people, there are spirals released as the sounding of the great sound of the AUM calls those whose time has come to be in light into that home of light, into that heart of the Mother.

Judgment, the Hastening of Opportunity

Even so, the sounding of the sound marks the hour of judgment for those who have pursued the rebellion against the law for aeons—aeons of energy spirals far beyond the ken of mankind. Therefore judgment is meted, and judgment is in our hands. Judgment brings forth justice—a hastening of the return of karmic cycles and also a hastening of opportunity.

Opportunity, that golden open portal to unity, is now on the crest of the year. Skirmishes have been won; skirmishes have been lost. But the light shines forth from the summit of life! And to those that have that light and receive that light, more is added; and those who have lost the light, those who have turned it to darkness, see that that which they have is taken from them.[3] This is justice according to the law of the Ancient of Days.[4] The battle for the minds of men, of women and children rages in every area of human endeavor. Where there is the sword of truth, where there is determination, there awareness, true soul awareness, coalesces souls in the divine mandala of the age.

Saint Germain Pleads the Cause of Mankind

Saint Germain stands forth this day before the Lords of Karma to plead the cause of mankind! He stands reading that petition which he has also written from his heart, pleading for time, pleading for energy, as he has done for hundreds and thousands of years. Saint Germain is a familiar face to the Lords of Karma. He is that one, that advocate for mankind, who frequents our chambers most often on behalf of mankind. And thus mankind have been, by the grace of this one standing for a planet and a lifewave, the recipients of dispensations of violet flame and of freedom, to carry on, to carry on a little bit farther into the age, into the years as the cycles pass.

A Petition on Behalf of the Holy Spirit

Now then, Saint Germain comes forth with a petition on behalf of the Holy Spirit and the Beings of the Elements, who are the servants of God and man in nature. He is isolating the instances of mankind's pollution of the elements—mental pollution, emotional pollution, and above all, physical pollution, nuclear wastes and by-products of all manner of chemicalization and industry. Saint Germain then lists before the Lords of Karma this day those areas of grave danger to the human race because of the pollution of the four planes of Mater.

In addition to this, the pollution of the etheric plane and of the beings of fire now takes place as there is an increase of hatred fanned in the hearts of the masses by those who continue to promote division and war and opposition even to souls of light. There is condensing in the very soil of Terra a hatred of the Divine Mother, a hatred of cosmic purpose, a hatred that is a fierce energy that must be challenged by those who know how to challenge, in the name of the living Christ, all spirals that misqualify the energy of the Logos.

Resistance to the Rise of the Feminine Ray

Understand, then, that as there is the rising of the feminine ray and freedom to womankind and freedom to the soul to be the feminine counterpart of the I AM Presence, so the resistance to that rising is borne as a cross by man and woman. That cross is the hatred of the Divine Mother, of the body temple, of the place prepared for the coming of that virgin consciousness.

Understand, then, that the Lords of Karma have consecrated this century, this cycle of the years, and this generation to the fulfillment of the divine plan of the Great Divine Director. For that plan to be implemented, devotees must be called forth from every walk of life who will face that hatred and pour forth the healing love of sacred fire, a burning desire, an energy coil that

consumes on contact that hatred directed against the rise of the
true feminine attribute of the Godhead. Come into union! Come
into alignment in the flame!

A Petition for the Purging of the Body of the Mother

Now Saint Germain presents that petition, asking of the
Elohim dispensations to purge the body of the Mother, the body
of Terra, the body of all mankind, of these spirals of hatred
coalescing as disease, disintegration and death, and the overturn-
ing of the cups of light, the liquid light of the Mother, the cups
of the chakras that ought to contain that purified energy crystal
clear.

Mankind know not what they do! According to the survey
taken by the Keeper of the Scrolls, we have seen again and again
that mankind abort the law of life, abort cycles, abort the incoming of avatars who are sent by the Lords of Karma to rescue
mankind—all of this in ignorance. And underneath the ignorance
is the rebellion of the fallen ones who incite mankind unto acts of
infamy untold since the days of Noah when the wickedness of
mankind rose to the heights of darkness.[5] As a plague of locusts in
the sky was the wickedness and the perversion of mankind in those
days and even also in the days of Sodom and Gomorrah.[6]

So that hatred directed against the seed of Woman in this age
comes forth as record and memory of past ages as energy spirals
come for transmutation. And you see, as mankind are ignorant of
the laws of transmutation which the Aquarian master has given
into their hands, so it befalls then the elemental kingdom to
transmute this hatred. It comes to them as the torch is passed; and
they must bear the burden not only of the initiation of the Divine
Woman and of the feminine ray, but also of the transmutation of
the cycles that make up that initiation of the crucifixion.

Elemental Life Bear the Brunt of World Karma

Nations in their time undergo that crucifixion—planetary
bodies in their time and starry bodies. So this is the hour. And
therefore, the beings of the elements, according to Saint Germain,
ought to have equal opportunity to receive dispensations of the
violet flame and of freedom's flame, inasmuch as they bear the

brunt of karma in this period. Therefore the Lords of Karma do act upon the petition of the Lord and the Knight Commander Saint Germain this day. And whereas in the past, dispensations of freedom have been given to mankind, in this hour our vote unanimous is to give unto elemental life spirals of freedom and energy.

And therefore that energy is released in this moment by the Elohim through the hand of the hierarchy of Cancer, the hierarchy of the Mother.

Vials of Violet Flame to the Beings of the Elements

And it is given now unto the beings of the elements, Oromasis and Diana, Aries and Thor, Neptune and Luara, Virgo and Pelleur. These beings stand before the Lords of Karma in the Grand Teton Retreat receiving the vials of violet flame which shall be unto the salamanders and the sylphs, the undines and the gnomes, and the angel devas working with them. And thus the forces of nature shall know a new freedom—freedom from the witchcraft and the black magic imposed upon them as mankind have sought in many ages to imprison elemental life.

Even as you have noted that those who practice the black arts have that familiar, that animal form which is an imprisoned elemental which they use as an electrode of energy, so in this moment when the flame of freedom is delivered unto elemental life, know this, O mankind—that with a new freedom, the elementals may very well put upon mankind energies also requiring transmutation and changes in nature, an adjustment in planetary cycles as elementals themselves undergo the rising and the spiraling to a new freedom.

Pray Daily for the Liberation of the Servants of the Holy Spirit

If you could see these beings who are utterly devoted to the service of mankind, how their auras are weighted down and burdened so that the little gnomes walk as hunchbacks in the forest carrying that weight of karma even as Christ also carried that weight upon the cross, you would pray in your heart daily for the liberation of these servants of the Holy Spirit.

Now let us turn the page of our report. Let us turn it and see

how the nations, one by one, are also receiving that energy. And
because it is not transmuted, that hatred of the Mother flame is
causing distortion in government, distortion of the cosmic honor
flame, distortion in the economy. And there is not a nation upon
earth that does not suffer from that energy.

Flame of Hope Anchored in Shasta

We see, then, that the hope of the world, as the flame of
hope anchored in the snowy peak of Shasta,[7] is the invocation of
light, the carrying of light, and the correct and accurate knowledge
given unto the Keepers of the Flame of those certain cycles which
change, which are specific in each of the twelve months, requiring
the challenging, requiring the flow of energy from the Elohim
anchoring that energy in your four lower bodies and releasing it
unto those areas of specific need. There is great need for the intercession of Archangel Michael and all the angelic hosts that
mankind might know the one true flame of life and the one God
as the God of freedom.

Distortion through Wedges of Consciousness

Distortion, the bending of the mind, the warping of the
mind, the pressing-in upon the minds and the emotions of
mankind through the mass media of those wedges of darkness, is a
serious challenge. For you see, the fallen ones have sought to
program mankind to the lie of the fallen ones.

And as they are programmed to certain behavior patterns in
their ignorance of the true law, when they receive dispensations of
light, the light flows into the cups of their consciousness. And if it
be an imperfect cup, it is all the cup they have; and therefore the
light that flows takes on the pattern of that cup. Even as the cookie
cutter of the Mother forms the bread of the Woman for her
children, so the cups of consciousness take the precious flow and
mold it again and again—not after the pattern of the divine, but
after the pattern of mortality, death and dying, sorrow and travail.

Kali Shatters the Clay Vessels

You see, then, that the Lord God of Hosts, and even Kali as

she swings her sword, comes down then to the children of mankind to dash those cups, to shatter those clay vessels, and to bring forth the new chalice of the new age, the new consciousness, and the new vibration. For how can we, as Lords of Karma, with all of the responsibility of a planet and a people entrusted to our care, give unto mankind that energy which is immediately distorted by that imperfect cup?

See, then, that if mankind do not answer the call to the marriage feast, if they do not come willingly to receive that energy and come dressed in the wedding garment signifying that they have exchanged the old cup for the new chalice, then they shall remain in outer darkness, in weeping and gnashing of teeth.[8] And when the energy flows, it will flow then to the canceling-out of an identity that is not forged in the light of the law of being. The light must come! The light is inundating as cycles fulfill a cosmic destiny!

What will you will in answer to the report of the Lords of Karma? What will you do to cause mankind to exchange their ignorance for the divine way, the Buddhic way, and the Christic way? What can you do but pray this day and pray tomorrow and tomorrow and tomorrow, and then go forth and speak the Word and hold onto the hands of those children of light who come near the flame and yet do not understand that flame because of the shroud of the impostor of the Divine Woman that has been placed upon them?

The Great Whore, the Impostor

Yes, that impostor named as the Great Whore has sought to take the children of the Mother from her hand before they could understand her word, before they could decipher the meaning of her coming and her teaching! See then that they are torn not from the crucible of life! Hold their hands! Talk to them and walk with them, O children of the light! See how they know not and understand not the way, for the light of the Mother shone in the darkness of the human consciousness and the darkness comprehended it not.[9]

A Jewel of Emerald Fire

I release the jewel of my heart unto your heart. It is a jewel of emerald fire! And in the jewel a seed atom of cosmic purpose for each one. I implant it now within your heart, O souls of fire! I place it there if you will receive it by your free will that there might be released to you day by day, week by week in the months to come, the knowing, the seeing, the understanding of taking the bread of the Mother, assimilating the bread and taking the wine of the Anointed One and drinking the cup, the whole cup, of cosmic consciousness.

O humanity, be transformed! O humanity, be transformed in living fire! Be transformed by coming into the union of the Mother! Then all will go well and all mankind shall know the truth, the truth that shall make them free.[10] I thank you and I bid you a good evening.

July 4, 1975
5:31-5:54 P.M. PDT

The Flame of Freedom Speaks

*A soul-stirring 4th of July message
from Elizabeth Clare Prophet delivered
in a mountain valley retreat
in Montana before a crowd of 5,000*

I hear the world singing a hymn of hope.

I hear the soul of America singing an anthem of freedom.

Singing the song of the pilgrims who settled on the East Coast.

Singing the song of the patriots who fought to secure the sacred fires of liberty.

Singing the song of our fathers who established and ordained the Constitution of these United States of America.

Singing the song of the pioneers who struck out toward the setting sun across the mountains, hills and plains to conquer the wilderness.

Singing the song of native sons north and south around a hundred circling camps.

Singing the song of the men and women who have labored generation after generation to form a more perfect Union—who lived and laughed and cried and fought two wars to make this world safe for freedom.

Yes, I hear the soul of America singing the song of freedom. But I also hear the souls of this mighty people crying out as tyranny stalks.

"*T*YRANNY?" YOU ASK. "In the land of the free?" "We have our freedoms," you say. "We can speak, assemble, pray, petition for the redress of grievances, and publish what we will. We do not have gulags. We are secure in our homes. We do not fear the midnight knock of the secret police."

Perhaps not. But we are victims of a tyranny whose shackles are subtler and thus more difficult to break.

Who will be the Flame of Freedom that speaks in America today?

I hear the cry of mothers and fathers whose children are being led into the lifelong bondage of ignorance through a failing system of education—children who cannot draw an inference from written material, solve complex math problems, or write a persuasive essay (some cannot write an essay of any kind)—27 percent of whom will not finish high school, who are part of the first generation of young people whose educational skills "will not surpass, will not equal, will not even approach, those of their parents."[1]

I hear the groan of the 13 percent of all 17-year-olds who are functionally illiterate. Though uneducated, they know very well that they are being left behind in a world that is becoming ever more technically sophisticated.

I hear the cry of a generation of youth which has had to run the gauntlet to reach a maturity that many may never know.

Who will be the Flame of Freedom that speaks for them?

"We will!"

Do we no longer care for those who are helpless? In ancient Greece female infants were left to die. Today it's Baby Does. I feel the awful pain of rejection piercing the hearts of newborn children left to die because of some real or imagined handicap, or for the convenience of their parents.

Who will be the Flame of Freedom that speaks for them?

"We will!"

Have we turned our backs on our children?

Did you know that over one million American children will run away from their homes this year? That 50,000 of these children will never be heard from again?—they will simply disappear. That almost 6,000 children will take their own lives this year rather than enter the conveyor belt of the mechanization-man syndrome?

Why do you suppose more and more are leaving home? Some children leave for the adventure, some run away to escape the savage beatings of a parent or guardian, others because they are the victims of incest or sexual molestation. Still others—the "throwaway" kids—will be kicked out. The vast majority will end up on the street.

Where does a young runaway find a job? I'll tell you. In the sex industry—pornography or prostitution.

Incest, child abuse, abandonment, child pornography, and the procuring of children is illegal in every state. But the laws are seldom enforced. There are an estimated 600,000 child prostitutes in the United States today—half male, half female.

Who will be the Flame of Freedom that champions their right to live a decent life?

"I will!"

Consider the case of Gina, age 14. Born and raised in Seattle, her father died and her mother left her and her brother in the care of their stepbrother and his wife. This is her story in her own words. Let your heart open and feel her plight.

"Two and a half years ago, me and my little brother ran away together because of what my stepbrother done to us. He beat us up all the time. And

3

then he raped me three times. So we ran downtown. My stepbrother found out where we were. He broke down the door and smacked me with his hand and took us back. When he got us home, he started beating me. I jumped out the back window and went downtown. I was on the streets for about four months, and then my little brother ran away and found me. He lives with me."

Her brother is 11 and small for his age.

"We live in cheap motels. I bought him a TV, a black-and-white. He loves TV . . . He's all I got. I got to take care of him."

And where does she get the money to support them both?

"Hustling. That's the only way you can survive down there. I first heard about it from a girl friend. She knew how I could make $50. All this guy wanted was to see your body. He was about 40. He took me to this old hotel. I was scared. We had sex. When he was done, he took me back to Pike Street, where my girl friend was. That's how I got into hustling. I was 12. There's been a lot of men since him. You know something? I don't really like sex. And except for my little brother, I don't think anybody ever loved me.

"I'm a Catholic. A lot of times I think, 'What's going to happen to me when the world comes to an end?' I try to go to church. I get lonely, that's when I go, and I think about what God's going to do to me. But hustling's the only way I can support my little brother. I would've done *anything* else, but I couldn't get a job. There aren't any for street kids."[2]

A lot of runaway children die young from malnutrition and drugs, disease and violence. They start with marijuana, which disorients their minds and destroys the sense of self-worth, and then they move on to coke, speed, LSD, and other hallucinogens, Quaaludes, and sometimes heroin.

I see the bewildered looks on the faces of those whose only source of protection and affection comes from those who exploit them—the pimps and the Mafia who organize prostitution rings. I hear the souls of these children crying out to the Mother of the World for refuge.

If we permit this wholesale abuse of our children, is it any wonder we are tolerant of the mad scientific procedures called fetal experimentation?

Some scientists perform surgery on living aborted fetuses without anesthesia. Two scientists in Helsinki severed the heads of eight infants born alive following hysterotomy abortions, and then forced a liquid sugar substitute through the large arteries in their necks so they could study the way the brain uses carbohydrates!

This is going on on planet Earth today.

Did you know that a fetus can feel pain at $13^{1}/_{2}$ weeks and probably earlier? Do you know there's a soul in that body, just like there's a soul in your body?

I hear the cry of the World Mother weeping for her children. *Who will be the Flame of Freedom that speaks for the World Mother and her children?*

"I will!"

Friends of freedom, this is why we gather in the Heart of the Inner Retreat—to celebrate our freedoms, our victories, and our way of life, but also to freely discover what are those things that are eating away at the very fabric of our American life—at the very body and consciousness and soul of our nation.

"Who will be the Flame of Freedom that speaks?" Elizabeth Clare Prophet and concerned citizens from 50 states and 24 nations gather in the "Heart of the Inner Retreat" at the Royal Teton Ranch north of Yellowstone Park to celebrate freedom and decry planetary injustice.

Did you know that in the 1930s, U.S. Public Health Service investigators left blacks with syphilis untreated so they could determine the long-term effects of the disease? Did you know that? Is anyone telling you that? This is *our* government.

Or that in 1953 the people of St. George, Utah, were exposed to deadly nuclear radiation and were told, "There is no danger"?

This is our government. Yet we the people are the government. Are we going to stand by and be the guinea pigs of *some* people when the government belongs to *all* people?

"No!"

Did you know that between 1945 and 1962, 250,000 U.S. servicemen and 150,000 civilians on our own soil were exposed to high levels of radiation without their knowledge or consent as part of a government experiment to test human psychological and military responses to nuclear stress?

Did you know that the early batches of polio vaccine were contaminated with a carcinogenic virus called SV40 — *and* that the public was not informed?

Did you know that during the sixties, researchers from New York's Memorial-Sloan Kettering Cancer Center inoculated elderly patients with live cancer cells without telling them — in order to measure their immune response?

Even though we hear a lot of talk about improving the so-called quality of life, many people in fact have a callous disregard for life — from infanticide to the next stage of euthanasia (the "duty to die" pronounced by Colorado Governor Richard Lamm) to such unannounced experiments upon an unknowing civilian population to the simple fact that it is still legal to smoke tobacco.

Cigarettes are the leading cause of preventable premature death in the United States. Fifty-eight thousand Americans died in Vietnam, but 300,000 Americans will die prematurely this year due to cigarette-related lung diseases.

Is it surprising, then, that when an Agent Orange-exposed Vietnam veteran enters a VA hospital seeking an examination for cancer of the bladder or liver, he is given a psychiatric examination?

Who will be the Flame of Freedom that speaks for them?

"I will!"

Between 1975 and 1982 — seven years — the U.S. Defense Intelligence Agency has reportedly received over 1,600 reports about American

soldiers missing in action in Southeast Asia who are still alive. *Soldier of Fortune* wrote about gaunt, hard-working crews of Americans in prison camps who were wearing Asian clothing and who were kept apart from the rank and file.

Let the Flame of Freedom speak!

"Let the Flame of Freedom speak! Let the Flame of Freedom speak! Let the Flame of Freedom speak!"

I hear the cry of the black and Latino women who are involuntarily sterilized without their knowledge or consent.

Freedom of speech? Yes. But what good does that do a victim of radiation poisoning who will die from leukemia?

Freedom of the press? Well, we can write about these abuses all we want—if we can find out about it in time to make a difference.

I hear mothers and fathers of Marines weeping over the senseless death of their sons in Beirut. Who will speak for those Marines now silenced by neglect?

"I will!"

They did their job, but did our government do its job to protect them? No!

And I hear the outrage of 269 souls who lost their right to be the Flame of Freedom that speaks when KAL Flight 007 was exploded out of the sky.

I hear the stirrings of the souls of a nation as they slowly awaken to the fact that others have deprived them of the freedoms they came to believe were their birthright.

One of the rights most fundamental to the establishment and maintenance of our freedoms is the right to own private property and to determine its use. This right is being eroded daily.

I hear the cry of the people forced out of their homes by the federal government for a crime no worse than that they lived in or near a national park or forest.

The people of Cuyahoga Valley, Ohio, were driven from their homes when the National Park Service condemned their entire town—churches, schools, homes, businesses—and then reopened it as a museum to show what it was like when people lived there.

> *I hear the stirrings of the souls of a nation as they slowly awaken to the fact that others have deprived them of the freedoms they came to believe were their birthright...*

I hear the cry of Betka Lankovska, a retired single parent from the Malibu Canyon area. Since she lived in a high-risk fire zone, she could not get fire insurance on her home until she removed the brush and weeds from several acres of land behind her house. She was required to get a permit from the California Coastal Commission to clear the land. And for the permit she had to have a hearing.

She applied for the permit in the spring of 1978. In October she finally got a hearing, but the permit was held up until her property could be searched for a *potentially* endangered species of weed that was *thought* to grow in her area. She was told that if she removed so much as a bush from her land before the permit was issued, she could be imprisoned or fined for $10,000.

As Californians know, the wheels of the Coastal Commission grind slowly. While Betka was still waiting for her permit, the Agoura-Malibu fire of 1978 swept through the canyon and destroyed her home and everything she owned. She had no insurance.

Who will speak for the common people so loved by Abraham Lincoln? Who will speak for these people who are defenseless against the bureaucracies and the gaining momentum of the power elite? *Who will speak for them?*

"I will!"

I hear the cries of despair groaning from the spirits of the one-quarter to two million homeless Americans plagued by hopelessness and shame. While we give out billions in foreign aid and our banks give away billions in loans to Communist countries that will not pay them back, Americans themselves are living in some of the worst conditions that can be found anywhere.

I hear the cry of the unemployed—the steelworker, the miner, the

8

lumberjack. I hear the cry of the farmer who hangs on to his land, hoping he will be in business this time next year. Foreclosures and bankruptcies are mushrooming in the farm industry.

Take the case of David Denly—a talented, aggressive, 41-year-old farmer whose 850-acre spread is going under—who "suffered an $80,000 loss on his livestock in 1981, a lowland flood in '82, and a drought in '83. It was even a greater brutality that drove him out of the business"—high interest costs.

Who sets those interest costs and rates? Who is tampering with the farmers of America—with their money, with their livelihood, with the value of their land? Who is it?

Let them be exposed by the Flame of Freedom that speaks!

When Denly found he

could no longer service debts of more than $600,000, he decided to sell out. "Denly hopes the sale of his assets will cancel his debts so he can get a job and start fresh." He says, "I'm back to zero, right where I was in 1966. When I'm in a crowd at church or in town, that works on me. I get this feeling that we failed. I suppose we did."[3]

My friends, this is still the United States of America, and these things ought not to be! Someone must speak out. Someone must take a stand and summon the strength to defend the helpless against these encroachments. And that must come about through the union of those who are determined, those who will *be* the Flame of Freedom that speaks at any price, at any cost. The Flame of Freedom must speak in America before it is too late!

Even though we're in the midst of an economic recovery, 10 or perhaps 20 percent of the breadbasket farmers in America are in the same danger. In most cases, the primary reason for the failure does not lie with the farmer. As in the case of the homeless, the unemployed miner, the steelworker, the black teenager, the electrician, or the mechanic, the

9

overriding culprit is the state of the economy—with which these people had nothing to do. They are the victims of the manipulators and the spoilers in our midst.

The cycle of boom and bust, of inflation and recession, is not a natural part of the economy. It is created artificially by the Federal Reserve System and the federal government, and it is exploited fully and to the hilt by the banking industry.

Although most people don't completely realize how it operates, they understand the effects. "When the money runs out, we have to rely on the mission," says Michael Hartwell, an unemployed fork-lift driver from Flint, Michigan. "Kids don't understand 'recession' and 'depression' and all the big words adults use. They just know their stomach's empty and it hurts."[4]

Someone must take a stand and summon the strength to defend the helpless against these encroachments.

And in the land of plenty, their stomachs ought not to be empty. Who is depriving the people of their rightful and lawful inheritance?

Let them be exposed by the Flame of Freedom that speaks!

The Fed is an elaborate instrument created by the bankers to manipulate the economy by either increasing or decreasing the amount of available money and credit. Its actions influence the health of markets and inflation and interest rates.

The Fed is supposed to "fine tune" the economy. It is debatable whether it does or even *can* do that. But there is no question about the Fed's ability to influence the economy and the lives of individuals.

Did you know that each half-point increase in mortgage rates disqualifies about one million potential home buyers from getting loans? A few men's decisions can alter the life of millions of Americans. And these men were never elected by *we the people*.

I hear the cry of the people of America held in bondage by the gross mismanagement of the economy.

I hear the cry of the people who put their money in Bank of America, Citibank, Chase Manhattan, Manufacturers Hanover Trust, Morgan Guaranty, the Chemical Bank, and Continental Illinois, whose irresponsible directors turned around and loaned it to nations that will never pay them back. That money comes out of the deposits of hard-working Americans who have lived by the ethic of being thrifty and saving and watching their savings grow, not expecting that those very savings would be stolen by thieves within the banking system.

Bankers and government leaders are busily looking for a solution to the world banking crisis brought on by the 800 or so billion dollars of international debt owed by Third World and Communist nations to Western banks.

Why is all this money going out of the country? What is the stated goal and purpose? Is it greed only? Or is it a madness for power and power to control the world—or for the power to create a one-world economy?

What is the grand design of those who send away America's money and do not feed her own poor, do not take care of her aged, and have to debate whether or not it's worth paying the medical bill to keep a child alive who needs extensive care upon being born?

Who are these great creators of our destiny who do it with our money, yours and mine? Who are they?

Let them be exposed by the Flame of Freedom that speaks!

I'll tell you one thing: *They* don't plan to take the rap. *They* are not going to suffer the loss when bad debts don't get paid. And *they* expect, with a reasonable amount of certainty, that the government will bail them out. That means the taxpayers will bail them out, either through direct infusions of dollars from the U.S. Treasury or through credit pumped into the banks by the Fed—that is, artificial money.

And the more money they print, the more money there's around and the less your dollar is worth. And therefore, a bite of your dollar is going to support these big bankers, supported by a federal bureaucracy that you did not vote for, a machine and a decision that is not your own—and that ought to be controlled by Congress.

Our republican form of democracy is slipping through our fingers through these monopolies, through these bureaucracies, and through this power elite who think *they* know how to run *our* lives, *our* pocketbooks, *our* jobs, *our* industry, *our* country, *our* families, and *our* children!

Whether it's created dollars or created credit, it's the government's policy not to let the big banks fold. Little banks, savings and loan companies can and do fold every day. They represent the work and the dreams of the little people. They are the heart of private enterprise. They're usually bought up by one of the megabanks like Chase, but a big bank has the power of the federal government behind it.

Why? Why doesn't the federal government stand up for the little people? It was founded in order to guarantee the rights of the people against tyrants. Have we forgot? Now it's the tyrants who are being defended by our government. And who is the voice of the people?

Who will be the Flame of Freedom that speaks for this nation— "I will!" *—before it becomes a dictatorship not unlike the Soviet Union or Nazi Germany?*

You think that is so far away? You don't know. It's subtle, it's creeping, and it happens to little people everywhere, every day. They cry out to God, but do they have the money to defend themselves? Can they fight the monolith of power that is emerging in this nation—*heartless*—to crush the individual?

What's the matter with individualism? What's the matter with the identity of the individual person? Why can't he be unique and different? Why does everybody have to be a number in *their* computer system? Are we going to allow *them* to stamp out the personality of our souls, the creativity of our hearts, our right to be individuals?

"No!"

Well, let's look at what the Fed is doing—one of the greatest monopolies in this country.

The more money the Fed pours into the large banks, the more inflationary the economy becomes. As a result, the government is destroying, or at least wounding, the small- and medium-size businesses of America and creating the conditions for a strong inflation, a deep recession, or both.

A lot of the experts on money and banking today predict an economic cataclysm any minute. *"Any minute,"* they say. "Maybe they are the prophets of doom," you say. I believe there is hope, but I believe that that flame of hope has to move into action on the part of an enlightened, educated citizenry that does not allow the very key to the abundant life to be destroyed in this manner.

The little people may lose their jobs, their homes, their farms—and their hope for the future. But the big banks will be rescued because their failure would be bad for the economy.

I hear the fears of the people who wonder if the debt bomb will destroy the economy and ruin their future. How did it all begin? It started with the Congress giving its control of our money system to the Fed in 1913, which enabled what have become the megabankers to control the system covertly.

After the Great Depression of 1929—caused in large measure by the Fed—the federal government became increasingly more protective of the banking industry, particularly the big banks, so that we would not have a repeat of the Depression. This was the rationale for increased government control.

So the bankers have turned the government's guarantees to depositors into an insurance policy to cover the bad loans they have been making to foreign governments and to give them the confidence to make so many bad domestic loans. Since it's not the government's policy to let large banks fail, they can count on being bailed out when the going gets tough—on *your* money, *my* money, or funny money that isn't even real and makes us feel wealthy when we're not.

Did you know that in 1982 the federal government gave Western banks $177 million to keep Poland from going into default by covering the interest on loans the Polish government owed to those banks?

You wonder why Solidarity didn't make it—why World Communism hasn't collapsed? Because *this* government decided to protect the international bankers instead of the freedom fighters in Poland—that's why!

Did you know that the federal government extended $120 million in credit to Romania at seven percent interest to enable their Communist government to build nuclear steam generators?

How about backing the faltering steel industry? How about helping our farmers? How about shoring up America? What do *they* have in mind?

There is no need for a man, woman, or child in this nation to go hungry or jobless, to be undernourished, to be wanting in medical care or in the finest education in the world. We are determined to reverse the tide. *We are* determined to reverse the tide!

There is enough room in this great land for every baby aborted annually to live, to grow up, to be free, and to have a livelihood and a job—to enjoy a fruitful life.

There is enough room for all of the aged whom we are told ought to die. There is enough room for the handicapped. There is enough room for all of us who come into life together and must share the grand burden and the noble experiment of a free people—and, by doing it right, fulfill our duty to export that example to all nations.

We are the Flame of Freedom that must speak for a world! And if *we* do not speak, who else will? Who else will speak if we do not? Shall we be dumb dogs that will not bark, as Becket said—will not protest in the face of heinous crimes against humanity? Shall we be those dumb dogs or shall we speak out?

"Speak out!"

We have a Goliath in our midst. Did you know that in June of 1983, Congress, in what has been called the "Big Bank Bailout," gave the International Monetary Fund $8.4 billion to help cover loans to Communist countries that were not paying back what they borrowed from U.S. banks? Who would suffer if the Communist countries were allowed to default? The bankers would collapse. The Communist regimes would collapse. And the little people of the world would rise up in the Flame of Freedom to once again claim their nations, their banks, their institutions, and their industries for freedom!

Why do our boys have to fight in Vietnam in a no-win war when our government, the power elite, and the banking houses are supporting an international Communist system? They're supporting it for managed conflict so they can also manage the outcome. That's what they're doing!

Why should our Marines die in Beirut? Why should they die anywhere? Why should any freedom fighters of any nation have to die fighting World Communism when it's already a dead beast? We just need to let it go!

Did you know that the United States government—that's us, remember, not *they*. (They think it's them, but we know it's us!) What *they* did in *our* name was to guarantee more than $70 billion in direct loans from private bankers to the Soviet Union and other members of the Warsaw Pact. That's what they've done with *our* money and *our* Flame of Freedom!

At $17.67 billion, the Soviet Union is the largest recipient of loans subsidized by Western governments. As the *Wall Street Journal* recently asked: "The Soviet subsidy loan level, never before acknowledged by the lending countries, raises an interesting question for Europe's political and business leaders: When did taxpayers in the lending countries ever decide to subsidize communism?"

"Never!"

I hear the cry—**I hear the cry and you hear it**—of the people who are paying more and more of their annual earnings into a bankrupt Social Security system. In order to honor its obligations, today's workers may have to pay a payroll tax of more than 40 percent—that is an increase of over $5,000 a year in the employee and employer tax for each worker earning $20,000.

As it is, the Social Security system lives from bailout to bailout. And there are great inequities in the system. Listen to this: A black male born today has a life expectancy of about 64 years. But based on current legislation which has pushed the retirement age to 67, on the average that black male will not live long enough to receive any benefits at all! But he will pay into the system all the days of his life and owe his soul to the company sto'.

How's that for manipulation? Create the retirement age above your life expectancy and promise you, "*In the end,* you'll get your benefits!"

I hear the cry of the unemployed and the underemployed who are being deprived of their sacred labor by the deindustrialization of America caused by the intentional diversion of investment capital away from the United States to foreign countries. Did you know it was intentional? Did you know there's a plan behind carrying industry and money out of this country?

Corporations have money to invest. U.S. Steel just spent $6 billion to acquire Marathon Oil Company instead of rebuilding its steel plants. Don't you think that's odd, seeing as how many steelworkers are out of work today? One of the great crimes of America today: that our government and the moguls of industry have allowed our own steel industry to go down. I think it's one of the worst things that has happened to this nation in this century, leaving us vulnerable and disadvantaged in time of war.

General Electric added 5,000 workers to its payroll by adding 30,000 foreign jobs and reducing its United States employment by 25,000 jobs. Who are the heads of these multinational corporations who neglect the Flame of Freedom in America, and by their deeds prove themselves untrue to her divine destiny?

In part, deindustrialization is motivated by a plan to develop international specialization of labor in order to make it easier to establish a "new world order." The economies of the nations are being rearranged by international bankers and multinational corporations. They want a new world order where the little people have nothing to say about what they do—in fact, where the little people are the slaves of the State.

I hear the soul of George Washington who declared, " 'Tis our true policy to steer clear of permanent alliances with any portion of the foreign world, so far, I mean, as we are now at liberty to do it."

We are giving away bites of our soul when we give away *our* money, *our* economy, *our* industry, and *our* Panama Canal. The net result of this deliberate policy to disinvest in America is the loss of somewhere between 32 and 38 million jobs during the decade of the seventies.

> *The net result of this deliberate policy to disinvest in America is the loss of somewhere between 32 and 38 million jobs during the decade of the seventies.*

It's not just a job that's lost, it's one's life, one's self-esteem, one's dreams—all that one has worked for for one's children and one's family. The work of generations gone before, knocked out because *someone* is rearranging *our* life and *our* world according to *their* design, not ours. We'd better find out who they are and what they're doing through the Flame of Freedom that speaks in our breasts.

The people of America are caught—caught between the debt bomb, the inflation-recession cycle, and the deindustrialization of America. The dollar, although it appears to be strong, is nearly worthless. It's only stronger against other currencies of the world that are more worthless. And the economy—not only of this nation, but of other nations—is on the verge of collapse.

Take note of this: Communist and Third World governments can't pay back their loans, so the frantic ones at the top create more paper money. It is worthless and ultimately the whole deck of cards must come tumbling down. And they want it to come down on *our* heads. And we say, "Let it be upon *their* heads!"

This is the American Revolution 1984. It is an economic revolution and it is waged not for this nation alone, but for the people of the whole world! It is a revolution where we say once more, "No!" to the tyrants.

We the people of planet Earth do have certain inalienable rights derived from Almighty God, which rights are life, liberty, and the pursuit of happiness. The abundant life, guaranteed and vouchsafed to us by our Creator, is ours. And *we* are given the mandate by our God to "take dominion over the earth."

But there are those who do not want us to take dominion over this earth. There are those who have not believed that "the earth is the Lord's and the fullness thereof." They want the world and its control for themselves, for their little nuclei of power elite.

Beloved hearts of freedom worldwide, I address you. Our first premise: Greater is He—the Almighty One—who is in you, than he that is in the

world! The second premise: Our numbers *far* outnumber and outweigh by Light the oppressors, the manipulators, and the destroyers; and *they fear* the people as they always have.

The tyrants of this world, the monied interests, they have their power by *your* consent and *mine,* by *your* money and *mine*— or by our combined lethargy. *They* exist only by the will of the people. The will of the people, enlightened and educated, withdrawing their support from these demagogues *can* turn the world around, *can* ignite a revolution and win it!

Their tactic is intimidation by reverse psychology. They make *us* believe that we need *them* when the reverse is true—*they* need *us!*

Economic slavery is one of the greatest forms of tyranny over the mind, the body, the soul, and the health of one's psyche. We, the American people, should be enjoying the abundant life God gave to us. And instead, we the people of the greatest nation on earth are being oppressed by the gangsters and sociopaths who have been playing with our money for decades.

Even though the Soviet Union has the best-equipped army ever assembled, the "hawkish" Reagan administration is actually spending slightly less on defense than the "dovish" Carter administration had planned to spend if Carter had been reelected! Carter's administration had planned to spend $210.4 billion on defense in 1983. The Reagan administration spent $209.9 billion. Even though that is a lot of money, do not rest easy. Much of our defense budget is wasted.

I hear the groan of the American taxpayer serving a wasteful bureaucracy. On May 30, the House of Representatives took note of the excessive prices the Department of Defense pays for spare parts: the Pentagon is spending $9,000 for a 45¢ wrench, $436 for a $7 hammer, $466 for a $1.49 socket in a tool kit.

Do you think my figures are in error? They're not. I will tell you where they come from. They come from greedy middlemen. They come from paying experts who have to make sure that the wrench or the hammer or the socket in the tool kit are in fine working order—and all kinds of people pushing paper.

Everyone wants to get rich from the defense budget. And those at the top want to justify bigger and bigger budgets.

It is not money, as many Americans think, that gets a job done. It hasn't done the job in education and it doesn't do it in nations more socialistic than our own.

Money is not the key to a nation. It's the Community of the Holy Spirit. It's the Mystical Body of God. It's hearts one in the living Christ who understand that there is more than dollars and cents to life. And that's why the little people always survive in these debacles—because they weren't living on money and material goods in the first place! They never did have enough.

We hear the cry of the American people undefended by a civil defense system or an anti-ballistic missile system. Has anybody knocked on your door and said, "I'd like to tell you what to do in case of a national emergency or a nuclear war"?

Well, if you were a Soviet citizen today, you would have been instructed thoroughly. You would know to go to underground bunkers in Moscow. You would know where your place of safety was. You would know how to survive a nuclear war—yes, you would—but not in the United States of America.

Who are the representatives of the people who care not for the preparation of a nation? "The Day After" was calculated to convince us that nuclear war is inevitable—if we don't freeze. On the contrary, it ought to convince us that our government doesn't care a whit as to whether or not *we* survive. That's the point of the film!

Let us look, then, to the sparks of freedom that fly as the communicators of the divine ideas that will win in this war of Armageddon. These sparks move heart to heart. And the people who are in chains in the Soviet Union today or in Red China or in Afghanistan or anywhere in the world—*they* feel our hearts' fervor, *they* feel the Flame of Freedom! It is in their breasts. And that is the greatest communication system of the whole world. It's the *power* of the Holy Spirit for a world to be won.

I hear the cry from the subconscious of the American people. At that basic level they know they are undefended by a civil defense system or an anti-ballistic missile system. Some people think that such preparations will provoke the Soviets. They have not studied history and they have not learned its lessons. And it goes back to the school systems.

They have not been taught what is the real, what is the declared intent of the Soviet Union and what has been declared since 1917—which is the unrelenting determination to take over the world. *Nothing* can provoke them. They are already provoked! They have an overall plan and we do not. We are reactors instead of the prime movers of the freedom revolution on planet Earth.

Mind you, the Soviets are not the only threat. What happens when Kaddafi gets a bomb and a delivery system? Did you know that in 1983 U.S. intelligence reports said that Libya already had five crude but effective nuclear weapons? Wouldn't it be worth the trouble to have a system that could save Washington, D.C., or New York or Chicago in the event that some madman tried to destroy one or two of our cities?

"Yes!"

After all, one interpretation of the prophecies of Nostradamus—and he was pretty accurate—says that a leader would arise in the Middle East who would overrun Europe and ultimately launch rockets against America and destroy New York City. Experts on the sixteenth-century seer say the time frame is within the next 20 years.

What happens when Kaddafi gets a bomb and a delivery system? Did you know that in 1983 U.S. intelligence reports said that Libya already had five crude but effective nuclear weapons?

We know that a people one with God can change a psychic prediction or even undo the prophecies of God when they spell calamity, because the only calamity that God ever allows is that which has to come tumbling down upon people's heads to wake them up and make them realize they're out of alignment with the universal law of harmony. If people will wake up without having to learn their lessons through war and cataclysm, God will spare the hand of his dire prophecy. For he sends his prophets only to warn us so we can save ourselves before it is too late.

Now, if we had an orbital defense system of the kind proposed by Gen. Daniel Graham, not only could we knock down a large percentage of a massive incoming Soviet attack, but we could also defend ourselves in the event of attacks from a variety of smaller enemies. And in the unlikely event that a Dr. Strangelove fired our missiles at the Soviets, we could shoot them down rather than leave the Soviets with the choice of passively accepting an American first strike or returning fire.

I hear the cries of those who fear a nuclear war—an unnecessary war with the Soviet Union. And I see the reaction of fear in a pacifism that is unwarranted and unwise because it is a peace without honor—a false peace that invites invasion and takeover, as has been shown over and over and over again in thousands of years of the history of military strategy and wars won and lost.

Pacifism never wins. Peace backed by the Flame of Freedom that speaks *is* power and it's the *real* power of the *real* people!

I feel the Flame of Freedom burning in my heart as you do—burning as a fire of such an intensity of God's love that it awakens me in the night. I feel that flame desiring to devour world hatred of the Christ in his little ones who will suffer under some kind of calamity, nuclear war or economic disaster, if *we* do not act.

Did you know that the Soviet military-industrial complex was built almost entirely by Western capital and technology? Did you know that "The Order," a conspiratorial group that has positioned itself as the power behind the American establishment, creates wars and revolutions for its own purpose—world economic takeover and a one-world government—with themselves, not us, at the helm?

Well, before you deny it or scoff, you better read about it in the exposés on "The Order" by Antony Sutton. You owe it to yourself to examine the documents and the irrefutable evidence that he presents. According to Sutton, The Order evolves its strategy around the Hegelian dialectic. They support—financially, militarily, and otherwise—conflicting systems, pit them against one another in war, economic strife or ideological clashes, driving brother against brother. And they're confident of gaining greater power and control over the nations by manipulating both the conflict and the outcome.

The financial powers of Wall Street built up Hitler's Germany *and* the Soviet Union. If you don't believe it, check the facts before you deny it. We can't remain ostriches forever. This has been done and it's well known. This is the international power elite (not the common people, not our fellow Americans) creating and managing conflict—and that for their own un-American ends.

World War II, with its 35 million deaths, was the result of managed conflict—industry in the United States, at the impetus of the bankers, backing both sides for a predetermined and predesired outcome, while the little people became fodder in the schemes of world conquest of these blackguards.

Now the same financial and industrial powers are building up the Soviet empire. The Soviets, of course, believe war with the West is inevitable and they're preparing for it. They're setting up their people psychologically to believe that the American leadership wants that war and they're bringing them to the brink—in a kill-or-be-killed frenzy—where they can do naught else but fire the first shot in that ultimate conflict.

We say from the heart of the American people to the hearts of the people of Mother Russia:

"Let the Flame of Freedom speak!"

Let the Flame of Freedom carry our message far and wide! Let the people in the Soviet-bloc nations know that we are their brothers and sisters in this fight for world freedom, that we *are* one, that we *do* know they suffer, and that they suffer because Western governments do not act—not because Soviets torment and torture, but because *we* do not say, "Thus far and no farther!"

Our representatives in Washington have become spineless. The people must now learn that they must speak for themselves, not through intermediaries. The people in Mother Russia must know that we do not trust their government, but also that we do not trust our own. And we see through the spoilers on both sides of the ocean and we *know* what's happening!

I hear the cry of freedom in the soul of Andrei Sakharov, sent into internal exile in the closed city of Gorky on account of his human rights activities. Sakharov has been on a hunger strike designed to force the Soviets to allow his wife to go to the West for medical treatment. There are rumors that he is very weak or even dead. Is he alive? We do not know. But whether in or out of the body, we know that the spirit of Andrei Sakharov is the Flame of Freedom that speaks!

Well, the Soviets say he's fine. Being fine is a matter of definition. They said Andropov had a cold—and then he dropped off. They're liars and we don't happen to believe a word they say!

As a matter of necessity, the Soviets crush any form of dissent. They have a wide variety of prisons in which they put dissenters—extermination camps, special camps for women and children. Or they can put them in a psychiatric prison where inmates are injected with drugs which can turn a healthy person into a vegetable. It's happening every day. And their souls are the souls that cry out in the Flame of Freedom.

Who will answer them as they waste away in this incarceration?
"I will!"

We will surely answer them with the greatest love, the greatest action, the greatest prayer force and the most dynamic decree momentum that the world has ever known. God is going to save this world for the little people because he made it for them.

Sometimes Soviet hospital prisoners are bound in a wet straitjacket and tied to a bed. As the jacket dries, it compresses the body with vicelike force. Who are these archfiends that enjoy the torment of human souls and bodies? Who are they? *Let them be exposed by the Flame of Freedom that speaks from the hearts of their victims!*

Soviet citizens are often arrested for their belief in God. Now hear this. The medical superintendent of one of the psychiatric hospitals believes that "people who believe in God belong in a mental ward."

Well, pretty soon it's going to be the people who believe in God in a certain way or the people who believe in God not in the way everybody else thinks. If you believe in their system, their orthodoxy, political or religious, you're OK. But if you seek the path of the individual and you're willing to listen to the voice of the Flame of Freedom alive in your soul, the flame that is God's divine spark, then watch out. Sooner or later, someone else who believes he knows better than you is going to restrict or attempt to restrict your comings and your goings.

That's the reason why on July 4, 1776, a group of people got together and signed the Declaration of Independence. That's the reason — because they knew the tendency of power, power that corrupts and corrupts absolutely. And they knew the tendency of tyrants to become insensitive to the needs of the people and what they and their ancestors had gone through in Europe. They came here to see to it that no rights or freedoms, human or divine — unless they would encroach upon the well-being of all — should be denied any individual.

We are here today to see to it that those rights are championed in America and then extended to the whole world. We have known the meaning of persecution. And we have known the meaning of the victory of our God. And we are satisfied that he is the defender of the oppressed and those against whom injustice has been brought. We know the power of the Flame of Freedom that speaks, and that's why we are satisfied to be God's instruments in this Revolution for Higher Consciousness.

There are 100,000 Christians in Soviet prisons today. We pray for them. Some are incarcerated for the crime of organizing prayers at funerals, organizing baptisms without prior registration with the government, and giving religious instruction to children.

Here religion is our divine and human right. There it is controlled by the state. Is that what we want?

"No!"

Then we must see to it that we do not allow it to happen by those who think that they are ordained to decide whether the people shall enjoy the use of their private property and when their speech or religion or assembly or press shall be limited.

An eyewitness of one of the prisons in the Soviet Union near the city of Archangel wrote: "We were transported...to the camp by train and then by...river barge. The hold of the barge was overfilled with prisoners, who were forced to sit in a doubled-up position. There was hardly any air to breathe. We were not allowed to go to the toilet....We were issued old camp clothing, and...herded off to the logging area. We were driven there in such a way that, by the time we arrived, we were half dead from exhaustion."

I bring these things to our attention today as we celebrate our independence lest we forget, *lest we forget* that while we enjoy freedom, some people suffer the abject degradation of their very humanity — lest we forget.

"For fear of ending up in the isolation cell or at being put on hunger rations, we devoted all our energies to doing the work assigned to us, sinking into the deep snow in the process....After work we were escorted...back to the camp. We ran all the way back to the camp so as not to become numb from the cold. We ran, we fell, we cried."

And today we cry also. We shed a tear for Mother Liberty as we feel the pain of this planetary outrage.

"There were times ...where [the guards] were absolutely bestial. Spotting a new prisoner, they might send him to fetch something...outside the working area, which was marked off with red signal flags. On reaching the marked-off area, the prisoner would be shot for attempting to escape. The guard who fired the shot would then be given leave as a reward."[5]

My beloved, this earth *is* the Lord's. Why do we allow it? We may not be able to stop those guards, but we ought to be able to challenge our own government and bankers and monopoly capitalists. We ought to be able to challenge them to stop feeding the money and the technology and the wheat and the gold to the Soviet Union that supports a system that treats our brothers and sisters in this inhumane fashion.

Where are the activists for human rights?

My heart is filled with the joy of the Flame of Freedom today, but I do not block out the suffering of my soul, which I allow to be sensitive to pain so that I will never forget to pray for these ones. And I pray that you, also, will not drown out the sensitivities of the World Mother in your own being—drown it out through entertainment and the pleasure cult and drugs and all manner of surfeiting and endless noise bombarding the senses.

It is time to go within and *feel* a planet in distress, *feel* the pain of the World Mother as she is in travail to give birth to the Christ in the hearts of her children.

Members of Solidarity in Poland have been asked by the Communist regime to emigrate—"Get out of the way so you're no longer a nuisance, so we can keep the less revolutionary ones under our control." They have refused to leave their country. The price they pay: They're in prison. They're fed a low-protein, low-vitamin diet because they will not leave. This regimen will slowly turn them into vegetables, or is calculated to do so.

I believe that their faith and oneness with the Blessed Mother and with the sacred heart of Jesus and the Flame of Freedom within their souls will be a mighty power to defend them against becoming those vegetables.

But we know that ultimately those who are so subjected *must* be liberated, *must* be freed—whether by God or man, whether in death or in life. And it is high time that we as Americans stopped turning our backs on the fact that the regime in Poland is alive and well today by the federal government of this nation, by the monopoly capitalists, and by the international bankers. That's why the system didn't come tumbling down. That's why Solidarity didn't win. That's why.

I hear the cry of Barbara Sadowska whose son was beaten to death at a Polish police station in May of 1983. We are all mothers at heart. Can you imagine for a moment the suffering and the loss of your son or daughter, beaten to death, dying in battle, senselessly.

Why isn't it clean and fair? Why aren't the Forces of Freedom on the march to win? Why don't we wipe out World Communism, beginning in our houses of education!

Why not? Because the ones who manage our lives *don't want* Freedom to win—because if the people are free, they won't have their money and they won't have their power. Therefore, they'd rather have money and power with the people enslaved.

Just go out and look at the world and prove me wrong if you will. I'd like to see some evidence that it isn't so. Tell me it isn't so, and I'll know it's a dream.

These people in Poland, in Russia, and other countries have to wait in line every day for the necessities of life—the bread that ought to be theirs, withheld by control. It is inhuman. It is degrading. It is designed to break the will and the creative spark of anyone.

In Poland they ask, "What is three miles long and eats potatoes?" The answer: A Polish meat queue.

There's a joke about a Russian woman who, tired of standing in line for bread, turns and says, "I'm going to go and kill Andropov!" to the horror of everyone else in line. She comes back six hours later and, in answer to their question "Well, what happened?" she says, "The line was too long."

While its own people do not have meat or bread or the necessities of life—this, mind you, being the result of the 1917 Bolshevik Revolution that promised life, peace and plenty for all and has delivered only death, war and deprivation—the Soviet Union today is defending itself against six insurgencies, forces fighting against the Soviets in Afghanistan, Mozambique, Angola, Nicaragua, Ethiopia, and Cambodia. Today people in these nations are offering armed resistance to Soviet hegemonism.

Six areas of Soviet conquest. Are they haphazard? They are there by design—the design of Communist world takeover.

In Mozambique, the MNR guerrilla movement seems to have the upper hand over Marxist president Samora Machel.

In Angola, UNITA, led by Dr. Jonas Savimbi, has control of a large portion of the country. But 30,000 Cuban troops keep the Soviet- and Cuban-backed Marxist-Leninist MPLA government in power.

And who pays these 30,000 troops in Angola? Gulf Oil, which provides Angola with about 80 percent of its revenues, keeps the Cubans there. Since the Communist government of Angola could not afford to give Castro the $100 per soldier per day it is reportedly paying for his mercenaries, we know where it comes from.

This is a very simple example of a Western multinational corporation *funding* the Communist takeover of a free nation. And the peoples of that nation bound by that economy must act independently of that subsidy to the Communists, which does not make it a fair fight. And still UNITA is in control of areas of the country.

Now *who* of all free governments of the West has offered to help the people defend their free land? Who goes out to help them? Not even a capitalist corporation will throw its weight into the side of the freedom fighters.

This is the great tragedy and travesty of our time—that bit by bit the world is being devoured by Communism. And the American government is not preaching to its people that soon there will be only one nation left that is free.

Or will it be free by the time the whole world is enslaved? Will it be too late? I think we should act today—not wait for ourselves to be surrounded, not wait for the whole world to be subjugated.

And you know, as I know, that the first to die when the Communists march in are their lists of freedom fighters. And thus, they kill off generations of professionals, the educated people, and the daring revolutionaries. And so far, in this century it has worked. Very few nations

where Communism has taken over have ever recovered and become free again, thanks to the hands-tied policy of the West.

Who do the Western powers think they're saving? They think they're saving their own statist system, but they're not. They're creating an international sorcerer's apprentice, and one day in the not too distant future they will not be able to control it...

Unless we the people make the difference. One day there'll be another reign of terror and their heads will roll and they will find out that they could not control their managed conflict, that one side or the other got out of hand. And, of course, there's no love lost among the rivalrous power elite. That is the characteristic trait they have shown in all ages.

So much for Mozambique and Angola—freedom fighters holding their own.

In Nicaragua, a variety of groups—the FDN, the ARDE, the Miskito, Sumo, and Rama Indians, the Catholic church, and a business group are trying to oust the Sandinistas. And our Congress debates whether or not we should help the freedom fighters in Nicaragua, while students in our institutions of higher learning are told that it is the Communists we should fight for and support.

If they knew the real history, if they knew the truth, they would stand on the side of the Flame of Freedom because they would know that the Communists perceive anyone who betrays his own government as the first who must go when they take over because he will also be a traitor in their system.

In Cambodia, the Khmer Rouge and two non-Communist groups — the Khmer People's National Liberation Front and the National United Front for an Independent, Neutral, and Peaceful Kampuchea — are trying to oust the government of Heng Samrin, which was installed by the Vietnamese Communists in December of 1978.

Who will help them? Who will help the people of Cambodia? I can tell you one thing. I know a lot of red-blooded Americans who would fight for the people of Cambodia — and fight to win! — if their own government would not stab them in the back and betray them in the process.

In Afghanistan, the mujahidin control about 90 percent of the country — at least by night. They are in desperate need of military supplies such as anti-tank and anti-aircraft weapons and food, shoes, and medical supplies.

The CIA is reported to have a $100-million plus aid package for the Afghans. But about 95 percent of the aid, which currently passes through Pakistan, gets skimmed off on the way. And the freedom fighters of Afghanistan today do not have what they need to liberate their nation from Soviet takeover.

And *then* is it going to be the Marines that have to go back to the Middle East because now the Soviets have their passageway to control the oil and the economies of the Middle East? They are moving in from every direction.

At what point does the United States of America and the free nations stand and say, "Thus far and no farther! You shall not pass!" Where do we draw the line? That is the question each individual must answer. Will you have to answer it when a Chinese Communist or a Soviet or some foreign army is at your door, at your border, in your state capital? Then will you answer?

People all over the world cry out to us. They cry out to us, and it is a planetary shame. It is a disgrace beyond disgrace that we who have won our revolution are not still fighting for freedom. It's the whole planet now. It's not just a nation half-slave and half-free.

The question is: Can a planet survive half-slave and half-free? We say it cannot. You cannot have a slave economy dependent upon a free economy and trading back and forth, because the free economy is going to be at the disadvantage. You can't have proper competition in life when one side is propped up by the other.

Nikolai Ryzhkov, a 19-year-old private who deserted the Soviet Army, says the morale of the 100,000 Soviet soldiers in Afghanistan is extremely low and that the drug problem among those soldiers is large. He says, "You can imagine how happy the rebels are to sell their hashish for guns to kill Russians."[6]

Russians selling their guns for hashish. Sounds like the corruption of Vietnam, only then it was the Communists corrupting our men with hashish. Ryzhkov was told that he would be defending the Russian border from Chinese and American mercenaries. But he saw none.

The Soviet Union exports franchises of totalitarian government, somewhat like we export McDonald's or Kentucky Fried Chicken! The Soviets provide the overall coordination and planning. East Germans help develop the secret police. North Koreans and Eastern Europeans handle the military training. The Cubans provide the muscle where needed. All that a would-be dictator would have to do is be willing to cooperate with the Soviet leadership.

Well, we all know that just as we can make our vow to Almighty God and receive the intercession of his angels, we could also make a pact with the devil and he would rush in to build up such a dictatorship and an empire. And we know that in every nation there are those who will sell themselves to the Soviet Union for power and for money. And we see it all over the West, including in our own country as our own people trade with the Soviets, selling our military secrets and our technology.

> *At what point does the United States of America and the free nations stand and say, "Thus far and no farther! You shall not pass!"*

I don't drive down Malibu Canyon without thinking to myself, "Right here at the turnoff to Hughes (or due north in the Silicon Valley), over this same road where my tires are now plowing, are American betrayers selling us down the river, giving away our edge in the nuclear age and perhaps sealing the deaths of millions." And Soviet spies are always there tempting them with money or compromising them and then using blackmail.

Right where we are — not in some far-off world, not on another planet, but on the very roads we use — there are KGB operators subverting our nation, with the full knowledge of our government, for filthy lucre. I say it's treason! And let those who let KGB agents have the run of our fair land also be exposed and tried for treason!

The nations where there are the anti-Soviet insurgencies all occupy key spots on the geopolitical map — Mozambique and Angola sit astride key sea lanes. Ethiopia sits on the approach to the Red Sea. Nicaragua occupies a key position in Central America. Afghanistan is the hub of the Eurasian land mass. Indochina is key to the Soviets' plans to encircle China.

A Soviet defeat in any of these areas, especially Afghanistan, would be extremely damaging to Moscow. It would destroy their image of invincibility and set back their plans for global hegemony.

Let free people everywhere act *even* when their governments refuse to defend their brothers and sisters under Communist oppression. Let a free people act while they are yet free!

I hear the people of the world crying out to the Mother of the World! I hear the cry of 1.5 million people who have fled Indochina to freedom in the last nine years. The United States alone has taken in about 654,000 refugees from Vietnam, Laos, and Cambodia. Another 414,000 are virtually prisoners in camps in 10 Asian countries.

Vietnamese boat people continue to risk their lives in flimsy sea vessels, but fewer are reaching safe havens. About 44,000 boat people reached safety in 1982. Last year the figure dropped to 28,000. The number left to drown at sea is thought to have significantly increased.

All this because of the manipulation of the war in Vietnam by the international power elite. And our own men have suffered as much as the people of Vietnam themselves in degradation, disorientation, and having to deal with the raw fact that they were betrayed by the government and the people of this nation in Vietnam.

I hear the cry of the people of Cambodia who were devastated when from 1975 to 1978 the Khmer Rouge killed 2.5 million of the nation's 7 million people. And *we knew* it was going on. And *we knew* it was because *we* pulled out of Vietnam. And then in '78, they were invaded by the Vietnamese.

We hear the cries of thousands of souls who disappeared in Argentina between '74 and '82 — who were abducted, tortured, and murdered by extremists.

I hear the Flame of Freedom crying out for a haven through Xia Yuren, who two years ago climbed out of a window in the Chinese Consulate in San Francisco and asked for asylum in the United States. Receiving escapees from Communist nations is one thing we can do with impunity. It's one way we can hold out the Flame of Freedom. "If you can get here, we'll take you."

Not so. Last January, at the urging of the Reagan administration, which noted that a "Chinese official assured a State Department official that Mr. Xia would not be penalized" if he were returned to China . . . Would any of you believe that?

"No!"

I don't think the State Department believed it either. Then why did the administration want to play footsie with Red China? Why does it want to get along with those who torture their people? The Chinese physicist, Mr. Xia, was denied asylum by a federal immigration judge. Where is he and what has happened to him today! We the people have the right to know and to act when any one of us is betrayed by the big boys!

I hear the anguished cries of the people of Central America as the blight of war spreads from Cuba across their lands. I see the repression and militarization of Nicaragua taking place where the right to dissent is denied, where freedom of the press and assembly have been abolished, and where religious freedoms have been curtailed.

Three thousand Cuban soldiers who have taken over the security police have helped make the Nicaraguans captives in their *own* land. Just imagine yourself held captive in your own country—imagine Cuban troops marching in today and saying, "You have no right to be free in America."

Since the Sandinistas have taken over, Nicaraguan Jews have had their rights systematically violated. The Protestant Miskito Indians were slaughtered or herded into concentration camps and their crops and villages were destroyed. Members of Somoza's National Guard have been hunted down and killed, often by the "vest-cut"—the cutting off of the arms and legs and leaving the victim to bleed to death.

How do men become worse than animals when indoctrinated by Marxism? What is it about this slimy system that causes people to maim others? Fanaticism in the extreme Right or Left succumbs to the ungodly nature and propensity that all of us must extinguish by the Flame of Freedom.

From '79 to '83, Communist guerrilla attacks have caused $826 million worth of damage to the Salvadoran economy. Right- and left-wing death squads terrorize civilian populations while the nation struggles valiantly toward democracy.

What does a Communist system have to offer when all is said and done—*when* by its very actions it can be seen as an ideology of death whose ends and means are always death and destruction?

Mexico today is so riddled with corruption and displays of wealth by party leaders that the CIA thinks the disparity between the haves and the have-nots could create a situation like Iran under the Shah. José Lopez Portillo may have banked a billion dollars when he was president of Mexico between '76 and '82, and his predecessor may have banked nearly as much.

What can you expect the people to do when the supposed representatives

The Flame of Freedom Speaks!

The Flame of Freedom speaks—the Flame of Freedom within each heart. The Flame of Freedom saith unto all: Come apart now and be a separate and chosen people, elect unto God—men who have chosen their election well, who have determined to cast their lot in with the immortals. These are they who have set their teeth with determination, who have said:

I will never give up
I will never turn back
I will never submit
I will bear the Flame of Freedom unto my victory
I will bear this flame in honor
I will sustain the glory of Life within my nation
I will sustain the glory of Life within my being
I will win my ascension
I will forsake all idols and
I will forsake the idol of my outer self
I will have the glory of my immaculate divinely
   conceived Self manifesting within me
I AM Freedom and
I AM determined to be Freedom
I AM the Flame of Freedom and
I AM determined to bear it to all
I AM God's Freedom and He is indeed free
I AM freed by his Power and his Power is supreme
I AM fulfilling the purposes of God's kingdom

of a free-enterprise system rob them blind? It's a setup—stemming from corrupt rightist elements—for the takeover of Communism. Four hundred years of dictatorships are karmically accountable before Almighty God for keeping the little people of South America poor and uneducated! Therefore, neither extreme Right nor extreme Left will get our vote, but the living Christ in the hearts of the people. For the prophet said, "The government shall be upon *his* shoulders!"

Sending forth sparks from the torch of freedom to light a world from the Heart of the Inner Retreat—"We have a dream of freedom...and a vision of what life on earth can and should be."

We believe that by the divine spark—the Christic light that God has placed in our hearts—we have the right and the ability to be self-governed. We look not for the kingdom here and the kingdom there, or for a saviour out of a political ideology or system. We do not think we are going to be saved by socialism, by Communism, *or* by capitalism. We believe that we are going to be saved by the living Christ with us, The Lord Our Righteousness!

He said, "The kingdom of God is within you," and I believe him.

We hear the cries of the victims of terrorism arising from the conflict in India between the Sikhs and the Hindus in the Punjab, taking more than a thousand lives and causing over a billion dollars of damage to the economy of the Punjab. Strife among brethren proves that they follow a religion of the letter and not of the Spirit. A religion has become a fanaticism when, in the name of it, people can kill or deprive others of their rights or destroy their countries and still believe, upon death, they will be received into the arms of Almighty God.

Beloved ones, this world hatred coming upon us was prophesied by Jesus, not because it has to be, but to tell us that we must invoke the sacred fires of the Holy Ghost for the consuming of world hatred that is intended to divide us.

It is not religion that divides us; it is the hatred of the devil whispering in one another's ears, "So-and-so thinks this way, therefore he is evil." God's people are good people everywhere, but sometimes evil forces move against them. Instead of fighting one another, let us defend one another against those forces of world hatred and fanaticism.

What is evil? It's that which destroys and kills. It's that which breaks the human spirit. It is that which puts out love and engenders fear—fear through misunderstanding. It's all over the world, and it must be consumed by that Flame of Freedom—not only as it burns in us, but as it speaks through us.

God gave us the power of the spoken Word and placed us above all other creatures. *Because we can speak, we can create.* The Word is the creative power.

Jorge Valls is a *plantado*—that is, he is a die-hard Cuban patriot who would not be reeducated nor compromise in any way with Castro or his regime. He was imprisoned for 20 years by Castro. He wrote frantically, secretively, using scraps of paper and cloth and ink made from spittle and dust or his own blood. He documented the full horror of life in Castro's prisons and endured the last 4 years of his 20-year sentence incommunicado, in solitary confinement.

He was released from prison—praise God and not Castro—on June 21, 1984. He is an example of what the *Washington Times* called "that special spark which inhuman adversity has been unable to extinguish." Castro allowed him to leave Cuba. And today he is the Flame of Freedom that can speak freely, and he is finally and at last rejoining his wife.

Lou Peters had an auto dealership in Lodi, California. When the Mafia tried to buy him out, he went to the FBI. He helped them gain enough information on Joe Bonanno, a Mafia boss, that Bonanno was convicted of conspiracy to obstruct justice in 1980, which led to a five-year sentence in federal prison.

In the course of his dealings with the mob, Peters voluntarily divorced his wife, Marilyn, for the safety of his family. This is the heart of a patriot. Although his wife was aware of the circumstances, Lou told no one else, including his daughters. For Lou, the challenge of the Mafia was a matter of "basic old-time patriotism." He said, "If I don't do this, who will?"[7]

That's the attitude: **"If I don't do this, who will?"**

Several weeks after Bonanno's conviction, Lou Peters remarried his wife. And then he contracted cancer and died on July 20, 1981. His tombstone was engraved with the following words: *"Honor thy country."*

Honor thy country.

We who are believers in a continuity of life, in the law of reincarnation, can appreciate the inner life of the soul of Lou Peters. We can imagine mighty angels strengthening him for this sacrifice—made for you and me. He realized that the economy is under attack by gangsters, not only the Mafia but the types we have named. And somehow, in the equation of his lifespan and that which was coming upon him, his soul determined to make a sacrifice which his wife and daughters and all of us can be proud of. I can assure you that in that soul there is the satisfaction: **"I have fought the good fight and won."**

May we all see to it that we ourselves remember the words, "That these dead shall not have died in vain." For all who can no longer speak — for they have fought their battles and gone on — for the saints who wait under the altar of God, we must say, "These dead shall not have died in vain. *We* will be *their* voice of the Flame of Freedom that speaks today!"

We have a dream of freedom, and *we* have the right to dream. We have a vision of what life on earth can and should be. And we have a right to have visions.

We have a land that is free, and we are freeborn. And here from this Heart of our Inner Retreat, which God through our spirits has consecrated to the spiritual and moral and human victory of our people, *we* will send forth sparks from the torch of freedom that will truly light a world.

Thank you.

1. The National Commission on Excellence in Education, *A Nation At Risk: The Imperative for Educational Reform* (Washington, D.C.: U.S. Government Printing Office, 1983), p. 11.
2. Dotson Rader, "Who Will Help the Children?" *Parade,* 5 September 1982, p. 5.
3. John McCormick, "A Riches-to-Rags Story," *Newsweek,* 2 April 1984, pp. 60–61.
4. Peter McGrath with Richard Manning and John McCormick, "Left Out," *Newsweek,* 21 March 1983, pp. 32–33.
5. Avraham Shifrin, *The First Guidebook to Prisons and Concentration Camps of the Soviet Union* (New York: Bantam Books, 1980), pp. 169–70.
6. "Soviets' 'Dirty War' in Afghanistan," *U.S. News & World Report,* 19 December 1983, p. 13.
7. Bruce Henderson, " 'Honor Thy Country': The Lou Peters Story," *Reader's Digest,* June 1983, pp. 103–8.

13

A CONFIRMATION OF FREEDOM

A Dictation by the Ascended Master Saint Germain

Hail, friends of freedom! I AM come in the flaming presence of the one fire that kindles the spark of liberty in the hearts of humanity! I AM come in confirmation of the fleur-de-lis within your hearts! I come in answer to the call of light-bearers all! I come in the flame, and I come in the starry body of the One.

The Defender of Freedom

Lo, I AM come! Lo, I AM the defender of freedom in every heart, in every nation, and in all mankind! Earth is destined to be a star of freedom, a star in the crown of the Cosmic Virgin! And I AM the champion of that flame, that light, and of the seed, the sons and daughters of God who walk the earth.

I send forth this messenger to deliver the word of hierarchy and I set my seal upon the brow of all who espouse the cause. You who will go forth in the name of freedom, claiming my flame and my momentum, which I have bequeathed not alone to America, but to all who fervently pursue the vow of unity, you who will go forth carrying that fire, will also have the momentum of my flame! For I stand this night to sponsor once again the patriarchs, the patrons, and the patriots of freedom. I sponsor those who will take the mantle and the fire and the sword. I sponsor those who reckon with the responsibility of an age.

The Discipline of Freedom

I come to place, then, the authority of my life in those who
will give their life also to that cause. I am looking for recruits; for I
am organizing the order of those light-bearers who will be the
catalyst of world freedom transcending, yes, the national boundaries, yes, the planetary boundaries, yes, transcending even the
finite thimble cup of consciousness which cannot see or understand
the plan and yet desires freedom.

Take my hand, for I have walked of old among those who
have served on this and other worlds defending freedom. And I,
too, have gone the way of Zadkiel's retreat where the crystal fires of
Holy Amethyst, of your own meditation, are there focuses of the
violet flame coming forth from the Great Central Sun, dispensing
through the consciousness of an archangel and an archeia the light
of freedom and of far-off worlds.

The hosts of the Lord are encamped round about the soul that
is willing to accept the discipline of freedom. This discipline is the
holding of the rein of God-power and wisdom and love; it is the
holding of a grid of consciousness to ensoul a civilization. Have
you the determination and the discipline of those who have gone
before you who have kept the flame?

We champion individuality; and yet when mankind manifest
that individuality, they are ridiculed. Men call for freedom, and
when those who dare to be free manifest that freedom, then the
masses cry out, "He is a nonconformist! He doesn't fit!" and there
is the heckling of those who dare to stand apart, to do something
of sacred worth that brings forth a unique flame. And therefore,
those who would walk in the discipline of freedom must be willing
at times to walk alone and apart, knowing full well that the Lord's
hosts walk also with the soul that stands alone, feet firmly on the
rock of the Real Self, the Christed One, the Anointed One.

A Flame That Must Be Borne

I dare to speak of freedom! I dare to speak of America as that
place where freedom has been enshrined as a flame! I dare to speak
of Jesus the Christ as the example of the individualization of that
Christ flame and the Wayshower. And so I come to say, you who
have not understood the way of freedom, know also that nations,

each and every one, have a flame that must be borne to all the other nations as the individuality of the Godhead.

Will you complain, then, that America is the cradle of freedom even as every other nation brings forth some facet of the jewel of the mind of God? How grateful am I to stand upon that ground consecrated by Elohim and archangels to the liberation of the souls of mankind! Here we are free to set forth the teachings of the ascended masters! Here that freedom has been won! And therefore you have come to declare, "I AM THAT I AM!" I tell you, there are places on earth this night where you would not be allowed to utter the name of God in public.

Omri-Tas and the Violet-Flame Balls

Precious hearts, let us champion freedom first within the soul, then within the soul of a planet! Let us see now earth saturated with the violet flame from the heart of Omri-Tas! For this night as you watch the release of fireworks, the 144,000 priests of the sacred fire, in their annual release, will send forth the violet-flame balls—those spheres of violet fire—and they will roll those spheres into the earth! And they will also burst! And the fire inside, a sacred fire, will be the anointing of the Holy Spirit to draw a planet unto the victory of light.

Glory to the flame! Glory to the thirteen who compose the mandala of light! Glory to the five-pointed star whereby all mankind learn the testing of mighty Cosmos' secret rays! Glory to every achievement that God has won in manifestation, that man and woman have won in God, in each and every nation upon the planetary home! Let freedom resound! Let spiritual freedom be found!

I Contact the Chakra of the Soul

As I raise my hands, I contact the chakra of the soul, the chakra of freedom. And from my hands now I release through the hands of the messenger a ray of fire that will penetrate your soul. Let it come if you will! Let it realign that forcefield if you will! Let it bring the consciousness of soul freedom into balance so that you will know the meaning of true freedom. This is a dispensation in answer to the calls of light-bearers that I might contact your souls with an increment of my causal body and reinforce there your desire to be free.

Soul Awareness

Marvel not that when the fires of freedom come, the elements of a not-freedom and a false freedom feel the grain and feel the friction of the entering-in of the pure wine of that fire, the pure and concentrated elixir that is the alchemicalization of soul consciousness. You have heard of cosmic consciousness; you have heard of God consciousness, Christ consciousness. Now I say, understand that soul consciousness is solar awareness, is the penetration of the fiery core of the Son of God and of starry bodies, of the heart of Elohim and ascended masters.

Your soul awareness, when purified, when aligned, when quickened by the seventh-ray action of the Holy Spirit, will give you unerring perception and a reading of vibration. Take care that you do not anticipate that correct reading before you have been cleansed. For many vibrations of deception have invaded the souls of mankind; and many are they who have said, "I feel this or that within my soul," and they know not that they are registering a reading not of the soul, but of that substance of the carnal mind that is the perversion of soul awareness.

The Teaching Is a Living Flame

Wait then upon the law of being! Wait upon the influx of the violet flame, and be diligent in application! Not everyone who declares "Lord, Lord" enters into the center of the I AM Presence.[1] Beware, then, the talking about the teaching and the living of the teaching! Let the doers of the Word, then, become the Word incarnate! And let them show forth that the teaching is more than conversation! The teaching is a living flame, a living vibration!

Let those who call themselves chelas of Saint Germain prove that stewardship of the flame! Let their auras now vibrate with violet fire! Let them feel the quickening, and let them impart that quickening unto mankind! Let those who claim association with the ascended hosts be ready to deliver the goods! For mankind in this age are perceptive, and they know the real from the unreal. And therefore, let truth ring clear!

Let liberty proclaim that every man is free to pursue the

Almighty according to conscience! This is the meaning of freedom of religion. Therefore, let not the state, let not the organizations of the councils of the churches or the elders of the people confine the souls of this or any nation to the doctrine and the dogma of the past, the timeworn beliefs. Let mankind be free! I declare it, and I send forth the thrust of the fire of cosmic purpose! I AM the champion of the light and of the right and of the force of freedom!

The Mantle of Freedom

Now I say, prove unto the ascended hosts that you can wear the mantle of freedom, that you can cut the rebellion of the fallen ones and pierce the night of gloom and condemnation and the tearing apart of the precious thread of contact. Now see how you can take the light, the fervent light of freedom, and mark a path that is clear that all who walk may follow in the footsteps of the ascended hosts.

Out from the Great Central Sun magnet come the angels of freedom, come the angels bearing the banner of freedom! Let that banner be known as the banner of the new order of the ages! Let it now blow in the breezes of the heavenly winds of the Holy Spirit! Let that banner blow! And let the light glow in hearts of fire.

Soul Training in Saint Germain's Retreat

I have more to say to you, yet I will reserve that teaching of the Word for the inner temple of the heart. And if you call to me, I will come to you and take you into my retreat for that special training this night unique to your own soul. And I will also reinforce the singing of the atoms and electrons in those who would espouse freedom yet know not yet the vibration of freedom.

I release it unto all! And I stir the fiery caldrons of violet flame. So angels of light from the central sun: Go north, go south, east and west, and carry the fires of freedom, quickening hearts in every walk, in every place! I AM freedom! I AM come, and I remain within your heart a living flame, if you will allow me to tarry there. In the name of the Christed One, I bid you adieu.

July 4, 1975
8:41-8:57 P.M. PDT

The cult of the Mother, destined to come into prominence in the twentieth century, was the foundation of the civilization of Lemuria. The fall of Mu was the direct result of the Fall of Man, which reached its lowest point in the desecration of the shrines to the Cosmic Virgin. Through the worship of the motherhood of God and the elevation in society of the functions of the feminine aspect of the Deity, science and religion will reach their apex and man will discover the Spirit of God as the flame enshrined upon the altar of his own being.

14

RAISING THE FLAME OF MU
AND THE CULTURE OF THE MOTHERLAND

A Dictation by the Ascended Masters Surya and Cuzco

An Increment of the Ray of Sirius

I come out of the Great Central Sun to deliver unto earth this day an increment of the ray of the God Star Sirius for the raising of an increment of the flame of Mu and the culture of the Motherland! I beam that ray from the fiery core and the central dais at the Court of the Sacred Fire on the God Star simultaneously as it is being beamed from our retreat on Terra at Viti Levu in the Fiji chain through the master Cuzco. Our hearts now form that nexus of light and that fulcrum of energy to release a forcefield of the Great Central Sun magnet over Lemuria to continue the raising, by the action of the great raising fires of the Mother ray, of all that is of noble worth, of all that was energized there by stalwart hearts, souls of fire, and the early root races of Terra.

This dispensation, which comes from the Four and Twenty Elders, is made possible by the fact that numbers among mankind in this decade are turning to the purity of the flow of the energy of the Mother and to the consecration of the sacred energies of life to purity and to the raising-up of that purity unto the plane of the heart, the mind, and the all-seeing eye. Now with the renewal of the adoration of the Mother ray as is given in the Hail Mary [1] and with the renewal of desire to set free the feminine aspect of the Godhead in every living soul, these devotees of light become a Great Central Sun magnet to draw the equivalent of that light from the shores of Mu.

Electrodes for Transition

As in all changes, transition on a planetary body requires that there be electrodes, transformers who receive the old and the new and provide the place for the adjustment. Therefore, light-bearers who will, who know that this is the hour to serve: Come forth now and receive the anointing to be that rod of power that is required for the transmutation of energies that have held back the Mother flame, that in the original crisis caused the cataclysm of the sinking of Lemuria—this misqualification of Eva, the Mother of living, of that life-force.

Angels for the Adjustment of Planetary Cycles

Now let it be redeemed in the nucleus heart chakra of those who have determined to keep the code of the Great White Brotherhood! Those who volunteer silently now within the heart and those who are worthy as disciples wherever they may be across the planetary body now have the visitation of an angel from Sirius, one of the angels who form the band that you call the mighty blue eagle—symbol of the God Star, symbol of the soaring of consciousness and the raising of the Mother, symbol of judgment and of vigilance and of the quickness of the all-seeing eye of God.

So the angels that make the formation of the eagle now come! And each one goes to the place where a heart is consecrated, where a life has been retained on Terra for this supreme moment of the adjustment of planetary cycles! So the rod is placed within the heart and the electrode is set. Henceforth, those who have this electrode shall be the direct outposts of the retreat of Cuzco, the retreat that is dedicated to the adjustment of planetary cycles in the four lower bodies of Mater.

At any hour of the day or night, then, you can expect the rushing-in of fire for a purpose, for transmutation; and you will know when you feel the fire flow that a corresponding energy of misqualified substance of Terra will also come into that vortex for transmutation. And in that moment you will hold the balance of Libra, of the Holy Spirit, of the cloven tongues of fire; and you will keep the balance of that hierarchy for the renewing of levels of consciousness and the stabilization of all mankind. This is a special action and a special dispensation whereby unascended mankind are drawn into that service heretofore reserved only for the ascended hosts.

Meeting in the Fiery Core of the Heart

But this is the age of the meeting of all parts of life in the fiery core of the heart. Therefore, when I went before the Four and Twenty Elders to receive this dispensation, I said: "Let us prove now the word of the devotees. They are young; they are full of the fervor of freedom. They desire to give of themselves to a planet, to a people. Let them prove their sacred worth! Let them prove, by an action of supreme import to elemental life and even to the perpetuation of life in Terra, how their hearts are full of love—a love of action, a love of submission to the divine will, a love that fuses with the wisdom of God and knows the Logos and becomes the law and is willing then to raise the hand and to make the pledge 'I will serve thee, my God, unto the end of cycles!'"

Proof of Commitment

Will you stand and make that pledge this hour? [Audience rises.] Will you say: [Audience gives the following pledge with Surya] "I will serve thee, my God, unto the end of cycles! I will serve thee, my God, unto the end of cycles! I will serve thee, my God, unto the end of cycles!"

And so I, Surya, went before the Four and Twenty Elders and I said: "I will prove that my faith in these souls is a valid faith. I will show you, O beloved hierarchies, that a thousand or more will raise their hands at Shasta to declare the service of the one true God!" And therefore I thank you; for you have redeemed my word and you have manifested the proof, the first proof, of commitment whereby the Four and Twenty Elders can extend to Terra new dispensations which come as a unique energy flow apart from and yet a part of the judgment of the Lords of Karma.

The Idling of the Flow

Now let us see how action will follow the word! Children of the one flame, the only thing that stands between word and action is the idling of the flow. I say, let not the flow idle! For in that idling of the energies of God, there is the loss of memory of commitment, the loss of the blueprint. Let all idling as indecision, as self-pity, as the justification of a self that is outside of the fiery core, be consumed now!

The Consuming Action of Love

I release that fire to consume the cause and core of chaos and confusion and debris that surrounds the Mother chakra of each one! Let it be consumed now! Let the energies of light from Sirius and the heart of the I AM Presence *purge* the planet, and especially the devotees so consecrated by their love! Be now burned by the consuming action of our love of life as above, so below! The Great Divine Director stands to arrest the spirals of all misuses of the sacred fire. Now let us see how the arresting of those spirals will result in even greater freedom for elemental life, for mankind and the crystal-clear seeing in the all-seeing eye—the place where the virgin consciousness is consecrated unto purity and unto victory.

Now let the wings of Mercury be upon the brow! Let them be upon the heels of all who run in the race! Now let us see how the word flows into action by the fire of Mem as you have emblazoned upon your consciousness the will to be a co-creator with Life!

Be Thou Made Whole

I AM the energy that ends all strife, all schism within the four lower bodies! I AM the flow of Mother that heals the separation of consciousness, that heals the wounds in the emotional body and the scars in the mental and etheric body! I AM the healing of the cells of the physical body! I come to make you whole! Won't you accept that wholeness, O souls of living fire? [Audience answers yes.] So be it! Be thou the wholeness of the God Star and see how the cosmic cross of white fire, designating the place where God incarnate is the Christed One, now *seals* you to *be* a blazing sun— and that sun the magnet for the raising of Lemuria!

O Lady Venus, now raise thy flame! O Sanat Kumara, holy Kumaras, our twin flames: Raise, O raise the energies of victory that all mankind and Terra might rise into the sun and the swirling fires of ascension's flame! I say again: *Be* thou made *whole! Be* thou made *whole! Be* thou made *whole!*

July 5, 1975
12:02-12:15 P.M. PDT

The key to infinity is won through the mastery of the lesser self (the microcosm) by the power of the Greater Self (the Macrocosm). This is the power of the Superconscious Ego over the ego, of God the Macrocosm over man the microcosm.

15

THE COSMIC CLOCK:
PSYCHOLOGY FOR THE AQUARIAN
MAN AND WOMAN

A Lecture by Elizabeth Clare Prophet

As we contemplate the love of hierarchy and of the master for the chela and we feel that love whereby the master says, "I cannot leave thee, I will not leave thee," we see how that love comes forth from the Father-Mother God as when Jesus took his leave of his disciples and said: "I will not leave you comfortless. Behold, the Comforter will come who will teach you all things."[1] The Comforter as the Holy Spirit gives us that teaching whereby we are not left alone to drift in our own sea of impurities, our own subconscious, our own karma. We are not left alone, because the teacher has left us the teaching.

One of the greatest examples of the love of hierarchy that I have found is the teaching on the cosmic clock. The cosmic clock is the comforter. It is that agency of the Holy Spirit that remains with us after the master ascends, while the angels ascend and descend on the ladder of life.

Cycles of Love Whereby We Ascend

It gives me great pleasure, then, to give you today the teaching on the clock. The cycles that unfold in this clock are cycles of love—the love whereby we ascend, the love whereby the consuming fire of all who have gone before us transmutes those elements that are not desirable, that are not permissible in the hallowed circle of the AUM. May I begin with a poem by Robert

Frost that has always been dear to me, and I'm certain dear to you, which conveys the cycles and the fiery core and the burden of karma that is upon us.

"Stopping by Woods on a Snowy Evening"

Whose woods these are I think I know.
His house is in the village, though;
He will not see me stopping here
To watch his woods fill up with snow.

My little horse must think it queer
To stop without a farmhouse near
Between the woods and frozen lake
The darkest evening of the year.

He gives his harness bells a shake
To ask if there is some mistake.
The only other sound's the sweep
Of easy wind and downy flake.

The woods are lovely, dark, and deep,
But I have promises to keep,
And miles to go before I sleep,
And miles to go before I sleep.

The snowy evening represents the fiery core of the I AM Presence out of which the soul descends—cycling through the cosmic clock, its cosmic destiny. And here we find ourselves at a certain point in that destiny. We stand on a point of the clock; and we cannot tarry in our cups, for we have miles to go, promises to keep. We have cycles to turn, commitments to meet to Lords of Flame, to hierarchies, to humanity. And before we lay this mortal form to rest and shuffle off this mortal coil,[2] we must fulfill those promises; and we have many miles to go.

The Hallowed Circle of the One

The first impulse of the cosmic clock that I was given came to me very early in this life. As a tiny child, as I lived the year I saw myself walking on a circle; and around the year I would walk, day by day. And I would remember dates and experiences according to where I had stood on this giant circle where my soul was walking. After I became a messenger for the Brotherhood, Mother Mary came to me and showed me this cosmic clock.* It begins with the fiery core of the AUM and your own twin flame. It begins with a circle—the hallowed circle of the One (fig. 1). Out of this hallowed circle, the ovoid of your I AM Presence and the I AM Presence of your twin flame came forth (fig. 2).

The fiery ovoid, the wholeness of God, produces that focal point of the twain (fig. 2), of Alpha and Omega (fig. 3), Father-Mother God carrying the torch of life, going forth to carve a cosmic destiny. Therefore, out of the whole single circle that represents infinity, there emerges two Monads each having the polarity of Alpha and Omega, the plus and minus of Being, each having the same electronic blueprint of life for twin flames with a cosmic destiny (fig. 2). Out of each of these halves which in turn has become a whole, each one an I AM Presence, there descends a soul—counterpart of the Spirit of the living God.

The Four Quadrants of the Whole

The soul then descends into Mater and is clothed upon with coats of skins[3]—an allegorical term used in Genesis meaning the four lower bodies—four lower bodies, frequencies for the realization of the four aspects of the circle, the four quadrants of the whole (fig. 4). The four lower bodies that surround the soul enable us to experiment with the alchemy of fire in the first quarter of the circle, the plane of the memory, with the frequency of white; with the alchemy of air in the second quarter of the circle, the plane of the mind, with the frequency of yellow; with the alchemy of water in the third quarter of the circle, the plane of the feelings, with the frequency of pink; and finally with the alchemy of earth, the plane of the physical body, with the frequency of blue. And so we come, trailing clouds of glory.

Those who have gone before us in the early root races, who descended into form, did not put on the density which we now wear, because their consciousness never entered into the area of relativity—of the energy *veil* that is called *evil*, which is created by man, by his free will, through the misuse of the sacred fire. And so twin souls descending from the twin flames of the I AM Presence

*See Diagrams of the Cosmic Clock, figures 1-16.

in the early root races ascended back to that fiery core without ever having created what we are going to diagram today, which is known as the electronic belt.

The *electronic belt* is a circle of energy that is below the heart, that is a negative spiral of all misuses of the sacred fire that have ever gone forth from your being, consciousness, and world, from your chakras, from your four lower bodies during your sojourn in the planes of Matter. When we chart this cosmic clock of karma as Mother Mary gave it to us, we have the opportunity to see day by day what the initiations of the sacred fire will be—how we will meet, challenge, conquer, and transmute the cause and core of every form of misqualified energy that we have deposited in Matter as an energy veil, as an illusion, as a chimera, as that which seems to be but is not.

As long as we are going out from the center of oneness sowing the seeds of karma, we do not have these daily confrontations of initiation. But when we determine, at a particular point on the path of that sunbeam going from the central sun, that we will turn, make an about-face, and go back to the fiery core of the I AM Presence, then we find, strewn along the path that we have walked for tens of thousands and hundreds of thousands of years, all of the sowings, all of the things that we have carelessly dropped—our idle words, cruelties, sins of omission and commission, thoughtlessness, strife—not only that which we have done individually but that which we have done collectively as part of the lifewave, or of the group of souls, with which we came into incarnation.

And so going out from God is like going downhill. It's easy going out. It's easy to be careless about how we treat life. But going back, it's uphill all the way—uphill over the bumps and the boulders and the mountains of our karma. We take the mountain of karma, as the masters have told us, and by the alchemy of the cosmic clock won by fervent application to the fires of the Holy Spirit, we create the pyramid of life. This great pyramid of life is the ascending spiral of our oneness.

The cosmic clock is marked according to twelve cycles. From the whole to the half to the four to the twelve is simply a further breaking-down of the individualization of the God flame. It means that frequencies are becoming articulate; they are becoming defined. And solar hierarchies are holding the pivot point for the release of that cosmic energy from the fiery core of Alpha and

DIAGRAMS OF THE COSMIC CLOCK
Dictated by Mother Mary to Elizabeth Clare Prophet

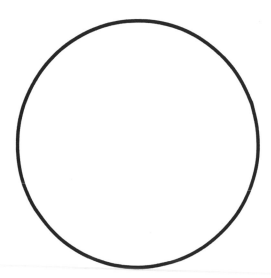

Figure 1
The All, the One
the Undifferentiated Whole
the White-Fire Core of Being
the Hallowed Circle of the AUM

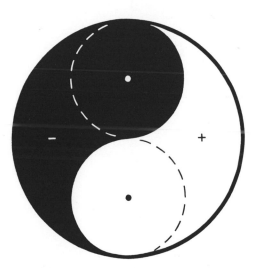

Figure 2
The T'ai Chi, the Polarity of Wholeness
Showing the Flow of Energy from Spirit to Matter,
Matter to Spirit over the Figure Eight

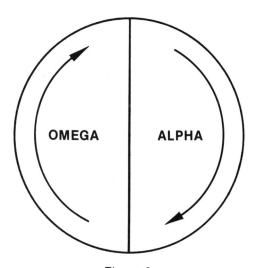

Figure 3
The Father-Mother God
The Going Out and the Coming In
of the Cycles of Alpha and Omega

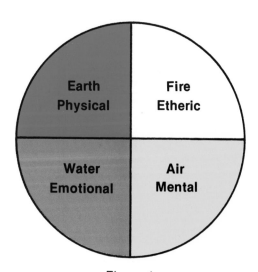

Figure 4
The Four Elements
Corresponding to the Four Lower Bodies
and the Four Planes of Matter

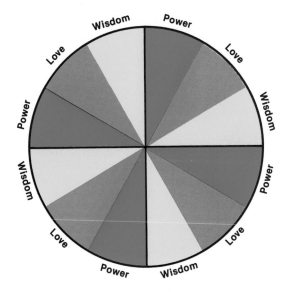

Figure 5
The Balance of the Threefold Flame
in the Four Quadrants of Being

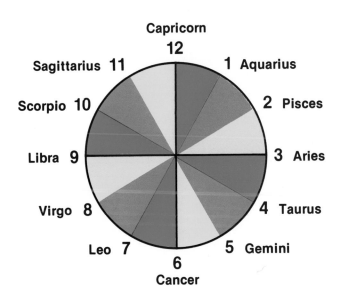

Figure 6
The Twelve Solar Hierarchies
Focus the Mastery of the Trinity
in the Four Quadrants of Being

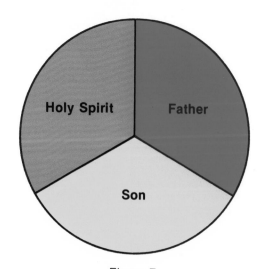

Figure 7
The Trinity of Being
The Creator, the Preserver, the Destroyer
Brahma, Vishnu, Siva
Father, Son, Holy Spirit

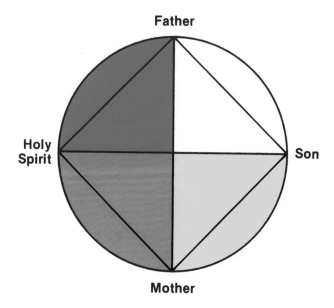

Figure 8
The Squaring of the Circle
The Three Become Four
through the Mother

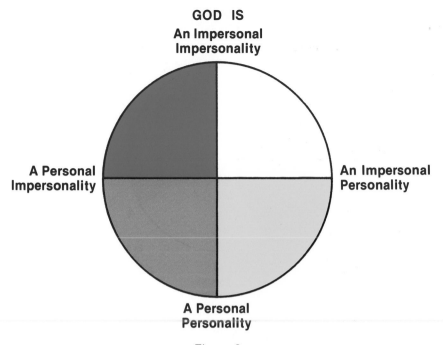

Figure 9
The Alchemical Nature
of the God Consciousness

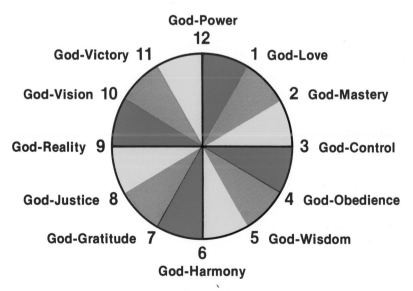

Figure 10
The God Consciousness, or God-Qualities,
of the Solar Hierarchies

Figure 11
The Ascended Masters of the Great White Brotherhood
Who Initiate Earth's Evolutions
in the God Consciousness of the Twelve Solar Hierarchies

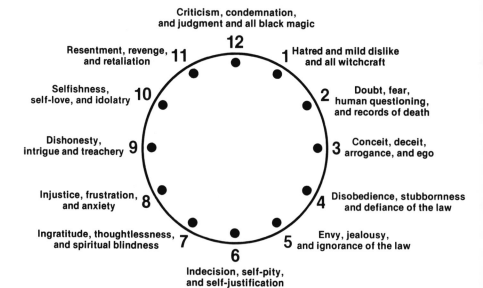

Figure 12
Human Perversions of the God Consciousness
of the Twelve Solar Hierarchies

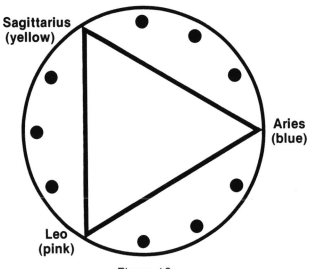

Figure 13
Triangle of Initiations in the Fire Signs

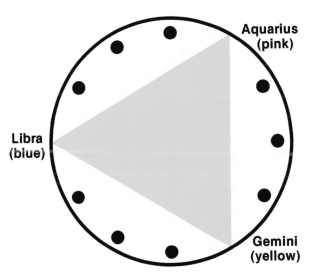

Figure 14
Triangle of Initiations in the Air Signs

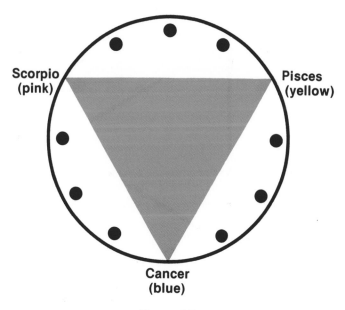

Figure 15
Triangle of Initiations in the Water Signs

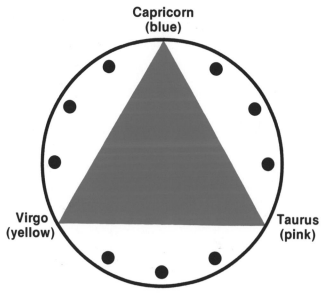

Figure 16
Triangle of Initiations in the Earth Signs

Omega. We see, then, that our cosmic clock divided into four quadrants becomes the twelve; and each of four quadrants becomes a threefold flame (fig. 5). This threefold flame is the same flame that burns within our hearts.

This diagram shows us that on each side of the pyramid—in each of the four lower bodies—we must balance the threefold flame; we must balance the expression of the threefold flame. The threefold flame is what it is according to our qualification. Because of the energy veil, or what we call effluvia, lodged in each of the four lower bodies, the threefold flame does not always shine with the same balance in the memory, the mind, the feelings, or the physical body.

We all have our strong points. Some of us are strong mentally. Some have a very strong etheric body—the fiery body, the fiery blueprint. Others are strong in the heart and the feelings, and others have the maximum health and flow of energy in the physical form. All of the four lower bodies must be perfected as vehicles of the sacred fire, of the threefold flame in the heart. The impediments which block the flow of the sacred fire in these four lower bodies also block the flow of light within the chakras. Therefore, the cosmic clock is a means of diagraming the mastery of the chakras as well as the transmutation of karma and the charting of the daily initiations.

The Twelve Solar Hierarchies

Taking these twelve points, we see that they are governed by twelve solar hierarchies (fig. 6). Some of you may be accustomed to making a chart for the world's astrology. You will note that the cosmic hierarchies are placed on the chart in a clockwise direction, beginning at the 12 o'clock line with the hierarchy of Capricorn. That is a hierarchy, let us remember. It is a hierarchy which releases the light-energies, the fohatic light, of God-power through the constellation, the configuration of stars, that we see and call Capricorn. The stars are not the hierarchy. The hierarchy simply uses these, as well as many other stars, to release that energy. Your causal body has a focal point for the release of energy of the hierarchy of Capricorn, and your four lower bodies are capable of releasing that flow if you can transmute all impediments to that flow.

Drawing this diagram of a circle, then, you would place the hierarchy of Capricorn on the 12 o'clock line, the hierarchy of Aquarius on the 1 o'clock line, the hierarchy of Pisces on the two, the hierarchy of Aries on the three, the hierarchy of Taurus on the four, the hierarchy of Gemini on the five, the hierarchy of Cancer on the six, the hierarchy of Leo on the seven, the hierarchy of Virgo on the eight, the hierarchy of Libra on the nine, the hierarchy of Scorpio on the ten, and the hierarchy of Sagittarius on the eleven. Each of these hierarchies releases a frequency of the Godhead.

We are intended to become this sundial, this cosmic clock. We are intended to create the spiral within the heart, to release the spiral that forms the clock, to become that pinwheel that whirls in time and space, delivering into the planes of Mater all of these frequencies in exact measure, in the cadences of the cosmic heartbeat. This is cosmic flow! It is flowing now, this very moment, from your causal body. Yet very meagerly are we the recipients of the flow unless we have that attunement which is called cosmic consciousness.

The Squaring of the Circle

Let us consider now the four quadrants as these become the action of Father, Mother, Son, and Holy Spirit. These four aspects show into which four categories the twelve hierarchies flow. The Trinity of Brahma, Vishnu, and Siva—or Father, Son, and Holy Spirit—is a trinity that corresponds to many aspects of the flow of energy (fig. 7). Here on this chart we show it corresponding to the four lower bodies (fig. 4).

The Mother is the key in Mater and in Spirit to the release of the energy of Father, Son, and Holy Spirit. The Mother is the catalyst; she is the fiery core out of which these energies flow. Therefore, the Mother has a particular relationship to Father, to Son, to Holy Spirit. And through her, the trinity becomes the squaring of the circle in Mater (fig. 8).

The trinity is the spiritual threefold flame, the sacred-fire aspect of the Godhead. To bring this into manifestation in the planes of Matter, we must have what is known as the squaring of the circle, the crystallization of the God flame. The Mother is the crystal whereby the trinity becomes physical, tangible, workable in the four lower bodies and in the chakras.

Four Aspects of the Circle of Life

Saint Germain, in his *Studies in Alchemy*,[4] has noted the four aspects of the circle of life; and he has given to the Father the name "Impersonal Impersonality" (fig. 9). This will give you a concept of the first quadrant and an idea of what the three hierarchies who govern that quadrant consist of. The hierarchies of Capricorn, Aquarius, and Pisces fall in the first quadrant, the fire body. The Impersonal Impersonality is the pure fiery energy of the law. It is the fohatic energy that flows.

We all think of Father as being a little less personal than Mother. We think of the Father aspect of God as remote even though he is not remote. This remoteness is not a "far-offness," but it is an impersonal quality which is contained in the Lawgiver and in the absolute perfection of the I AM Presence.

If we move one turn, one 90-degree angle of our 360-degree circle, we come to the second quadrant, the place where the Impersonal Impersonality, as flow, becomes the Impersonal Personality, the Christed One, the Word incarnate. This is on the Aries line of the clock. And under this frequency of the mind of God that has become the mind of Christ is the mastery of the hierarchies of Aries, Taurus, and Gemini.

We see in the figure of Jesus the Christ an impersonal personality. He is a personality and yet he is impersonal. It is that midpoint between Father and Mother, the place where Alpha and Omega meet to give birth to the Divine Manchild, the Christ, personified in Jesus with the warmth and the love and yet a certain distance, a certain quality of sternness. This moving between the Father and the Mother which we find so satisfying in the man Jesus also defines the individual Christ Self. That is the 3 o'clock line.

Coming to the 6 o'clock line, which marks the third quadrant—the emotional body, the feeling world, the love aspect of being—we find the Mother and the Personal Personality. The Mother is the most personal personality of the Godhead that we can conceive. We know her intimately; she is one with us all of our lives. The one we are closest to is Mother. We live in the womb of the Cosmic Virgin. Our earthly mothers portray that vibration and that light. When mastering the feeling world, then, it is the Personal Personality of the Godhead which we become aware of.

Finally, in the fourth quadrant we come to the mastery of the physical body through the Personal Impersonality of the Godhead. Here the Holy Spirit manifest as the cloven tongues of fire gives us the action that is necessary to coalesce atoms in the plane of Matter, the plane of earth.[5] Here is the blending of Alpha and Omega as the union of twin flames, the wholeness of the AUM, whereby we can bring into manifestation below all that is above.

As we study the cosmic clock, we will see that at different periods of our lives, during different initiations, we are required to put on the mantle of and become each one of these phases of the Godhead. Under the Mother we are mastering the energy of the hierarchies of Cancer, Leo, and Virgo; and under the Holy Spirit, that Personal Impersonality, we are mastering our initiations under the tutelage of the hierarchies of Libra, Scorpio, and Sagittarius.

I say "under the tutelage" because these cosmic hierarchies are the supreme teachers of mankind. And they give their teachings to us through ascended masters in the scale of hierarchy who have volunteered not only to hold the flame for these hierarchies for the evolutions of this solar system, but also to teach the way of overcoming through the testing of the masterful beings from the central sun who comprise these twelve solar hierarchies.

The Ascended Masters Who Occupy the Twelve Points on the Clock

We will see, then, that ascended masters with whom we are familiar occupy positions on the twelve points on the clock to lower into manifestation the twelve qualities of the solar hierarchies (fig. 10). The 6.04 decree (see page 205) shows you these masters and their God-qualities. In section A you will see that the 12 o'clock line is presided over by the Great Divine Director, and you will see in section C that the quality on this line is God-power.

This means that the Great Divine Director is holding the focus of the hierarchy of Capricorn and their flame of God-power for the evolutions of this world (fig. 11). This means that when our initiations come under this hierarchy, we face the Great Divine Director directly and receive our teachings, our examinations, under his rod. The seven archangels assist him in this discipline of the evolutions of Terra.

Standing for the Aquarian age under the Aquarian cycle is beloved Saint Germain, holding the focus of God-love on the 1 o'clock line with the angelic hosts of light. Beloved Jesus stands on the 2 o'clock line for the Piscean dispensation and that hierarchy holding the flame of God-mastery which he proved. Assisting him in this task are the great hosts of ascended masters. On the 3 o'clock line—the line of the Son of God, the only begotten One— is the Sun Presence of Helios and the Great Central Sun messengers focusing the quality of God-control, which they amplify by the power of the Great Central Sun magnet. This magnet *is* the God-control of the flow of life through us, the flow of the energy of the Logos. This is the quality we must outpicture under the hierarchy of Aries.

On the 4 o'clock line under the hierarchy of Taurus is God Obedience, the ascended master Godfre, whose mastery of the flame of obedience makes him eminently qualified to deliver to us the flame of God-obedience and to give us the initiations of love under the hierarchy of Taurus. The seven mighty Elohim serve with Godfre to train millions of lifestreams in the law of conformity to the inner blueprint.

Beloved El Morya holds the position in Gemini on the 5 o'clock line, governing the energies of God-wisdom and testing us, with the reinforcement of the legions of Mercury, in those twin flames of Gemini, the Alpha-Omega cycle which comes through on that 5 o'clock line.

Serapis Bey, hierarch of the Ascension Temple, working diligently with the great seraphim and cherubim, initiates us in the white-fire core of the Mother, the flame of purity which we call God-harmony. To master the Mother flame on the 6 o'clock line, we must master the flow of harmony. We must be able to hold the reins of harmony in our four lower bodies. This is not an easy testing, inasmuch as it is a testing of the water element, of the *energy-in-motion*. It requires that we keep harmony while in motion—in action—when for some it is difficult enough to keep harmony while standing still.

On the 7 o'clock line is the Goddess of Liberty, who is the spokesman of the Karmic Board. Together with the Lords of Karma, she holds the key under the hierarchy of Leo to the quality of God-gratitude. The Goddess of Liberty once said that immigration is *"I AM gratitude in action."*[6] As she holds her lamp in the port of New York welcoming immigrants, so gratitude on the 7 o'clock line is continually affirming all of the gifts and graces of the Spirit and our appreciation for life. Each time we say, "I AM grateful," we increase the flow in the feeling body. This plays a tremendous part in the factor of balancing karma. The flame of gratitude is an important key in the turning of the cycles of the cosmic clock.

Beloved Lord Lanto in the Grand Teton Retreat, with the Lords of Wisdom, keeps the flame of God-justice under the hierarchy of Virgo on the 8 o'clock line. On the 9 o'clock line of the Holy Spirit, the hierarchy of Libra is served by mighty Victory from Venus and the Lords of Individuality, who keep the flame of God-reality for mankind, giving us our initiations in what is real and what is unreal.

Beloved Cyclopea and the Lords of Form hold in Scorpio on the 10 o'clock line the balance of the power of God-vision. The action of this energy is released to us as the testing of the all-seeing eye. On the 11 o'clock line, Lord Maitreya, the Great Initiator, and the Lords of Mind keep the focus for the hierarchy of Sagittarius, testing us in the flame of God-victory, the eleventh hour, the hour of God-victory.

Now what does all of this mean? The revelation of the cosmic clock is a magnificent concept. It is the most liberating concept— after the knowledge of the I AM Presence, the Christ Self, the ascended masters, the violet flame, and the science of the spoken Word—that we have received.

Remember, we were speaking about all of this karma that is due on Terra in the next twenty-five years and that which we are about to face, which we are facing even now. This karma is not punishment. It is opportunity. God does not desire to see mankind fail the tests, and he does not create tests out of whimsy, contrived, that we will fail. Karma is *never, never* punishment! It is opportunity to experience that which we have sent forth as a co-creator with God, as a scientist, an alchemist in the laboratory of Mater. We have a right to know the fruits of our experiments. When we let energy flow, we must have a clear indication of the result of our experiment or we will not know in the future how to duplicate that experiment or whether it is desirable to duplicate it or to cancel it out.

The return of karma must be seen as a joy, an anticipation in the heart, a flame of gratitude that runs to greet the master who comes carrying the weight of karma on the way. How can we have that rejoicing when we are burdened day by day by what seems an enormous punishment, a burden that we do not yet understand is light? The way to understand the joy of the greeting of the master on the way of life, of running to greet the Lords of Karma, is to realize that the flame within the heart, the I AM Presence, is a spiral of energy so intense, a vortex of light infolding itself so as to have the momentum to draw into it and to consume every last jot and tittle of the law of that karmic recompense—every last vibration, every burden of that karmic weight, whether it be a million years old or it happened yesterday. That flame is a flaming flame that will not be quenched.[7]

So at the fiery core of the circle is that flame of your heart. And as the wheel of the cosmic clock turns day by day and you experience the return, you do not sigh with the burden of the lines of your destiny, but you greet them with the joy of the flame. We see, then, that God, desiring to see mankind pass these tests, has given us the supreme science of the Divine Mother—the cosmic clock.

The First Twelve-Year Cycle

Take the 12 o'clock line and place there the day, the month, and the year of your birth. If your birthday is July 4, place July 4 on the 12 o'clock line. At the hour that you were born, you began your first initiation, the initiation of the hierarchy of Capricorn, of God-power. The initial thrust of God-power was your first breath and your first cry, and the initiation you passed was to seize the flame of life and take it and claim it as your own. As you know, some unfortunately do not pass this test. All through the first year of your life, you were serving under the Great Divine Director and the hierarchies of Capricorn, testing the power as that power manifested in the stretching of the limbs, in the flow of the energy of the heart, in the exact working of the physical body.

On your first birthday came the first initiation in this life under the hierarchy of Aquarius, and God-love infused your soul with a new wonder. Your identification with love and with loved ones increased. On your second birthday come the initiations of Pisces in the water element. It is a testing in the etheric body of the flow of water—the emotions. It is the flame of God-mastery. In this year you master many things. Scientists tell us we learn more in this year than at any other time in our life—in fact, in the first several years of our life. So the flame of God-mastery comes with a great thrust to the two-year-old, who is eager to master everything in sight.

Then at three comes the awareness of the Christ Child. The child gains a tremendous sense of identity, of "I AM WHO I AM," the awareness of the name, and "I want to do it all by myself!" This is the development of the ego; it is the Divine Ego aborning in the child. The greatest mistake the parent can make is to do for that child what the child diligently desires to do for himself; and when the child cries that you have done something for him, quickly undo it and let him do it himself. It is terribly important that the flame of individuality develop in this third year under the hierarchy of Aries. It is focusing the balance for a lifetime. All the while, the records are being recorded in the subconscious; and all that occurs on these lines—all of the impressions, all of the sounds we hear, the interaction with life—all of this is going into the record of the four lower bodies.

In the fourth year comes the test of the hierarchy of Taurus. More and more we are precipitating into the physical, gaining mastery of the physical. There is now that certain stubbornness which carries through the flame of individuality—the stubbornness that is not a bad stubbornness. It is a will to be, to have a separate identity, to forge out that mind which is beginning to work. Children are reading and they are working with numbers. They are mastering the physical element, the earth plane of Taurus. The entire year is marked by this energy.

As we see in the aspect of the circle that shows the threefold flames, Taurus is a sign of love (fig. 5). It is by love that we precipitate determination, and it is actually a determination within the soul of the child to conform to the law of the inner being. The problem here is that not all children have the sense of the inner law, and they have laws imposed upon them from without that society and parents and schools deem more important than the inner law of the child. So the child is taking into himself, line upon line, whatever he contacts and composing the law of his life at subconscious and conscious levels.

At this period of time and earlier, the Montessori system[8] is able to give the child the contact with the inner law; but many other educational experiences which children have at this age are to the detriment of the child. These experiences tear from the child his contact with the inner law of life. This, then, will be a pattern that is set for life, for good or for ill. The cycles come; the cosmic clock is unfolding.

On the fifth birthday, the child comes under the hierarchy of Gemini, which tests the wisdom of the Christ mind. It is a sign of air. The mental development increases. The child is precocious. The child wants to learn. Most of our educational systems hold the child back in games and playing, saying, "This is what children do!" But Maria Montessori found out that children are brilliant, have a tremendous desire to learn, and have the keys whereby they *can* learn. Though she did not describe it in this way, she shows in her system how children can draw forth from the causal body and the I AM Presence the inner genius of the soul.

On the 6 o'clock line, on the sixth birthday, the child learns under the hierarchy of Cancer the flow of energies-in-motion, the flow of harmony. This is a time when parents must take care to see that the child is not allowed to have tantrums and to throw energy in order to control others. For the next three years the child will be testing the emotional body and the flow of energy: What can the child get away with? What can the child do with energy?

The child discovers that if he throws energy through the solar plexus or through screaming, he can command a whole group of adults. So the child becomes very powerful and at that very moment begins to control the mother. This is the time when the mother as well as the father must define their positions, and it is the time when the child must be taught how to govern energy-in-motion. Many of the tools in the Montessori system teach this governing, this control which extends to the physical body and the mental body and sets the correct patterns at the etheric plane.

At age seven the child is dealing again with an action of love under Leo and the mastery of God-gratitude—learning manners, learning politeness, learning to say "Thank you," developing an awareness of social action and interaction. On the 8 o'clock line, the hierarchy of Virgo anchors into this earth sign the flame of God-justice, the equality of the flow of energy in the four lower bodies. At the age of nine, the child comes again into a new increment of awareness—awareness of life as the Holy Spirit and the flame of God-reality. A greater measure of independence is coming here, and parents must take care to see that the child is taught what is real and what is not real.

There is a confusion which results from the media today whereby children are given all kinds of cartoons and stories and fantasies with which they identify; and they float in and out of the astral plane, in and out of illusion. Here we define reality. And we find that in our educational institutions there is also a desire to define reality. Yet in their ignorance, educators tell our children that that which is unreal is real and that that which is real is not real. My children came home telling me that their teacher said: "There are no angels. There isn't any God. No one believes in God anymore." This shows the importance of the role of the parent, who must reaffirm reality and the standards of the Holy Spirit, the cosmic honor flame that *must* be inculcated in this early cycle.

The tenth birthday marks God-vision, dealing with the energies of Scorpio, the test of the ten, selflessness, a lesson of giving, a lesson also in the water element. In the eleventh year the flame of God-victory—a flame of light, a flame of illumination— dealing with the energies of Sagittarius, the fire of Sagittarius anchoring in the earth quadrant the sign of victory, the development of the physical body.

Each twelve years marks the turning of a cycle of the cosmic clock. On the twelfth birthday the child returns to the place of origin and now has a set of records to be dealt with from the first turn of the clock. The child faces the initiations of puberty on the 12 o'clock line in a new cycle of God-power surging through the four lower bodies and he will also deal with all of the records of impressions of the first year of his life.

Now 12 o'clock also marks the year when the first increment of karma from previous lifetimes descends. Unless the child is an advanced soul, an initiate, or has requested that the karma be given earlier, it is the plan of the Lords of Karma to allow children to have twelve years and to allow parents and teachers to have twelve years to correlate in the child's consciousness the blueprint of life, the mastery of the mind, the standards of culture, the standards of religion—all the right things that children should be taught as the legacy of the thousands of years of culture on this planet.

Unfortunately, today parents are sometimes ignorant of this culture and of this teaching. Our educational institutions do not ensoul it; and we find many times that in the first twelve years of the life of a child, more harm is done than good. Nevertheless, these twelve years are the supreme opportunity to pass to the children the torch of all of the values we hold dear, spiritual knowledge, and an understanding of the cosmos. Maria Montessori found out that little children are enthralled with astronomy and the study of the stars because they have the commeasurement with the infinite. Mathematics and physics and chemistry also intrigue the child.

The Second Twelve-Year Cycle

During these twelve years, the pattern of what the child will bring forth is set. Ideally, the child will have developed a strong sense of cosmic law, which parents call right and wrong. But right and wrong, of course, move on the scale of relativity as the decades roll by; and so we prefer to speak of cosmic law itself as the measuring rod of right and wrong. After the child is given that supreme contact with the soul in the first twelve years, when he has that grounding, he faces the tests of karma and the tests of puberty. With a firm foundation in the law, he is equipped to face that energy which is oncoming and which presents a great testing in the next twelve-year cycle—the years between twelve and twenty-four.

Let us study these years as we take up an examination of the perversions of the twelve hierarchies of the sun. On the twelfth birthday, the child receives the impetus—actually a sphere of light that descends from the causal body—of God-power. It is a blue sphere of energy. It is delivered to the Christ Self, to the Christ flame, just as cosmic hierarchies deliver a sphere of light at winter solstice for the turning of the cycle of the year.

So this gift of energy now is within the heart of the child. How will the child use this energy? The child will use the energy as he has been taught. If he has been taught obedience, he will use it in obedience. If he has been taught God-control, the energy will flow with God-control. If he has been taught the proper behavior patterns, the proper discipline and learning techniques, all of this God-power will be used as an adornment to amplify all of the other twelve aspects of the clock. However, the child is also going to deal with the first increment of karma in this year. And this frequency of energy that is the misuse of God-power we define as *criticism, condemnation, and judgment* (fig. 12). It is the misuse of the etheric body and the alchemy of fire.

Now this condemnation manifests in many subtle ways, including self-condemnation and self-belittlement. It may be a period when the child withdraws, feels uncomfortable with his peers, doesn't know quite how to interact. The self-belittlement and sense of worthlessness at this age, which may continue all the way through the twelve years of attempting to integrate with peers, can be the result of past karma delivered on that twelfth birthday. As the I AM Presence delivers the sphere of fire, of God-power, so the Lords of Karma, through the Christ Self, also deliver the package of karma that contains his misuses of God-power in previous lifetimes.

Now these misuses do not fall strictly into the category of these three words, yet they can be sensed as such. When initiations of Capricorn are prevalent in the life of the individual, there is that feeling of being weighted down, of being condemned, the feeling you can't do anything right anytime no matter how hard you try, the feeling that people are speaking ill of you—and perhaps they actually are, but it can become a burden to the point of a psychological complex of paranoia. All of this is often the result of the misuse of God-power in past incarnations.

The wise parent who has the teachings of the clock will take the child in hand. The twelve-year-old has the complete capacity to understand this clock. He will understand, then, that he has choices to make. He can choose to increase his momentum of power by invocations to the blue flame and to the masters who serve on that ray, especially to the Great Divine Director; or he can choose to indulge that condemnation as it cycles back to him for transmutation. Instead of letting it go into the flame, he may take that condemnation and begin to condemn his parents or his brothers and sisters or children at school. He may become hypercritical of everything and everyone, including himself. When parents observe this trend, they should warn the child, "It is time to give an invocation to put into the flame all that is less than the perfection of God-power and your divine plan that ought to be fulfilled this year." Children will see the difference, and they will also run to greet the opportunity of balancing this karma.

Now where there is ignorance of all that is taking place, you find that people can go through an entire year of taking all of that momentum of karma and re-creating it. *People re-create karma.* For an entire year they can be misqualifying the flame of God-power. And when the cycle turns and that flame and that torch which ought to have been carried is to be exchanged for the flame of God-love on the line of Aquarius on the next birthday, the flame which has not been carried cannot be exchanged for a new flame. We see that initiation is cumulative. What we earn on one line has to be carried to the next line, and it becomes the foundation for mastery in that line.

Therefore, on the thirteenth birthday, the child who has correctly used the flame of God-power lays it upon the altar; and the momentum of God-power gives him the mastery to claim the love of Aquarius and to anchor that love as purity, as divinity. The age of thirteen, then, is for the adolescent the testing of love in many ways. It is a time when love must be garnered in the heart, when the wise parent will show the child how to raise the energies coursing through the body, how to release that energy in the heart, how to expand the heart chakra, to begin to understand life as a path of service, and to continually be giving in love in order to use these new energies which are arousing new feelings within his form. These energies can be used for the service of life, and the child can gain a great sense of mastery of that flow in this year.

However, with the release of that flame of love, the karma of hatred and mild dislike, which are the misuses of love, also comes up for transmutation. We find that young people at this age like to get together in groups and cliques and clubs, and there is the stratification into social levels. Some are left out and some are included, and intense likes and dislikes build up. They move in groups, and there is the feeling that some are on the inside, some are on the outside. There is that substance of intensity in relationships. All of this, of course, can be dissolved by the alchemy of divine love when parents and teachers are there to show the child how to use these energies.

As we go around the clock, then, to the fourteenth birthday on the 2 o'clock line, we find that there is mastery to be gained, especially over the increments of karma coming at this age—a very important age, especially for the devotee who is born to attain God-mastery in this life. The training in the walk of Jesus and of the Christ will be a tremendous bulwark in the life of the adolescent, the teenager—understanding the teachings of Jesus, his words, his counsel; understanding Jesus as the guru, the master of the age; understanding that there is a very intimate communion that we can have with Jesus giving us the strength to overcome temptation, to walk in the way of mastery. The entire Piscean dispensation is the gift of Jesus to the fourteen-year-old. As wise parents, we will see that our children understand and develop a very personal relationship with this beloved master.

With that increment of God-mastery and the walk with Jesus, there comes the increment of karma that is a momentum of fear and doubt, including all past records of the experience and the initiation of death. At fourteen there is a great deal of torment that the adolescent faces in coming to grips with past records of death. In this year we find young people across the world even considering suicide and the forms of violence that come from these records of death.

Coming to the fifteenth birthday on the 3 o'clock line, the child enters into his own sonship—his awareness of himself as the Christ. He truly comes into the awareness that "I AM a son of God!" He is not simply affirming this, but he is realizing what it means to be a son of God. The Christ Self releases an increment, a momentum, of the Great Central Sun; and the Christ flame actually blazes forth through the child. With proper guidance, even miracles can happen in the lives of children this age, for they are pure and of the virgin consciousness. They have a very special contact with the angelic hosts and with Mary and Jesus which they have not lost since their incarnation, since they were little children and had that attunement in the fiery core of life.

When children at age fifteen face that awareness and potential of the Christ, they also are faced with that increment of karma which is the ego, or the carnal mind. We find that it is an age when young people become aware of themselves as personalities and they move and push the personality and the ego first—with all of its demands and flirtations and movement and interaction—to the neglect of the soul, to the neglect of the development of the Christ flame.

At age sixteen, there is a supreme opportunity for building, for anchoring the talents of the child in the earth plane. This year falls in the mental quadrant. It is the year when application in school is very important; preparation and decisions for the sacred labor are being made. "What will I do with my life? What is my divine plan? How will I forge a future for myself, for my family?

How will I bring forth the talents of my causal body?" All of this the hierarchy of Taurus shows the young adult of sixteen. And this application of the flame of love, in study, will bring the reward of the foundation that is necessary for life.

Unfortunately, there are many distractions at this age. Besides the increment of the flame of love and God-obedience that is given on this birthday, there is also that package of karma—the record of all that the Lords of Karma require the sixteen-year-old to transmute of past records of rebellion, disobedience, stubbornness, and defiance of the law—the inner law of being. The age of sixteen (and even younger) is the age when experimentation with all forms of abuses of the body takes place—the taking-in of drugs, the taking-in of impure substance, impure foods—all of this misusing the flame of the law and the action of love in Taurus. We find that because of the way the foundations of civilization are made, young people of this age going with their peers do not have the guidance needed to pass the tests on this line; and usually they make more karma than they balance.

With the seventeenth birthday on the 5 o'clock line comes an intensification of God-wisdom by the hierarchy of Gemini. The age of seventeen is an age when a great deal of knowledge can be gleaned from the causal body, when all of the hierarchies of heaven stand waiting to impart to the soul its inheritance of the yellow sphere of the causal body. The increment of karma that comes up for transmutation in this year is the increment of envy, jealousy, and ignorance of the law. We find that when the individual is personality-oriented and doesn't get out of that socket from age fifteen on, there are envies and jealousies and vying for relationships. Sometimes this all-consuming energy takes all of the young person's time in relationships with the opposite sex—in determining whether or not this is going to work out or that is going to work out—which is a part of the testing of the hierarchy of Gemini, the twin flames of Gemini.

If this energy can be transmuted and placed in its proper perspective, the right relationships can bring about the fusion of energies for the drawing forth of a vast amount of wisdom. The mind of the seventeen-year-old, when freed from these other concerns of personality, has the capacity for amazing input, study, and accomplishment, especially accomplishment in the sacred labor.

At the age of eighteen, on the 6 o'clock line, comes the testing in the flame of God-harmony and the Divine Mother. Eighteen marks the beginning of a three-year cycle—eighteen, nineteen, and twenty. In these years the feeling body is at its prominence and there is the testing of that feeling body by the substance of karma up for transmutation that must be consumed if we would gain the mastery under the hierarchies of Cancer, Leo, and Virgo. The karma which comes to the fore under Cancer is indecision, self-pity, and self-justification—feeling sorry for oneself for not being accepted in college, not going on to higher opportunity as others are going, feeling sorry for oneself because of one's own failures, that idling of energy, the inability to make a decision. "What will I do with my life? I'm out of school. Now where will I go?"

The mastery of this flow is necessary to forge ahead into the higher learning of advanced educational institutions, which were destined by the masters to be the focal point for the release of the culture of the Divine Mother. The high-school years are intended to be for the release of the energies of the Christ Self, the Christ mind. Entering college, vocational school, business school, or some training after high school is a time to glean from the hand of the Mother the knowledge of your sacred labor and to complete this training in the four years which culminate on the line of the Holy Spirit.

And when we come to the line of the Holy Spirit after that training, it is time to go forth into the world of form to make our mark, to get a job whereby we precipitate with our hands, with the correct use of our energies, that which we are intended to manifest in this life. The years twenty-one, twenty-two, and twenty-three are periods when we can take advanced training, mastering further phases of postgraduate work in the increments of the Holy Spirit; or we can go forth, our training completed, to take our place in the world community.

Now, the misuses of these lines to watch for in those years: At nineteen, under the hierarchy of Leo, ingratitude and disturbance in the emotional body. There's a certain anxiety and nervous tension. Then at twenty the mastery of Virgo—the sense of injustice, the sense of *human* injustice, the outrage of particular experiences or particular individuals you are interacting with who you feel have been unfair. It's a time to take up social causes, social justice and injustice. It's a time to be careful that we don't squander the increment of light that is given from Virgo for God-justice by getting completely caught up in a sense of injustice whereby we recreate and amplify injustices in our personal life and on a planetary level.

At twenty-one the testing of Libra, of God-reality, comes again. On this line we find the perversion of Libra, of reality, as unreality. It is that deceit—the deception, the intrigue, and the treachery—which the ego uses to justify its position. We must be careful to correct in children the tendency to lie, to fib, to expand on the facts so that they are slightly distorted so as to suit our needs. And we must see that we do not allow our imagination to make us believe that we have an attainment we do not have or to make us rationalize the deliberate betrayal of the laws of society to the detriment of the interaction of lifestreams.

Twenty-two, the year of Scorpio, is the year of the testing of the sacred fire, the testing of the uses of the sex energy, which of course comes all through adolescence. But the testing in this year comes as the release of the karma of many misuses of the sacred fire in the past. This is also a year when people start families. It's a year for the mastery of the flow of the sacred fire and the using of that energy to bring forth children. It is the year of vision, of seeing the plan of life, carving out that vision, selecting one's life partner.

The momentum of selfishness of the past is very strong in this year. We must see to it that we do not base our lives, our plans, our marriages on selfishness, on possessive love. Partnerships based on residual karma that is not transmuted will not be lasting. We must call forth the sacred fire from the hierarchy of Scorpio and the Elohim Cyclopea for clear seeing, for the transmutation of these misuses of energy so that we can make our decisions based on clear seeing.

Finally, completing this second twelve-year cycle with the twenty-third birthday, we have the hierarchy of Sagittarius giving us an impetus for the victory of life. Opposing this victory is the entire dragon of the carnal mind—our own human creation symbolized in the form of the dragon in the Book of Revelation. And this energy comes with a momentum of resentment, revenge, and retaliation. When we are eleven years old and playing, it is the year when we have the hostilities and the cruelties that children are noted for—the fights and so forth, the resentment, the revenge, the getting even with So-and-so because he did this to me. Well, it comes again at age twenty-three. And we must see to it that we do not allow resentment in its subtle form of silent seething to take from us the crown of victory, which is a release of victorious, golden illumination.

The Third Twelve-Year Cycle

Coming back, then, to the 12 o'clock line, we are at the twenty-fourth birthday. The next cycle of twelve years is for the mastery of the Christic light and the Buddhic light. In these twelve years we have the opportunity to become the Christ and the Buddha. At age thirty-three, Jesus manifested the victory of the Christ consciousness and earned his ascension. At age thirty-six, Siddhartha attained enlightenment. We have the opportunity to do likewise.

Thirty-three is the number of the initiation of life that begins at birth and culminates in the thirty-third year. On the thirty-sixth birthday is the initiation of Buddha; and from there on in life, if we have passed the tests of Christic initiation, we are given intimate contact with Gautama Buddha and other Buddhas who have gone before him in the testing of our souls according to the Buddhic light.

Now if all follows like clockwork and all we outpicture throughout our lives is the God-qualities of the twelve hierarchies, of course we ascend. And that is the spiral of the ascension that you weave with the threefold flame in each of the four quadrants. The threefold flame becomes the fire in the center of the base of the pyramid that begins to turn as a spiral when you are nigh your ascension. It envelops your form, your four lower bodies, and you are completely consumed and return to the heart of the Father-Mother God.

Jesus came into embodiment with 93 percent of his karma balanced. As he went through the cycles of his clock during the years from his birth to the age of twelve, he received from his causal body only increments of the flames of God-power, God-love, God-mastery, God-control, God-obedience, God-wisdom, God-harmony, God-gratitude, God-justice, God-reality, God-vision, and God-victory. He, the avatar of the age, was, however, required to balance planetary karma even while increasing the sphere of the Christ consciousness during these first twelve years.

At the age of twelve, he was given the opportunity to balance personal as well as planetary karma and to begin the initiations for Christhood. His acceptance of this responsibility even when it conflicted with family obligations is evident in his statement to his parents when they found him discoursing with the doctors in the temple, "Wist ye not that I must be about my father's business?" [9]

During the next eighteen years—one and a half cycles on the cosmic clock—he prepared for his three-year mission, both in and out of the retreats of the Great White Brotherhood in the Near and Far East. Each line was a major initiation under Lord Maitreya, who was his guru and who put him in contact with the Cosmic Christ. With each increment he was fortifying himself with the God flames of the solar hierarchies for the three-year ministry which culminated in his crucifixion, his resurrection, and his ascension.

If we come into embodiment with karma and yet qualify God's energy and the returning energy of our karma with the flames of God, we have the opportunity to consume that karma by invocation to the sacred fire, by the momentum of light in our causal body, and manifest considerable attainment in the Christ consciousness by our thirty-third birthday. This is the year that we enter our divine mission. We go forth with our ministry able to deliver the teachings of the ascended masters to the world, to serve the souls involved in the karma of our mandala of life.

The ascended masters are concerned that the youth coming into the teachings at this time come in at an early age—in their teens, in their early twenties—so that they will have a decade to prepare for that cycle of life when the tremendous culmination of victory in the thirty-third year can anchor within them the full complement of the mastery of Jesus the Christ, Lord Maitreya, and other ascended masters, such as the guru of the chela or the chohan of the ray on which the chela serves. The three-year mission following this year then culminates in the fulfillment of the power of the three-times-twelve. Three times going forth in the cycles of the cosmic clock brings us to the age of thirty-six and the Buddhic initiation.

Applying This Teaching

Now when we train children in our schools from the age of

two and a half in this teaching, when they grow up with the training of Maria Montessori all the way through high school and then enter our institutions of learning such as Summit University, when they have this training combined with a liberal arts or a specialized education and all that must be mastered in the fields of human endeavor, they will be truly equipped to face the initiations of the ascended masters, to take dominion over the earth and focus the energy within their chakras to bring about the manifestations of alchemy that will be the mark of the sons and daughters of God in the Aquarian age.

As we are dealing with ourselves as we find ourselves at this time in space, as we come to grips with our karma and our karmic cycles, we can make the most of the clock whatever age we are, because the sacred fire, the transmuting flame, can consume the cause and core of all past misuses of the qualities of God on all lines of the clock.

Now as I was saying, if all goes according to clockwork and we earn the flame of our God-mastery, then we walk the earth as teachers, as unascended members of the Great White Brotherhood. If we fail our tests year by year, making more karma than we balance, accumulating not only the increment of the past which we vowed before the Lords of Karma to balance in this life but also the increment of karma from present infractions of the law, which pile up into another mountain of karma in this embodiment, when we finally surrender our life to the path that is set before us, the path of initiation, we will have to intensify our decree momentum, our action of invocation to the flame of life, and our momentum of service to the cause of the Great White Brotherhood in order to fulfill our divine plan in this life.

It is still a supreme opportunity! It is still a supreme moment of victory! And Saint Germain has promised us that if one applies this teaching and the law of the violet flame and all that the masters have given through their teachings, through the Keepers of the Flame Lessons, the soul can ascend either in this life or in the next life—the requirement being the balancing of 51 percent of all misuses of these twelve flames and the fulfillment of the divine plan.

The Clock of the Months of Your Birth Year

In the first part of our lecture, we discussed how the clock unfolds year by year from the day of birth. Now we will discuss how the clock unfolds month by month. The clock we will look at now is the clock of the months of the year. We will chart one year in your life—any year, this year. We will chart one year in the life of the Christed one.

Draw a circle, which will represent a year, for the chart of your birth cycle. Divide your circle into twelve months. The first month on the chart of your birth cycle is the month of your birth. The first day on the chart is your birthday. Place the day and the month of your birth on the 12 o'clock line. Your birth year always begins at the 12 o'clock line, which is governed by the hierarchy of Capricorn. On the 1 o'clock line, place the next calendar month, but the same date of your birth. Then simply continue around the clock, placing the succeeding months and your birth date on the remaining lines. For instance, if your birthday is July 4, put July 4 on the 12 o'clock line, August 4 on the 1 o'clock line, September 4 on the 2 o'clock line, and so on. This is your birth calendar, a chart of your birth year. This will tell you, month by month, how your initiations fall under the twelve hierarchies of the sun.

Wherever your birthday is, three months later to the day (e.g., October 4), on the 3 o'clock line, you will be initiated under the hierarchy of Aries. And for one month you will have the initiations of the Divine Ego versus the human ego, the opportunity to transmute the human ego and develop the Divine Ego, which is your own Real Self, the Christ Self as it represents the I AM Presence. This testing comes under the hierarchy of Aries, under Helios. And what greater ego do we have in our solar system than our own sun, the brightest spot we know? That which has the greatest exaltation, that is your own Christ Self.

Six months after your birthday to the day (e.g., January 4), you will have the testing of the hierarchy of Cancer, the testing of the Mother flame, the testing of your harmony; and you will have the testing of the flow of water in the emotions. Nine months after your birthday to the day (e.g., April 4), on the 9 o'clock line, you will have the test of the hierarchy of Libra—the test of the Holy Spirit, the test of reality, the opportunity to prove what is real and to transmute all kinds of karma of unreality that comes to you to be cycled into your flame for transmutation.

Is this clock accurate? It is so accurate, it is awesome! It would be frightening if we did not understand and love the law that governs a cosmos. It is so exact that if you actually know the hour of your birth, every month at this hour you will actually be able to observe the shifting of the cycle. The exactness of the flow of energy-spirals in the cosmos is a wonder. It's like the wonder of the human body and of cells and of the flow of life and the vastness of the design of the body temple we live in. But the wonder of wonders is to perceive how this cosmic clock works.

The Cycles of the Moon

During the month (approximately twenty-eight to thirty days of these initiations), day by day there is an accurate unfoldment of the initiations under the hierarchy of the sun. Also to be considered in that month of initiation are the cycles of the moon.[10] The moon is moving through the cycles of the twelve hierarchies even as you are moving through your karmic cycles.

The moon presents an additional testing. It is the testing of your soul. It is the testing of the personality. Therefore, while you are in the month of initiation under Aries, for example, and the moon is going through its twenty-eight-day cycle, you will have an opportunity under the hierarchy of Aries to prove your mastery over what we call *moon substance*. Moon substance is misqualified substance, energy that has been misqualified under the influence of the moon.

The moon governs the astral, or water body. In the perfection of cosmic astrology, the satellites of planets, the lunar bodies, are intended to be reflectors of the feelings (the pure feelings) of the lifewaves of the planet. They are like giant screens that reflect and amplify our feeling body. As soon as mankind begin to misqualify their feelings and to have layers in the astral belt (the subconscious of the planet)—layers of hatred, layers of mild dislike, and all of these distortions of the feelings of God—then the moon begins to amplify this energy. And therefore, there is no longer the pure reflection of the light of the sun from the moon; instead, the light of the moon is the reflection of man's misuses of solar energy. Well, this is what we have to contend with in our solar initiations.

As it passes through the house of Aries, the moon will amplify the substance of the ego, the conceit of the ego. When we have a full moon in Aries or any phase of the moon in Aries, you will notice—and I usually take note of these things when I go shopping or somewhere where there are a lot of people—people's interactions with one another are very much at an ego level. Everyone is putting forth an aspect of the ego and relating at the level of the ego.

Recently we had a Capricorn moon, and I noticed a very heavy weight upon the people of the substance of condemnation. And that condemnation, amplified by the power of the full moon, was sort of a bristling energy of people criticizing and picking each other apart and looking down on each other just for nothing—just for breathing the air or walking by in a dress that maybe someone didn't like. That energy saturates the astral plane. When you are aware of it, you instantaneously make a call: "In the name of the Christ, in the name of the I AM Presence, I call to mighty Astrea and to the Lords of the Violet Flame to consume the cause and core of all misuses of the hierarchy of Capricorn, of God-power, and of all moon substance that is a misqualification of that energy."

Anticipate Your Tests

This science of the cosmic clock, when we understand it, enables us to make very specific, precise, scientific calls. There is no point making a call for something that is not prominent or, as we say, "up for transmutation." There are certain cycles of energy that are there, energy that needs to be transmuted at a particular time because of the configurations not only of the sun and the moon, but of the planetary bodies—all of which have their influences of misqualified energy, not only because of the forcefield they occupy in time and space, but also because their lifewaves (those which have evolutions in either the etheric, the mental, the astral, or the physical plane) have polluted the sacred fire. We feel that flow of energy from bodies within our solar system and from bodies beyond.

So, going back to the birth cycle, during the third month of your calendar birth year, when you are undergoing the testings in the hierarchy of Aries, you will have to be aware of the cycling of the moon as a secondary testing. Now, if you know that that is your initiation, that Lord Maitreya, the Great Initiator, and your own guru are going to be allowing energy to come to you to see what you will choose (will you choose the Divine Self or will you choose the human self?), if you are aware of that just as you are aware of a stony path or a dangerous crossing, you anticipate and prepare for it. It's like being ready to catch a ball when it's pitched to you. The astrology lets us know specifically—it pinpoints in the cosmos—where the testing is so that we can put our attention upon it, so that we can prepare for it, so that we can invoke the violet flame to consume the cause and core even before the test comes.

In the days just before the turn of the cycle of the month, you begin to prepare for that testing. You anticipate it. You give your calls to Astrea, to the Elohim, to encircle the cause and core of all misuses of the sacred fire, of ego substance, and you have certain meditations which you give on the violet flame. And you clear the ground, which makes the testing that much simpler because you are there ready to seize that energy, ready to welcome the Lords of Karma and your Christ Self, who deposit that energy on your heart's altar for its transmutation.

Now let me go over this birth cycle once again. You put the month and the day of your birth on the 12 o'clock line, and you put the next month and the same date on the 1 o'clock line, and so on. And thus you go around the clock, following the months of your birth year. You walk, as it were, around this circle once every year. You walk through the twelve hierarchies, spending approximately twenty-eight to thirty days under each hierarchy.

Balancing Both Personal and Planetary Karma

You are carrying a flame from the point of origin, which is Capricorn. You carry the flame, and you carry it to each of the twelve houses of the hierarchies. You carry the torch of Capricorn and you deposit it in the house of Aquarius; you lay it upon the altar. You take up the torch of Aquarius, and you carry it to the house of Pisces, and so on. You are carrying the flame of each hierarchy as an emissary of that hierarchy during that particular month of your year. You are a Christed one—one anointed with the flame of Christ—accepting the challenge of going forth to consume the cause and core not only of personal karma, personal misuses of that hierarchy, but also of planetary karma.

The influence of your I AM Presence moves from the microcosm to the Macrocosm when you begin to manifest the God-mastery established through a daily ritual of decrees and invocations. Thereby you invoke enough fire so that when you give forth your calls in the morning, your energies are sufficient not only to transmute your own karma for that day under a house and sign, but also to make a considerable dent in planetary karma on that day.

The path of Christhood and of Buddhahood should be considered as the parallel lines of personal and planetary initiation, a movement to the right and to the left, to the right and to the left—the right signifying the balancing of personal karma through service, self-sacrifice, and surrender and the left signifying the taking-in of planetary karma and the balancing of this karma in the sacred fires of the heart. So right and left, right and left, we must walk these parallel lines of self-mastery.

We cannot ascend back to the heart of God unless we contribute to the balancing of planetary karma. Everyone who has shown us the path of mastery has demonstrated that it is necessary, at a particular point, to go from the personal to the planetary phase. The significance of Jesus dying for our sins on the cross was that he was transmuting planetary karma. And everyone who attains that mastery must go through the initiation of the crucifixion—not necessarily surrendering the physical body, but being willing to take into that body spirals of planetary karma to balance, or justify, them in the threefold flame within the heart.

Your Personal Cosmic Clock

Now this is your calendar year. In addition to your calendar year, your twelve months on the clock, you must always keep track of how old you are; and whatever your age is, find that age on the clock, by putting zero on the 12 o'clock line, age one on the 1 o'clock line, and continuing around the clock until you come to your age. If you are thirty-six years old, you are on the 12 o'clock line of Capricorn for the whole year. Or if you're forty-eight or if you're sixty or if you're twelve or seventy-two, you're on the line of the hierarchy of Capricorn for the year. Within that year you will walk through the twelve hierarchies month by month.

For example, if you are twenty-six, you are on the 2 o'clock line for your year; but on your birthday, you started the first month of your year under the hierarchy of Capricorn. Remember, all cycles begin in Capricorn. It's like two dials on the meter that measures electricity—all those little dials. Well, one dial is for the yearly cycle and the other dial is for the monthly cycle.

Now this is your personal cosmic clock. There are other phases to it; there are other ways to break it down. There are other things that you can learn about it, such as the trines and the polarity of the signs. For example, when you are having a test in Aries, you have to remember that there will be secondary tests of Libra because it is the polar opposite, the polarity of Aries on the clock; and you can be aware of this testing. Simultaneously, there's the testing in the fire trine because Aries is a fire sign. The triangle, the grand trine of testing in the month or year of Aries, comes on the 3, the 7, and the 11 o'clock lines, which are respectively the fire signs of Aries, Leo, and Sagittarius (fig. 13). And they form a threefold flame, as you can see by the colors on the chart. Aries is the blue fire sign, Leo is the pink fire sign, and Sagittarius is the yellow fire sign, according to the unfoldment of the threefold flame. So each of the four elements that come through the twelve hierarchies gives us an opportunity to balance that element in the threefold flame.

The water signs—Pisces, Cancer, and Scorpio—come together, and they are the 2-6-10 (fig. 15). The two is the yellow, the six is the blue, and the ten is the pink. This is your threefold flame for the mastery under the hierarchies of water. If you are in a Scorpio year, you will also have some testing of Pisces and Cancer substance, because that is the grand trine of your testing—to balance that triangle and that threefold flame.

You can study the cosmic clock that you have drawn; and through your own Christ Self, you can figure out all kinds of information about yourself, about your life. I encourage you to make a general outline of your life's history, of what you can remember of the most crucial events, positive as well as negative, and to put them on the clock. What happened to you when you were two or five or ten? Perhaps there was something very important that you remember; and if it wasn't so good, if it was a bad record, call for it to be consumed by the violet flame under the hierarchy in which it happened and under the ascended master serving on that line. If it was a great event, note it as a key cycle in your cosmic destiny. Make the most of it. Amplify its momentum by calling to the hierarchy of that sign to purify and perfect that happening in your life.

The Cycles of the Planet Earth

The earth is also undergoing initiations under the cycles of the cosmic clock. The birth-year cycle of the planet earth begins at the time of the change of signs from Sagittarius to Capricorn, which is winter solstice. Winter solstice (approximately December 22) is actually the new year which we celebrate on December 31. And that new year commences with the testing of the entire planetary body under Capricorn.

Now if you're watching the papers—as much as they tell us of what's happening—if you are watching the news media and simply being observant in the world, you will see how nations and their governments and their economies and every phase of human activity will come under the testing of the hierarchy of Capricorn in that month. And if you're working for world order and for God-government and you are interested in helping society and serving in your community, you will notice that leaders, important people, are burdened by the weight of light and darkness peculiar to Capricorn and that their functioning is hindered by the mass consciousness' misuse of the sacred fire in Capricorn. So when you are giving your decrees for world action from approximately December 22 to January 21, you should take care to make invocations for the transmutation of the world karma of criticism, condemnation, and judgment—misuses in the etheric body of the flame of God-power.

The season of winter corresponds to the etheric cycle—the fire element, the going-within to the fiery core. The season of spring and the testings on the planetary body that come with Aries symbolize the mind, the element of the mind, the new birth, the resurrection fires that come with Aries. With summer comes the testing of the emotions. Wars and demonstrations and sometimes rioting and all kinds of turbulence happen in the summer to the planet as a whole and to people as they find that their emotions are being tested. Even the heat we experience is a product of mankind's misqualified substance in the astral body of the planet; and in our coping with life in the summertime, we must take into account the ever-present tests of the emotional body. In the fall comes the earth cycle, the harvest, corresponding to the Holy Spirit and the recycling of energies; and we see the fruits of the Spirit made manifest in the fruits of the earth.

    [For further instruction on the cosmic clock, see the lecture
"Charting the Cycles of Your Family According to the Cosmic
Clock" by Elizabeth Clare Prophet in the tape album "Family
Designs for the Golden Age" (A7440) published by The Summit
Lighthouse.]

July 5, 1975
2:41-3:52 P.M. P D T
4:10-4:50 P.M. P D T

6.04 Round the Clock Protection

In the name of the beloved mighty victorious Presence of God, I AM in me, Holy Christ Selves of all mankind, all great powers and legions of light,

A (12) Beloved Great Divine Director and the seven archangels,
  (1) Beloved Saint Germain and the angelic hosts of light,
  (2) Beloved Jesus and the great hosts of ascended masters,
  (3) Beloved Helios and the Great Central Sun magnet,
  (4) Beloved God Obedience and the seven mighty Elohim,
  (5) Beloved El Morya and the legions of Mercury,
  (6) Beloved Serapis Bey and the great seraphim and cherubim,
  (7) Beloved Goddess of Liberty and the Lords of Karma,
  (8) Beloved Lord Lanto and the Lords of Wisdom,
  (9) Beloved mighty Victory and the Lords of Individuality,
  (10) Beloved mighty Cyclopea and the Lords of Form,
  (11) Beloved Lord Maitreya and the Lords of Mind,

Beloved Lanello, the entire Spirit of the Great White Brotherhood and the World Mother, I decree:

Seize, bind, and lock! Seize, bind, and lock! Seize, bind, and lock!

B (12) all criticism, condemnation, and judgment,
      and all black magic
  (1) all hatred and mild dislike and all witchcraft
  (2) all doubt, fear, human questioning, and records of death
  (3) all conceit, deceit, arrogance, and ego
  (4) all disobedience, stubbornness, and defiance of the law
  (5) all envy, jealousy, and ignorance of the law
  (6) all indecision, self-pity, and self-justification
  (7) all ingratitude, thoughtlessness, and spiritual blindness
  (8) all injustice, frustration, and anxiety
  (9) all dishonesty, intrigue, and treachery
  (10) all selfishness, self-love, and idolatry
  (11) all resentment, revenge, and retaliation

and all that is not of the light into mighty Astrea's cosmic circle and sword of blue flame of a thousand suns, and lock your cosmic circles and swords of blue flame of thousands of suns from the Great Central Sun and blaze megatons of cosmic light, blue-lightning rays, and violet fire in, through, and around all that opposes or attempts to interfere with the fulfillment of

C (12) my God-power and my divine plan fulfilled in all cycles
  (1) my God-love and my divine plan fulfilled in all cycles
  (2) my God-mastery and my divine plan fulfilled in all cycles
  (3) my God-control and my divine plan fulfilled in all cycles
  (4) my God-obedience and my divine plan fulfilled
         in all cycles
  (5) my God-wisdom and my divine plan fulfilled in all cycles
  (6) my God-harmony and supply and my divine plan fulfilled
         in all cycles
  (7) my God-gratitude and my divine plan fulfilled in all cycles
  (8) my God-justice and my divine plan fulfilled in all cycles
  (9) my God-reality and my divine plan fulfilled in all cycles
  (10) my God-vision and my divine plan fulfilled in all cycles
  (11) my God-victory and my divine plan fulfilled in all cycles

and my victory in the light this day and forever.

    And in full faith I consciously accept this manifest, manifest, manifest (3x) right here and now with full power, eternally sustained, all-powerfully active, ever expanding, and world enfolding until all are wholly ascended in the light and free! Beloved I AM, beloved I AM, beloved I AM!

Note: The decree may be given one of four ways: (1) Following the preamble, give sections A, B, and C straight through, ending with the closing; (2) give the decree twelve times, using one insert each time from sections A, B, and C, beginning with number 12; (3) give the trines on lines 12, 4, 8; 1, 5, 9; 2, 6, 10; 3, 7, 11, in sections A, B, and C; or (4) give the crosses on lines 12, 3, 6, 9; 1, 4, 7, 10; 2, 5, 8, 11, in sections A, B, and C.

The Brotherhood of Mount Shasta is a part of the Great White Brotherhood. Its members hail from an ancient hierarchy of light-bearers who were there when Mu went down. They are ascended and unascended masters who keep the flame of purity in the mountain and receive chelas who meet the measure of their rod. They are devotees of Buddha and his light. They are disciplined priests and priestesses who tended the flame of the Mother on the altars of Mu before she sank. They are Zoroastrians and Confucians, Taoists and Zen monks. They chant the chant of the AUM and are well acquainted with the mystery of the Christos in the I AM THAT I AM.

The Master of the Brotherhood of Shasta will speak through the messenger and for the first time reveal his name to a public audience. Since names are keys to energy flow, the revealing of a master's name is a gift to be treasured by all chelas of the ascended masters.

16

I AM RA MU

A Dictation by the Master of the Mountain

I AM the voice of the mountain. I come to bear tidings of the Brotherhood of Mount Shasta unto all who have been called and all who have answered the call at inner levels and in outer manifestation. I come forth from the heart of the mountain and from the heart of your own I AM Presence to welcome you into the fiery core of purity, to welcome you into the fraternity of souls of light-bearers.

Hail, children of Mu! Hail, children of the Motherland! You have come home to our abode, and here we have kept the flame for many thousands of years. Here we have coalesced fiery energies of consecration from the altars of Mu and placed them upon the altar of the mountain.

A Chalice for the Ray of the Motherland

I AM Ra Mu. That is my name. I release it unto you that you might give the chant that is sung by devotees of our holy order, that you might intone the name that God has given unto my own I AM name, a name that is a chalice for the ray of the Motherland to be drawn forth now from the heart of a mountain into the hearts of devotees assembled in the physical octave. And therefore those at etheric levels who are members of our order who have intoned that holy sound rejoice and look forward to the intoning of that sound with you that day—that day that has come now as the day of rejoicing here at the foot of our holy mountain.

As you have listened unto the music and the singing and the voices, know that choirs of beings, devotees of ancient Lemuria, ascended masters and their chelas who have gathered in the retreat of Mount Shasta, were anchoring through that sound—by the action of the light and sound ray—into this octave choruses of the ancient music of the Motherland that you might be quickened in the intonation of the AUM, into the divine memory of your origin and your life on Mu and how you served the Ancient of Days and how you served the holy Kumaras and Lady Master Venus.

A Chant of Love

Now then, as I have given to you my name, will you not use it as a chant of love whereby the light of Mu and of Shasta and of the momentum of devotees of the ages can be anchored in a moment in your heart for service? And my own causal body I place upon the altar of the Great White Brotherhood, that it might be used as a magnet to draw the souls who serve together in the mandala of the Motherland once again to that point of intimate communion in the Holy Spirit so that that light can stream forth in all of its intensity, in all of its love, to capture souls—young souls on Terra, older souls and embodied angels, elemental life—to capture them all in the central flame of the Mother which we enshrine. [Audience joins the master in chanting "Ra Mu" three times.]

Devotion to the One Fire of Shasta

The sounding of the word rolls up the mountain, and the sounding of the word by the devotees of the mountain resounds and flows down the mountain. And the meeting of the waves of light is the rejoicing of light and of the waves of Alpha and Omega as devotees ascended and unascended, devotees of inner planes and outer consciousness, merge in the devotion of the one fire of Shasta. Wherever you are, wherever you make your abode and your altar, know that there when you sound the name that I bear, the light will flow from Shasta, from my causal body to your own fiery heart. And thus the oneness of cycles and the ritual of that oneness is commenced this day.

The Mystery School

I pay tribute to all who have served the light, and I acknowledge many friends of light and of the mountain who have been a part of the inner experience of the mystery school that is conducted here in our retreat. Coming in the physical to this conference, making the pilgrimage to the physical focus, will also serve to anchor in your outer mind those experiences which you have had here, the instruction, and also that which has been given in the Grand Teton Retreat.

Evolutions Inhabiting Various Planes in Terra

Now I would speak to you of other evolutions and of other lifewaves coming nigh Terra and the signal of those lifewaves as the signs written in the heavens, written in the stars, and written in the clouds. I would speak to you of great civilizations of light-bearers, of nuclei of souls who inhabit various planes of consciousness in Terra, of the beings who inhabit the earth itself—a masterful race—those who also descended from Lemuria. And the interconnection of these lifewaves to our retreat is secure.

Mankind do not realize how Terra is honeycombed with retreats and lifewaves and evolutions. You are on the surface. Many are within. Many enjoy the light of the sun of the fiery core even as you enjoy the light of Helios and Vesta. The Brotherhood of Mount Shasta seeks the integration by the action of the eighth ray of all hearts who are afire with the love of bringing earth into that point of initiation of the resurrection and the ascension.

Adjustment of Atomic Frequencies

There are souls serving diligently in many planes of consciousness having the celestial body, the etheric body, as you have the terrestrial or earthly body. Simply by dialing a frequency of consciousness, as many evolutions in this and other solar systems are able to do, you could advance to their plane of awareness. You could pass through the mountain by the adjustment of the dial of frequency and even enter, retaining physical consciousness, our retreat.

And yet this knowledge has not been vouchsafed to the

majority of those living on the surface of Terra; for they have not shown the mastery of the God-control, the God-harmony, of the fiery core. For once that fiery core is released for the adjustment of atomic frequencies, tremendous power comes into integration in the four lower bodies. And the awareness of God-reality in the face of all that assails that power must be the mastery of the chela on the Path.

Love, the First Requirement of the Aquarian Age

On the path then to our retreat, if you would come retaining physical awareness, there are yet hurdles to be passed. Others have passed them; others are studying. You may be counted among them. You may become initiates of our retreat, but there are requirements. And the first of these is love. Love must sound the new tone of the Aquarian age. Love is a word that is used. Let it now be a vibration that is pure. Let it be purified in the heart chakra! I send forth the light of my heart! I challenge all misuses of the fire of love! I say, let those energies now cycle in for qualification by the sacred fire!

We will not allow the desecration of our holy mountain. We will not allow the impurity of that vibration of the misuse of love which manifests as rebellion against the wisdom teachings of the ages, against the Lord God and the Logos, against the sacred fire. We will not allow those enemies of the Real Self to camp upon the holy mountain of God.

A Volcano of Golden Liquid Fire

Therefore, from the summit of Shasta there rolls now a sacred energy rolling down the mountain as golden liquid fire. So it purifies! So it inundates! So it carries the flame of devotees! And if you look in akasha, you will behold in former times the record of volcanic eruption when that was a physical manifestation; and you will see the counterpart as the action of the overflow of the golden honey, the elixir from Venus that comes forth from the mountain of the Mother, tribute unto Mater. You will see how the etheric level of that overflow is a penetration of fire, a cleansing and an anchoring.

So let it be this day from etheric levels that energy goes forth!

It is the energy of victory—mightier than an avalanche of snow and ice. So the golden oil rolls with a power that will not be stayed. It is a sacred fire purifying the holy mountain, challenging those who misuse the energies of our abode.

An Accounting before the Hierarchy of Shasta

Henceforth, then, all who walk upon the mountain shall give accounting and shall be called by the Lords of Karma for their abuse of that sacred energy. And that judgment will not be turned back, and there shall be a quickening of that victorious light contacting the heart. And those who resist it, those who blaspheme it, those who turn against the messengers of the Brotherhood—these will have their time, their place to give an accounting before the hierarchy of Shasta.

We seal Shasta in Mother light. We seal this day physical atoms, atoms at every plane. So let it be the focal point, then, for the raising of the culture of Lemuria even as that focal point is the place of the heart of the devotee.

Shasta, Crown Chakra of Lemuria

O Shasta, crown chakra of Lemuria, of Lemurians focusing the light of God-consciousness, now release thy flame of golden light! Now release that energy! Now let mankind know that the one true God is able to raise up a mighty people, a mighty continent, a mighty following unto the glory of the I AM THAT I AM. And this precipitation of the golden elixir shall be a monument to the Great Divine Director. And it shall be for the seventh root race, for the incoming souls, a focal point of mastery and of light and of homecoming and of the welcome of the Mother flame.

Crystal clarity of the mountain, now let the fire ascend! Now let the smoke be the vapor of the Holy Spirit! Now let it be the rising of the incense from the altars of the devotees of fire! Now let that incense be pleasing unto the Lord, a celebration of the communion of hearts "as above, so below." Now let it be that all evolutions and lifewaves have the contact from the physical unto the etheric, unto the ascended-master octaves, of a new momentum, a new vibration which your coming has made possible in the physical octave.

Destiny at the Summit of Shasta

Hail, children of Lemuria! Hail, children of the Mother! Hasten to greet the sunlight of the dawn! Hasten to seize the energy of the sun! Then run with the sun! Then run with the wind! Then run to greet your cosmic destiny at the summit of Shasta!

I am standing at the summit—my heart, my head, and my hand forming the trinity of light. I stand to receive you. Come! Come into the heart of the holy of holies. And the way is through your I AM Presence; the way is through the open door of the Real Self. So find reality and find me standing in the snowy fires of the Mother light.

I AM Ra Mu.

[The audience joins the master as he chants his name.]

July 5, 1975
5:10-5:28 P.M. P D T

The Old Man of the Hills, a great patriot of light who works with Godfre and Saint Germain to expand the fires of freedom from the heart of the mountain to the hearts of mankind, will also address the audience.

17

FIERY VORTICES OF CONSCIOUSNESS BECOMING GOD

A Dictation by the Old Man of the Hills

In Search of a Chela

And I AM the Old Man of the Hills. You have not known my flame, and yet you have known my name. Orion I am called, and you have sung to the aureole of the dawn. You have called me Old Man, and I have laughed with a twinkle in my eye; for if you could see me, you would wonder whether or not I am an old man, a young man, or perhaps something in between. I come scaling the summits of life. And I work with elemental life and with God Tabor, spanning the mountain ranges of North America. I am in search of a chela, even as I was once in search of a guru, even as I met my master in the mountain.

I am a devotee of freedom, and I am proud to be called a patriot of life! For I release the fervor of my heart, and that fervor is a sphere of pink light around every star aborning—the star of your soul, the stars of the flag that blows in the wind, the stars of the nations, the stars of planetary bodies. And I walk with Godfre; I walk with Saint Germain, ever kindling, with the fervor of my heart, the precious concepts of freedom which they hold for mankind. And as I walk, many times in silence, meditating upon the words of God Obedience and of the master of freedom's flame, I hear them also in search of a chela—not one, but many.

And as the fires of the Almighty flash to these masters concepts of freedom, plans for the golden age, projects for America, for Canada, for Central America, for South America, for the entire hemisphere—as this hemisphere is being prepared to play host to the evolutions of the seventh root race, my prayer unto the Cosmic Virgin is spoken: O Mother of the World, send thy sons, send thy daughters! Send them unto these selfless ones, these masters who require a hearth, a home, a place to come to be free, to talk with chelas, to present their plans, a heart that can be trusted, a heart that will not fail for fear, for hypocrisy, for cowardice.

The Summoning for Service

Patriots, I summon you in the service of the light! Now let us see what that fire of love, purified from the heart of Shasta, can do within your hearts as you bring the votive light to Saint Germain, to Morya, to Godfre, with a vote of confidence, saying unto these avatars of the age: "I love thee, O my Lord! I serve thee, O my Lord! I would walk and talk with thee! I will not leave thee, O my Lord! I will not leave thee until the victory of freedom to every man, woman, and child upon this planetary home!"

Let this be the fulfillment of your AUM! Let this be your promise! Let this be your caress of the wind and of the stars and of the mountains! Let this be the flowing light from your robe as you scale the heights of God consciousness!

Preview of the Ascension

When I was yet unascended and in contemplation of the vast Sierras, as I gazed upon the mountains, I was inspired with the exaltation of the soul. And one night as I lay in camp alone, hearing the music of the stars, my soul took flight from my form and I consciously left my body temple for the first time. Lying there in the mountains looking unto the stars, the gaze of my eyes contacting whirling fiery centers transported my soul unto the causal body of ascended beings and my own I AM Presence, and I had a preview of the soul's flight unto the ascension.

And how I rejoiced to know that which God holds in store for every living soul! How I rejoiced in that moment, transcending planes of consciousness, to see the servants of God as angels and seraphim and sylphs and masterful beings! And I saw how a cosmos is a succession, one by one, of body temples, of fiery vortices of consciousness becoming God, of God becoming self-hood in manifestation through the cycling of the stars and fiery bodies.

The Descent of the Soul

And my own guru upon that holy night came with a visitation of the birth of the Manchild; and I saw the Christ being born, and I saw the record of the descent of the soul of Jesus into that form. Even as I had risen from my body temple to experience planes of causal bodies, so I saw how the soul of the avatar of the age had descended from his own starry body into form. And so I saw the cycles of life ascending and descending, descending and ascending, and souls upon the ladder reaching for the stars.

The Initiation of the Stars

Cosmic purpose was born! And I thought: "I must take the record! I must take it to all those below who have not seen the vision of initiation and of freedom." And the master said to me: "My son, when they are ready, they will have the same initiation that you have been given. And until that hour and that moment, let your communication be with the fiery core of self and let it be the affirmation of reality. Let it be the tutoring in the outer of souls—not of the ultimate, but of the next step on the Path.

"Do not burden souls on Terra with the knowledge of the steps high upon the mountain where the rocky crevices are formidable indeed. They cannot equate with higher initiation. They are concerned with the next step; and that step may very well be how to pay the light bill, and how to buy the groceries, and how to comfort the sick child, and how to earn a living, and how to bake the bread. These are initiations that pave the way for the mystical union of the body of God on earth and the body of God in heaven."

And so with these words and more of a teaching so profound and so joyous that I leave you to the communion of your own Master of Life to receive it, I descended once again to my body temple high in the Sierras, and I found myself once again gazing upon the stars in the firmament of God's being. And I rubbed my eyes and I said, "Was it a dream? Was it a dream?" And I knew in my soul that I had contacted a vastness and a plane of mind where the few are privileged to be.

God Is All-in-All

And when morning came and the sun and the sound of the birds, I remembered the sound of the stars, and I saw even the birds as emissaries of hierarchy speaking to ears that will not listen to the inner sound, singing of a lost chord, singing of hierarchy! And I looked at the birds and all of the kinds of birds and I said: "This is hierarchy. This is the physical manifestation of all the beings who inhabit the spheres." And as I thought upon nature and the trees and the mountains and the rock and particles of being, I knew profoundly: God is All-in-all. God is All-in-all! Simple words, I know; but when experienced, profound beyond the word. And what can you say to a friend along life's way when you have had the initiation of the stars? Better keep the silence and say, "God is All-in-all!"

A Focus of Starlight: Orion's Retreat Opened

I maintain a focus of starlight, of the God Star Sirius in the mountains of North America. And now by permission from the Lords of Karma, I am able to welcome you to my abode. And this is a day for me—the opening of my house of light to chelas who will call to be taken to this retreat. And when you come, prepare to be received by angels of freedom, angels who are devotees of Saint Germain! And in my house, my house of light, you will find mementos of patriots of freedom who in every nation have won for the cause of the Great White Brotherhood some noble gain for the Aquarian cycle, for the master of freedom, and for the soul of humanity.

Training in the Retreat: Mastery of the Soul Chakra

When you come, I will teach you in the way of the mastery of the soul chakra; for my dedication is to all who walk with Godfre and Saint Germain. I serve them in the heart of the mountain. And so I say, come if you will! Classes are beginning, and the first round of souls is being taken for a special training, mine to impart by the grace of God. And you can also expect training in mountain climbing and in survival—survival of the soul and the four lower bodies, survival in transition, survival when energies mount from Sirius, when they intensify.

And when the step-up of frequency comes and you are required to be in the light, you will have the knowledge of turning the dial of frequency and blending with the new order of the ages. And in that moment, souls who have the flame and the fire and the movement and the mastery of the soul will find themselves elevated to a new consciousness, a new plane where priests and priestesses of Lemuria and sons and daughters of Shasta are gathered, holding the laurel of the Lord of the World.

Circle of the AUM: Laurel Wreath of the Buddha

And this laurel wreath which they have woven of sacred energies of the chakras is their floral offering unto Buddha! And they hold this laurel wreath of the victor garlanded also with the roses of the Mother ray and the daisies of the field and the lilies of the valley and the poppies blue and the violets. They hold it in a giant circle! And I just had to tell you about this laurel wreath, because at each conference when I see the devotees forming the hallowed circle of the AUM at the conclusion of the class, I see the merging of the devotees of the order, the Holy Order of Mount Shasta, also forming the circle and lowering the ring of light of the laurel wreath of the Buddha unto those who make that circle.

And so then, when you form it at the conclusion of Shasta 1975, know as you hold the hand of one another that you hold the hand of God and of devotees in the mountain and that that laurel wreath is shared among you and that it is yours to place in honor and in tribute upon the head, the crown chakra, of the Lord of the World. This is your gift, your spiral of energy of all of your devotion and your attention and your singing and your decreeing of a class. The laurel wreath of the one who took the flame of Sanat Kumara to keep it again until children of the Mother should respond and come forth to be keepers of the flame!

Anchoring of the Master's Flame in a Physical Body

Now rejoice! For I am close at hand; and I take my walking

stick and I hike into the mountains, and I anchor my flame in a physical, tangible body. And by and by, one of these days when you are hiking in the mountains, you may see afar off a form of one—perhaps an old man, perhaps a young man, perhaps the flame of Orion! From my heart to your heart the flame of the mountain glows. We are one in the purity of the love of Shasta!

July 5, 1975
5:29-5:49 P.M. P D T

18

WHEREVER YOU ARE IS INFINITY
The Co-Measurement of a Cosmos
Slides and Meditations
with the Microcosm and the Macrocosm

A Lecture by Elizabeth Clare Prophet

Wherever you are is infinity. What an exciting concept! Let us draw consciousness into the fiery core of the heart and let us know infinity. Let us know it as the threefold flame. Let us know that we need not wait to pass from time and space to experience the Infinite One. Let us define that as the lie of procrastination, putting off God, putting off cosmic consciousness. Why can't we have it here and now? We can. We have only to claim it.

I AM WHO I AM

Infinity is the converging of Alpha and Omega within the heart; it is the cosmic cross of white fire; it is the sum potential of you in the center of the AUM. Morya has said, "Cosmic consciousness is the realization of self as the galaxy of light which declares from the very center of the atom of being, 'I AM WHO I AM.'" Let us declare it together: I AM WHO I AM! I AM WHO I AM! I AM WHO I AM!

Forevermore down the corridors of eternity the formula of be-ness echoes as the mathematics of the spoken Word: I AM WHO I AM. This, the very first equation of being and consciousness, is the foundation of your alchemical experiment that leads to the fullness of that life which is God.

I say, then, come with me. Expand the field of the mind. Tread the cosmic highways which I have trod which lead to the throne of Almighty God. If you are to become a messenger of the gods, you must get out of the finite consciousness and the confines of the mortal dilemma. You must be able to see beyond the finite self, beyond your lilliputian world, and by commeasurement perceive the vastness of the plan—the vastness of God's being which you can make your own. . . .

Let us declare it again: I AM WHO I AM! I AM WHO I AM! I AM WHO I AM! I AM WHO I AM!

In order for mankind to break the cycles of a dead and dying world, in order for mankind to refrain from identifying with the spirals of disintegration and to ride instead the spirals of integration that lead to the source of life, they must be given a new perspective of life. This comes through the conceptualization of commeasurement whereby the measure of a man is measured against the measure of a cosmos.[1]

I AM Everywhere in the Consciousness of God

Wherever you are is infinity! One of the first statements of the newly ascended being, the one newly born to absolute God-freedom, is "I AM everywhere in the consciousness of God." By the flow of the ascension spiral, we can be everywhere in the consciousness of God.

The cycles of yin and yang are the cycles of the concentration and diffusion of light. Consciousness in meditation, like the swing of a pendulum, is also like the cycles of life, the undulations of going within and coming out from the fiery center. When we declare, "I AM WHO I AM," in the fiery core of the heart there is a surging of intense light from the I AM Presence in concentration. When you say, "I AM everywhere in the consciousness of God," there is the bursting of the atom, and you feel all these particles of light going out and bursting and filling a cosmos. And because the burst is from your heart, because your electronic blueprint, the frequency of your I AM Presence, is impressed upon each fragment, you can say truly, "I AM everywhere in the consciousness of God."

The concept of concentration and diffusion we understand in terms of time and space. And in being everywhere, we think of the vastness of cosmos and commingling with it. We must remember the definition of infinity: the allness of the One in the oneness of the All. Can we define a cosmos without time and space, without the coordinates of the stars and the atoms? Can we imagine a cosmos that has dimension, that has commeasurement, yet has not time and space? It is difficult. But we understand infinity as being altogether apart from our finite understanding of movement and of being.

Let us try this experiment of going within the heart and then expanding out just to establish movement and flow, to get rid of the calcification of sitting in this body. Let's get the concept of the soul leaping into the stars, of being free to come and go. It is something that the masters teach in the Keepers of the Flame Lessons, an exercise which they give for soul travel.

Morya says the sign of the advancing chela is mobility—to be where the I AM WHO I AM is in time and space, at the right time and in the right place. Mobility means you are defining energy in cycles of awareness of God and you find yourself in the place where God desires to release the greatest concentration of light at a particular point. Mobility means moving for the masters, moving in service, being able to respond to the Holy Spirit, the wind that "bloweth where it listeth."[2] So is the coming of the Christed ones. This movement begins with elasticity of consciousness.

The Fiery Core of the Heart

Now let us see how concentrated we can become. Let us visualize the fiery core of the heart the size of a pea; let it be now an intense white-fire center. And let us feel all energy of being going to that center as we declare, "I AM WHO I AM." Remember, it is your I AM Presence uttering the fiat concerning this sphere of fire, declaring "I AM WHO I AM," affirming being here below through you. Together: I AM WHO I AM! I AM WHO I AM! I AM WHO I AM!

Intensify your meditation now in that fiery sun. Enter there. Stand in the fiery sun the size of a pea within your heart. Stand within it now. Feel the intensity of the sun. In the center of this blazing sun, let us give the chant of the AUM.

Now meditate upon identity as a sphere. This is the only way you will be able to penetrate all of cosmos and all of time and space. You are a sphere. Standing in this fiery core, know that you can, as energy, as light, go out in all directions if you choose, when you decide. You can burst forth; and with God-control and even measure, you can expand in all directions and fill all time and space with this energy. Now for the concentrated fire again, let us give "I AM WHO I AM." I AM WHO I AM! I AM WHO I AM! I AM WHO I AM!

Penetrating All Time and Space

When I say "Now," you will feel the bursting of the pea and energy going in all directions and yourself the energy, the identity of the energy. You'll feel yourself penetrating all time and space. After I say the "Now," let us declare, "I AM everywhere in the consciousness of God." And as you declare that, you will feel that spherical flow outward in all directions. Now let us be silent in concentration in the heart.

Now! I AM everywhere in the consciousness of God! I AM everywhere in the consciousness of God! I AM everywhere in the consciousness of God! I AM everywhere in the consciousness of God! I AM everywhere in the consciousness of God! I AM everywhere in the consciousness of God! I AM everywhere in the consciousness of God!

Now continue to expand out through the stars, through the Milky Way, through the galaxies. Again. I AM everywhere in the consciousness of God! I AM everywhere in the consciousness of God! I AM everywhere in the consciousness of God! Now we will seal this sphere of cosmic consciousness with the intoning of the AUM. This will set the matrix of your everywhereness. AUM! [Chanted]

When I say "Now," you will take this entire awareness of self as cosmos and draw it instantaneously back to the fiery core of the heart. And all galaxies and stars and energies and cosmic beings will be contained at that point of infinity in the fiery core of the heart. And we will declare after I say "Now," "I AM WHO I AM." Now continue to feel yourself commingling with the starry bodies, passing through them. See the suns, the planets, comets, spirals of light. Feel the tremendous peace and the stillness of this

everywhereness. This is the vibration of the Mother and the Holy
Spirit.

Now! I AM WHO I AM! I AM WHO I AM! I AM WHO
I AM! During this meditation, feel free to continue the concentration in the heart; and when you feel the pressure and the
natural release, feel yourself leap into the cosmos again and repeat
the ritual which we have enacted.

I AM beholding
    Nature where'er I look.
The Tree of Life I shook—
    And tumbling down,
Visions of Source reveal
    Sunflowers God's radiance steal.
Shells of restless tides reveal
    The golden ratio
In universes twinkling from afar.

Life in me beats freely.
    I see a tree or man
Walking into Reality
    As robin's egg in spring,
Holding Cosmos all inside,
    Does bring to mind a sun.
The warmth of love from Above
    Makes me sing of Source
Far greater than I understand.

And covering land, I see
    A million snowflakes blending bland
Into a million faces,
    Daisies in the field of earth
Gazing spherelike.
    A billion grains of sand, of worth
Do lead me to a sunbeam,
    Raylike with its Light,
A Golden Thread—

From heart to mountain height
    Does lead me to my Home delight
Where each ray ne'er alone
    Does find aright
The palm of God, our goal—
    Perfection bright,
Dazzling white!
    Serenity—
The balm of Victory! [3]

July 5, 1975
9:09-9:35 P.M. PDT

Alpha is the personification of the God flame as Father in the core of consciousness we call life. Alpha is the highest manifestation of God in the Great Central Sun. He is also the most humble. His complement is Omega, the personification of the God flame as Mother. Together they focus the beginning and the ending of all cycles of life. Welcome, Alpha and Omega!

19

THE JUDGMENT:
THE SEALING OF THE LIFEWAVES
THROUGHOUT THE GALAXY

A Dictation by Alpha

Hail, sons and daughters of flame aborning in the cosmos of the Mother! I AM come to claim my own. I AM come to draw the flock into the heart of love. I come to seal the eye and to set the mark of victory upon my own for the day, the everlasting day, when the fire shall stream forth and the separation shall occur and the rays of God shall be drawn back to the heart of the Great Central Sun! I come to seal lifewaves not alone in this solar system, but throughout the galaxy; for the initiation of light draweth nigh!

To Renew the Ancient Vow

Fear not! I AM with thee! I AM thy Father-Mother God. I AM in the center of a soul and I AM in the seed of the whole of creation. I come to renew the ancient vow. I come that you might know that God is, that God cares, that God is here where you are, and that you can always be where I AM. I AM the answer to a prayer before you have called. I AM aware of all aspects of life. I know the light that flows. I know the darkness that must be consumed ere you can come into the throne of Alpha-Omega. I know what is required of thee, line upon line.

And inasmuch as I AM that awareness, will you not call to me more often for the revelation of that plan of life and of the scheduling of initiation and of the exercise of light within the chakras? I yearn to hear the voice of my children even as my children yearn for the flow of our love. Know then that Alpha is not as far as you think—and yet far, far, far removed from mortal consciousness, from confinement.

I AM Where You Know the Law

I AM where you know the law. I AM where you discover the fire that glows. I AM beyond all reaches of consciousness, yet in the heart of every consciousness. The magnet of our love is sufficient to polarize you now, to seal you in that original vow—not the vow of this lifetime or many lifetimes, but the vow you made in the far distant beyond in the cycles beyond the stars when you, a soul, born, caressed in our arms, made preparation to go forth.

The Cradle of Our Love

Do you remember the cradle of our love? And do you remember the day when you chose to go forth and to descend in form? We remember well—and the tear in the eye of the Father-Mother, knowing all that the soul would traverse, yet the soul rejoicing, not knowing the travail of separation, but only the joy of going forth on a mission of discovery, of experiment, of probing the all of God. For the soul knew not that it had already the all of God, but determined to go forth to rediscover that self of the I AM THAT I AM.

The Grand Return

Now the tear is in the eye of the soul as the soul contemplates how many cycles have turned since the fond embrace and the fond good-bye. And the time has come for the return! The fire burns on the hearth of Home. Brothers and sisters are waiting. Angels tarry at the gate, looking longingly into the heavens and into the planes of Mater, searching for prodigal son and daughter, searching to see the soul appearing as a fiery glow in the distant scene—angels waiting to announce to Father and to Mother the homecoming of a soul, of souls, of lifewaves, of planetary evolutions and solar systems. And so in the fiery core of being, we anticipate the wholeness of love when all will be found in the oneness of unity, when all will know that the rays of our oneness have fashioned the myriad paths back to the central sun.

How could we leave any soul bereft? And therefore many paths have been woven and the golden thread has gone from our altar. And in all directions the golden thread goes forth as a lifeline unto souls reaching up, reaching for the grand return, reaching for the grand cosmic moment of the swell, the swell of life and then of the fire infolding in the center. And by the impetus of the fiery vortex, souls moving in the current seize the thread—at last the thread! They have the thread—they are coming!

The Moment of the Investiture

We see them now following the thread, the golden thread of the law—the law of the Mother, the law of the anointed ones whom we have sent forth again and again in all systems of worlds. We have sent forth our chosen ones to signal the hour and the law and the love and to remind the souls that God above awaits the return and the supreme moment of the investiture when the soul is vested with the immortal flame sealed in that fiery sphere of the I AM THAT I AM. Then we are satisfied. Then we take our rest, knowing that the soul shall be immortally blessed, sealed in fire, nevermore to roam into the planes of experimentation leading unto temptation, leading unto experimentation and the fire that burns and the fire that can singe the souls and the wings of the soul.

A Ray of Light to Every Threefold Flame

We are Alpha and Omega! Now the circumference of our embrace includes all who have sealed the light of the Father-Mother God. And now those who are sealed by our hand in this hour, in this moment, shall know no fear, no loss when there comes the mark of the beast, the mark of the dragon and the Fallen One;[1] for these are sealed and they are marked for immortality. [Silence] From the chakras of my hands an infinite flow— threads of light contacting all of life! I send a ray to every threefold flame in the all of creation that you might experience here, being in the center, the very hub of a cosmos where all are one in the flow of love.

The Second Death of the Fallen One

I come to announce the second death of the Fallen One and the judgment of that one known as Lucifer.[2] And I impress upon all Mater the record of the judgment of the one who has rebelled against the law of the fiery core of life.[3]

Let it be known by proclamation of Alpha and Omega sent and signified by our hand, delivered unto all the nations and the starry bodies and the lifewaves, that the Fallen One, as identity, as energy, as consciousness, has passed through the fires of Alpha and Omega, whose flaming reality consumes all that is in rebellion against the one Source, Almighty God. And many who followed the Fallen One have also passed through the judgment hall of the God Star Sirius. And there are others whose time has not yet come for whom the judgment has not been sounded.

Seeds of Rebellion: The Challenge of the Hour

Now let all evolutions and lifewaves know: The challenge of the hour is the consuming by the sacred fire of the cause, effect, record, and memory of all that has been impressed upon the body of the Mother—that body the entire cosmos—by the fallen ones. Now let us behold how the Fallen One has left seeds of rebellion even in the four lower bodies of the children of God. And so the Evil One came and sowed the tares among the wheat.[4]

Now let the sons of light go forth! Let them go into the fields white with the harvest. Let them, as the reapers with the angelic hosts, separate the tares from the wheat. And let it be done by the fiat of Alpha and Omega! Let it be done by the action of the flow of sacred fire from the I AM Presence of each one!

Release of the Light of the Fiery Core

More dangerous even than the Fallen One are the seeds of rebellion that remain to be consumed, for the seed contains within itself the pattern of the whole. And therefore I release the light of the fiery core of the flow of our oneness for the canceling-out of the seed of the Fallen One. I release this energy to the level of the etheric plane, the plane of fire. Farther it cannot go without the assent of your free will and your invocation, for the sacred fire will burn and consume the wheat with the tares unless it first be assimilated in the consciousness of the light-bearers.

Withdraw All Consent of the Carnal Mind

Let the sacred fire, then, in the increment that can be borne by each one, be sealed in the third eye and the crown and in the heart as a trinity of action that can be called forth and released in the plane of the mind and the mental belt of a cosmos. It is the mind of Christ that the fallen ones have determined to seize, to misuse. They have no power from Alpha and Omega; yet the fiery core of life within the children of the sun has been used to affirm that power, to acquiesce to it and to reinforce it.

I say then, withdraw by the authority of your free will all affirmation, all consent that you have given unto the fallen ones, unto their rebellion, unto the seed, and unto the carnal mind of your own creation. Only thus will the mental belt be cleansed of the remnant of the Fallen One.

Challenge the Dweller on the Threshold of Your Own Cosmos

Now let the beast that occupies the bottomless pit of the subconscious and the desire body be exposed also! And let it be seen that this creation instigated by the fallen ones has also received the seal of your approval. For that which remains untransmuted, which you have failed to challenge, that which exists in consciousness, is therefore the creation of free will. And until you will to call it back, to undo it, to restore it to the fiery core for transmutation, it remains a blight on the whole of cosmos.

Judgment to Every Living Soul

Only when you challenge the dweller on the threshold of your own cosmos and your own consciousness—the rebellious one—can you breathe the breath of life and know "I AM free!" Therefore, that judgment that has come to the Fallen One, meted out by Alpha and Omega, must also resound within the consciousness of every living soul. And the Alpha-to-Omega, the atom of identity in the fiery core of your own being, must release the spiral that renders the judgment whereby the dweller on the threshold passes through the second death and is no more and has no longer any habitation in the whole consciousness of that life which you call your own, but which I am here to tell you is my very own—mine to give, mine to take. And I can claim that fiery core, that replica of the Great Central Sun, when the cycles roll and the law of being returns the drop unto the Ocean.

Be Purged by Free Will

You have a cosmos! You have an energy field assigned to you! Let the four quadrants of your creation be purged of every residue of the Fallen One! Let them be purged by your free will aligned with my own, aligned with the Four and Twenty Elders who render judgment in the God Star. And let the earth body as well be free of the impressions of rebellion and the ego that is set apart from the Divine One!

Confirm the Judgment in Your Own Being

Let all be alert! Let all know that the passing from the Macrocosm of the one who instigated the rebellion of the angels is a point for the release of great light in the Macrocosm. You are globules of identity suspended in the Macrocosm of my own self-awareness. And that light which inundates the cosmic sea cannot penetrate the sphere of identity which you are unless you will it so. Therefore I come to say: Ratify and confirm the judgment within your own being; and only then be satisfied in the law and in the victory.

Judgment is nigh. Understand that unless you release the judgment in your own microcosm and withdraw all support of the energy veil, when the judgment comes and the skeins of consciousness are found to be woven inextricably with skeins of evil, then the entire globule must pass through the spirals of Alpha and Omega. And this is the ritual, then, of the canceling-out of that which cannot be absorbed into the sea; for by free will it has not willed it so.

Determine the Fate of Your Own Cosmos

You are set apart as a diamond suspended in crystal,

suspended in ruby, suspended in agate. See how the crystallization of the God flame which I am must be made your own. You determine the fate of your own cosmos. So let it be. So receive the warning that perhaps there is even greater danger now than when the adversary was personified before you; for now it remains only the subjective awareness, and that subjectivity is the burden of the soul that longs to be extricated from that substance that has no part with light.

Forge Your God-Identity

I AM Alpha! I AM Omega! When you know that you are Alpha, that you are Omega, then—and only then—will you find yourself in the white-fire core of the Great Central Sun. Children of the One: Forge your God-identity!

July 5, 1975
10:58-11:25 P.M. P D T

Is there a counterfeit creation and a false hierarchy? Is there an invisible government of darkness? Who or what are the dragon, the beast, the false prophet, and the great whore as depicted in the Book of Revelation?

THE DRAGON
Perversion of the Father

THE FALSE PROPHET
Perversion
of the Holy Spirit

THE ANTICHRIST
AND THE BEAST
Perversion of the Christ

THE GREAT WHORE
Perversion of the Mother

20

ANTICHRIST: THE DRAGON, THE BEAST, THE FALSE PROPHET, AND THE GREAT WHORE

A Lecture by Elizabeth Clare Prophet

Will you draw a circle on a sheet of paper, full size? The topic of our discussion is Antichrist and the categories of Antichrist as outlined in the Book of Revelation: the dragon, the beast, the false prophet, and the great whore.[1]

Free Will

Beloved Alpha spoke to us last evening of the judgment of Lucifer, the Fallen One. In explaining the counterfeit creation, we must zero in on the concept of free will. If there is free will, then there is the freedom to choose light or darkness, God or not-God, reality or unreality, the Self or the not-self. Now if you deny the premise of free will, what are you doing here? Who made you come? Are you a puppet on a string or did you walk here of your own free will?

Free will is an essential element of the cosmos and of understanding the law of cosmos. Even the electron has free will. The electron is the smallest particle of energy that has elected to do the will of God. Souls came forth with the gift of free will leaving the fiery core of Alpha and Omega. Among the souls that went forth, some exercised that grace of free will to choose to merge with the will of God, and some chose to merge with the will that was the direct opposite of that will.

The First Three Root Races

The first root races on Terra, evolutions of souls coming forth for the first time into incarnation in Matter, used their free will to elect to merge with the light. They did not experience what has been called the Fall—the descent from the fiery core to the periphery, to densification, to the plane of relative good and evil. They did not depart from the third-eye consciousness of the all-seeing eye of God, of ever beholding the absolute perfection.

Three entire lifewaves came forth and chose to do only the will of God with full awareness at the mental level of the consequences of a not-choice, of choosing the Antichrist. But they never entered into the choice. They never fell for the rationale that you have to experience evil, or the energy *veil,* in order to understand it, in order to distinguish it, in order to choose. For them, the analysis in the laboratory of the soul was enough. They chose the light; they remained in the light; they returned in the ritual of the ascension.

The Fourth Root Race and Lucifer's Rebellion

It was with the coming of the fourth root race that there was the interference. This is described in *Climb the Highest Mountain* in the chapter called "A Heap of Confusion." We look around at the confusion on the planet and we say: Where did it all start? Where did it all come from? How did we get into this realm of twilight where we do not have the vision of the Whole?

The Fallen One, Lucifer, elected to use the tremendous light of God that had been given to him to glory in his own image, in his own selfhood, and to enter into competition with the Creator. It is sometimes difficult to understand how such an exalted being, one called "son of the morning" and "Lucifer" (meaning light-bearer), one so close to the very heart of God, could rebel.[2]

There is a story in the Apocrypha of the New Testament—religious writings that have been handed down from the early Christians but which have not become a part of our Bible—that God created man in his image and likeness, that he created sons and daughters. He sent forth Christed ones and he said to his angels: "Now I have formed man out of my own image, out of my own likeness. Therefore, this image is myself incarnate. Now, therefore, worship the image of God."

And the story goes that the archangel Lucifer, or perhaps Satan, refused to worship the image of the Christ, the reflection of God across the vast cosmos. That reflection, that image borne in the Divine Mother, borne in the Son, the Christ, became an anathema. You might say that the Fallen One became jealous that the Lord God did not require that the creation worship him.

We see the mark of the Fall, then, as ambition, pride, egocentrism. And this mark of the Fall, as it is spun into a veil, into a mist that surrounds the ego, becomes an intellectual rationale, a philosophy that is devoid of God in the center. It becomes a materialistic science that needs no God. It becomes intellectual reasoning. It becomes a self-sufficiency that says: "I don't need God. I can do it better than God."

When all of this took place in the consciousness of Lucifer, he still had great light; and that great light was the result of his momentum before the Fall. So great was his light that millions of angels were in his service; and when he made the decision to separate from the fiery core of being, the angelic hosts, so accustomed to obedience to their leader, followed after him.

We read in the twelfth chapter of the Book of Revelation that Michael fought the dragon and his angels, and the dragon prevailed not; "neither was their place found any more in heaven." We read that a third of the angels were cast out of heaven with the dragon, with the Fallen One.[3] A third of the hierarchies serving the light in a certain sector of the cosmos followed the way of the rationale of the intellect.

Michael the Archangel comes with his angels to challenge the adversary, this one who is now anti-God, Antichrist. And there is war in heaven. John the Revelator, who received the Book of Revelation as a dictation from Jesus the Christ sent and signified by the angel of Jesus, witnessed the record of that war in heaven. And so it is written that they were cast out of heaven. And then the warning goes forth, "Woe to the inhabiters of the earth . . . for the Devil is come down unto you, having great wrath."[4]

The Fall of Lucifer
and the Contamination in the Planes of Mater

"Come down" signifies the fall of Lucifer, the descent into

Matter and into maya. It signifies that his place is no longer in the plane of Spirit, where only perfection can dwell. He is cast out of the fiery core of being and he dwells in the planes of Mater consciousness. These include the four quadrants—the etheric, the mental, the astral (or emotional), and physical planes of consciousness—in other words, the entire habitation, the dwelling place of our own souls. We find, then, that during the epoch of the fourth root race, there is contamination in the planes of Mater in this solar system and throughout various sectors of this galaxy and other galaxies. The fall is system-wide.

Now we see souls of the fourth root race, innocent souls who have just come forth from the heart of God. They have not the aeons of experience of the mastermind of the Fallen One. They hear his argument. They hear the argument of the Serpent depicted in the Book of Genesis: If you eat of the fruit of the tree of the knowledge of good and evil, "ye shall not surely die."[5] This is what the carnal mind said unto the woman. The Lord God had said, "If you eat of it, you will die." The carnal mind says, "You will not *surely* die." It is an intellectual argument. It is meaningless. It is sophistry.

The death that is spoken of is the potential for the death of the soul, or the second death.[6] When we partake of the knowledge of evil, the knowledge of the energy veil, by taking it in, assimilating it within our consciousness, the seeds of the second death are sown. From that moment on, the warfare is in the four planes of Mater of our own microcosm. We have allowed the Devil that is cast down into the plane of earth, the plane of Matter, to gain entrance into our four lower bodies.

The Descent of Energy:
The Fall of Man and Woman

Adam and Eve are symbolical of man and woman—the average man and woman living on Lemuria during that epoch. Many fell for that lie; they allowed the descent of energy. And it is written they knew that they were naked. They knew that they no longer were wearing the wedding garment, the seamless garment of the virgin consciousness of the all-seeing eye of God.[7] And therefore they, too, were cast out of paradise. As Lucifer had been cast out of heaven, so they were cast out of that circle of fire where only the laws of perfection heretofore had been outpictured by the first three root races.

The Invasion of the Fallen Ones

Once the mankind of Earth had responded to the lie of the Fallen One, they broke the seal of the virgin consciousness of the entire planetary body. No longer was Earth protected from the fallen ones. And therefore they came—the angels who had fallen and those whom they had influenced on other planetary bodies, influenced to the extent that on the planet that once was between Mars and Jupiter, the fall was so great, the rebellion so complete, that there was, as a consequence of rebellion, schism.

The divide-and-conquer tactics of the fallen ones were successful. There was war on that planet. There was the use of atomic energy. And the outcome of that war was the total destruction of the planet—the blowing-up of the planet that has been called Maldek. The remains of this planet are the asteroid belt between Mars and Jupiter. There are the remains of another fallen planet, another destroyed planet, an asteroid belt closer to the sun that has also been discovered. We have, then, clearly the record, right within the physical, right within our own solar system, of the consequence of the misuse of free will.

Now Alpha warned us in his dictation that even though the judgment of Lucifer has come, this does not guarantee our safety, this does not mean that the battle is o'er, because the battle is now being waged in the microcosm of each individual soul on the planet Earth.

With the coming in of laggard evolutions that had destroyed other planets and the coming in of the fallen ones, the planet Earth then became a conglomeration of lifewaves. The consequence of that fall was the total degradation of life almost to the plane of the animal—the point that finally resulted in the decision of cosmic councils to cancel out the planet Earth, because not a single solitary soul remained to acknowledge or adore the threefold flame within the heart.

The Coming of Sanat Kumara
and Many Light-Bearers

At that moment Sanat Kumara came. Many light-bearers

came with him, legions and hosts of light. Many of you numbered among those who came with Sanat Kumara, who saw the plight of the fourth root race, who saw the action of the fallen angels influencing them, who saw the laggard generation lowering the life standard of Terra. And so there was quite an array of souls who volunteered to come and assist the raising-up of the life-force, the raising-up of the sacred fire, the restoration of the feminine ray that had been destroyed, desecrated on Mu—who volunteered to restore the Christ to the position of prominence within every individual.

We see how long the fallen ones and their arguments have held sway, how long it has been since the Fall that mankind have failed to acknowledge the I AM Presence, the I AM THAT I AM that was revealed to Moses.[8] That teaching was known on Lemuria before the Fall. It has been lost. And even though great avatars have come, mankind en masse has never been restored totally to the awareness of the I AM Presence, the flaming monad. This shows how entrenched the consciousness of the fallen ones, of Antichrist, and the laggard generation is upon the planet Earth. How long has it taken, even with the coming of Jesus the Christ, for the restoration of self-awareness as Christ in every man, woman, and child?

The Fallen One, Lucifer himself, has convinced mankind that there is only one Son of God, only one Christed One, and that all the rest of us are sinners—that we have no right to be sons and daughters of God. This lie has been continuing century by century. This is the lie that has been the watering-down of true Christianity, of true Buddhism—the taking from the children of the East, the children of the Mother, their right to be the Buddha, their understanding that they hold that potential of Buddhahood here and now, not in the long distant future.

The Sinking of Atlantis

We see, then, that relatively speaking in the relative plane of maya, Antichrist and the fallen ones have had their day. They have had their day of preeminence where the serpentine mind has held sway in mankind—all through the Dark Ages, all through that period when mankind did not know the one true God. Their consciousness contributed to the wickedness that was accomplished in the days of Atlantis, which led finally to the edict that went forth from the Lords of Karma that resulted in the flood, the sinking of Atlantis.

That edict went forth because science had reached such a state of advancement (with these laggard evolutions coming from other planets plus the fallen ones who had an extensive knowledge of the control of the life-force, the DNA chain, the creation of life in the test tube) that the creations of the Atlantean scientists were grotesque—all types of hideous forms and even the mixing of the seed of animal and human life. And we read in mythology of those creations that are half goat and half man. These were the product of the experimentation of the fallen ones. And therefore the flood came.

But according to the laws of creator and creation, all of the animals were not destroyed. Those that were the mixture of the seed of man and animal were destroyed. The remainder were paired off and had to be taken by Noah so that they could propagate once again, because elemental life had become a part of that creation, a part of that manifestation.[9]

We see, then, that the influence has been for thousands and thousands of years. Now the question is: Why did the Almighty allow such an infiltration of the consciousness of the souls of mankind? Why did he allow it? Simply because he respects his own laws—the law of free will and the gift of free will. Now this law is an exact mathematical formula. It means that to each and every living soul, to you and to me and to the archangels and to the angels who follow them, to the laggards and to those who rebelled against God, to all there is given a sphere of energy, a nucleus of energy, that is released cycle by cycle, lifetime by lifetime.

The Final Judgment to Come

When we went forth as living souls from the flame of Alpha and Omega, we were given an allotment of energy equivalent to a certain number of cycles of evolution in time and space. This could amount to several hundred thousand years, several million years—the figure doesn't matter. The principle is that we have free will and the right to experiment with free will only for a certain span of time and space. At the conclusion of the soul's passing through these cycles (and the going through the cycles according to the cosmic clock is exact; over and over again we pass through those twelve hierarchies of the sun, facing their initiations in the planes of Matter)—at the conclusion of that allotted time, then, is the judgment. And that judgment is known as the final judgment—the final tallying of what has been done cycle by cycle.[10]

If 51 percent of the energy allotted to the soul has been qualified with light, the soul has earned the right to retain an identity. It is accorded the ascension in the light. It becomes a part of the I AM Presence and then a permanent atom in the body of God forevermore. One with God, sealed and fired in God, it can nevermore go out. It remains in the consciousness of God, expanding throughout eternity.

If there is not the sign of a sufficient amount of effort placed on the side of light, if the soul cannot show just cause as to why its existence ought to be perpetuated, if it has been continually using light to reinforce the ego and the worship of the ego, at the end of that cycle the soul stands before the high tribunal of the Four and Twenty Elders, which is located, in this sector of the galaxy, on the God Star Sirius. It is the Court of the Sacred Fire. The Four and Twenty Elders are cosmic beings, twelve sets of twin flames who represent the twelve hierarchies.

The soul stands on the dais of the Court. If the Court decides, in consonance with the Christ Self of the soul, that the soul has not shown just cause why its identity should be continued, then the flame of Alpha and Omega is passed up through the dais and the identity of the soul is canceled out. The Christ Self of that lifestream merges with the universal Christ; the I AM Presence of that lifestream merges with the universal I AM Presence. And the energy that was used to create the soul, the energy that was used by the soul in its miscreations—all of that is withdrawn back to the God Star for requalification. The requalification occurs in a giant forcefield of the sacred fire that is named in the Book of Revelation as the "lake of fire."[11]

The Lake of Fire

The vision of this lake of fire and the knowledge of the lake of fire by the fallen ones has resulted in their development of the doctrine of hellfire, damnation—eternal punishment in the fires of hell. It is the fallen ones who have created this false theology.

They have purveyed it to the holy innocents.

In fact, the moment that any misqualified energy comes in contact with the lake of fire, the sacred fire consumes the cause and core of the misqualified substance. The energy is restored to the perfection of God, returned to the fiery core of the Great Central Sun magnet as part of the Source of life, and used again, even as the potter remolds the clay that he has fashioned into a form which he desires to now cancel out. So as far as eternal damnation goes, this is the desire of the wicked to threaten the children of the light with eternal suffering. Nevertheless, the children of the light need to be concerned with the fate of the soul, not with the doctrine of the Luciferians.

Time in Space to Repent

Alpha explained that Lucifer, the Fallen One, at the time of his rebellion, had a certain quantity of light that had been qualified as good, as light, while he had been in the service of God. That momentum of energy plus his attainment before the Fall qualified him to have a certain period of time in space to repent, to return to the worship of Almighty God. That period of time has been very long for the innocents, for the children of God. It has been going on for thousands of years upon the planetary body.

During that period of time, because of the tremendous attainment of Lucifer, his ability to manipulate energy, and because of the nature of the fact that young souls do not have that attainment, it was Lucifer and the fallen ones who actually controlled life in the planes of Matter—not to the extent, however, that souls could not rise. During that period of tribulation, many souls overcame the carnal mind within and the Fallen One without; and through suffering and trial and temptation—overcoming all—they passed through the ritual of the ascension and returned to God as ascended beings.

Lucifer's Time Is Up

Now it is the end of the Piscean dispensation, the end of the period when Jesus came to prove the Christ, to manifest the light which Lucifer could not challenge, could not defeat. So at the end of this dispensation, it has come to pass that Lucifer's time was up—no more cycles allotted to him, no more opportunity.

Furthermore, he misused his position in hierarchy, which he was not permitted to do, by coming forth and challenging the messengers of the Great White Brotherhood. The manifestation of the law is such that those who represent the Great White Brotherhood have protection from the Fallen One. Likewise, the Fallen One cannot be touched by the messengers, because it is up to mankind to choose whom they prefer—the messengers of the Christed ones or the carnal mind. At any moment, then, when the Fallen One, Lucifer, would go forth in a direct attack on the messengers, a certain allotment of his opportunity and energy would be taken. Over the last fifteen years, this has occurred increment by increment, until finally that full portion of 51 percent of the darkness of Lucifer was seized from him by the Lords of Karma.

The Judgment of Lucifer

It happened, then, that he was called to judgment, bound by Archangel Michael in answer to the calls of the Christed ones, and taken to the Court of the Sacred Fire to stand trial before the Four and Twenty Elders. His trial lasted for days, and during that period an examination of the total record of the actions of Lucifer and the fallen ones was taken by the Twenty-Four Elders.

A review was made. At the conclusion of the review, the opportunity for repentance was given to Lucifer to bend the knee before the Christ, before Almighty God, and to worship the I AM Presence. He blasphemed before the Twenty-Four Elders and declared he would never worship the image of the Christ. His time was up. As he stood on the dais, the energy of Alpha and Omega passed through his form and canceled out the one that was once known as son of the morning. This, then, was the announcement that was brought by Alpha last evening.

The Seed of Antichrist

Alpha was very concerned in making this announcement that the children of the light, the students of the ascended masters, do not become complacent, do not consider that the victory is won. This is only the beginning; the warfare is now in the soul of everyone. In the four quadrants of being, we are required to exorcise the Antichrist, the seeds of Antichrist, of rebellion, that have been planted there by our association with the fallen ones, with the laggard generation.

May I mention that when the fallen ones were cast down into the earth, many were forced to take embodiment by edict of the Lords of Karma; and therefore they walk among us. There are fallen angels in embodiment who are the ones who instigate the philosophies and the movements that are Antichrist, leading the children of God into all manner of perversions, instigating corruption in government, in the economy, in every nation on earth. They are a very dangerous group of individuals, because they have that power of the angelic hosts and they convey tremendous feeling through the feeling body because that was their momentum before incarnation.

After they incarnated, many of the angelic hosts of light who did not fall volunteered to take incarnation to offset the work of the fallen angels. And therefore we have also abiding on earth many angels of light who serve the light, who help mankind, who carry the flame of love, who are teachers. And many of these angels of light are among the student body of the ascended masters' chelas, because they are the ones who desire to have the teaching to teach mankind the way.

Now therefore, since our incarnation upon the planet, no matter what category we fit into—whether of the sons and daughters of God, the children of the fourth, the fifth, and the sixth root races, which subsequently incarnated, whether we are of the angelic hosts who came to rescue mankind or whether we came with Sanat Kumara or whether we came from other planets on the rescue mission—whichever category we fall into, most of us, until this time of the revelation of the ascended masters' teachings, have forgotten all of this history of the Fall, all of this history of why we are here, what is happening, why we love the light and yet find ourselves entangled with skeins of darkness and in a situation of having karma with souls of light and souls of darkness.

The Lie of the Fallen Ones

We come to the place, then, of seeing that after we came on this rescue mission one way or the other, after taking incarnation, we forgot why we were here and who we were. No one told us we had an I AM Presence, and the veil of maya became very thick.

Without a teacher, we could not know the way. We believed the lie of the fallen ones that there was only one Son of God. We accepted the mass condemnation of the Luciferians, of whom it is spoken in the Book of Revelation, "This is the accuser of the brethren which accused them before our God day and night." [12] The "accuser of the brethren" is another name for Lucifer, who accuses, or condemns, souls of light, continually amplifying and magnetizing condemnation until the children of light feel totally worthless, allow themselves to be absorbed in the mass consciousness, and no longer take a stand for truth because they do not understand that the truth is within them.

We find that through intermingling, we have made karma. We have reacted to the fallen ones. We have been seized by their anger; we have responded in revenge. And therefore the skeins of karma have woven us, tied us, to the fallen ones, sometimes in a very personal way in a family situation. This is why you see in many families people of light and people who don't love the light; you see schism and division.

We find, therefore, that almost without exception—and it is important not to have that spiritual pride that makes us think we are the exception—the children of the light on Terra have absorbed the influences of the fallen ones. Without even realizing it, we have taken in at subconscious levels their philosophies, their way of life, their morality, their accentuation on "the good life." "Eat, drink, and be merry, for tomorrow you die" is the byword of the Luciferians, because they know ultimately they will pass through the second death. So they teach that doctrine to the children of light and they draw the children of light into a pleasure cult, a cult of sensual thralldom, and thereby cause the children of light to lose their souls.

The fallen ones, knowing that they will be canceled out, have only one goal. They say, "If we're going, we're going to take the children of light with us." And so this is why they continue in their ways. They would destroy a planet in order to take with them souls who would give them allegiance in the destruction of that planet.

They have set up false forms of government. They have drawn individuals into their camp. Nazism is a clear example of a government of the fallen ones, of a black magician incarnate being used to take millions of children of light into the camp by the sounding of the fierceness of the voice, the beating of the drum, the military rhythm, and the exultation of the concept of a superrace.

Appealing to that pride which the Luciferians had already implanted in the children of light, they make them come into this mass hypnosis; they draw them in by the magnetism of pride. This has happened over and over and over again. Civilizations have risen and fallen as the result of the Luciferians entering into the top echelons of government and only slightly perverting the true philosophy of the Christ and of Almighty God.

Individualism That Excludes the Christ

The philosophy of the Luciferians is an ultimate individualism; but it is an individualism that excludes the Christ, that excludes the merging of the Christ flames of all for the good of the many. Luciferians are individualists to the point where they will not cooperate with society. But they milk society. Through the perversion and corruption of capitalism and communism, they have milked the masses of the light of their divine inheritance. They have taken the wealth of nations and they have put it into their pockets. They have organized an inner false government that is known as the Illuminati.

This Illuminati was begun in Bavaria in about 1776 by one known as Adam Weishaupt. It is an organization of the fallen ones who have infiltrated the banking systems of the world, the governments, the economies. They always operate behind the scenes; and they attempt to draw into their camp the young, the brilliant, the children of God. They flatter them; they appeal to that spiritual pride, that intellectual pride. They tell them that they are going to make them rulers of mankind. They tell them that they are of the elite and that the masses are not worthy to rule themselves and therefore they must be ruled by the intellectual elite and the men of science. Thus they deprive the people—the children of the light who have the threefold flame—of their God-given opportunity to rule themselves according to the dictates of conscience.

And whether it is in the West or in the East, no matter what the form of government, no matter what the rationale, the movement is toward more and more power in the central government, less and less authority given to the individual people. We find that the power of concentration of wealth is hoarded in the hands of the fallen ones, the Illuminati. We find that it is hoarded in every nation.

Divergent Political and Economic Systems

We find that the varying systems of government and economic systems, political and economic theory, are all contrived, that they are used by the fallen ones to get the children of light in opposing camps so that they will fight one another, so that the Luciferians don't have to do anything about destroying the children of God. They just prop them up on the battlefield and let them destroy one another in a war that is supposed to be a righteous war for some great cause. But the cause never comes through; no side wins. Who is Vietnam saved for? Is it saved for the Vietnamese? Who is it saved for? Either side. Nobody wins. But who is destroyed? The children of God on the battlefield. Their blood is taken at the hand of the fallen ones and those who profit by war—the Luciferians, the munition makers, the people who build the planes, build the armaments, and so on.

There is a real plot that is a skein of maya across the planetary body like a spider's web. The worst thing about the plot is that the Luciferians have successfully divided the children of light. They have divided them on the religious scene into camps of opposing and warring factions, until the viciousness and the fanaticism of those who call themselves this or that religion—against one another and against the teachings of the ascended masters—is an absolute tragedy. But it exists and we must face it.

We see the same thing in the political arena. The Illuminati seek to control the elections. They would let the children of God think that it is a fair thing and that the opposing views are being represented in the two-party system; but who wins? The one who wins is often the plant of the fallen ones in whichever party that they decide to back. All of this is camouflaged by nice words, nice speeches, quoting all of the right phrases. And the people think, "He's a good guy because he believes in freedom of speech and he believes in democracy and he's asked us to pray for him—so he must be a good guy."

Let Us Bury Our Differences

Well, here we are. We're talking about the dragon, the beast, the great whore, and the false prophet. We're talking about that which has infested the souls of mankind which must be exorcised. We see, then, that when the judgment of Lucifer comes, the one great boon that is given to us is a period of time when we can launch forth with the teachings of the ascended masters without having the key adversary opposing every step we take.

We find that there is an opportunity in the next twenty-five years for a tremendous expansion of the light, a tremendous transmutation by the action of the Holy Spirit. If we will unite, if we will bury our differences, if we will see that differences are always contrived and that if we will stay in the teaching long enough we will resolve all aspects of difference, we will find in the fiery core of being the basis for our unity. We will understand in the light of cosmic law that all that is right and good is agreed upon by all of us. And we will see through the philosophy, the temptation, the lies of the fallen ones that have been imposed upon us to separate us.

If we are truly desirous of forging a golden age, we will stay with the sacred fire, we will stay with the violet flame, we will stay with the masters. And we will clean up our own consciousness, our own chakras, our own worlds, until we can see clearly the light that unites us and the energy veil that separates us, which can be thrown into the flame. We must exorcise all that causes division. This is the greatest weapon of the fallen ones—their divide-and-conquer tactics. And they divide us over the silliest of issues!

I could not believe it! In 1968 when we were traveling, we visited two of the most magnificent cathedrals in Nuremberg. I was taken to see these cathedrals. They were two Protestant cathedrals. We went in one and we went in the other, and I asked my cousin: "Now what is the difference between the beliefs of these two churches? Why do they have two cathedrals? Why don't they build one great cathedral and worship together?"

He said: "Well, one group believes that the bread and wine in the Communion ritual is only a symbol of the body and blood of Christ; the other group believes that the wine and the bread through the ritual of transubstantiation become in fact the body and blood of Christ in the ritual of Communion. Over this difference they split—I don't know how many hundreds of years ago—and they each built their own cathedral."

Now can you imagine, in the face of saving a planet and

saving souls, what difference it makes? What difference does it make? Can we not give the freedom to each individual soul who worships in the church to believe as his conscience dictates without separating ourselves and thereby opening the door for the wedge, a further schism, to be driven in by the doctrines and dogmas of the fallen ones? And so it goes. I'm certain that you have seen the pettiness of the division and the nature of the division.

What concerns me is the vision that Alpha gave to me as he was speaking. He spoke of the great cosmic ocean of the being of God and he spoke of us as souls suspended in that ocean. He spoke of the Macrocosm and of Lucifer's second death and his influence being transmuted in the Macrocosm. But I saw that the soul, a globule of energy and light, a forcefield of identity, was sealed in a membrane, the membrane of identity, the membrane of free will, and that all of the light of God and of the whole Macrocosm could not penetrate that membrane unless the soul inside willed it so.

And of course this explains how people in the world can be so surrounded by the love of God and never acknowledge it. It is the membrane of identity. Granted, it is a temporary identity, because it is not yet forged as a permanent atom of being in the ritual of the ascension. It is the soul gone forth with an allotment of energy, biding its time in Mater, determining what the choices will be.

The Dragon, the Beast, the Great Whore, and the False Prophet: Perversions of God in the Four Lower Bodies

I saw, then, that unless people understand clearly and accurately that the battle is in the four lower bodies and the soul, the second death of Lucifer, the entire victory of Armageddon, even the victory of a golden age, will not mean the winning of immortality by the individual soul.[13] Each individual soul, because it elected to go forth from the fiery core of oneness, must make the decision itself. It must sit in the center of the Christ flame even as the Four and Twenty Elders sit in the Court of the Sacred Fire on Sirius. The soul must invoke the Christ Self to manifest the judgment of the dragon, the beast, the great whore, and the false prophet. Now each one of these perversions of the Godhead control one of the four lower bodies. I want you to diagram this on the circle you have drawn.

Now I suggest you study the Book of Revelation. Beginning

with chapter eleven, you can read of the mission of the two witnesses who are the messengers for the Great White Brotherhood—
the two prophets which bring the teaching of the ascended masters to the age.[14] They come and they deliver the teaching and they
also face the challenge of the dragon.

Then there is the coming of the Woman in chapter twelve—a
"Woman clothed with the Sun, and the moon under her feet, and
upon her head a crown of twelve stars," the twelve stars denoting
her mastery under the twelve hierarchies of the sun.[15] Chapter
twelve is the sign of the Aquarian age, the coming of the feminine
ray, the elevation of the feminine ray. And when the feminine ray
is elevated, it brings forth the Christ, the Manchild, that is the
fulfillment of the mission of the Divine Mother in all of us.[16]

Chapters thirteen, fourteen, fifteen, and sixteen go on about
the dragon, the beast, the great whore, and the false prophet, and
they go on at great length. And of course, the Book of Revelation
is written in code. It is cryptic. It was delivered by Jesus. The final
verse says that if any man should tamper with the Book of
Revelation in any way, his name should be removed from the Book
of Life.[17] That's a pretty strong warning to all of those who were in
their cells in the last several thousand years rewriting the sacred
scriptures and to the fallen ones who infiltrated the churches and
removed from the teachings of Christ and the teachings of the Old
Testament those scriptures which clearly revealed the nature of the
fall of the Luciferians, the nature of their creation, which clearly
revealed the teaching on reincarnation, the laws of karma. All this
was in our sacred scripture. All this has been tampered with.

Now there are some who say that sacred scripture is the absolute Word of God. Well, where it is the Word of God, it is the
Word of God. Where it isn't there, it isn't there. And that is the
problem we face—that people try to piece together a theology and
a doctrine that they say we cannot stray from, when they do not
have the whole writing of the law and the Word.

Jesus, of course, knew that they would do this. Jesus didn't
even bother to write the books—did you notice? He gave the
teaching; he let his disciples write it down. He knew that the
teaching would carry only in the flame within the heart, from fire
to fire to fire. That is what apostolic succession is intended to be:
the carrying-down of the tradition of the true teaching of Christ—
not of the dead ritual, not of the untempered zeal, not of the

fanaticism, but of the flame. That is what the true priests and priestesses at the altar of God are intended to convey to the people.

Instead, the flame was lost. The teaching was tampered with. So when Jesus dictated that Book of Revelation to John on the Isle of Patmos just shortly before John's ascension, he included in it, "Anybody that changes one word of this book, his name will be stricken from the Book of Life." And so they didn't tamper with it. It's there intact. But it is cryptic. And the reason it is cryptic, in code, is that you can't tamper with code, because those that would tamper with it are actually too ignorant to know what to change.

And that's what happened in the visions of Ezekiel and of Daniel in the Old Testament.[18] Those writings couldn't be tampered with, because they seem inane on the face of it to the fallen ones and the rebellious ones, since you have to be in the Holy Spirit to understand them. Well, I'm not here to give you a complete exposé on the Book of Revelation. This we do in upper levels of Summit University. But I am here to show you about the battle of Armageddon in your forcefield.

The Dragon on the Twelve O'Clock Line: Perversion of the Father

Please divide your circle into four quadrants. We place the dragon on the 12 o'clock line. The dragon is the ultimate perversion of God as Father, God as lawgiver, God as power. The dragon, in its immensity, symbolizes that forcefield, that vortex of energy that has taken the power of God and created the image of the beast; it has created this monstrous form. And that dragon consciousness, the direct opposite of God the Father, initiates dark cycles and gives the perverted power to the beast. The dragon is the counterfeit of the Impersonal Impersonality of the Great Divine Director. On the 12 o'clock line is the accuser of the brethren referred to in the Book of Revelation.

The perversion of God-power is condemnation. That condemnation is the pounding, the aggression on the mind that is continually downing you, telling you you can't succeed, permeating the mass consciousness with the will to fail and the will to failure. It is the pressing-down of the crown chakra, the pressing-down of the energies of the crown into the lower chakras and then, by the action of the dragon, causing those energies to be misused in lust and sensuality.

Now this is the quadrant of the etheric body, the fire body. We learn that the dragon is the perversion of fire, of the fohat of creation. The creation of the beast itself and the dragon is the misuse of the sacred fire of man and woman, of the Elohim, of the seed and the egg of the Father-Mother God, creating this monstrous form that is seething with all of the accumulation of the rebellion of the fallen ones. This vibration will act in the subconscious, in your own etheric body, as self-condemnation, as condemnation of others, as the denial of God.

Now see how many among mankind under the influence of this dragon within their own subconscious deny God. Maybe it's not an outright denial—"God doesn't exist"—not as blatant as atheism. But maybe it comes under a perversion of Pisces—doubt in the existence of God, fear that God will punish us, fear that he will not be just, a trembling, or a consideration that God is remote, that God is a hateful god (the perversion of Aquarius), that he is not a God of love.

Relegating God to a distant cosmos where he has no part of our personal lives—this is the denial of God. This is anti-God substance, very subtle. After all, if the dragon popped out of your subconscious, appeared on the screen before you, talked to you and said, "Now I'm the dragon, I'm the perversion of God, and I'm going to see to it that you fail," why, you'd take up your sword and you'd slay the dragon! But the dragon is very subtle: it is our own carnal consciousness.

It is simply the doubt that the I AM Presence is real. It's the doubt that the I AM Presence can fulfill the law of being within us. It is the doubt that the I AM Presence will come through every time we make a call. It's the doubt that the I AM Presence will be able to completely defeat the world dragon, the world momentum, and the mass collective subconscious.

Let us understand, then, when we feel that momentum of condemnation of ourself or other parts of life, of hatred of ourself or mild dislike of ourself or other parts of life, of doubt and death and belief in death—all of this is the dragon consciousness stealing the fire of our etheric body, depriving us of the glorious victory of the light of the solar hierarchies in that body.

This is a consciousness, a very subtle consciousness, of *malice*. It is malice beneath the surface. It is not often active except in the insane or those who are suddenly seized to commit mass murders and crimes. But it is there. It's like a silvery black forcefield at subconscious levels that comes up and pricks and incites these sometimes aggressive emotions and energies that we suddenly feel coming through us. We actually don't come face-to-face with this type of force until we challenge it, until we totally and wholeheartedly accept God and the teachings and the Path and the goal of the ascension. Because as long as we are not on the Path, we are part of the mass consciousness.

There are only two places you can be—either on the Path or in the mass consciousness. There is no middle ground. The middle ground is a very deceptive place. People think they are in the middle, but they aren't. They're really in the mass consciousness. So only when you decide to go against the mainstream of the mass consciousness do you confront all these forces, who then become very, very uncomfortable and begin to bellow their death cries and their death throes within your consciousness. And that's when you experience the battle of Armageddon.

People come into the masters' teachings and they think: "When I was in this or that church, I didn't have any problems at all. Now I'm in the masters' teachings, and all kinds of things are happening to me and it's really a struggle to maintain my own and maintain my light. What's happening to me?" And so because people don't like the struggle, they often go back to the calm and the ease and the downstream of orthodoxy, that aspect of orthodoxy which is the perverted teachings of the Brotherhood.

The Exorcism of the Dragon

To set the record straight in the etheric body, the dragon must be exorcised. How do we exorcise it? You have the 6.04 decree, "Round the Clock Protection." You have the violet flame. You have mighty Astrea. You have your own Christ Self and your own I AM Presence. And you can release the fiat: "In the name of the Christ, in the name of the I AM THAT I AM, I demand the binding of the dragon within my etheric body. I demand the transmutation of the cause and core of the consciousness of the dragon, the seed of the dragon and the egg of the dragon, and all that remains of the influence of the dragon in my subconscious. Let it be done this hour in the name of Jesus the Christ! And let Archangel Michael and mighty Astrea come into my etheric body this day and purge me of the cause and core of all that is less than my I AM Presence and my Christ Self! I accept it done this hour in the full power of the threefold flame within my heart."

Now you make your own prayer, you make your own call, and you make it fervently. You apply the teachings of the Brotherhood. You get down on your knees, if necessary, when you feel the temptation and the force of the dragon, and you refuse to let it overtake you. You call to Archangel Michael to take his sword and slay that dragon. The entire Spirit of the Great White Brotherhood will reinforce the call of the son of God who desires to make secure the forcefield of his own microcosm.

The Antichrist and the Beast on the Three O'Clock Line: Perversion of the Christ

Standing on the 3 o'clock line challenging the Christ is Antichrist himself. This Antichrist, from that point of the 3 o'clock line of the Christ, is that which gives birth to all of the perversions of the Godhead—the dragon, the false prophet, and the great whore. Antichrist is the fulcrum of all that is "anti-." That which is on the 12 o'clock line is anti-Father. That which is on the 6 o'clock line, as the great whore, is anti-Mother. And that which is on the 9 o'clock line opposing the Holy Spirit is anti-Spirit, or anti-Holy Spirit. It is simply a frequency which is the exact opposite of the frequency of light, which opposes the forcefield.

Now on the 3 o'clock line, serving under the Antichrist, is the beast. And in the Book of Revelation there are two beasts which are listed—the beast that riseth up out of the sea and the beast that cometh up out of the earth.[19] These are the two beasts who, under the Antichrist, pervert the emotional body and the mental body. The beast is the carnal mind—the serpent that crawled on its belly before Eve, come fullgrown now. The beast of Revelation is the mature adult of that serpent of Genesis. And it grew by the acceptance of souls. As we accepted the lie of the compromise of relative good and evil, we fed the serpent, and the serpent grew into the beast.

The beast controls almost the entire astral belt and mental plane of the planet. Not quite, because those who are the Christed ones and who have the true light and have the true teachings (and

I don't mean only those who are students of the masters, because in every walk of life, in every religion, there are real souls who have the real light, who are real devotees, and I know because I've met them in every church and in every teaching and in every walk of life)—they are there and they hold the flame and they do not allow the emotional body or the mental body to become polluted.

But for the most part, the mental plane is polluted with the beast of intellectual pride and ambition and competition; and the beast polluting the astral plane is the pollution of all misuses of the flame of the purity of the Divine Mother. Saint Germain has said that the astral plane is the sewer of mankind's consciousness. And by the temptations of the beast leading to all forms of perversion and misuse of God's energy, the astral plane is what it is today.

Many people who study the Book of Revelation go into naming names of people in embodiment who personify the dragon, the beast, the false prophet, and the great whore. I don't think it's necessary to do that. In fact, there may be one or several individuals on the planet who can claim a greater concentration of the beast, the dragon, the great whore, and so forth, than the rest of us and might stand out among us as having that greater mastery and forcefield of the energy veil. But I think pointing the finger at anyone, even pointing the finger at Lucifer, diverts us from the victory and from the battleground of our own soul.

I think it's very dangerous to say, "The Devil made me do this and the 'force' made me do this and So-and-so made me do this, and so I sinned and so I fell." That's exactly what Adam said. You know: "Eve gave me the apple and I ate it." And Eve said, "Well, the serpent tempted me and I ate it." And everybody blames everybody else for the departure from consciousness.

Now this really isn't funny. I've recently had a letter from a student who told me of a departure from the laws of God. And this student did not take the responsibility, but said: "The force was working against me. It was a plot. I was surrounded by opposition and I succumbed." It's the old lie. Paul said, "Who did hinder you that ye should not obey the truth?"[20] Who did it? If you don't own up to your own responsibility, you'll never get on the path of the ascension. You'll be tricked right out of your life, tricked right out of your soul, and you'll find yourself standing on that dais for the last judgment.

So we look within. We examine our own mental body. We look at the lines of our own clock. We say: "Am I outpicturing God-control in the Divine Ego or am I prancing around like a peacock with my human ego, trying to impress everybody with my spiritual knowledge, getting myself all kinds of titles and things so that I can become a teacher and let everybody see how great I am?" Have you asked yourself, "Is it the human ego or the Divine Ego that has set itself up?" We have to think about these things. We have to know that when we are on the Path, nothing is going to be obvious: everything is going to be subtle.

That is why the masters' teachings are so intricate. That is why they keep on releasing *Pearls of Wisdom* and dictations. Because the fine points of the law—when you hear them, when you read them—they click. They burst as a fire in the mind and you say: "Aha, that's what that vibration was! That's what was manifesting in me! It was not of the light! I'm going to kick it out and put it in the flame."

That is why we have to study to show ourselves approved unto God—because these are subtleties of vibration.[21] And the ego goes around looking benign, smiling and saying that it is so wonderful and so lovely and such a perfect example of this or that teacher or teaching, making a great impression on all kinds of people. But it doesn't have the flame. That's why Jesus warned of the false teachers that come as the Antichrist—come in the name of the Christ and yet have not the flame.

The question is, Can the teacher deliver the flame? Does the light flow? The teacher can only be a clear pane of glass. If the teacher takes any credit unto himself, the glass has a smudge on it. If you and your soul take credit for anything and give not the glory to God, you are reserving an identity separate from God. "The Father worketh hitherto, and I work. I of my own self can do nothing. It is the Father in me which doeth the work."[22]

Let us beware of the Antichrist within. Let us see that it does not manifest as that puffed-up pride carefully hidden on the 3 o'clock line or as rebellion against the law of God on the 4 o'clock line or as jealousy and envy of the sons and daughters of God who have attained, on the 5 o'clock line.

Spiritual envy and jealousy is a wicked thing. It is what divides movements. It is what divides students of the ascended masters into little groups here and there. And yet it never comes out at its face value. People will never admit that they are jealous of another teacher or another path, and yet that jealousy manifests.

I have seen again and again how teachers, various types of teachers, have felt threatened by the ascended masters' activity in The Summit Lighthouse, by the messengers. They have felt the enormous power of the light and the dictations. Instead of coming in, uniting, rejoicing, and realizing that no one can possess the light, no one can possess a student, they are afraid that their students might hear about the teaching, might feel the light and desert them and come into the great company of the saints. And therefore envy and jealousy at spiritual levels causes division in the body of God. It's the old plot: divide and conquer. They fall for it because they haven't surrendered the ego.

This is Antichrist. Let us know it for what it is. Let us heal it by the light of the Christ! We do not condemn it; we understand how the ego feels threatened. Anybody who's ever had an ego—and that's all of us—we know how the ego feels threatened. The only way we're going to get rid of envy and jealousy is to throw that ego into the fire and let the Christ come down in all of the majesty of the Logos and be God in us. Then we can't be threatened; we can't rebel. We are God. We can't go against the law of God; we can't be jealous of anyone, because the same God which is in us can be in all teachers, is in all disciples. So who needs to bind disciples to himself? Who needs the burden of controlling other people's lives? Who needs it, when we have the magnificent flow of God in our midst?

Chelas of the masters have to be free to come and go like the electron. They have to be free to elect to worship at the altar of their choice. And let their choice be the altar of their own heart and not the altar of the false prophet. Let us see, then, that we clear the mental belt and clear the way for the coming of the teaching, clear the way for the sacred fire of Alpha to be lowered into the mental plane.

The Great Whore on the Six O'Clock Line: Perversion of the Mother

Now let us see on the 6 o'clock line how the great whore swallows up the image of the Cosmic Virgin. The signet of the

Cosmic Virgin is the teaching of the Divine Mother, the wisdom of the Mother. We are counseled in the Book of Proverbs to seek out Wisdom, to follow her.[23] This is the counsel of the Father to the son—counseling him to seek out the learning of the Divine Mother. It is the Divine Mother who holds in her hand the teachings of the Father whereby the children of God can return to the flame of Alpha.

Coming in the name of the Mother is the great whore. It comes as organizations. It comes as large mass movements that, almost like a giant blowfish, suck the children of God into a teaching, into a doctrine, into a political theory that, instead of taking them to the sacred fire, takes them outside the circumference of God's being. The great whore is all that goes against the purity of the Mother within us. It is the perversion of the Mother flame. It is the perversion of the life-force.

It takes courage to kick out the great whore. Every perversion of the feminine ray in man and woman must go. On a mass scale we see it as pornography. We see it as the abuse of the body of the Mother in advertising, the playing-up of sex everywhere, the misuse of sex. We see it in the destruction of the children of the Mother of all ages in this period when the Mother flame is rising.

It is rising like a continent, like Lemuria. It is pressing up in all mankind relentlessly. It cannot be turned back. But as it rises, it comes in contact with all that has opposed it in all centuries. And so there is cataclysm in consciousness, there is upheaval, there is insanity; and that flame keeps rising and it keeps rising. We either blend with it, move with it, determine to govern our energies, or we will find ourselves aligned with the great whore and not even realize that the precious energies of the Mother have been seized from us.

So let us beware the subtleties—all inharmony in the feeling body, ingratitude, anxiety, nervous tension, the sense of injustice. When we shake our fist at God and say: "It isn't fair! It isn't fair what you've done to me! You've killed my mother, you've killed my father, you've taken my child, you've given me this terrible disease, this terrible misfortune!"—that sense of injustice, of rebellion against our karma, is rebellion against the Mother, rebellion against God, against the law of life that coalesces in us through the Mother. Let us beware then. The entire astral plane of the planet is the great whore, the perversion of the Mother.

We had a dictation on the binding of the great whore by beloved Astrea:

> You have heard of the fallen ones and that many have been brought to judgment in recent months. Now comes the judgment of the great whore and the impostors of the Divine Mother and the impostors of Kali and Durga and Mother Mary and all who implement the will of the Cosmic Virgin! Now judgment is spoken this day and the action of Astrea goes forth to *bind* the great whore!...It is done in the name of the living Christ by the action of Purity and Astrea according to judgment and justice this day implemented by the Four and Twenty Elders. Those impostors of the feminine hierarchy, those whose time has come, must go to the Court of the Sacred Fire for judgment in this hour. [24]

This judgment parallels the judgment of Lucifer. It means that key impostors of the Divine Mother on the astral plane—as Lucifer was on the astral plane, not in physical embodiment—have been taken to judgment. The judgment of those who live in physical bodies awaits the time of the fulfillment of their cycle, of their allotment of energy. Judgment has come in the Macrocosm. The fiat has gone forth. The judgment will not come within our four lower bodies until we ratify it, until we kick out the great whore and enshrine the Divine Mother. So it is the same thing: God acts, and we must act to ratify his actions or we will find ourselves separated and apart from the flow of the great cosmic sea.

The False Prophet on the Nine O'Clock Line: Perversion of the Holy Spirit

On the 9 o'clock line is the false prophet and all of the line of false teachers. When each avatar, each Christed one, takes his leave of the planet in the ritual of the ascension, the threefold flame within the heart, merging with the threefold flame of the Christ, merging with the threefold flame of the I AM Presence— this trinity of action, assuming the totality of the soul back into the I AM Presence, takes place. When this goes up, there is a release from the Presence that comes down to fill the vacuum and fill the void, to comfort those who are left, to comfort the disciples.

Hence, the Holy Spirit is known as the Comforter.

In the last days of Jesus' mission on the earth, he told his disciples what would come—that he would leave, that he must go, that he must be crucified that the law and the prophets should be fulfilled. But they should not be heavy and sorrowful, because when he would go he would send them another Comforter, and "he shall teach you all things." [25] So it was ten days after the ascension of Jesus, on that day of Pentecost, that the disciples were gathered and there was the rushing of the mighty wind and the coming of the Holy Spirit. [26] It was the same vibration of the ascension spiral. And that Comforter which came gave them gifts of the Spirit to be teachers, gave them the gift of tongues, gave them the gift to go forth and fulfill their mission. It was the anchoring in their hearts of the mantle of the Christ.

The true teacher of all mankind is the Holy Spirit. When we pray to the entire Spirit of the Great White Brotherhood, we are praying to the focalization of the Holy Spirit that each and every ascended master has left behind for the comfort of the disciples on the way. That Spirit appears on the 9 o'clock line under the hierarchy of Libra for the precipitation of God as Father, God as Christ, God as Mother in the physical plane. We cannot understand and receive the teachings of the ascended masters unless we have the Holy Spirit. Unless we have the flame, the essence of the radiance, we cannot sit in a room and even comprehend or retain the words of the dictations. We cannot even read the words of the masters and click into them unless the flame within our heart and soul responds.

Now Jesus also knew that inasmuch as the Comforter would come, all manner of false teachers and false prophets would also come. So throughout the New Testament we are warned of the false prophets, the false teachers. "Wherefore by their fruits ye shall know them." [27] They say all the right things, they quote all the right words; yet they set themselves up independent of hierarchy, independent of the Great White Brotherhood. And they draw disciples to themselves, and they allow their disciples to give them the glory for the light. They control the lives of their pupils; they interfere with the free and natural flow of the light of the Presence and the Christ Self.

Some of them even know of what I speak and that that is the mark of the false prophet. And therefore they carefully camouflage the fact that this is taking place. With their mouth and with their words, they say they give glory; but in their feelings and in their subconscious and in their hearts, they are puffed up with the vanity of the fallen ones.

The only way to isolate the false teacher is by the flame of the Holy Spirit within you. Only by the testing and the continual testing of the vibration, only by keeping yourself unspotted from the world, by going through the battle of the four quadrants, by exorcising these four aspects of Antichrist, will you be able to identify those who have not exorcised these forces. As long as they remain within, you may very well be the victim of these forces in the subconscious of others. But the innocence of your soul will always be protected by fervent prayer, by the intercession of Archangel Michael, by the Great White Brotherhood, until you come of age in the wisdom of the Mother whereby you have that perfect discernment and Christ-discrimination.

The Challenge of the Hour

So, my friends, I present to you what is the challenge of the hour. I consider that I could not have you come to this conference without telling you where things really are, what the stakes are, what the challenge of this embodiment is, what you must do to seal that soul that is yours in the flame of God.

I trust you will take the seriousness of the hour not as fear—for what is there to fear when you have the full knowledge of ascended-master law that can be applied to give you the victory? Where is there fear when God is real, when you have an I AM Presence and a flame and the heartbeat of God within you?

You have only to speak the Word, and the entire panoply of the fallen ones will crumble before you. That is the gift that God has given into your hand as the threefold flame and the I AM Presence. Won't you take it and won't you use it? Claim it! And by freeing yourself, won't you free a planet and a people for the Divine Mother?

July 6, 1975
10:38 A.M.-12:02 P.M. P D T

To be in the aura of one whose Self-awareness includes an infinite aspect of the mind of God requires some adjustment of consciousness. We remember the Psalmist's query when contacting the Elohim whose vastness equates their energy field with the Lord of Creation himself: "What is man that thou art mindful of him and the son of man that thou visitest him?" Man the infinitesimal against the backdrop of the infinite ones. Elohim—the living definition of cosmic consciousness.

What dost thou know of man, the manifestation, to be mindful of him—to even acknowledge his presence in the universe so boundless with the glory of God? Is it because thou knowest that man is a potential god—an Elohim in the becoming? Dost thou contain the measure of a man against the measure of a cosmos? Is the equation one of the dot becoming the sphere of God? Dost thou contain the formula whereby the drop can become the ocean? Oh, to penetrate the mind of an Elohim and become the mind of God!

21

AN INCREMENT OF LIGHT FROM THE HOLY KUMARAS

A Dictation by the Elohim Apollo

Hail, Lords of Flame from Venus! Hail, sons and daughters of God! I AM come in the fire of the central sun to release to the mankind of Terra an increment of light that is the seed of Alpha, of cosmic illumination to raise the fires of awareness and to increase the penetration of the Infinite One.

Once in Ten Thousand Years

So come, Sanat Kumara! Come, holy Kumaras of Flame! The hour has come for mankind to receive that increment that is delivered only once in ten thousand years for the elevation of consciousness and the centering of that consciousness in the crown. And so we have prepared these forcefields, and so they have willingly prepared themselves. And the crown begins to flow with the holy oil of wisdom's flame.

Implanting of the Rod by the Solar Logoi

Let mankind know again contact with the law! Let them know the yellow diamond light without flaw! Now the rod coming from the central sun by cosmic edict—the stepping-up of the mind of humanity! And the Solar Logoi implant that rod in consonance with the Christ Self of each one. And it is done! And mankind may, if they choose, employ the rod to enter a new era and a golden age! And the rod is sealed in the blue fire of our momentum for the protection of that energy.

A Magnet of the Father to Polarize the Mother

Now I say, this dispensation is not accorded to the fallen ones nor to those who have not the threefold flame of life. Only the creation of God, and the loyal creation, is the recipient of the impetus that will draw, as the Alpha lodestone, the Mother light. Therefore, let the magnet in the crown be the increase of the awareness of God as Father, God as the masculine ray! For this is the awareness that will polarize the true feminine. Therefore, let the tyranny of the perverted masculine go down! Let it be consumed by Cosmic Christ illumination! From the heart of the Elohim, let all that has hindered the true expression of the Divine Mother be consumed!

We release the light and you have the option of taking that light or leaving it suspended in the ocean of God. How wondrous is the creativity of the soul! How wondrously has God placed himself as opportunity in life! Wherever life responds, life is blessed. All of elemental life this day looks with the renewed hope of the archeiai for Wisdom to claim her own, for Wisdom's children to seek her out, to know the law.

Expose the False Teachers, Demand the Cosmic Christs

Let the children of Terra be dissatisfied with their teachers! Let them expose the false teachers! Let them demand the Cosmic Christs, and then we will see the Cosmic Christ come forth. If you are content with the stubble, then you will be left with the stubble! I say, raise your standard and a cosmos will rush to meet that standard!

Why tarry in mediocrity? Will you stand for the nonsense that is being delivered to you in the higher institutions of learning on this planet? I say, will you stand for it or will you do something about it this day? It is high time that the money changers' tables be overturned in the temples of learning! Let the real teaching be proclaimed!

A Vow to Release Wisdom's Ray

I say, those who turn their backs on this dilemma will give

answer to me! For I am the Elohim of wisdom's ray, and you have promised to release that ray! I remind you of your vow. I hold you to it! At least if you forsake your vows, do so with ceremony and come before the Lord God and have courage to say, "I desire to be relieved of my vow this day." Then go your way and we shall pass the torch to another.

Let wisdom pierce the coward and the hypocrite and let them be exposed! Where there is injustice, go forth with the flame of justice! Where there is doubt and fear, carry the torch of mastery! Where there is ignorance, be wisdom's fire! Where there is darkness, be victory! Be the cross of illumination! Be willing to carry that cross, to live for the cross!

Your Flame Must Do the Work in This Age

If you do not like what is happening on Terra, change it! Do not condemn it; do not join those who reviled the Christ upon the cross, saying, "If thou be the Son of God, come down and save thyself!"[1] I say to you, you are the son of God! You are the daughter of God! Go forth! Crack that cement of that intellectual learning and stand in the seat of the philosopher of the age and deliver the true teachings to those who come for truth! Go back to school! Take up the torch! Pass your tests! Become qualified to take your stand, for you must have at least equal credentials to overthrow those who are teaching the luciferian system.

Lucifer is taken, but his philosophy impregnates the consciousness of the children of the light. Who will exorcise it? We have not the authority to enter Terra unless bidden by yourselves. Yours is the flame which must do the work in this age! Our Father has consigned that flame to your altar. We bow at that altar. We adore the flame within you. And we wait...and we wait...and we wait for action!

God Needs Action

Let there be action then! Not the grumbling and the gossip. We don't need that! The children of light do not need that! God needs action! A planet in distress needs men and women fired with a cause, fired by wisdom's flame. Children of the light, *do* something about the predicament of mankind! I appeal to the

God within you even as you appeal to the God within me. You are the hope of hierarchy even as we are your hope. You are vested with the authority of the I AM Presence. It is the all-power of a cosmos.

What Will You Say?

When all is said and done and you report at the conclusion of a lifetime to the Lords of Karma, what will you say when you look back and see what might have been, what might have been? What will you say? Will you say, "I'm sorry; give me another chance"? Then will come the thunder of the Lords of Karma: *"It is too late! A civilization has been lost! A planet has been lost! It is too late!"* There is a time and a tide. There is a space for opportunity. Do not postpone the victory, for the victory is a torch suspended in the atmosphere within your grasp! Seize it! For when you look again, another may have taken it on to the fore and another may also have let it drop to the ground.

There is a saying on Terra, "When you want to get a job done and get it done right, do it yourself, because you can't count on anyone else to do it exactly the way you want it done." Well, I am telling you, precious hearts of light, had the avatars of the ages turned over to another that calling, that supreme moment of service that was theirs and theirs alone to give, the planet would already be a vacuum, a nonexistence, canceled out in this solar system. No one can do the job that is yours to do.

Contemplation Fused in Action

Let none think that wisdom's fire is a ray of contemplation! Our contemplation is fused in action simultaneously. As we think, we do! Ours is the instantaneous precipitation of the mind of God. We do not tarry in a dream world, imagining what the future will be. We make the future happen now! For in the now the mind of God is the crucible for the alchemy of souls.

Forge a Light Civilization

Forge a light civilization! Forge a new science! Go out and establish that school of light, that Montessori International! Let it be a reality! Why do you wait? Do you wait for ten million dollars? Teach the children! They are not concerned with funds. They are happy in the flow of wisdom's fire. Turn over to me then the requirement of abundance and of flow and of precipitation, and I will see to it that the flow comes forth from God through hands of willing servants! Call to me and I will back the masters of precipitation for the City Foursquare.

Energy to Energize the Blueprint and the Plan

Time marches on! *Tempus fugit!* Every hour and every week is for a cosmic purpose. Be infired this day! Wisdom's angels are on the march, and they march north and south, east and west! And they go where the crown is waiting to receive the golden glow. O mankind, how we love thee! How we love thee, O mankind!

I AM Apollo! I AM Lumina! I AM the spark of fire that goads you to the progress of the ultimate truth. I AM the Elohim of God! I AM the fire of the Logos! I AM the flow of energy to energize the blueprint and the plan. Now let that plan be quickened and fired as we receive the Divine You as Christ-potential! I release my flame for the liberation of the Divine Us in you. Be released then by the action of Jophiel and Christine and all of the hierarchies of wisdom's flame!

This day Terra receives the initiation of the holy Kumaras. Let us see now how mankind demand the real teaching—the truth, the law, the life! And let us see through whose hand the hand of God will feed the children of the Mother! I AM with you in the fervor of light's fruition, light's accomplishment, light's fulfillment in the crown. I AM the devotee of the Buddhic One! I AM the light of the sun!

July 6, 1975
12:50-1:06 P.M. PDT

Summit University is sponsored by Gautama Buddha, Lord of the World. Lord Maitreya and the World Teachers, Jesus and Kuthumi, are directly involved—teaching, counseling, raising consciousness. Summit University is an experience in God. It is an encounter with the Real Self. It exposes the synthetic self at the same time as it reveals the greater glory of the inner man, the inner woman. Then it lets you choose between the two. Its premise is that the world, with its built-in illusions, does not allow the souls of mankind to make an accurate choice between the real and the unreal. To clarify the issues, to point the way of freedom side by side with the way of bondage, to give you the opportunity to choose and choose well: this is the action of Christ and Buddha. This is the work of the Mother in the mystery school.

22

THE WORK OF THE WORLD TEACHERS IN THIS AGE
Summit University: A Mystery School
of the Great White Brotherhood

A Presentation by Elizabeth Clare Prophet
and the Students

This afternoon our lecture, "The Work of the World Teachers in This Age," will be on the subject of Summit University, a mystery school of the Great White Brotherhood founded by Gautama Buddha. I'm going to ask our Academic Dean to speak to you about Summit University, so I'll turn the podium over to him now.

Thank you, Mother, and good afternoon. Most of you by this time have probably had the opportunity to visit the bookstore and to pick up a Summit University information package, which are available in the bookstore to all people who are interested in the university. We would like to take this opportunity this afternoon to bring to you a closer contact with the university, to bring to you more definition as to the goals and the theme of the university.

I would like to do that by answering a basic question that many people have asked, and that is: What will Summit University do for me? If I attend Summit University, how is it going to enhance my life and further me along life's way and more properly bring me into my divine plan and the fullness of that which I am supposed to do in this life? It's a very pertinent question, and I would like to answer it by discussing five points that lead to the preparedness of an individual on his walk on the path of life.

The first point I would like to make is that Summit University is preparation for a greater understanding. By greater understanding, I mean an expanded awareness of life, an expanded consciousness, an awareness of God and all that is taking place around us. Attending Summit University enables an individual to go out into life's ways and to experience all of the experiences that one can encounter during a lifetime; it enables the student to be able to discern between reality and unreality, which is very difficult. Of course, the higher we get on the ladder of attainment, the more subtle the differences become. So this discernment enables the individual to go out into the world and interpret the experiences that come to him while living this life. So, preparedness for greater understanding.

The second point I would like to make is that Summit University is preparation for your life's work, whatever that work may be, whatever your profession or your livelihood, whatever you're going to do to make a living—what the masters refer to as your sacred labor. The world has created somewhat of a mechanical society where the joy of working and serving in a profession has become to many mundane boredom and routine that has resulted in many people wanting to leave jobs and not work at all—simply because of the lack of the flame of joy that's missing in many of the occupations and the work that is available in the world today.

At Summit University, the ascended masters' teachings enable a person to align himself with the divine plan and thereby maximize the opportunity of his sacred labor. And when one understands cosmic law and the teachings as the masters bring them forth, there is really no need for dissatisfaction or discontentment with the work which we do in this life. But rather, those who leave Summit University have a sense of joy, a sense of accomplishment, a sense of responsibility, and a sense of fulfillment when they go out and they work, whatever their job may be— whether they're an engineer or a doctor or whether they're weaving baskets or they're a professional mother.

Whatever life's calling, Summit University prepares a person for that calling and enables the person to become involved in a calling and a job that is in alignment with their own divine plan rather than something that would be counterproductive to that which they are intended to do. So Summit University is preparation for your life's work.

The third point I would like to make is that Summit University prepares the individual for greater service. There are those who have determined that they will devote their lives, one way or another, to serving their fellowman, to serving humanity. And some people, while searching for this service, whatever it may be, become involved in things like the Peace Corps and VISTA and working with local volunteer programs. Many opportunities are available. We've contacted people like this. We've had people come to the school who have had such a background.

But Summit University provides the training whereby the aspiring student becomes an effective light-bearer, doing more than rendering a mere service of one's energy in labor to a cause; but rather one learns to devote his *entire being* to the betterment of humanity, to the betterment of mankind. And through the science of the spoken Word and special invocations that are given to the students, regardless of one's service, an individual learns to become a world-server.

Whether you're working directly with the masters' outer organization or whether, because of age or other limitations, you're perhaps forced to stay at home, a person can learn to render greater service to mankind through the use of the teachings and the invocations that are given at the university. Those of you who have felt at one time or another that you're just not doing enough to serve because you're not working in the outer organization and something is limiting you from doing that, you can learn to become an effective light-bearer, learn to become as effective as anyone else doing any other kind of job, regardless of your age, your background, or what you are or what you're doing. And that's extremely important in the world today. So Summit University prepares the individual for service.

The fourth point I would like to make is that Summit University is preparation for initiation. And initiation is the real theme of the university. It is the essential theme of the masters' teachings, for it is by the successful en-countering of initiations that we ascend in consciousness and we rise in attainment. At Summit University, the masters, through Mother, outline initiations and teach the student to see and understand these initiations when they manifest.

Now the masters initiate many people, and many people receive initiations from the masters; but many are unaware of the fact that they are being initiated. And here is where the essential element comes in, because at Summit University the initiations are stepped up. The students have a closer contact with the masters; they have a closer contact with the messenger. And through the office of the messenger, the masters are able to give initiations to students that they would not ordinarily receive—initiations that can be administered only by an appointed representative of the ascended masters, initiations that truly are not available in like manner anywhere else on the planet. Coming this close to the masters and coming this close to their representative is extremely valuable, and I really don't think that enough emphasis can be put on that point. So, Summit University is preparation for initiation.

The fifth and last point that I would like to make is that Summit University is preparation for the ascension. Whether you've been studying the masters' teachings for a decade or whether this is your first conference, whether you are eighteen or eighty or over, the tools for a more rapid acceleration on the path of attainment are given forth at Summit University.

For those of you who are aspiring to make your ascension, the knowledge, the teachings, the experiences that come forth are invaluable; they are experiences and teachings that have never been released at conferences. There is instruction that has never been printed in a book.

And, at least for some time to come, many of these teachings people will receive only by attending Summit University. So for those of you who feel like you've just begun to scratch the surface in attending this conference, I'd like to say that there's much, much more. This is just an infinitesimal portion of that which is available. So, my fifth point—Summit University is preparation for the ascension.

Regardless of your background or your calling in life or your level of attainment, the point we would like to make is that Summit University has something for you. No one has left Summit University, has completed one or more quarters, that has not noticeably and extensively benefited from attending the school. I think that every student that is here at this conference would attest to that. I feel that probably the greatest illustration that we could give you at this time is some living examples of people who have gone through the transformations that all experience at Summit University. So today we have some students with us who are going to talk to you briefly about their experiences at the university and what this close contact with the masters and Mother has meant to them.

Aloha!

Aloha! I say "Aloha" because last December, just shortly before Christmas, my husband and my five-year-old daughter and I left our island home to have a short visit with family and friends on the mainland. Around January 5 we went to the Motherhouse in Santa Barbara to see what The Summit Lighthouse was about. We heard a dictation, our first dictation. It was delivered by Sanat Kumara and Lady Master Venus at the conference in Los Angeles at Christmas or at New Year's time. It completely changed our lives.

We had been living in the lap of the Divine Mother in the most beautiful place we had ever lived in, in the islands—totally blissed, as you might say, with the natural beauty of our home, of eating off of a campfire, of swimming in crystal-clear waters—and yet something was missing. It was that sense of incompletion, of "where is that place we can return this energy? What can we do to show our gratitude?" And we couldn't really verbalize it. It was hard to talk about. But we had difficulty in overcoming some of the little trivial trips that assail every parent, every family that is upon the face of the planet.

Three months later I found myself at the Easter conference quavering back and forth in my Cancerian manner of waterhood—the old way of going up and down (what's going to happen next?)—whether I should go to Summit University or not. I heard and witnessed and felt the flames of students from the previous quarter, and my soul just leaped, knowing that this was something that I had to do—not only for myself, but for my family and for everyone who I would ever meet that day and onward. And I was afraid. I was scared, I have to say.

I knew that it was the greatest thing that had ever happened to me in the way of education and the way of experience. And every single day that I passed at Summit University, I knew more and more that I was gaining the tools that would help me master that flow of the water.

At this point, it's an honor and a great privilege to speak to you and to be able to share with you the joy of having the tools to master that which used to cause problems, that which used to be the basis of inharmony, of doubt and fear, and all the things that we encounter along the Path. Try as we might to overcome them, unless we have the right tool for the task, it's very difficult to overcome them.

I look in the faces of my husband and daughter now and I can see the change that I have undergone in their response to my ability, through the grace of God and through the grace of the masters and the tools that I have received, to meet every need and every obstacle and every little problem in an everyday sense, with the greatest amount of love and understanding and the right thing to do, so that that person doesn't feel like, for instance, when they're five years old, that they're being stepped on, that they're under too much discipline, that something's going on that's unjust in their life.

It's so important for us, the Mother in all of us, to nurture every other part of life and let them know how important they are as they're blossoming. I am so grateful for this awareness, for this expansion of perspectives so that those trivial things, instead of being one big problem, can all be so tiny now. You can put a whole bunch of them in one little bag, call upon the masters who have promised they would help in that particular instance, and just sort of dispose of it, the whole time keeping the harmony in the family and feeling that love and that illumination and that truth flowing from the arms of the masters.

It's such a practical experience! If you're never going to go to another school, another seminar, another anything, a quarter at Summit University can clear up so much and fill so many gaps and so many cracks and expand your awareness so much for meeting the world and for meeting all the people that you meet every day who need that little something. It's just the most glorious experience to know that there's that and even more, and that as you go back on the three months experience and start applying it, you pull out of the memory bank those things and use them in everyday life. You see that you really are the hands and the feet of the masters and of divine will and of the love of the Mother.

I'm very grateful for this opportunity to thank you, to thank the masters, and to thank Mother, the Mother of the Flame, for her service, for her dedication to all of us. And I think I have an inkling of that fire that burns in her heart to want to welcome you all to Summit University and to the arms of the Divine Mother. Thank you so much.

T.M., Portland, Oreg.

Gold Is Precipitated Sunlight

It is also my privilege to welcome you here. It's a really fulfilling part of my life, because I was here for a month and a half before this all got together and I can see how it's been formulating. To see you all here from all parts of the earth and especially from our America—it's quite fulfilling. Being a guard, I've noticed on your name tags where you've been and where you've come from, and it's really thrilling.

It's a thought form that I would like to place in your minds and in your hearts—of how much actually there is at Summit University to gain and experience. Every day for those twelve weeks, the masters place just thousands and thousands of little seeds in our minds. Just one of those seeds was that sunlight itself was precipitated gold, or gold itself is precipitated sunlight. Maybe they work both ways. But it's true. Gold is a valuable source of our monetary well-being and we must have it in order for the monetary system to work.

Gold is found everywhere. It's found in the earth, right beneath your feet right now. The scientists can pull it out, even in places where we can't see it. It's in the air that we breathe, because if gold is precipitated sunlight, then that sunlight is with us every day and we're actually breathing and living gold. It purifies our systems and it purifies the system of worlds that we're in. It's something more special than perhaps we really know about.

We think of the presence of that gold and the desire that so many men have had to have that gold in their pockets. Perhaps they don't really want it in their pockets for the right reasons, but they still want it in their pockets. I think we all know that. We've watched enough Western movies and everything. And perhaps we've even felt that we want something as precious as gold ourselves. We desire something more precious than gold.

Well, that gold under your feet right now is also available to you, perhaps at the bottom of that lake out there behind me—nuggets maybe the size of your fingernails. And if you look long enough, you might find them. They might somehow fall into your reach. You might even stumble upon them in the night and come up with one in your hand in the fistful of dirt that you happened to grab. You might search for years and find a vein of gold out in the hills out there that runs three weeks. You might mine it for that long and become sort of rich.

And then perhaps one day after you've searched for a long time, you go to the heart of say, Mount Shasta, and you find a vein thirty feet wide, thousands of feet long—just pure, solid, rich gold shimmering in, say, rose quartz—something that beautiful—and you find it. What are you going to do with it? It's too beautiful to dig out of the mountain, but you do value it.

I would like to say that Summit University is like finding the vein of gold in that mountain. It's endless. You couldn't spend it in your lifetime. All you can do is reach it and use it. It's there and you're at the threshold of it right now if you so choose to be. You've perhaps come a long way—thousands of embodiments, thousands of miles to come right to here where it is. The knowledge is gold because the knowledge is light. And if light precipitates gold, then I would like to say that you're all very rich right now. I thank you very much for this opportunity to speak to you.

V.S., Oceano, Calif.

Wisdom's Angels Are on the March

Good afternoon. I've had the privilege of meeting some of your children in the children's program, and I would just like to say to you that I know all of you are having a marvelous experience here and we're having a marvelous experience with the children. And the children are so beautiful. They're a little bit like the souls who come to Summit University, I guess, but perhaps a little less tarnished by the world this lifetime. They're so beautiful; they're so receptive; and I feel that it's been such an honor and a privilege to be able to work with them.

As I was sitting in the dictation this morning, I asked Apollo to tell me what I should say this afternoon and I got the keynote. It was "Wisdom's angels are on the march." And Summit University students are on the march, and so are all of us on the march to truth on our planet. At Summit University we get armed with a certain sense of fearlessness and a great love for our fellow

children of the light on the Path and for each other, and
with the golden two-edged sword of illumination, that
sword which cleaves asunder the real from the unreal,
light from darkness, truth from error, and immortality
from death. We take that out with us.

And as Apollo spoke to us all this morning—and he
was imploring us to impart the true teachings—I was
thinking to myself, we have such a need to awaken
mankind from ignorance. Summit University has been my
own awakening, and I want to pass that on to you. The
flame just leaped within my heart—and I know all of
yours—as we heard our beloved Apollo this morning; and
I reconsecrated myself, as I know most of us did, to the
flame of wisdom and to saving a planet. And it's to the
flame that leaped within my heart that I give honor and
glory and the gratitude of my heart for the experience that
I've had at Summit University and that I'm having at the
conference now with all of us, and especially with your
children.

I really never had such a tremendous experience in
my lifetime as I had at Summit University. It's the experience of being taught through the heart and the Christ
mind of our beloved messenger, the teachings of the
ascended masters coming through our messenger and
through the other instructors at the university. You've
never attended a university like Summit University, I'll
tell you! When I finished my doctorate in clinical
psychology in 1966, I said to myself, "Well, that's the end
of school, thank goodness!" You know, no more school
for me—twenty-one years of it's quite enough! And that
was, of course, before I had come into the awakening and
gotten to know something of the ascended masters, as you
might gather.

Well, I'm standing here to tell you that the experience of Summit University and our beloved Mother of
the Flame and the ascended masters' teachings have completely lifted that veil of ignorance when I said, "No more
schooling for me!" I realized that life is schooling, that
our whole embodiment is learning more and more of God
and of the creation. And I'm really ready to go back

tomorrow—and we just finished a few weeks ago, right before the conference!

For me it was being taught in heart and soul and mind. It was satisfying the longing that my soul has had all my lifetime. And I never found it anywhere—to have a complete learning experience, a God-directed learning experience. And I hope that many of you will give your souls this same opportunity. It's like getting that cup of cold water after you've crossed that burning desert of the human wasteland that we've all been crossing for many, many years.

Words are really kind of inadequate to express the joy and gratitude that I feel from my experience, but I do hope that you're feeling some of what I'm saying to you. And I do want to add, too, to the professional people who may be here, that it's the first time that I feel my professional training is going to be adequate. I don't feel that my work as a psychotherapist could have been anywhere near complete. To have the teachings of the ascended masters has been the true psychology and the integration of all of the training that I've received all of my life.

I think I've known since I was a little girl that I was to work and serve people and to catalyze other souls somehow, but I didn't know what that meant. I thought for a while that it meant a lot of graduate school and it meant working in the "world" kind of psychology. Now I do know what it means. And I know that this would be true for professional people in many other areas—that with the ascended masters' teachings, you will find that true sacred labor that God wants for you and that your soul is yearning for.

So I just want to say, come to Summit University and be armed with wisdom's ray as we go out into the world in the flow of the love of the Divine Mother and the power of the Father. And we're going to all go out, we're going to slay the dragons for Mother and the masters, and we're going to save the planet and bring the earth into the golden age! Thank you.

M.B., Boulder, Colo.

"I Represent the Grayhairs!"

And I represent the grayhairs! I received just such an
inspiration from someone months ago who invited the
grayhairs to come and take ascended-master university
training. And I thought, well, could I do it? I'm pretty
well along. But then a member of the staff gave me
another nudge; and finally my own soul, I suppose,
wouldn't give me any peace.

So I just completed that same first level that you've
just heard about. They've told you all of that. And that
word "level," when I first heard it, well, I thought that
that was a commonplace word. But all of a sudden I found
myself up a level! And you'd never go back after you're up
a level!

All the wonderful things that have been said are so
true. And I have experienced that one level so far. When
the next or what the next will be I'm just leaving to the
Powers that be to direct me, as we've been told to do. And
so we don't have to worry about it. Whatever we're
supposed to do, the avenue will present itself and there we
find ourselves. And so with that same spirit of enthusiasm
that you've already heard and with the gratitude that we
feel towards our precious Mother of the Flame and the
wonderful teachers and the masters who prescribed all
this, we say, thank you.

Thank you, God. Thank you, all. Thank you.

A.B., Oakland, Calif.

I can only glow with a mother's joy to see all of the beautiful
people coming through Summit University, to know that God has
made them what they are and I've had the privilege of helping the
petals to unfold. It is truly the greatest experience of my life to be
at the point of Summit University where I see the transformation
taking place in souls who come.

We have a picture that is taken for the application and we
have a picture that is taken at the end of the twelfth week and we
put them in the folder for our records, and usually you can't tell
it's the same person. You have to be sure and mark the second
picture so you know which folder to put it in.

The Gift of Initiation

The transformation, I can only say, is by the grace of God. And as I was meditating on what that transformation is, Maitreya showed me that it is the gift of initiation. It is the gift of the hand of God working through my heart and hand and imparting to the students something from their own causal body, something from their own I AM Presence, which must come according to hierarchy from teacher to disciple and be handed down. And so levels are niches—i-niche-i-action (initiation)— as Mark used to talk about it. And that is what the gift of Summit University is.

The studying, the decrees, the invocations—all of these are outer forms whereby the inner soul and flame can be drawn to the surface and spill over, as it were, like the oil of Mount Shasta and inundate the entire being and soul and consciousness for that life of service. I know that there isn't anything greater that has ever happened and that I am the observer and the instrument and God is the doer. This is the dream of the ascended masters and the beginning of universities of the Spirit, and all I can say is how privileged I am!

A Declaration of Independence of Terra

At the end of each quarter, we have a president's reception; and all the students come and we have a good time, and we sing and we talk about our togetherness. And Saint Germain gives a dictation to each concluding class. This last class was under the direction of Lady Master Nada and the sixth ray; and they have a tremendous sense of service and the meaning of karma yoga— balancing one's karma through service on that sixth ray, as Jesus taught us. And this class put together a Declaration of Independence of Terra and presented it at the president's reception.

They put together their hearts, their heads, their pens, and determined that they would declare before Almighty God and Sanat Kumara the independence of the planet, just as our forefathers declared the independence of this nation and this soil for us to prove the Christ consciousness. And when that was read, my thoughts went to Sanat Kumara, to the cosmic councils, to that moment when they had decided that earth should be snuffed out. And I thought to myself: "Sanat Kumara, you are redeemed in this hour! The few and the many are responding. And for all the fiats and the dispensations and all of the input of hierarchy, a new generation of light-bearers has risen up to take their stand, to claim this planet for the light."

I'd like you to hear a student read this declaration of independence. And if any of you care to sign it, as I signed it and Lanello signed it, we'd be happy to have you do so. I think it's a tremendous fruit of the Spirit, of the union of masters and their students.

If I may add just one thing to what everyone has already said about Summit University: The one thing that it's really done for me is that it's filled my soul so I could become myself; and I think that's the whole point to it— to discover your individuality and your God-identity. And so it's with our hearts that we put our energy into the Declaration of Independence of Terra. Hear ye, hear ye!

When in the course of cosmic events it becomes necessary for a planet to be set free and for Terra to assume a perfect rotation by which the laws of cosmos and the grace of God entitle her, it becomes necessary for those who claim the light to unsheathe the sword of truth and release through the power of the spoken Word the reasons that impel them to come apart and be a separate and chosen people.

We hold these eternal truths to be self-evident, that all men are created to realize God and to one day ascend back to their I AM Presence, that they are endowed by their creator with certain unalienable rights, that among these are a balanced threefold flame, a Holy Christ Self, and the rights of free will to choose the light. That to harmonize these perfect energies, decrees are issued amongst men, deriving their just powers from the untapped sources of the cosmos. That whenever any form of darkness is encountered, it shall be challenged by the power of the light.

And citadels of truth shall arise, laying their foundations on such principles of love and molding their powers with such wisdom of the divine that to them shall seem most likely to raise a planet and its people back to the fiery destiny from whence they came. We, therefore, as just representatives of the light, appeal to the Goddess of Justice, beloved Portia, for the rectitude of our intent. And in the name and by the authority of the Christ consciousness of each soul of this sacred mandala, we solemnly affirm and decree that Terra is, now and forever, a God-free planet.

By affirming the ark of the covenant within our hearts, we are now and forever lively stones in the Church Universal and Triumphant. For the support of this declaration, with firm reliance upon the protection of Archangel Michael, we mutually pledge to each other, on the cube of white fire within, our hearts, our heads, and our hands. By the grace and will of God, we accept this done in the year of our Lord, nineteen hundred and seventy-five. Amen.

J.V., Seattle, Wash.

Now you know some of the joy that I experience as I see the I AM Presence coming into full manifestation in the hearts of those who come to Summit University and in all of you as you keep the flame across the planetary home. This magnificent scroll, a gift to cosmic councils, is received with gratitude by the entire hierarchy.

A Way of Life

Before closing our presentation on Summit University, I would like to show you this brochure called *A Way of Life*. It is part of the entire packet that is given to those who are interested in Summit University, which you can procure at the Summit University booth. *A Way of Life* is the code of conduct for students of Summit University. It was compiled under the direction of El Morya and Serapis Bey, our two key disciplinarians. I'd like to read you the introduction to this pamphlet, which we would like to pass out to all of you so that you can understand what it means to be a disciple, what it means to be disciplined by the ascended masters.

Discipline is a way of life, and that way begins with the teacher. The ascended masters present an alternative to chaos, personal and planetary—the order of the cosmos. Order is God as energy moving in spirals of patterned identity—in you, in time and space, in eternity. The discipline of hierarchy challenges an age. It calls the true devotees of the law of selfhood to reach the acme of self-awareness as God.

Discipline is a rod of iron magnetizing components of individuality into the polarity of the Real Self. Discipline when self-imposed is the instrument of self-perfectionment. When imposed by a master, it becomes the means of self-liberation. Those who have walked the way of self-discipline know that the crumbling of civilization comes when men fail to walk in the way of ordered being, of disciplined consciousness. They know that where there is no self-will to discipline, little by little people lose touch with reality. They become incapable of defining individuality, and they utterly fail to come to grips with personal and planetary karma.

We live in a world where, for want of discipline, people neither know themselves nor each other. The ancient teachers foresaw the end from the beginning. Hence they inscribed upon the temple wall, "Man, know thy self!" To know the self necessitates finding the way of life that will discipline the self. Moreover, it requires a teacher—one who has disciplined the self and thereby defined the self.

The purpose of Summit University is to teach disciples of the ascended masters scientific methods for discovering reality, defining identity, balancing karma, and knowing the True Self of all. To achieve this goal, the code of conduct was outlined under the direction of the Masters El Morya and Serapis Bey specifically for men and women desiring to place their feet firmly on the path of initiation.

Without discipline, there is no path and no disciple. For the one who would be disciple is the one who willingly submits to the discipline of the teacher within and the teacher without. The teacher within is the Real Self; the teacher without is the ascended master. Both are given preeminence at Summit University. Elizabeth Clare Prophet is the focal point for the student's realization of both aspects of hierarchy. Through her flame, students learn to define the inner guru and they merge with those who, having defined the inner guru, have become that guru. These are they who have thereby mastered time and space and entered into the reunion of the One.

The ascended masters are the real teachers of the age. They preside at Summit University. Sponsored by Gautama Buddha and assisted by Lord Maitreya and the World Teachers, Jesus and Kuthumi, the masters of the Great White Brotherhood are using the forum of this mystery school to contact their chelas throughout the world. Step by step, they outline the path so that all who sincerely want to know God and to experience being as life, truth, and love cannot fail to increase, measure for measure, their awareness of self as God.

The goal of attainment is set for the few, that the many might follow the standard of a new age and a new energy. Summit University is the catalyst of cosmic consciousness. It is a twelve-week spiral that begins with you as self-awareness and ends with you as God Self-awareness. As you traverse the spiral, light intensifies, darkness is transmuted. You experience the rebirth day by day as the old man is put off and the new man is put on. To implement this alchemy of self-awareness, initiations are given by the masters through the Mother of the Flame individually to the students as one by one they present themselves a living sacrifice for love. Energies are aligned, chakras are cleared, and the soul is poised in the four lower bodies for the victorious fulfillment of the individual divine plan.

The premise of Gautama, teacher of teachers, is: "There is an escape from darkness unto light. There is a way wherein the soul takes flight. I point the way. I AM the way." Jesus said the same; for he, too, found the way through the flame within. At Summit University we teach the way of self-mastery according to the ascended masters' teachings for their disciples in this age. Those who would walk in that way rejoice as a flame that leaps into the fire of God to follow the disciplines outlined in the following code of conduct. They have accepted the master's way and the master as the way. They rejoice to behold the day when, through discipline and self-mastery, they can say to souls along life's way, "I AM the way."

July 6, 1975
2:56-3:45 P.M. P D T

23

CHURCH UNIVERSAL AND TRIUMPHANT

A Lecture by Elizabeth Clare Prophet

This morning we spoke about the challenge of the four quadrants of Matter, of the four lower bodies, and the intrusion—the thrusts of Antichrist—into those four lower bodies. We see very clearly that this is our challenge, this is our responsibility for a lifetime. The ascended masters, the Great White Brotherhood, and the Darjeeling Council have also seen this plight, this dilemma, and they have offered a solution. I have come this afternoon to present to you the ascended masters' solution to the challenge.

If you would draw a circle and divide it into four quadrants, I will show you the diagram and the plan for world action (see p. 301), which we are going to present to you in a fuller outline in the two-day leadership seminar. But for all of you who have newly come into the teachings and are desirous of seeing how we can take Apollo's flame and carry the torch into action, I will give the outline in the next hour.

The Father: The Summit Lighthouse

The Summit Lighthouse was conceived in the heart of Morya, the Chief of the Darjeeling Council. He contacted his representative Mark L. Prophet in 1958, after having trained him since a child, and said, "Go to Washington, D.C., and found The Summit Lighthouse!" The founding of The Summit Lighthouse was the first step in the master plan. Morya had the cosmic conception. And as all cycles begin at the 12 o'clock line, he began there at the point of God the Father, the Impersonal Impersonality, with The Summit Lighthouse, designed to be that organization which would publish the teachings of the ascended masters. In other words, The Summit Lighthouse was founded to set forth the law, cosmic law, for the Aquarian cycle. The ascended masters would use it as a forum for the Lawgiver. Later Summit University Press was inaugurated as a department within The Summit Lighthouse to distribute our books nationally and internationally on a wholesale basis. Today hundreds of bookstores distribute the teachings of the ascended masters.

The Son: Montessori International
and Summit University

We have labored many years together setting forth that law, writing and publishing; and at this time the Word has gone forth over the face of the earth. Many, many souls have taken up that teaching. The time came, however, when the law itself and the torch of the Father should be passed to the Son. And so on the 3 o'clock line the inspiration of the Christ flame, that focal point of the Impersonal Personality of the Christ, was taken up in the founding of educational institutions that would teach the law, demonstrate the understanding of the law; for this is the office of the Son of God. The bursting forth of the flame of illumination, then, in the mental quadrant, the second quadrant of the circle, manifested first as Montessori International. This was the school that Mark and I founded in Colorado Springs in 1970; we held it in our retreat there.

At its zenith, Montessori International had almost one hundred students from preschool (age 2½) through the eighth grade. We had one of the most fantastic programs that has ever been devised: foreign language programs, skiing, science experiments for little children in the early grades, language training, even Latin for fourth graders. We had a class where Spanish was spoken exclusively with English only to assist the child to learn Spanish.

We consider our Montessori school the most vital activity on the line of the Christ, which forms a part of our fourfold effort.

Now second to that, Gautama Buddha came in his 1973 New
Year's Address and delivered into my hand "a torch charged with
the vital fires from God's heavenly altar and the conveyance of a
vast mission to illumine the world's children and produce the
blessing of true culture to the age and unto all people everywhere."
That flame of the Buddha was passed to me as a torch, and I have
been running with it ever since. As a result of this dispensation,
at the Freedom '73 conference we announced the opening of the
doors of Summit University. Summit University and Montessori
International, on the 3 o'clock line, are the institutions which will
carry forward the statement of the law that has been given through
The Summit Lighthouse.

I'd like you to notice that the statement of the law is that
which defeats the dragon. It sets the blueprint for a golden age; it
exposes the Liar and the lie; it exposes the accuser of the brethren.
This is the purpose of The Summit Lighthouse – to set the etheric
blueprint and to withdraw the power of the dragon. On the 3
o'clock line, the institutions of learning restore the Christ consciousness to mankind. They defeat the Antichrist and the beast that
comes out of the sea and the beast that comes out of the earth.[1]

It is one thing for the law to be stated in books; but as you
well know, we have schools upon the planet because people need
to be taught what is in the books. The teaching has to be made
alive by good teachers; and we have the finest in the cosmos – the
ascended masters – and they do illumine their own pages. And they
are continually dictating. Whenever I take the platform at Summit
University, one or another of the ascended masters is giving
enlightenment on a vast host of subjects. The most thrilling thing
is to have a student ask a question and an ascended master answer
the question. When you're a student and that happens to you, you
will know what a thrill it is.

The Mother: Church Universal and Triumphant

Now, with these first two quadrants covered in an organizational manner, functioning and reaching out, we come to the
line of the Mother, to the holding of the Mother flame at the 6
o'clock line. This is the line of further expansion of the masters'
work at the organizational level. John the Revelator had the vision.
He beheld the New Jerusalem coming out of heaven as a bride

adorned for her husband.[2] This is a most fantastic conception of the Cosmic Virgin! He's speaking about a New Jerusalem, a City Foursquare, and in the same sentence it is "a bride adorned for her husband." The Bride that is adorned for the Father is the Cosmic Mother, and it has ever been in the tradition of world religion that the Church is the Bride of the Holy Spirit.

The Church is the feminine aspect. The Church represents the squaring of the circle. The New Jerusalem is the City Foursquare. It is the squaring of the Trinity of Father, Son, and Holy Spirit. The Church comes forth so that the Mother flame can be enshrined upon the altar; and with the Mother flame enshrined upon the altar, the Church is the magnet that draws the children of God back to the ritual of ordered service and worship whereby they pass through the gate of the victory of the ascension.

The statement of the law and the teaching of the law could not be complete without organization in the Mother flame, which is the Church. Accordingly, the ascended masters made the announcement over the last two years, in many dictations and documents that we have received, of the founding of what is to be known as Church Universal and Triumphant.

The vision of the Church was given to me as I saw beloved Jesus the Christ in heaven standing at the altar of a mighty cathedral. And I saw assembled by the thousands those whom we call the saints—those souls at the etheric level and above in the ascended octaves who form that part of God which is known as the body of God in heaven. And Jesus revealed to me that it was time for that Church, that conception as a cosmic conception, to be lowered into manifestation. The time had come because the cycles had turned. The time had come because disciples had made themselves ready.

And so Jesus appointed me to inaugurate this Church; and he placed upon me the mantle of the Vicar of Christ, which means simply the representative of Christ. Mother Mary was the head of the Church when Jesus left. It is the Mother flame that is the center of the Church. And subsequent to that anointing, which took place several years ago, we received the dictation from the ascended master Pope John XXIII, who, as the Vicar of Christ, came forth in February of 1974 to announce that it was time for the Church Universal and Triumphant to be formally inaugurated, to have legal status in the world, to have a set of articles and bylaws and a formal board of directors and categories of members and communicants. The dictation in which he outlined this is included in a Keepers of the Flame Lesson. When you arrive at that lesson, you will be able to read it in its entirety.

He said in this dictation that the Church Universal and Triumphant was to be the feminine aspect of our mandala. It was to be the nucleus and the white-fire core of those devotees who had a more than ordinary desire to be devoted, to become part of the ritual of the true Church, participating in the sacraments to be dictated by beloved Jesus, who would accept a body of tenets, who would bind together and form the cosmic cube. He explained that although The Summit Lighthouse had been functioning as the Church, as the Father aspect, it was like the white sphere; and the wholeness of Alpha and Omega as the whole sphere would now be divided in twain. Now the Alpha-to-Omega would function in polarity as The Summit Lighthouse, representing the Father of God, and Church Universal and Triumphant, representing the Mother of God.

So The Summit Lighthouse would be, as it always has been, the publishing arm; the Church would be the house, the cosmic cube to receive the children of God and the place where those who would undergo the disciplines of the Mother would then be able to take the initiations step by step—through the sacraments, through the holy orders—of ascending in consciousness, in vibration, and preparing for the ascension.

Church Universal and Triumphant is a circular stairway that we take step by step. It presents the outline of the thirty-three initiations that are required of everyone who takes the ascension. And it presents a nucleus, an order, a foundation whereby we can take our families, our loved ones, our children, and give them the training that is necessary.

Just as the Mother flame is not the first thing that we discover when we come into the teachings, so Church Universal and Triumphant is not that which is most obvious about the work of the Great White Brotherhood. Rather, it represents the fiery core, the inner devotees—those who hold the flame of the Mother and are concerned with the raising of the culture of Lemuria and being part of the body of God on earth and who are willing to undergo the disciplines to so become. It is Church Universal and Triumphant that sounds the death knell to the great whore, to the total organization of the misuse of the feminine ray on the planet. I am very pleased to report, then, to this company that on the anniversary of Saint Germain's ascension, on May 1, 1975, Church Universal and Triumphant was officially incorporated and has status as a corporation in the United States of America.

The Holy Spirit: Keepers of the Flame Fraternity

Completing the four quarters of the circle, we look to the 9 o'clock line to see who will carry the flame of the Holy Spirit, who will undo the teachings of the false prophets, the false hierarchies. This is the line of the Keepers of the Flame. The Keepers of the Flame are those who keep the flame of life, which is the flame of the Holy Spirit. The Keepers of the Flame Fraternity has been the fraternity of Saint Germain within The Summit Lighthouse since the early 1960s. The obligations in the Keepers of the Flame Fraternity are simply to study the lessons, to practice them, to apply them, and to offer to Saint Germain regular monthly dues of three dollars to support the publishing through The Summit Lighthouse. The Keepers of the Flame represent that body of the Lord which goes forth to contact the masses through the Holy Spirit.

A Place for You in the Four Aspects of the Circle

We see that in each quadrant, hierarchy has answered, hierarchy has given forth the counterpoint to each attempt of the fallen ones to usurp the planes of Mater. Now, for each and every one of you, there is a niche, there is a place, there is a time and a place for you to find yourself in each one of these planes.

The first contact a person has with the ascended masters' teachings is normally through something published by The Summit Lighthouse—a book or a pamphlet. And books and this type of teaching suffice until you want more. And when you want more, you decide to become a Keeper of the Flame, to take the lessons, and to have a certain amount of initiation; but your direct contact is with the ascended masters, not so much with the organization. To intensify that activity of the Holy Spirit, you may decide to take training at Summit University. And of course our quarterly conferences are mini-courses that come on the 3 o'clock line of the Christ. So we see, then, the Father, the Son, and the Holy Spirit in these three aspects.

Finally, should you really decide to become part of the foundation of the Mother flame for the Aquarian age, you would consider membership in the Church Universal and Triumphant. Pope John XXIII explained to us that those who are members of the inner Church, the heavenly Church, already have the cube within their heart. The cube is the sign of membership, and it cannot be gainsaid: you either have the cube or you do not. It is the mark of the Godhead and the mark of your service to the light in previous incarnations. You may earn the cube by affiliating as a Communicant of the Church.

It is very interesting that since we have begun initiating members in the Church, as the prospective members have come before me for an interview, Jesus has shown me the cube in the heart. It lights up. It is a crystal. It is a perfect cube. And it encases the threefold flame. It is magnificent to behold, and we behold it in all of the saints in white robes who stand in that mighty cathedral. The Church Universal and Triumphant is designed to be the open door of the Divine Mother to receive individuals from every walk of life. There are individuals in every church on the planet who have that cube in the heart. Our concern is not so much that they join us but that we reinforce their light that we might be one in the flame.

Now these four aspects of the circle show you the inner workings of the Great White Brotherhood and what we are about and how we can go forth to realize the divine plan. Serving in any aspect of one of the four, you have the opportunity to include the rest for the purposes of expansion and of inundating the earth with the total circle of our cosmic consciousness.

The Circle of Oneness: Summit International

We have conceived under the direction of the Darjeeling Council a unifying principle—a name, a concept, a mandala that would mean to all of us the totality of the plan. This name is that which is to be used in centers throughout the United States and the world, centers for the teachings of the ascended masters. The name for the circle of the oneness of the four is Summit International.

We see that the Summit is the principle of the I AM Presence, the pinnacle of being which we reach through the teachings of the masters. We know that the Christ Child that comes forth from the

Divine Mother, the Manchild, has a purpose: He goes forth to rule all nations with a rod of iron.[3] The teachings of the ascended masters are for all nations, all peoples, and our scope is worldwide in its outreach. We see, then, that this name is fitting to include The Summit Lighthouse, Summit University, Montessori International, the Keepers of the Flame Fraternity, and at the fiery core, the Church Universal and Triumphant.

The two days of our leadership seminar will be devoted to showing you how you can organize nuclei, teaching centers of Summit International, and how you can incorporate in your areas the structure and the services of the Church Universal and Triumphant. I would now like to ask the Reverend Monroe Shearer to read to you the twelve tenets of the Church.[4] They are most enlightening. [Tenets are read.]

Membership in the Church

These are the twelve tenets of faith that form the foundation for those who would become Communicants in the Church. Communicants are those who desire to affiliate with the Church in an outer way by applying for membership and supporting the outer organization. There are several classes of membership within the Church. To be eligible to be a Communicant, we ask that you shall have passed through seven lessons of the Keepers of the Flame Fraternity.

Membership in the Church is not to be taken lightly, but with consideration of the responsibility of the totality of the mission. We feel it is important that people have time to consider the responsibility—to study the teachings of the masters, to read the books, to really come to grips with what membership means. The tenets can be passed out; you may have them. Keep them. Think about them. And when you have reached that point in the fraternity of making a more than ordinary commitment, you may consider applying for membership.

The holy order within the Church was founded by Mother Mary. It is called the Sons and Daughters of the Dominion of the Water Element. Sons and Daughters of Dominion are selected from the Communicants of the Church. They are appointed and initiated by the head of the Church. They are the holy order that expands the awareness and mastery of the teachings as released by

Mother Mary. And essentially, Mother Mary says that in this age we must have a body of souls who will master energy in motion — the water element.

Those who desire to become Sons and Daughters of Dominion must first become communicants of the Church. Then there are thirty-three vows that Sons and Daughters of Dominion take.[5] They vow to intensify the action of clearing the planes of Mater through invocation, through the science of the cosmic clock, and in general, to support the mission. They are either married or they maintain celibacy. A number of Sons and Daughters of Dominion have been initiated over the past several years.

From the Sons and Daughters of Dominion is selected the Council of the One Hundred Forty-Four. This is a special group of devotees that have certain responsibilities that are defined in the articles and bylaws. And finally, there are the Elders of the Church serving with the Vicar of Christ. They also serve with the board of directors of the Church and they have certain voting rights and certain powers of decision-making within the total running of the Church.

The law of tithing is something that is taken up by members of the Church, as they understand the law of the ten that has been set forth in the Old and New Testament in giving a tenth of one's supply to the support of the activities of hierarchy on earth. The law of the tithe is the foundation of individual spiritual growth. It is the science whereby when we take one-tenth of what God has given to us and give it back to him in his order on earth, in his Church on earth, he then takes that tenth, multiplies or squares it, and gives back to us 100 percent again.

Those who practice the law of the tithe — and there are many in the organization who do — find a tremendous flow of cosmic abundance, freedom, and blessings coming into their lives. When founding the Church, Jesus said that the sign of one's devotion is one's ability to trust the law of the tithe and to give that portion for the growth of the Church.

July 6, 1975
4:16-5:33 P.M. P D T

Activity of the Father
THE SUMMIT LIGHTHOUSE
SUMMIT UNIVERSITY PRESS
THE SUMMIT LIGHTHOUSE GROUPS

Activity of the Holy Spirit
KEEPERS OF THE FLAME
FRATERNITY
CHURCH UNIVERSAL
AND TRIUMPHANT
COMMUNITY TEACHING CENTERS

Activity of the Son
SUMMIT UNIVERSITY
MONTESSORI INTERNATIONAL

Activity of the Mother
CHURCH UNIVERSAL AND TRIUMPHANT

THE MANDALA OF THE
WOMAN AND HER SEED

"This same Jesus which is taken up from you into heaven, shall so come in like manner as ye have seen him go into heaven." As the voice of God spoke to the disciples on the mount of transfiguration, so we echo the fiat "This is my beloved Son, in whom I am well pleased; hear ye him."

Jesus the Christ and Kuthumi serve together as World Teachers. Kuthumi is known to western devotees of Christ as the Master K.H. or for his embodiment as Saint Francis. Jesus and Kuthumi will speak to us on world dilemma.

24

I COME TO CLAIM MY OWN

A Dictation by Jesus the Christ

The Corona of the Soul

Fear not, little flock; it is the Father's good pleasure to give you the kingdom.[1]

I come to call my own. I come to claim my own. I come to receive the little ones and those who have yearned for the oneness we shared in Galilee and in other times as over the centuries we have joined in the battle of light. I come with the golden light of the World Teachers to mark the corona of the soul. And the great Sower of Souls, the Almighty One, commissions me this day to seal that fiery light of the soul in the corona of my own causal body. And there is a golden light now that seals the soul of each one who has taken the spiral of our releases in this conference to the heart as a fire that will grow.

I come to protect the souls by the action of the living Word. I come to anoint you. I come to claim my own. And I am the same Jesus which was taken up from you, and so I have come in like manner as ye have seen me go. So is the coming of the son of man.[2] So is the coming of your own Christ Self, and where there is room to receive him, the coming of the Holy Comforter in the teaching secured by the Mother.

The Mandala of the Church

Now let the cube of souls be formed! Now let the mandala at

the fiery core of the Church be the sign unto the hierarchies of the sun that on Terra souls of light have provided the place where the Mother flame might be enshrined. Let the day of initiation be hastened and let the disciples make themselves ready.

The Wedding Day

Let the preparations be made as for the wedding day! Let the brides come with a veil of innocence purified by application! Let them come washed clean by the flow of the Logos! Let them accept mercy as the healing ray whereby that which has been fractured might be made whole again! And let the bridegroom come, the champion of the Cosmic Virgin! Let the Christed ones appear! Let those who are the framework of the masculine ray of the Godhead now clear the way for the coming of the bride!

And let the best man be there who will speak for the groom, who will keep the flame for him and voluntarily protect, as a keeper of the flame, the sanctity of the marriage vow. And let the matron of honor, carrying the bouquet of the virgin, be summoned as the one who guards the sanctity of the vow of the marriage and prepares by invocation and prayer for the coming of the little ones. Let all the bridal party be those who prepare for the coming of the Church and the Christed One. And let the family of God on earth reflect the holy family in heaven of the sacred trinity of life, even the threefold flame.

Let there be rejoicing! Let there be celebration! Let there be the fiery cube of the heart! I come to clear the way for the coming of the avatars. I come to bless Keepers of the Flame who would reconsecrate their vows. And I shall stand upon the holy mountain of the Lord and I shall release the blessing through the Mother of the Flame for the marriage that is made in heaven, that is dedicated upon earth.

Initiation for Reunion in the Fiery Core

For every marriage is initiation in preparation for twin flames and their reunion in the fiery core; and marriage is the crucible wherein man and woman come together to bear one another's burden, the burden of karma and the dharma of life. And thus as the masculine and feminine rays of Alpha and Omega are enshrined in the marriage vows, so the wholeness and the oneness of the twain provides the forcefield whereby the wholeness of the Father-Mother God might receive souls taking incarnation and all of mankind.

The Alchemical Marriage

I come then to proclaim the need for the laws of heaven to be dedicated as the laws of earth. Let all understand that the alchemy of the marriage ceremony is the confirmation of the alchemical marriage whereby in the ultimate sense the only true marriage is the soul's reunion with the I AM Presence in the ritual of the ascension. Let the moment of love, then, commemorate the ultimate reunion of the soul with the I AM Presence.

Let life be, then, daily the testing of that love and the inspiration of that love that will lead Father and Mother back to the point of origin, back to the place where the twain may become Father and Mother for a lifewave, Manus of a race, sponsors of a solar system, integrators of galaxies. This is the potential of souls united in love. And therefore, as the foundation of the Aquarian age, as I uphold the flame of Saint Germain, I sponsor the marriage and the holy family as the basic law and unit of society.

Prepare a Home of Love for Souls of Light

"Suffer the little children to come unto me, and forbid them not: for of such is the kingdom of heaven."[3] Let them come with their innocence! Won't you receive them? Won't you prepare a place for those who have volunteered to assist mankind in the upward movement of spirals? Won't you prepare a hearth and a home of love? Even that one—the Marquis de Lafayette—who assisted George Washington, who again came forth to assist Guy Ballard as his son, who has recently passed from the screen of life, is knocking again at the portals of birth.

Avatars Rejoicing to Come Forth

I say, then, let the Keepers of the Flame who have volunteered at inner levels to sponsor this patriot of love be blessed on the mountain and go forth to receive a soul of light. And let the avatars be known! And let the parents understand that so many souls of light who have been rejected in these years—unwanted, aborted in their spiraling—desire to be welcomed into families of light. They are ringing the bell, so to speak, at the door of life and the portals of birth. Brave souls are these! Some have tried not once, but twice and a third time to enter; and each time—by their ignorance, by their misunderstanding—they have been prevented and their incarnations aborted.

Precious ones, let your hearts be softened! Feel the tenderness of their love and let their tenderness be reflected in your own love. Receive them with open arms! For you see, they behold your joy; they behold the release of light at this conference. They see how the masters' teachings are coming to the fore; and they, too, can project into the future and know that by the time they are mature, this teaching will have inundated the earth and will be known in every nation and the I AM law and the ascended masters will be taught as the law of the Aquarian age.

This is my word and my prophecy and my vision that is your joy to fulfill. See then how the avatars would come forth, how they are rejoicing to take part in this holy manifestation, in this spiral of light that promises to draw all mankind into the opportunity of the ascension! Now that you have your university and the place of Montessori International secured by the Elohim and the Mother and all who are yearning to prepare that forcefield, now that the diadem of the Church is set as the crown of the Mother's rejoicing, now that Keepers of the Flame are taking their stand in a declaration of independence for Terra, won't you see how important it is that the souls of light receive the souls of light, that these precious ones make their way into your arms, into your care?

Consecrate Life as a Mother, a Father, of the Flame

I ask that you write to me to sponsor these souls and to Mary the Mother, who waits to form the precious diamond of the heart for each incoming lifestream. I ask that you consecrate life as a Mother of the Flame, as a Father of the Flame, and that you take the responsibility that others have taken for you. I have spoken and you have heard the yearning of my heart.

David's Vision of a Fiery Cross

My joy is great; my cup runneth over.[4] And as I knelt in prayer long, long ago, serving the children of Israel, and I wrote down the meditations of my heart as the Psalms which have been preserved, I remember the vision which I saw in the starry heavens, a fiery cross of light which God allowed me to see. And I knew that my soul would be perfected; and I declared with the prophets of old, "Yet in my flesh shall I see God."[5]

That prophecy came to pass in my incarnation in Galilee. And I experienced what you, too, can know as the miracle of the Word incarnate, as the essence of the Christ flame which flows, then, as the sacred fire through the body, the four lower bodies, the mind and consciousness. I was, as you can be, literally charged with the light of the Logos in that ministry; and it was the gift of God. As I strove to be the chalice, so God responded to my striving as he will respond to your own. He filled my cup and he allowed the words of my mouth and the meditations of my heart to be acceptable in the sight of the I AM Presence of all life.[6]

"Lord, Make Me an Instrument of Thy Peace"

In the words of Francis, who comes now to speak to you, whom I honor as the flame of peace and the fiery gold, "Lord, make me an instrument of thy peace!" This is my continual prayer as I expand the field of my cosmic consciousness. So know that the Elohim also pray—and elemental life—even as you pray the Our Father. Let our mutual prayer, then, be the prayer of Francis. Won't you say it with me? "Lord, make me an instrument of thy peace!" So let it be, precious hearts! So the call compels the answer.

Preparing the Body of God upon Earth

I seal you with a kiss upon the brow. I come to each one. May I also wash your feet? May I also anoint you even as Mary anointed me for the crucifixion? So may I prepare the body of God upon earth for the joy of the passion and the joy of the resurrection and the joy of the fulfillment of the dream of the Cosmic Virgin in the Church Universal and Triumphant?[7]

July 6, 1975
6:15-6:32 P.M. PDT

25

THE SUPREME MOMENT OF THE JOY OF OVERCOMING

A Dictation by Kuthumi Lal Singh

The Dynamic Flow of Chastity, Obedience, and the Love of Mother Poverty

I, too, am thrilled with the coming of Jesus our Lord! He was my master then and he is my master forevermore.

In those days of old when we called the brothers of Assisi and we went forth preaching in the squares, we sent forth the light of love from our hearts, the light inspired and ignited by Jesus. And as you look back upon the days of Assisi, almost romantically, thinking of those moments we shared, I would remind you that the weight of materialism and sensuality and the rejection of the way of the Christ was virulent. And therefore the Lord allowed me to infuse the Church with a dynamic flow founded on the ray of chastity, obedience, and the love of Mother Poverty.

Laws of Karma and Reembodiment Taught

We came to demonstrate what a band of devotees could realize when all else was set aside. And you know, we gave forth the teaching of Jesus set forth in the works of Origen on the law of reembodiment and the law of karma, for this was a part of the doctrine of the early Church; and therefore devotees of the Mother came to the retreat of the Poor Clares and they did give their invocations and prayers in penance for the sins of past lives.

The Church to Be Built of Lively Stones

How fortunate, then, that we are able to draw together again in this nucleus of chelas of the masters many of the souls who served in the order of the men and the order of the women! I welcome you! I welcome you, one and all! For this is also an hour similar to that day when the Church, as the body of God upon earth, requires the revitalization of the flame of the heart, when the Church must again become built of lively stones, of those who are ready to take that stand for purity and for obedience to the law of life.[1]

Our cause was unpopular. Do not expect that yours will be popular, at least not overnight. But I expect, as the cycles turn, that the flow of light from the I AM Presence will ultimately be welcomed by the masses of mankind because you chose to take your stand. Our rejoicing over the one and the two and the three who came to join us was very great; for we saw in the life reborn, in the lives reformed, how the victory of Christ in the soul was an alchemy able to reinfuse the entire momentum of Christianity with life, new life, as the real essence of the blood and the body of Jesus.

Let the New Wine Be Poured into the New Bottle

Now then, in this hour when there has been compromise of doctrine and dogma, there has come to pass that manifestation which does not allow for the new dispensation, the new wine of the Spirit and the law of the Aquarian age, to be received by that Church which we served. The doors are closed; and with the turning of the cycle of Pisces to Aquarius, we find and we have found it necessary to build anew, to let the old bottle be broken and let the new wine be poured into the new bottle of a new organization, a new foundation, a new concept.

I am happy to tell you that many who form the nucleus of this Church are the saints who built the old Church. Many who are prominent—in fact, many who have been canonized by the Church—have now incarnated again and have been among the first to take their vows. It is interesting how mankind recognize the virtues of the saints, and yet the Lords of Karma and Jesus the Christ require that these ones so recognized oftentimes return.

Saints in This Age

Their souls come back to the scene of earth, for they are the sons and daughters of God who carry the flame and transcend the ages and the cycles. And they come again, and the children of God rally to their standard; for they recognize the ones who led them in the past. And so, many times as the members of the Church have prayed to the saints, their calls have been answered by the I AM Presence and out of the great fount of light of the causal body of those who were canonized and yet who are presently or were then in incarnation. Thus to be a living saint in heaven and on earth is an opportunity which moment by moment you can ratify and fortify and pursue.

The Sign of Tribulation

I know because the Spirit moved upon me that God desires to make of you saints in this age, to let you walk the earth unascended and yet masterful beings clothed with the alchemy of Saint Joseph, your own beloved Saint Germain. And in the hour of suffering and temptation, of trial and tribulation, remember the lives of the saints—how they were persecuted, how they suffered, how they passed through their own dark night of the soul and the dark night of the spirit. Know, then, that the sign that you are marked for a more-than-ordinary mission is always the sign of tribulation, of testing.

The Hour of Your Crucifixion

The Lord does not will that you should suffer, but the Lord must determine if you are willing to suffer for the cause. And when you show your willingness to take that suffering whereby the sins of the world are borne for a time, then the Lord comes and he sends his legions and his angels to give you succor as you pass the long night in the Garden of Gethsemane, as you pass through that ritual of the cross whereby the old man is put down and the Christ is born in the living flame of the resurrection. No man, no woman, not God himself or the ascended masters will take from you the hour of your Gethsemane, the hour of your crucifixion; for it is the supreme moment of joy, of overcoming, of proving that you are the son of God worthy to be born again!

The Accomplishments of the Devotees

Oh, how we love the devotees! How we love those who are forging ahead, carving out the destiny and the path of the fourteen stations over which all mankind will one day walk! It is time to tell you of your accomplishments. It is time to tell you of attainment and that you are winning and that day by day your striving is noted by the Keeper of the Scrolls and the recording angels who keep the record in the great Book of Life. It is time to tell you that the agony of your soul, the longing of your soul for God, and the delivery of your soul into the arms of love by your own self-discipline has not been in vain nor has it passed unnoticed; for the Lord God himself has approved of the holiness of your consciousness, blessed ones.

And you know as I speak of you that I know of your prayers and I know of your agony and I know of your victory. And I claim your victory! And I set it as a golden stone, a diamond of yellow fire, in the crown of the Mother—a sign to all, to all the fallen ones and the demons of the night, that they dare not tempt the sons and daughters of God and the chelas of the masters! For they will be thrust aside and they will be cast down and they will be exorcised by the authority of the rod that you carry.

Earth Is Coming Home

And so your authority grows as you give the invocations. And so your light is sending forth a beacon that is heard as the sound and the light ray in the farthest stars! And do you know that there are cosmic beings and angels who have not even taken note of Terra for hundreds and thousands of years who have raised their eyes and beheld the wonder of souls on Terra coming Home through the wisdom of the Mother and the teachings of the ascended masters! I say, then, that with all of the sounding of the might of the materialism of an age, that sound becomes a din and recedes before the roar of the sound of the spoken Word of the devotees that is amplified by the Elohim, that is heard in the farthest corners of the cosmos!

Keep On Keeping On!

And as the little children say their prayers and their decrees, we stand as the World Teachers in approbation, in acclamation, in rejoicing. And we look to each other and we say: "Earth is coming Home! The children of the light have found the flame of the Mother!" And so we are gratified this day. And so we come to you in that rejoicing of wisdom's golden flame and we say to each one:

> Keep on keeping on!
> You are winning in the fray!
> Keep on keeping on!
> Prepare for the glorious day!
> I AM the golden white light,
> The array of the Cosmic Virgin,
> The veil of the Mother,
> And the wedding garment soon to be your own.
> Keep on keeping on,
> Keepers of the Flame and Communicants of the Church!
> For we behold the spiral,
> The golden spiral that is reaching
> Unto the star of the causal body of Terra.
> Keep on keeping on,
> For earth shall become a sun!
> Keep on keeping on
> For the day of the victory won!

The Sign of the Cross Formed by Elemental Life

I send forth the sign of the cross and the sign of the cross formed by elemental life as the birds of the air. I send you the flower of my heart, the white daisy of purity, chastity, and obedience—these three the vows of the brothers and sisters of Assisi.[2] Our love enfolds you, and I hold you in the fond embrace of illumined action!

July 6, 1975
6:33-6:49 P.M. PDT

Victory is a flame, a consciousness, an awareness of God which aeons ago a being from Venus determined to manifest. As Jesus determined to be the Christ, as Gautama determined to be the Buddha, so one whose name has long been dissolved into the flame which he became determined to be victory. Mighty Victory ensouls God's cosmic consciousness of victory for all evolutions and lifewaves in time and space. A vast array of legions bearing the same flaming awareness accompany this hierarch to champion the heroes and the humble, the conquerors and those who would be. The moment you determine to be victorious in this life, to be the Christ, balance your karma and make your ascension, Victory comes to your side to defend your God-victory to the end. Mighty Victory—deliverer of a planet and a people who maintain the sense of victory, who will to win.

26

THE WAVE OF LIGHT FROM SHASTA

A Dictation by Mighty Victory

Hail, legions of light! Hail, angelic hosts! Now descend in the flame of Victory! Now descend! Now descend! I call you forth from the Great Central Sun. Now encircle the devotees round about with the flame of Victory and let that victory be anchored within the soul!

Claim the Victory of the Light

Hail, children of the light! I AM come in the flame of Venus and in the flame of Sanat Kumara. I come with great joy! I come with victory! I come to inspire you unto that joy of victory which shall surely be your own if you will plant your feet firmly on Terra and plant your hands into the air raised up unto the star of your own I AM Presence. I say in this moment, this cosmic moment, claim the victory of the light! Claim the victory of your ascension! Claim it now I say, for this is the holy day of decision! [Audience rises and responds with cries of "Victory!" and "I AM America's victory now!"]

Angels of the Great Central Sun Seal Your Vows

Ladies and gentlemen, I thank you for your response. May you know that your response, heartfelt, reaches the angels of the Great Central Sun, who have come forth on a special mission this night to seal your inner vows, to seal your victory. And therefore by that decision and by that confirmation of the victory of Terra, so you seal your heart flame in a coil of fire, in a coil of energy that shall go forth to fulfill its cosmic purpose.

A Thousand Faithful Decreers

And so the Goddess of Liberty is redeemed and her call for a thousand faithful decreers to save this nation and save this planet has come home, for you have faithfully decreed in these days of victory and you have shown the cosmic councils what you will do for light. Now show me also, as the days pass into the years, how you will retain the fervor of victory!

Angels of Victory

Do you not feel the joy of my company? Do you not feel the great release and surge of angelic hosts who have known naught but victory for thousands and thousands of years and years and cycles beyond your ken? And their momentum is victory, victory, victory! So let it be your own; for these angels come forth in adoration of that flame, the threefold flame within your heart which they also used for the victory. And therefore they worship the flame as the flame of victory, for they know what that light can do.

Now see then how you have come from north and south and east and west; and many have not known even my name or even that such a being as mighty Victory existed before this conference, and many have not known of the violet-flame angels or of the gracious Sanat Kumara, our hierarch of light. You see, then, you have proven to the Lords of Karma what I said in my request for a dispensation of victory, that it would be possible to draw to Shasta 1975 souls sincere, souls yearning to be whole even though they knew but a small aspect of the law, and by the fire of the Brotherhood to draw them into the lodestone of the light of the Mother and the light of the I AM Presence.

Momentum of Victory Pledged as a Mantle of Protection

And thus you have responded! And so by the alchemy of your

fervent love, most precious to behold, there comes forth this night a momentum of victory for your soul. And I have stood before the altar of Almighty God in the Great Central Sun and I have made a pledge on behalf of every soul who has given of his energy and his light in this conference. And I have made that pledge that my momentum of victory shall be as a mantle of protection, as a sphere of light, and as a momentum that will draw not only your soul, but the souls of all whom you contact into the joyous flame of victory. So be it! It is my calling. It is my offering. It is my honor to bring to you the flame of my heart.

Scroll Foretelling the Day of the Ascension

And now angels of victory release unto each soul the scroll that foretells the day of the ascension in the light. Do you not know, precious hearts, that the day and the hour of your ascension as opportunity has been written by the Lords of Karma? And *if* you fulfill your calling and your election and *if* you apply your energies in devotion and remain in the center of the flaming will of your own I AM Presence, if you fulfill all that is required by the great law for your soul, you will come by the spiral of victory released this night to the day and the hour that God already knows for your victorious ascension in the light.

Think of that! The goal that you scarcely knew before you contacted the teachings of the law! Now you understand that God has first perceived the plan, that God has placed within your soul the conception of that plan. And now by the joy of victory with freedom's fire, you are free as the dove that soars unto the heights to move into the center of that mandala which the Lord God has so lovingly, compassionately created as your very own. Precious hearts, won't you please be seated.

An Open Door for Victory to Flow

With the announcement of Alpha of the judgment of the Fallen One, I come to announce an open door, an open opportunity for the blazing light of victory to flow across Terra unobstructed by the shadowy figure of that Fallen One who in that cycle was wont to challenge and to test and to accuse and to oppose the children of the light so blest.

Satan Is Bound for a Thousand Years

Now then, the cycles roll! And I would also tell you that that one, that Fallen One that is called by the name of Satan, a number of cycles ago was also bound and remains bound. And therefore, for that thousand-year period of the binding of that one, there is hope, there is opportunity, there is the most tremendous momentum for the expansion of the flame that the world has known for thousands of years. Now see how opportunity, as the golden door, stands before you! And you standing before that door may know that the knock and the opening and the entering-in is that which you have been called to, that which is your hope, that which is the fulfillment of hope, that which is a present reality here and now.

Challenge the Lie and the Seed of the Fallen Ones

See then that you understand that Victory's flame is the momentum whereby you challenge every lie and every remnant of the seed of the fallen ones. Do you understand that now is the moment to rush into the battlefield, to take the victory, to take the land for Saint Germain, to claim Terra for the light? Now is the moment when the general in the field gives the command "Onward! Onward! Onward to victory!" Now is the moment when the fallen ones will scatter at your footstep, at the drumbeat.

"I Claim That Energy for Saint Germain"

Mine eyes have seen the glory of the coming of the Lord! And I give to you that vision of the coming of the Lord's hosts. This is the time when although there is the rumbling and the grumbling and the raising-up of mighty armies in many nations and nuclear power and wars and rumors of wars—this is the hour of victory! This is the hour when light goes forth by the power of the spoken Word, when light goes forth! And in your name, the name of the I AM, in your name, in the name of the Christ, the fiat "I claim that energy for Saint Germain!" will cause the ones of the night to tremble and to falter and to fall. And then the inrushing of the angelic hosts as they bind the tares and take them to be burned at the harvest, the harvest of the Lord's hosts, the harvest of the children of the light.[1]

Challenge All That Opposes the Christ Consciousness on Terra

This is what I am saying. I am saying that by the fiat, by the command, challenging all that which opposes the Christ consciousness on Terra, all that you see as threatening woe, will go! I say it will go down before the authority of your I AM Presence! Now try me and see how that light will swallow up the darkness! See how the light of your Presence is able to restore the planet to the golden age! I AM Victory and I know whereof I speak! I have seen the conquering of worlds, of maya and effluvia by light, and I have seen worlds come into a golden age that many an ascended master had long crossed off the list.

Claim Terra for Saint Germain

I say this for you must understand that at any moment, at any hour, no matter how far the children of light have been taken into the lie of the fallen ones, when the truth is acclaimed, when it is spoken, when our light goes forth by the spoken Word, the souls of those children of the light know the voice, know the vibration, know the call! And they run and they leap and they come and they forsake their former ways and their former lives! And overnight you will see how the youth of the world will claim Terra for Saint Germain!

The Wave of Light from Shasta

So be the wave of light going forth from Shasta! Carry the light of Ra Mu and the golden oil of the crown of chakras! So be the wave going forth north, south, east, and west, even as you have come! So go forth as rays of the sun and claim Terra for victory, victory, victory! Victory, victory, victory! [Audience joins the master in saying, "Victory!"] Victory, victory, victory! Victory, victory, victory! So be it in the name of the living God! I AM that flame. I AM your flame to claim. I AM with you unto the end of the cycles of error and to the fulfillment of the cycles of truth. Be thou made whole in victory!

July 6, 1975
11:11-11:27 P.M. PDT

Divine direction is a state of consciousness in God. It is the perfect awareness of his plan for all life. Ultimately this awareness contains within itself not only the direction, but its logical conclusion in action-fulfullment. Long ago before our souls were reckoning with being God, an initiate of Solar Lords perceived the need of lifewaves here below to know the plan and to proceed with unerring direction from the polestar of being to complete the plan as blueprint-matrix, as thought conceptualized, as motive and willingness engendering momentum for completion, as Mater-realization, physical fulfillment, the completion of a cycle.

His name, too, became secondary to the flame he adored. And so the nameless one worshiping God as the law of unerring direction came to be known as the Great Divine Director, because through adoration he became the adored and then the Adorable One. And then the office in cosmic hierarchy, the Great Divine Director, became his God-identity.

27

LET US IMPLEMENT THE PLAN OF HIERARCHY

A Dictation by the Great Divine Director

An Examination of Consciousness

Good evening, ladies and gentlemen. I come in concern for the implementation of the plan of Victory. I come determined to leave with you the impression of the vastness of cosmic cycles and an understanding of spirals of consciousness—your consciousness, my consciousness, and even the consciousness of the fallen ones who have passed through the judgment in recent months.

I come with a close examination of the fabric of consciousness, of the warp and woof of consciousness on Terra. I examine the threads and the crosscurrents of life and I perceive exactly what must be done to perfect the wedding garment of Terra. I see the dark threads and how they must be withdrawn without disturbing the fabric of world thought or of the soul delicate, aborning in time and space.

I come to show you how to withdraw the elements of error— and this a most important tool of the light-bearer. Now then, you approach the soul upon the path who has light and devotion and yet is caught in the snarls of an erroneous doctrine coming forth from a false teacher or perhaps a well-meaning one who has conveyed a false teaching; and you see that soul and you say, "O my friend, may I show you a precious book of the law?" And the soul replies, "Thank you very much, but I have my own." And you say: "Hmm, [audience laughs] what shall we do here? This is a soul of light. I cannot leave him to the distresses of the fallen ones."

And then you perceive the fabric of consciousness and you see
how the fallen ones have come in the night to sow those tares
among the wheat, the golden grain of the Cosmic Christ light.
And you are determined, for you have the flame of Victory; and
you are determined then to impart that flame unto the soul. And
so you say, "Perhaps we can talk about the light of life." And the
friend replies: "Ah, yes, I know all about the light of life. And I
have all knowledge of the light of life." And you say, "Hmm."
[Audience laughs.] And then you excuse yourself, and you go into
the next room and you say, "Mighty Astrea, encircle that soul!"
[Audience laughs and claps.] And you return again to try another
round. [Audience laughs.]

<h2 style="text-align:center">Solutions</h2>

Now I AM the Great Divine Director and I do have solutions.
And I say to all, it is time that you refuse to let go of the children
of light. Catch them by the toe if you must [audience laughs], but
hold on to the children of the light! For I have a plan and that plan
is the divine direction of the light. And I say to you, one and all,
that the light *is* all powerful, that the light *is* flow, that the light
will claim its own! And therefore, speaking with that friend along
the way, know that the light within the heart of the friend *will* be
victorious. And when I say know, I mean decree it so with all of the
love and the fervor of your heart.

And now you say: "My friend, will you tarry with me? Will
you partake of bread, and shall we take together the communion
cup of our Lord?" And now the friend will listen, for it is the
mystical presence of the Christ in your midst who magnetizes the
soul unto the I AM Presence. And so you prepare the place for the
honored guest and you receive that one in hearth and home. And
you enjoy the freedom of love, of the I AM Presence, and you
know that only God can make that one whole.

<h2 style="text-align:center">Cycles of Sharing</h2>

There are cycles and there are cycles, and there are moments
to share the teaching and there are moments for the sharing of
love. When you know that the light cannot fail, that it will not
fail, then you place the emphasis upon the invocation of love that

consumes the cause and core of every deception. Moment by moment within your heart, let the prayer go forth that the divine plan of that soul be lowered into action.

Scroll of the Divine Plan

I pray also that you will call to me, for I have within my consciousness—think of this—the scroll of the divine plan for every living soul on Terra and in the vast beyond. And therefore the word of Jesus "Be not forgetful to entertain strangers: for thereby some have entertained angels unawares."[1]

Now then, make the call for the divine memory of the soul to be brought into outer manifestation according to the divine plan; and call for the quickening of the Christ mind and call for the penetration of the all-seeing eye!

The Breath of Divine Love

Let the ascended masters have their try with your friend! Let them have the opportunity! I have watched how many of you have let go too soon. And you have not been determined enough to make an impression of light, but a bit chary in your conversation, being willing to retreat at the first sign of rejection or belittlement of the teaching. I say, press on! For all that is of error that has been superimposed upon the free will of the friend can come to naught as the Holy Spirit releases the breath of divine love.

Liberation of the Will

There are many ways to approach the soul, many ways to release that soul. I am not concerned with interfering with free will. I am concerned with the liberation of that will! And I am tired of mankind being bound in the shackles of a false ideology and a false doctrine! At least, then, let us determine to clear the debris so that the soul can live and see and make right choices! As Saint Germain has said, we demand equal time! And if the ideology of the fallen ones must be proclaimed, then let the ascended-master teaching be shouted from the housetops! And let mankind make their choices; and let them make those choices fully backed by the love, the fervor, the invocations, and the determination of the chelas of the sacred fire.

"Feed My Sheep"

Now I say, the admonishment of the Lord "Feed my sheep" was never more important than in this hour.[2] For it is the nourishing of the souls who have been starved of the truth that is your opportunity—souls that have been fed that substance so far removed from the truth that you might say their taste buds have no longer any affinity for the light. So altered has the structure of consciousness become that they are as the ones who have been in the dark cave, and they come forth from the cave and they are blinded by the light.

You see then, the world is not only in ignorance, but it is in sore need of healing. Release the healing balm of love! And where the cup of cold water is required, extend that cup; and where comfort and compassion and a listening ear and an understanding heart, extend these as flames of the Holy Spirit and see how the soul, finding the warmth of your heart, will open to the teaching by and by!

Pray without Ceasing

Let us never let go of a soul until that soul has said, "Leave me alone! I will to go unto perdition." And then, even then, shall we leave the soul? We shall pray without ceasing.[3] We shall pray and continue to pray. We shall know that all mankind require that support in this hour. And so I say, let us implement the plan of hierarchy with compassion, with wisdom! And let us be ready for any eventuality, any alternative. Let us be flexible as teachers—not unbending, but willing to walk the way of souls crying out for that fire.

The Withdrawal of the Threads

Let us speak of the withdrawal of the threads. They must be pulled out delicately, carefully. See now, then, how the Mother employs the crochet hook to draw through the threads, and the needle, and the fineness of her skill. Understand, then, that in answer to your call, the sacred fire will rush forth as an arrow and it will pluck those threads that mar the image and that interfere with the design, the needlepoint of the Cosmic Virgin. What you cannot do, the sacred fire will do, I assure you!

Calls for Change

And you can conceive of the most fantastic invocations and calls if you will only look at the world. You can conceive of making calls for change, for the overthrow of darkness and the coming-in of light. And I tell you, no matter what the call, if it is the will of God, angels of the Great Divine Director will go forth. Therefore, make the call to consume every error in the economies of the nations, on the political scene, in the government, and where you have been distressed and discouraged and almost totally given up hope for victory.

There I say, pursue! Be relentless with your call! For you never know when one more call will cause the crumbling of that wall of Jericho, that wall of recalcitrance, that wall that seals the children of light behind the borders of the adversary's consciousness. See then that you understand that the call you make in the name of the Christ to arrest the spirals of darkness and deceit is a call that acts twenty-four hours a day to stop that action of the fallen ones even before it is manifest!

Mandala Sealed in Throat Chakra

Yes, I AM the Great Divine Director, and I am directing into manifestation now that impression of the mandala that is before you [see p. 327]. And I seal it in the throat chakra that you might utter fiats of the law given unto you by your own Christ Self, by your own I AM Presence, for the healing, line by line, for the all-consuming sacred fire, line by line.

Bind the Seed of the Fallen Ones!

Now it is time to preserve the culture, the science, the education, and the religion of the Mother and, in preserving that forcefield, to simultaneously withdraw all that has been implanted there. Now then, by the authority of your own I AM Presence, I send forth the fiat: *Bind* the seed of the fallen ones! *Bind* the spirals of the fallen ones! *Bind* their lethargy! *Bind* their boredom! *Bind* their compromise! *Bind* the false teaching! Let it be bound by the causal body which I AM! Let it be bound by the causal body of each one!

The Impetus to Divine Direction

And now let the fervor of mighty Victory be carried through divine direction, through discipline and freedom! For the discipline of the will of God and the freedom of the violet flame are the converging of the spirals of Alpha and Omega for the victory of a planet. I ask that you make calls for divine direction to all who are in a position of making policy and directing the affairs of mankind in every walk of life. Let the leaders receive from my causal body and your own the impetus to divine direction and not human direction!

Victory unto You, My Friend

And now go forth! Now go forth, O souls of light! Go forth to meet the friend along the way! And when you see the friend sent by the hand of God, determine unto that one and say within your soul: "Victory unto you, my friend! Victory unto you! Victory, victory, victory!" And receive that one in the name of the Christ and receive the reward of the Christed ones.

Follow the Course unto the Ascension

I AM forevermore the consciousness of divine direction! So receive that pulsation from my causal body and follow the course, the divine direction, unto the day, the hour, the fulfillment of your stars in the ascension in the light!

I salute you, one and all! I know you, one and all! I claim you as you have been claimed by Almighty God. I claim you for the flame of purity in the divine direction of all life. So *be* the wholeness of the law! *Be* the wholeness of the law!

July 6, 1975
11:36-11:55 P.M. PDT

The need for harmony and love between all the masters' chelas united in a common effort cannot be overemphasized. Working and serving together, we form a mandala of light through which the masters of the Great White Brotherhood will awaken humanity.

THAT YE LOVE ONE ANOTHER
AS I HAVE LOVED YOU

A Lecture by Elizabeth Clare Prophet

Good evening, everyone. The theme of our leadership conference has been love in action. The love that we bear is the fire of our heart, the kindling fire of a planet; and truly it is the torch that will light the world.

Jesus' Final Communion with His Disciples

I would like to talk to you about the love of Jesus and of all of the avatars who have gone before us, about Jesus' final communion with his disciples on the shores of Galilee and his appeal to their love and to the love flame within their hearts. He only said a few words, but the words that he said were the words that also kindled the torch of a planet and a people. These words were very precious to Mark, and he often quoted them to us as the disciples of the Brotherhood. I feel that if we can understand what Jesus was yearning for and longing for in these words, we can understand what we must have to go forth and be victorious.

You recall that they went a fishing and they caught nothing. Jesus came early in the morning and he told them to cast the net on the right side of the boat, and their nets were full. They came to shore and they found that he had prepared fish and bread for them; and after they had dined and after they had completed this ritual, then he spoke to Peter.

Note: This is the concluding lecture of the two-day leadership seminar, "Leadership Is Love in Action," held July 8 and 9.

"Feed My Sheep"

"Simon, son of Jonas, lovest thou me more than these? He saith unto him, Yea, Lord; thou knowest that I love thee. He saith unto him, Feed my lambs. He saith to him again the second time, Simon, son of Jonas, lovest thou me? He saith unto him, Yea, Lord; thou knowest that I love thee. He saith unto him, Feed my sheep. He saith unto him the third time, Simon, son of Jonas, lovest thou me? Peter was grieved because he said unto him the third time, Lovest thou me? And he said unto him, Lord, thou knowest all things; thou knowest that I love thee. Jesus saith unto him, Feed my sheep."[1]

I feel that in those precious moments, in the final words that he had with his disciples, Jesus saw the whole vision of what could happen to Christianity, what could happen to the mission if people would fall down and worship his person and fail to become the Christ, if they would enter into idolatry and build monuments to him and fail to meet the needs of the souls hungering for truth. All of this he saw, and he questioned Simon Peter three times.

Are We Willing to Make the Sacrifice?

Here we stand. Jesus is saying this to each one of us. Every ascended master who has left the planet is saying this to us. Lanello is saying this to us. There are so many things we could do, we might do; but do they contribute to this one commandment, "Feed my sheep"? Are we meeting the needs of the hungry souls of a planet? Are we getting right there where the soul is with our love, with our ministration? Are we willing to make the sacrifice that is necessary to tarry with those in need, by the hour if necessary, to carry them over the rocky places? Are we willing to go as Jesus did to find the one sheep that is lost, leaving the ninety and nine?

Are we willing to make that sacrifice to go all the way in contacting people on the Path? Do we hand them a brochure and go on our way? Or do we stop to acknowledge the flame, impart the love? Do we remember them when we go home at night in our prayers? Are we willing to take that fifteen minutes or a half hour and really pray for those who are in need of prayer, who need Archangel Michael, need the invocations? This is feeding the sheep. They need the spiritual bread. They need compassion; they need love; they need understanding; they need talking to. They need praying for; they need the intercession of Mother Mary.

Are we willing to get out of bed in the morning and give that rosary? And when we say, "Hail, Mother ray," are we giving our adoration to the Mother within those who are coming into the light? Are we actually bowing before the Christ in these sheep to the point of saying: "This is a god in the making. I will serve him until he becomes and knows that he is that god"? It's that calling which the Great Divine Director spoke of in his final dictation—of not letting go of souls who know not that they are in need of the light, but not burdening them with our personality or idolatry or placing ourselves in the way of the masters' teachings.

The Responsibility Is Yours

Jesus is saying to Peter, "The responsibility is *all* yours." And that is what the masters say to us. And when we go forth from this conference, we have to work and work and work as if everything depended on us, as if there were no one else it depended on. And when our work is done and we enter in the evening into the communion of the Holy Spirit, we pray as if everything depended on God. We know that except the Lord's Spirit fill the works of our hands with a flame, we build in vain. Therefore Jesus said, "My Father worketh hitherto, and I work."[2]

We work together with the Father. As John Kennedy said, "Here on earth God's work must truly be our own."[3] Here on earth *we* have the dominion; *we* have the opportunity. Sometimes I see people decreeing as if they thought that the decrees were going to do the work. Decrees are not a substitute for intelligent planning, for common sense, for surrender. The words won't do it. Putting in time and marking time and rolling fingers over beads— that is not going to do it.

A decree is a matrix; it's the instrument for the flow of your consciousness and God's consciousness. When you decree, you meditate on releasing and surrendering, on sacrifice, on self-discipline. You contemplate what you can give to God. When you decree, you create a matrix of purity and God lets his light flow; and you get inspiration and you know how to work the following day. You receive the plan; you commune with light; you go to the retreats. God builds on the matrix that you have set by your decrees, by your flow, by your energy. They go hand in hand.

The work is no substitute for decrees; the decrees are no substitute for the work. The decrees are restoring your soul with the life blood that you need. It's the flow and contact between you and hierarchy whereby you can feed the sheep. And your works are works that are practical. Jesus said that "the children of this world are in their generation wiser than the children of light" because the children of light get into the high vibrations of the masters,[4] they sit and meditate and somehow they think everything else is going to take care of itself, and they get very impractical.

I think we should prove Jesus wrong on that statement, and I think he would be very happy to have us prove him wrong and show him that we, the children of light, can be wiser than the children of mammon, wiser than those who are entirely engaged in materialism, that we can come forth with excellence and victory and achievement because we know we are the handiwork of God, we are not afraid to work and serve, and we know that as we do this, God will fill that matrix of our service.

Jesus did not say to Peter, "Pray for God to feed my sheep." He told Peter to "feed my sheep," and he's saying the same to us. God can't feed the sheep unless he feeds the sheep through you. That's the law of hierarchy; it's the law of planes of consciousness. So the command directly to our heart-core from the Brotherhood this night is "Feed my sheep." And we must understand that anything and everything that deters us from that practicality of reaching the heart and the soul of humanity is opposition to divine love in action; and we must meet it as the foe and we must slay that dragon, whether it is lethargy, procrastination, or other enjoyments that take our time. Whatever it is that prevents us from the contact is depriving us of the glory of meeting and answering the call of our Saviour.

God has set the goal. The goal is the total enlightenment of mankind. We have received that mandate from Gautama Buddha and we are in the midst of implementation. God has given us the freedom of our own creative potential to figure out how to implement the goal. By exercising our creativity, our free will, our God-given intelligence, we earn our own godhood, we earn our ascension. We are not robots to God's consciousness. We have to "forge our God-identity," as Alpha told us. Forge an identity!

Make it permanent as an atom of God. This means be creative and exercise your creative potential to the fullest.

Summit University: The Passing of the Torch

Jesus spent three years teaching twelve apostles and the other seventy and the women disciples to take the flame of the Christian dispensation to the world. I am asking you to give me twelve weeks so that I can impart the flame of hierarchy, of Gautama Buddha, of illumination, of love in action, to you. It is for the greatest calling that the world has ever known—for the Aquarian age, for the golden age, for the foundation of that age.

I feel the greatest single gift you can give to hierarchy in service is proper training. In twelve weeks of giving to hierarchy and following the prescribed plan, you submit yourselves at the altar of the masters; and thereby I am allowed to impart to you certain initiations which cannot be otherwise given—initiations of the chakras, of the alignment of your four lower bodies, of balancing or the setting aside of karma so that you can walk out of Summit University and enter into world service. The masters will set aside karma for you to be involved in world service; they will do that if you show forth effort.

I am yearning within my heart to give you the flame of Gautama Buddha. It is more than a thousand-petaled flame. It has an infinite number of petals. Each petal is to be imparted to those who come through Summit University. And that flame in your heart will grow and grow and grow until one day you are carrying for the Divine Mother and for the Buddha the entire torch for a planet and a people. The impartation and the passing of the torch is necessary. It is important. It is of the utmost importance in your life.

I am here sponsored by Maitreya, the Great Initiator, to directly impart initiation to you. I cannot overstate the meaning of that initiation. It is a gift that comes, and it does not come that often. The light that can be imparted to you must be imparted through someone who is unascended, who is in the physical. This is how the chain of Christ consciousness has gone on for thousands of years. If you will give a little obedience and a little service and a little time and energy to that discipline that we have there, the return to you by proportion is simply a geometrization of your input.

So as I stand before you, knowing within me as no one else knows what Summit University means, what the training means, what Gautama Buddha, Maitreya, and the World Teachers have in store for you, I cannot be silent. I must tell you that it is a gift that is burning in my heart as I yearn to impart it to you. It is the fire and love of the Solar Logos of a cosmos, yearning to burst forth and to be anchored in those who will come to avail themselves of that discipline. And therefore, I stand before you and I tell you, there really is nothing more important for you to do than to be prepared to answer the mandate of our Lord "Feed my sheep!"

You are willing; you are loving; you are determined. You have fervor; you have heart flame. I would like to see you crown all of that with a Cosmic Christ illumination that can come only through initiation and application as the masters have given it to us to be outlined. In order to receive initiation, which is an increment of hierarchy's consciousness, the chalice of your soul must be crystallized. Crystallized means Christ-realized.

I want to take you through the twelve weeks of initiations of the twelve solar hierarchies, and I want to leave you with the understanding that my heart is bursting to give you a fire that has been given to me that I must impart, that I cannot keep unto myself. I want you to know that I am keeping the flame for you until you are able to make that trek and to receive that flame. And you who have come, do not tarry to return; for God is waiting to ordain you ministers and to send you forth and to give you those initiations that are advanced in the Holy Spirit.

"That Ye Love One Another"

And now may I read the words of Jesus "This is my commandment, That ye love one another, as I have loved you."[5] How can we love one another as Jesus loved his disciples unless we know what his love for his disciples is? To know what the love of Jesus is for his disciples demands drawing in to the fiery core of the Christ consciousness. Jesus defined that love. He said:

"Greater love hath no man than this, that a man lay down his life for his friends. Ye are my friends, if ye do whatsoever I command you. Henceforth I call you not servants; for the servant knoweth not what his Lord doeth: but I have called you friends; for all things that I have heard of my Father I have made known unto you. Ye have not chosen me, but I have chosen you and ordained you, that ye should go and bring forth fruit and that your fruit should remain: that whatsoever ye shall ask of the Father in my name, he may give it you. These things I command you, that ye love one another.

"If the world hate you, ye know that it hated me before it hated you. If ye were of the world, the world would love his own: but because ye are not of the world, but I have chosen you out of the world, therefore the world hateth you. Remember the word that I said unto you, The servant is not greater than his lord. If they have persecuted me, they will also persecute you; if they have kept my saying, they will keep yours also. But all these things will they do unto you for my name's sake, because they know not him that sent me."[6]

They know not the I AM Presence. They know not that out of the I AM Presence comes forth the Christed One; and out of the Christ, the soul. If we love one another as Jesus loved the disciples, then he calls us "friend." And as "friend," we are in a working relationship with hierarchy. As long as we do not show forth that love for one another which Jesus had to the disciples, then we remain servants in a lower rank, because we have still shown hardness of heart to one another. And if to one another, how can we be trusted to love the ascended hierarchy?

Will you remember this—that the ascended masters are not interested in the love you have for them if you have cross words, condemnation, and judgment of one another on the Path? Because what you do to one another is what they take as the actual, factual manifestation of your devotion to the masters. And all else that you give the masters is hypocrisy and is rejected if you do this to one another.

Will you remember this key, then, in addition to feeding my sheep—that love for one another must burn as a fire in your heart as though you were meeting Christ on the road to Emmaus,[7] as though Jesus your Lord were standing before you and you had the opportunity to serve him? And will you have that love for your families and your friends, even if they are not in the teaching? Will you cease looking down upon anyone and recognize that whoever comes to you for any reason, the Christ within his heart is your Lord and your Master? By this flame of love we will conquer for Saint Germain, for the Aquarian age; and without this love, we are brittle. Our words are hollow and vain, and who will listen to us when we have not that pure love?

"Go and Bring Forth Fruit"

And finally, will you remember "Ye have not chosen me, but I have chosen you and ordained you that ye should go and bring forth fruit and that your fruit should remain: that whatsoever ye shall ask of the Father in my name, he may give it unto you." Saint Germain and Jesus, whom you see radiating through these magnificent pictures, have chosen you for this age, for making the transition from Pisces to Aquarius.

You have been chosen; you have been ordained; you have been anointed by the flame of your own Presence. And to what purpose? This one purpose: that you go forth and bring forth fruit. Fruit is action; fruit is results; fruit is multiplication; fruit is what comes on the tree because the tree has released the energy of God. Fruit is souls wedded to Christ because you have kindled the flame. That is fruit "meet for repentance,"[8] as John the Baptist said—fruit of multiplying your Christ consciousness, showing forth that fruit.

And your fruit will remain. Why? Because you have learned the key that Jesus gave: "Whatsoever you ask the Father in my name, he will give it you." That is a promise; it cannot fail. And this is how you exercise the promise: "In the name of Jesus the Christ, I call to the heart of the Father-Mother God for love to triumph on Terra." Whatever fiat you make, see that it is in keeping with the will of God. And if you are not certain that it is the will of God, when you make the fiat say, "Let it be done according to thy will, O God!" It is important to say that when you pray for healing or changes in people's consciousness, because you don't know what their karma is or what the will of God is.

Jesus made a covenant to those whom he chose; and he ordained that if you would bring forth fruit, the fruits of the Holy Spirit, anything you ask the Father in the name of Jesus the Christ, it will be given unto you. That is sealed, sanctified, ordained; it is in your hands for the asking. And the corollary to this promise is this—that the Christ in whose name we ask the Father—Jesus the Christ—is also the Christ of every man, woman, and child upon the planet.

Therefore you can say: "In the name of my own Christ Self, in the name of the Christ Selves of all mankind, in the name of Jesus the Christ, I implore the Father-Mother God to expand the teachings of the ascended masters throughout the planetary body; and I accept it done this hour in full power." That is a fiat. It will go forth on the wings of your devotion, on the wings of the Spirit; and the Lord God has said, "My Word shall not return unto me void."[9] That is the word and the promise that you speak.

Beloved hearts, go forth to feed the sheep in the love of Christ because you determine not to let down one ascended master who has gone on. You will not let down Jesus or Saint Germain, and that is the promise they have exacted from every true disciple. If you love me, feed my sheep. Go forth to feed the sheep! Go forth in the love of one another! Go forth in the power of the spoken Word! Go forth to bring forth fruit, and see how you will transform a planet as God in you works his works. Thank you and God bless you.

The Sealing of the Energies

May all the glory and the light and the love that has gone forth from your hearts in this conference be given as the glory of the I AM Presence and sealed in our causal bodies. In the name of the Father and of the Mother, of the Son and of the Holy Spirit, let every erg of energy from the entire Spirit of the Great White Brotherhood be sealed now in the causal bodies of all who go forth from this altar. Let it be sealed and let it be multiplied without limit for the use of hierarchy in the blessing and the implementation of the plan. So be it. We accept it done this hour in full power. Amen.

July 9, 1975
9:50-10:14 P.M. P D T

"What Man Has Done, Man Can Do"

Saint Germain, the Knight Commander of the Keepers of the Flame Fraternity, founded that order to begin the initiation of souls upon earth who could be counted worthy to be accepted into the Great White Brotherhood for this very purpose—that a greater portion of the consciousness of God individualized in the heavenly hosts might be anchored upon earth through His embodied sons and daughters for the blessing of mankind.

I trust that you will also recognize that other avenues have been provided for your preparation to be received into this Brotherhood that is sometimes known as The White Lodge—our releases in the Pearls of Wisdom, in our publications, in *Climb the Highest Mountain* and in the full course that is outlined at inner levels for the Ascended Masters' university. All of these have one goal in mind: oneness with the Brotherhood and then the ascension into Light for the Keeper of the Flame.

I have placed before you a goal that is attainable. Because some have attained, all can attain: "What Man Has Done, Man Can Do." This is the motto of Lightbearers in service to humanity. Man can succeed because he has the potential of Christ and of God—because others have made the sacrifice, have surrendered, and have overcome.

Nada
Lord of the Sixth Ray

29

A MESSAGE TO ALL
WHO WOULD KEEP THE FLAME OF LIFE

From the Darjeeling Council
of the Great White Brotherhood

The Coming of the Ancient of Days

Long ago the Ancient of Days* came to earth to keep the flame of Life that you and I might live to one day know the True Self as God. He was known as Sanat Kumara, one of the Seven Holy Kumaras who focused the Light of the seven rays.

When cosmic councils had determined that no further opportunity should be given to humanity—so great was their departure from cosmic law, their desecration of Life—Sanat Kumara raised his hand and offered his heart to serve the souls of mankind until the few and eventually the many would respond once again to keep the flame of Life.

Granted this dispensation by solar lords, Sanat Kumara came to earth with sons and daughters of God who volunteered to support him in his mission as Keeper of the Flame. He established his retreat on an island in the Gobi Sea, now the Gobi Desert. And there at Shamballa he would remain to tend the sacred fires until some among mankind would stir from the low estate to which they had descended by their ignorance (ignoring) of the Law of the One—until once again they would begin to call upon the name of the LORD† and give devotion to the Living Flame of the Most High God.

For at this dark hour of planetary history, *all* had forgot their God Source, *none* paid recognition to the spiritual fire in the temple of man. Therefore, through adoration and invocation to the one God, and service to the planetary lifewave, Sanat Kumara and his band of

*Dan. 7:9, 13, 22. †Gen. 4:26.

Keepers of the Flame magnified the triune aspects of Life which in the beginning the Father-Mother God had placed as the threefold flame within their offspring. This they did that the Children of the Sun might remember their reason for being.

The Flame That Burns within Your Heart

This flame that burns within your heart (one-sixteenth of an inch in height) is the divine spark, the potential of your divinity. It is the gift of Life of the Creator to the creation. "For God so loved the world, that he gave his only begotten Son . . ."* The consciousness of the Son is centered in the flame, which is thus called "the Holy Christ Flame." This Trinity of God's sacred fire focuses the primary attributes of Power, Wisdom, and Love—his bestowal, flame of his very Flame, to every son and daughter.

Truly this threefold flame is the tri-partite Light which lighteth every man and woman of God that cometh into the world.† This is the individualization of the God flame whereby the Word is "made flesh" in you and whereby you behold the glory of the LORD of all within your members.‡ The flame that burns within your heart is the seat of cosmic consciousness, the ensign of the son or daughter of God. It is your link to Reality, to Being, and to Life eternal. It is the anointing by the Real Self of all souls who choose to keep the standard of the Law of the One.

For the original Keepers of the Flame who came with Sanat Kumara it was the supreme joy of their service to fan freedom's fires in the hearts of earth's wayward children—to woo them back to their First Love.

Thus, in the first aspect of the flame, the blue, they taught the worship of God as Lawgiver, as Father Principle, showing the people how to internalize and amplify the will and the power of the First Person of the Trinity.

In the second aspect of the flame, the yellow, they sent forth praise to His Light-emanation—Christos—as the eternal Son, the Second Person of the Trinity, setting the example of the path of the incarnation of the Word through the wisdom (wise dominion) of the Law even as they outpictured the qualities of the Teacher.

In the third aspect, the pink, they ministered unto Love as the Third Person, the Holy Spirit, teaching the littlest children the self-realization of the fires of illumined creativity through a

*John 3:16. †John 1:9. ‡John 1:14.

compassionate individuality, unveiling the cloven tongues* as the twin flames of the Comforter and the seat of the Divine Mind.

These things they did. And as ministering servants, they sought to quicken the action of all three by awakening the soul's inherent devotion to the Divine Mother—she, the personification of the sacred fire, the white fire core at the heart of Matter creation—she,

*Acts 2:3.

the ascension currents, the vital force enshrined in the body temples of her sons and daughters, and everywhere in Nature the energy of purity that reignites the Trinity in the hearts of mankind.

The Torch of the Goddess of Liberty

Your threefold flame is, in fact, the flame of Cosmic Liberty enshrined in the heart of the Goddess of Liberty, the beloved Mother of earth's exiles, who with Saint Germain sponsors the Keepers of the Flame Fraternity. Her statue in New York Harbor is a reminder to the Children of the Sun of their ancient heritage and vow to bear the torch of illumined God Self-government to the peoples of earth.

This knowledge Saint Germain sealed in the hearts of the Light-bearers who had served with him in a golden-age civilization that existed more than 50,000 years ago in a fertile land where the Sahara Desert now is. This age of enlightenment, peace, plenty, and advanced technology declined when the majority of the people turned their attention from the acknowledgment of the God within to the selfish pursuit of sensual pleasure—and squandered the sacred fire.

But the faithful who had glorified God in their hearts and in their civilization were given a special protection unto the day when the opportunity to restore the Lost Word and the Lost Teaching would again be theirs. That day has dawned. For this once mighty people have reincarnated on American soil, called by Saint Germain from many nations to return to the Law of the One and rebuild the golden age. One and all—both the Lightbearers who had illumined the subsequent dark ages and the many 'children' who had turned from the Light and the Central Sun of Being—are called to raise on high the torch of Mother Liberty, that earth's evolutions and the youth of the world might survive a perilous night oncoming whose harbingers are the Four Horsemen.*

"Hold Fast What Thou Hast Received"

Your heart flame, then, is the Life and Truth and Love of an ancient mission whose hour of fulfillment is come!

A sacred fire kindled on heaven's altars and enshrined by the Cosmic Christ upon the altar of your heart, it is not native to the material plane. Anchored in time and space in an interval that is called the "secret chamber of the heart," the threefold flame is God's

*Rev. 6:2–8.

votive Light on earth. Because of mankind's ignorance of the Law and their neglect to tend the flame by love, angels of the Lord of the World have tended it for the salvation of your soul since the coming of Sanat Kumara aeons ago.

You see, someone on earth must keep the flame. It is not enough that it is kept in heaven. In order to be permanently retained—in order for it to be expanded unto *your own* God Self-awareness—the flame as the hallowed Presence of God within you must be daily acknowledged and adored *by you.* Through prayer, meditation, and the giving of divine decrees in the name of the beloved I AM Presence, you can expand the flame to magnify the LORD on earth as in heaven—and do for yourself what the Father intended you to do from the beginning and what holy angels have done in your stead for so long.

This, of course, is your free will to do or not to do. For God so loved you that he sent you forth on a journey into this "far country" to be a keeper of his flame of Life on behalf of millions who to this day remain unquickened by the God flame. Wherefore, in so doing he gave you the freedom to make this calling and election sure, and ultimately to choose to be or not to be—by exercising the power of the God flame.

And so, beloved, know that your application of the sacred fire in communion with the Father-Mother God and the practice of the science of the spoken Word will increase God Self-awareness in yourself and in all mankind; for the flame is God's will to be in you: it is consciousness, intelligence, intuition, love, understanding, and power. All attributes of your Real Self come forth from the flame, for the flame is the divine spark of the Word, the Logos, without whom was not any thing made that was made.*

All of this you must now make your own by the soul's active assent (ascent) to her divinity. Yes, it is your birthright as a joint-heir with Jesus Christ† to take part in the glorious ritual and attainment of God-realization—for though the Father sends many helpers along the way, the final work of salvation—*soul-elevation*—must truly be your own.‡

Now, beloved, is the accepted time for you to confirm God's will to be in your life—by your soul's own free will to be His instrument on earth.

To give you the knowledge of techniques for your self-mastery in and through the God flame, the understanding of the laws

*John 1:1–3. †Rom. 8:17; Gal. 4:7. ‡Phil. 2:12.

governing their use, and the direct tie to the Ascended Masters who sponsor students on this path—once they have acknowledged the inner desiring of the soul to be one with her LORD and to fulfill her divine plan in this life—is the purpose of the Keepers of the Flame Fraternity and Lessons.

"I Am My Brother's Keeper"

To be a Keeper of the Flame, then, is to live to preserve and uphold the sacredness of Life in all—beginning with oneself. It is the great calling of Jesus, who said:

> . . .Whosoever will be great among you, shall be your minister:
> And whosoever of you will be the chiefest, shall be servant of all.
> For even the Son of man came not to be ministered unto, but to minister, and to give his life a ransom for many.*

When men cease to be their brother's keeper, no longer serving to set life free, they cease to keep the flame. The consequence for the total disregard for the sacredness of Life is total cataclysm—of body, mind, and soul. Upon such neglect continents have sunk, worlds and lives have been destroyed.

Indeed, the karma of neglect, as a sword of Damocles, hangs over the nations and our planetary home today. It can be turned back only by those in embodiment who, in gratitude for a grace extended to mankind for tens of thousands of years, are willing in the urgency of the hour to receive with joy the LORD's calling to be a Keeper of the Flame of Life on earth.

For the Law has come full circle. Sanat Kumara and his Keepers of the Flame have paid the price many times over for an ungrateful humanity. The day of the LORD's reckoning is at hand:† All who have received the grace of the Ancient of Days through the Lord and Saviour Jesus Christ and other servant-Sons sent from God must now pay the price, not only for their own salvation but for the many who for too long have taken for granted the intercession of the heavenly hosts as well as the Lightbearers in their midst.

In this day and age men and women dare not ask, as did Cain, "Am I my brother's keeper?" but rather, when given the opportunity to account for sentient life, "How can I keep the flame of Life

*Mark 10:43–45. †Isa. 2:12; 13:6, 9; 61:2; Joel 2:1, 31, 32; Zeph. 1:7–9, 14.

KEEPER OF THE FLAME   *Nicholas Roerich*

for a planet and a people?" Jesus and Gautama and the avatars and saints of the ages have one and all laid down their lives for their friends. They are the true Keepers of the Flame. They have carried the torch and passed it hand to hand, heart to heart through the ages, that you and I might take it again to master Life's sacred energies for the healing of the nations, one day to take our place with the immortals.

Some who read and run are already Keepers of the Flame and have been for many lifetimes. Their affiliation with this branch of the Great White Brotherhood therefore confirms their soul's election even as it strengthens the inner and outer ties of a world body of co-servers in an indissoluble union for the victory of Light, Freedom and World Peace.

The Great White Brotherhood

And so, the immortals are those who have kept the flame and then become one with the flame in the ritual of the ascension. This is the same flaming presence of God that appeared to Moses, that Zarathustra adored, the same whirlwind which took Elijah and which as "a cloud" received Jesus from Bethany's hill.

All who have similarly merged with the flame through obedience to the inner law of their own God-free being, through the sacrifice of the lesser self unto the Greater Self, have, following their final earthly embodiment, taken their place among the hosts of the LORD. Because they have mastered time and space and accelerated, or stepped up, their vibration to the plane of the I AM Presence, they are called "Ascended" Masters. They, too, are keeping the flame for mankind. Together with their unascended disciples (*chelas*), they comprise the eternal order known as the Great White Brotherhood.

Dedicated to the salvation of the children of the Light through the World Teachers, its members Above and here below are marked by the white light of their auras. They are "purified and made white"* by the eternal Logos into whose I AM Presence they have ascended or are ascending. Regardless of race, creed, religion, or national origin, all children of God can walk the same path of initiation which the Ascended Masters and their disciples have walked: They, too, can ascend into the Presence of the living God—the Mighty I AM Presence—and become a part of the heavenly hosts.

*Dan. 12:10.

The Keepers of the Flame Fraternity
Founded by Saint Germain

Down through the ages, members of the Great White Brotherhood have come forth to sponsor uplift movements and to assist the lifewaves of earth in every aspect of their evolution. Great artists, inventors, scientists, statesmen, and religious leaders—as well as the pure in heart from every walk of life—have been overshadowed by various members of this spiritual hierarchy as they formed the avant-garde of achievement in their fields of service.

In this century, Saint Germain—patron of the United States of America and hierarch of the Aquarian age—stepped forth once again to sponsor an outer activity of the Great White Brotherhood. In the early 1960s he contacted his embodied representative the Messenger Mark L. Prophet and founded the Keepers of the Flame Fraternity in memory of the Ancient of Days and his first pupil, Lord Gautama— and the second, Lord Maitreya.

His purpose was to quicken all who had originally come to earth with Sanat Kumara—to restore the memory of their ancient vow and reason for being on earth today: to serve as world teachers and ministering servants in their families, communities and nations at this critical hour of the turning of cycles. Thus, Saint Germain recalled the original Keepers of the Flame to hearken to the voice of the Ancient of Days and to answer the call to reconsecrate their lives to the rekindling of the flame of Life and the sacred fires of freedom in the souls of God's people. We quote from the letter which he dictated to his students on the occasion of the inauguration of the activity:

Beloved Friends of Freedom,

The requirements of the hour are constancy, harmony, and loyalty. For centuries men have tasted of the treasures of heaven; and for an equal time they have debated, delayed, and strained at the proper use of those same treasures. The heaven that might have manifested long ago upon earth has been delayed solely by man, and through no fault of the Father, whose kingdom is still in the process of coming. Today the cosmic wheel has turned almost to the point of no return, and it is imperative for all mankind that the necessary unity and other divine qualities be forthcoming with expediency.

THE ASCENDED MASTER EL MORYA

In this hour of great testing and decision, I say there is no peril so great as that of impeding or stopping the progress of activities sponsored by the Ascended Masters. As long as there are men and women of faith and goodwill who will lovingly band together with almost fierce loyalty under the Father's aegis and our right hand of fellowship, we will continue to provide the assistance from our level that is so necessary in carrying out upon earth the cosmic-purposed actions that fan the fires of freedom and keep aloft the torch of God-liberty.

Recently the Darjeeling Council, through the beloved Ascended Master El Morya, your friend and mine, made known the formation of a spiritual fraternity to be composed of dedicated men and women who are willing to put their shoulders, minds, and hearts to the wheel of sponsorship in the coordination of the manifold activities under our direction. This voluntary group of the faithful is destined, if they will accept it, to be a part of the selective focus from which shall be drawn the permanent focus of beloved Morya's diamond heart (dedicated to the will of God) in the outer world of form. Now I am honored to acknowledge the first tangible gleams from the hearts of those blessed ones who have accepted with dignity and joy the real privilege of becoming Keepers of the Flame.

The purpose is clear: the fusion of fiery spirits ascended with souls on earth in a unifying action for and on behalf of the salvation of the children of the Light in this age.

For those aspiring to serve with members of the heavenly hierarchy, the Keepers of the Flame Fraternity provides the counterpart here below to the Great White Brotherhood Above. Keepers of the Flame pledge their support to the Ascended Master Saint Germain to assist him in the publication and distribution of the true Teachings of Jesus Christ as these have been delivered to mankind through the prophets, world teachers, messengers and avatars that have walked the earth on every continent for tens of thousands of years as emissaries of Sanat Kumara.

As Keepers of the Flame give their support to Saint Germain as the Lord of the Seventh Ray and the Seventh Age, he in turn sponsors their personal path of initiation, releasing instruction in cosmic law which, when applied, leads to self-mastery. The Keepers of the Flame Lessons, supplemented by the Pearls of Wisdom and other published discourses, set forth the Teachings of the Ascended Masters that enable the devotee to make the transition in consciousness from any religion or no religion to self-conscious awareness in God and to a true understanding of the laws of God affecting his life and world.

Initiations for Keepers of the Flame

Initiation is the only means whereby the Master can determine whether his disciple is ready to receive greater Light, greater Knowledge, greater Responsibility. Initiation is the testing of the soul according to a definite, predetermined course that is known as *the Path*. Some justify their system by saying there are "many paths." There may be many lesser paths, but there is only one Path that leads to the summit of Life, the I AM Presence. All other paths, as tributaries, must ultimately merge with the one Path which is the crystal river of the water of Life that leads to the source of Being.

Those who desire to enter into a true Guru-chela relationship with a living Master should understand that the Ascended Masters are the true Teachers of all ages ordained by God through the Ancient of Days as his emissaries. They have come to earth's evolutions in their hour of tribulation to teach them how to return to the innocence of Eden, how to solve the problems of their ecology and their economy and lay the foundations of a golden age at every level of consciousness.

Those who see clearly the need to make the commitment to their own Real Self and to the Path that leads to the soul's liberation will also see that only those who have walked the Path as Keepers of the Flame of Life, only those who have fought the good fight and gained the victory over the "beast"* of the lower self and the forces of Death and Hell are truly qualified to teach mankind the way. This the Ascended Masters have done. This they are supremely qualified to teach you to do. For they are empowered by God as his servant-Sons to take you where unascended teachers or so-called spirit guides cannot go—to the octaves of Light and etheric retreats of the Great White Brotherhood.

When the pupil is ready for this commitment to the path of eternal Life (having seen the futility of false theology in mainline religions or of false gurus' cults of idolatry or of such traps as psychic dictations from ego-centered Atlantean discarnates), then the Ascended Master appears—with his commitment to the pupil. This is the meaning of hierarchy, whose logical function and highest expression is sealed in the Guru-chela relationship originally sponsored by Sanat Kumara.

This is the purpose of the Keepers of the Flame Fraternity—to provide the open door whereby the Ascended Masters may contact

*Rev. 15:2; 17:8, 11.

Jesus Christ and Saint Germain
Wayshowers of the Aquarian Age

The Ascended Masters Jesus Christ and Saint Germain, passing the torch of the Christ consciousness and the I AM THAT I AM for the Piscean and Aquarian dispensations, stand in the long history of the earth and her evolutions as the great deliverers of nations and peoples by the sacred fire of freedom and the salvation of the soul through the path of the ascension. This is the path of initiation that leads to the soul's reunion with the I AM Presence through the mediator, the Christ Self—the open door of the eternal Christos which no man can shut—personified in the Christ flame of the Piscean Master Jesus. It is the path of initiation by the baptism of the sacred fire of the Holy Ghost revealed through the God consciousness of the Aquarian Master Saint Germain as he delivers to the people of God the dispensation of the seventh age and the Seventh Ray—the violet flame and its invocation through Father, Son, and Holy Spirit.

Saint Germain is the seventh angel prophesied in Revelation 10:7 who comes to sponsor the finishing of the mystery of God "as he hath declared to his servants the prophets." Saint Germain brings to the lost sheep of the house of Israel the remembrance of the name of the LORD God—I AM THAT I AM.* This Ascended Master, who was embodied as the prophet Samuel, calls the Twelve Tribes from the four corners of the earth and makes known to them their true identity as the Lightbearers commissioned to serve with the Ancient of Days to set the captives free by the Christ Self, their own Real Self—the Word that was the true Light which lighteth every man that cometh into the world.

Beloved Jesus Christ and Saint Germain, together with all of the heavenly hosts, Ascended Masters, Elohim, and Archangels—the entire Spirit of the Great White Brotherhood—have come forth in this moment of the turning of the cycles of Pisces and Aquarius to teach us how to call upon the name of the LORD in order that we may overcome the "dragon," the personification of evil, the *e-veil,* or *energy veil,* referred to in the scriptures as the carnal mind, the Devil, the Evil One, the Adversary, Lucifer, Satan, etc.

This great overcoming of the forces of Darkness by the Lightbearers was prophesied by Jesus Christ to his disciple John as he wrote in the Book of Revelation: and they overcame him "by the blood of the Lamb, and by the word of their testimony." The blood of the Lamb is the essence, or "Spirit," of Christ, which is his Teaching withheld from the people for thousands of years by 'false Christs'

*Exod. 3:13, 14.

THE ASCENDED MASTER JESUS CHRIST

THE ASCENDED MASTER SAINT GERMAIN

and 'false prophets', now brought forth once again by the Ascended Masters and their Messengers. The "word of their testimony" is the science of the spoken Word whereby through prayer, meditation, dynamic decrees, and communion with the LORD, his sons and daughters become the instrument of his Word as the fiat of the Logos.

Thus the knowledge of the true Teaching of Christ—brought to our remembrance, as Jesus promised, by the Holy Spirit in the person of the Ascended Masters as they release their dictations to the Messengers—combined with the decrees of the LORD spoken through the Ascended Masters and their unascended disciples, are the means whereby the Lightbearers overcome the world tyranny of the fallen angels in this and every century. This Great Overcoming following the "Great Tribulation" is decreed by Almighty God, as is the coming of the Ascended Masters, their Messengers, and their disciples. It is the teaching and the mission of the Ascended Masters Jesus Christ and Saint Germain that we must make every decree of the LORD our own and then stand fast to behold the salvation of our God.

As the deliverer of both Jew and Christian from the leaven (false doctrine) of the Pharisees, ancient and modern, Jesus Christ and Saint Germain proclaim the Messiah already come in the threefold flame of each one's heart and in Jesus, who as the Son of God came to teach us the way of the Christ, personified not in himself alone but in every son and daughter of God. Thus, in truth and in the true science of the religion he taught, all mankind can and shall declare with the blessed Sons of God, "I AM the Way, the Truth, and the Life" and understand that it is the I AM THAT I AM, the LORD our God, dwelling in our own temple who is, was, and forevermore shall be this Way, this Truth, and this Life.

These blessed Ascended Masters are the intimate friends, guides, teachers, counselors, and comforters on the way of Life, walking hand in hand with the Lightbearers in this age. All who will call upon them in the name of the I AM THAT I AM will be blessed with an immediate manifestation of their Electronic Presence—the fullness of their tangible Light body focalized in time and space within the aura of their disciple. The devotee may visualize himself with his right hand in the hand of Jesus and his left hand in the hand of Saint Germain. Calling upon these great wayshowers of the Twelve Tribes of Israel, devotees of Truth may know with the certainty of cosmic law, whereby the call does compel the answer, that these Ascended Masters will never leave him as long as he remains obedient to the principles and practice of Truth, Life, and Love, to the Law of the One, and to the inner God flame, the I AM THAT I AM.

their embodied chelas and the chelas may contact their true Teachers. Once the commitment is made and the contact is established, initiation commences. The student's earnest study and self-mastery of the Teachings, skipping no steps along the way—however advanced he may believe his spiritual attainment to be—is the sign of humility that to the pure in heart unlocks the mysteries contained even in the most basic instruction.

In addition to receiving graded lessons dictated by the Masters to the Messengers Mark and Elizabeth Prophet, the chela is taken in his soul consciousness (out of the body during sleep) to the aforementioned etheric retreats of the Brotherhood, there to receive special training under the Seven *Chohans* (Lords) of the Rays, who make up the spiritual governing board of the Keepers of the Flame Fraternity. As the disciple applies himself earnestly to every precept set forth in the lessons and other privileged communications, Lord Maitreya, the Great Initiator and Representative of the Cosmic Christ, gives to him the same initiations which were given to Jesus Christ, Mary the Mother, John the Beloved, and all who have ever overcome the world.

Step by step, the disciple is prepared for his soul's testings on the Path. These are sometimes given to him when least expected through family and friends. Whatever his environment, the disciple finds that the Master is acting either directly or indirectly through his associates to test his mastery of the law of harmony and his correct use of the Godly attributes of Power, Wisdom, and Love. And ultimately the testing is to see whether or not the chela is willing to make the required sacrifices concerning the lesser self that are necessary in order for him to receive the mantle of the Greater Self, his own beloved I AM Presence, as well as that of the Master.

Keepers of the Flame Lessons

In the Keepers of the Flame Lessons, the Ascended Masters have carefully set forth the true Teachings of the Divine Mother brought to earth by Sanat Kumara and taught by Jesus Christ, the prophets of Israel, Gautama Buddha and Lord Maitreya. Some of these Teachings have been held for mankind for thousands of years in the archives of the retreats of the Great White Brotherhood, waiting to be delivered to committed hearts. Many were originally brought forth in the power of the spoken Word by messengers of hierarchy. However, their disciples did not always record their words; and when they did, the written record was often lost or destroyed. In other cases, and this is frequently true in the sacred scriptures of the world, the record is incomplete because the Law itself demanded silence, for the mysteries could only be transmitted heart to heart by the Master to his disciple.

Whether by ignorance or malice or the constraints of the Path, some of the greatest Teachings, and indeed the Teachings that are key to the individualization of the God flame, have been omitted. It is these keys which the Ascended Masters give to their chelas as they prove they will use them wisely for unselfish and constructive purposes only. These are the keys to that self-mastery to which every form of self-idolatry must give way. Above all, the key to be treasured is the identification of the Real Self as God, which dispels the doctrine of the synthetic self wherever it appears.

In a Pearl of Wisdom in which he addressed himself to the subject of the Keepers of the Flame Fraternity, Saint Germain made the following statement concerning the Keepers of the Flame Lessons:

> In this day and age we have entrusted the Teachings to no one man, but we have given finite portions of the Infinite, segments of Reality, to the planet as cosmic cipher which the heart, when purified, can readily decipher. In the Pearls of Wisdom, the Keepers of the Flame Lessons, and other releases which comprise the Teachings of The Summit Lighthouse, we have sought to integrate the wholeness of all genuine uplift movements that have ever existed on earth.
>
> Ours is the intent, as God wills it—if man wills it, too, and serves with God—to elucidate through the Keepers of the Flame Lessons such standards of elder beauty as have never before been known and experienced upon this planet. The day will come when those souls who are privileged to receive these communications will esteem them as the golden illumined light of the hand of heaven reaching into the individual heart and saying, "Know God, know thyself, know the law of thy Being."
>
> As never before, we hope to open the ancient books—even the books of the Ancient of Days—to reveal that which has been kept secret since the foundation of the world. . . .
>
> There is so much that is hidden, waiting to be revealed, that we can scarcely contain ourselves as we work under higher guidance to raise the consciousness of the aspirant

toward the Light and away from the shadows that life has sought to impose upon him. . . .

The sunlight of God's love is the sunlight of God's freedom. Into the dimensionless, limitless world of the Spirit man must come, bearing in his hand the cup of his desire for God's wonderful revelation, for God's wonderful work to be made known unto him.

Justifying the trust of the Keeper of the Flame in the Ascended Masters, the lessons deal with a practical understanding of the law of karma and reembodiment, of the transmutation—through invocation of the violet flame—of the misqualified energies of this and all previous lives. And they set forth the instruction whereby, through earnest application and selfless, obedient service to God and his fellow man, the disciple may move toward the goal of the ascension at the conclusion of either this embodiment or the next. Thus, the necessary balancing of karma and fulfilling of the divine plan through one's special service to life, called the sacred labor, is clearly outlined by the Masters. The Path is plain, their guidance unerring, their presence unfailing. But the responsibility rests with the individual to prove it every day.

Privileges of Keepers of the Flame

In addition to receiving Keepers of the Flame Lessons and enjoying an intimate relationship with the Ascended Masters and their Messengers, Keepers of the Flame are invited to attend special sessions at quarterly conferences and weekend seminars. At these meetings, instruction by the Messengers Mark and Elizabeth Prophet is given, as well as dictations from the Ascended Masters on current world problems and their solutions.

Church Universal and Triumphant Community Teaching Centers and Summit Lighthouse Study Groups throughout the world are authorized to hold Keepers of the Flame meetings several times a week open only to members in good standing. These services include a Sunday morning ritual with dictations by the Ascended Masters and sermons and lectures by the Messengers, a Saturday morning Kuan Yin service, a Saturday evening Saint Germain service, a Friday evening ascension service, and a weeknight service for the youth of the world. Here decree sessions and prayer vigils are held and the taped dictations (audio and video) of the Ascended Masters are played.

THE ASCENDED MASTER KUTHUMI

Membership in the Keepers of the Flame Fraternity is a prerequisite to attendance at Summit University. The curriculum includes a full program of courses in Ascended Master law given in a twelve-week retreat setting. It is an in-depth study of basic, intermediate, and advanced instruction, combined with in-class training and initiation under Serapis Bey, Hierarch of the Ascension Temple, the Maha Chohan, Representative of the Holy Spirit, and Lord

Maitreya. Here Gautama Buddha and the World Teachers, Jesus and Kuthumi, preside and release the Teachings of the Ascended Masters through Elizabeth Clare Prophet, who holds the office of Mother of the Flame.

Those desiring advanced initiations on the Path may apply to become communicants of Church Universal and Triumphant. It is not necessary to be a church member to be a member of the fraternity. A Keeper of the Flame may retain his affiliation with any church or group whose beliefs and practices are consistent with the laws of God.

The Giving and Receiving of the Master and His Disciples

The Keepers of the Flame Fraternity is the giving and receiving of the Master and his disciples. As the Master freely gives his cosmic momentum as a mantle of light to his disciples to hasten the day of their soul's liberation, to shorten the days of tribulation (karma) for the sake of the elect, so the disciple offers unto the Master devotion to the flame, a life of service to the world community, and a determination to purify the self—his soul, his chakras, and his four lower bodies—as a crystal chalice for the Master's work on earth. Thus, the Master blesses the chela as his instrument. And through his chela the Master reaches out to those souls who will receive him, offering a cup of living water that they, having drunk of the true Teachings, may never thirst again.

To sponsor the worldwide outreach of Saint Germain, Keepers of the Flame pledge to the fraternity monthly dues which may be sent yearly or quarterly. These are used to publish the Keepers of the Flame Lessons and to promote the expansion of the Teachings through the weekly Pearls of Wisdom, other publications, and outreach through the Messenger's worldwide lecture tours. Over the years, dues, tithes and contributions of Keepers of the Flame have enabled the activity to maintain its international headquarters at Camelot in Malibu, California—including Summit University and Montessori International (meeting the needs of children pre-school through grade 12)—and to establish and maintain their Inner Retreat at the Royal Teton Ranch, a 33,000-acre self-sufficient spiritual community-in-the-making in southwest Montana, and Community Teaching Centers and Study Groups throughout the United States and the world.

The Story of the Two Witnesses

In every age the Brotherhood has sponsored twin flames, Messengers of the Word incarnate, who witness to the cycles of Alpha and Omega, the beginning and the ending, the Father-Mother God. Those who serve in the office of the "Two Witnesses" write down the law of the Manus, the guardians of the race and sponsors of each 2,000-year dispensation. They sound the warning of the conspiracy of the seed of the wicked and of the returning karma of the chosen people who have failed to come out from among them (the fallen ones) and be a separate people. They are the prophets of the LORD who stand as the representatives of the World Teachers to the chosen people and to the multitudes. Those who are chosen are those who choose to listen and to identify with the flame of that which *Is real* and to be initiates of the Brotherhood even while they are instruments of the LORD.

God has never left mankind without emissaries of his Word. They have often gone unrecognized, unheeded, and civilization and karma have taken their course. More often they have been "despised and rejected of men." But they have always been present—some known, some unknown.

The training of the Messenger takes place over thousands of years of the soul's incarnations on earth. It is something acquired not through human effort but through illumined, loving obedience to the law of the Inner Self and the word of the Teacher. The conclusion of the training is the gift of prophecy and more; it is the bestowal of the mantle of the Great White Brotherhood and the empowerment of the Word by the Holy Spirit. It is a commission from the Brotherhood, a divine ordination—and a dispensation, or grant, of energy and sponsorship to carry on the activities specifically accorded to their office in hierarchy.

Mark and Elizabeth Prophet received the anointing from Saint Germain, the Knight Commander of the Keepers of the Flame Fraternity, to wear the mantle of the prophets of Israel and to occupy in these latter days the office of the Two Witnesses, Messenger of the Great White Brotherhood. Summoned by their Guru, the Ascended Master El Morya, they were called by the LORD God of Israel in the same voice of the I AM THAT I AM that spoke to Moses out of the burning bush, saying, "Let my people go!" They were called together to stand "before the God of the Earth," Lord Gautama Buddha, and to prophesy "a thousand two hundred and threescore days." This empowering of their twin flames, "the two olive trees and the two candlesticks," was foretold by Jesus Christ in the eleventh

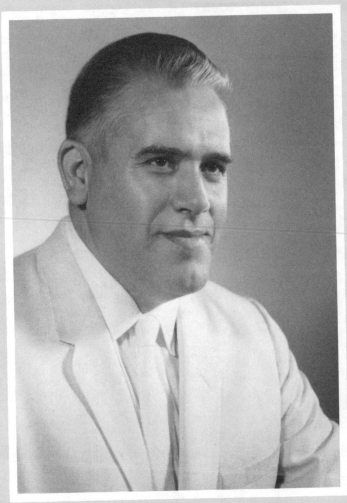

THE MESSENGER MARK L. PROPHET

THE MESSENGER ELIZABETH CLARE PROPHET

chapter of his Revelation to Saint John the Divine, a dictation "sent and signified" by his angel.

The Messenger is the one whom Malachi declared would be sent to "prepare the way before me," i.e., the way of the Lord—the Christ Self—who "shall suddenly come to his temple." The Messenger assists the children of God to make contact with the Christ Self so that the Christ Self can release to the soul the Teachings of the I AM Presence and the Ascended Masters. Hence, the Messenger stands representing the Christ Self until there is no longer any need for the Messenger, and all who have come forth from God once again behold the I AM Presence and their true Teachers, the Ascended Masters, face to face.

The dispensation of prophets and messengers is an intermediary dispensation. It is for that period when God's children, because of their disobedience, no longer hear the voice of God directly as they once did in earth's early golden ages and in the Garden of Eden. Ultimately every man, woman, and child will sit under his own vine and fig tree, as Micah said. The vine is the Christ and the emanation of the Word through the crystal cord; the fig tree is the I AM Presence and causal body—your own Tree of Life. And you are intended to commune with the entire Spirit of the Great White Brotherhood as you sit in meditation under your own vine and fig tree. That 'Spirit' is actually the cumulative momentum of the Holy Spirit. The testimony of the LORD through this witnessing Spirit is available to all who make contact with the hierarchy of the Ascended Masters, Elohim, Archangels, and the hosts of the LORD through their own Christ Self and the embodied Messenger.

On February 26, 1973, the soul of Mark Prophet made the transition from the planes of time and space and ascended into the sphere of the I AM Presence. Known as the Ascended Master Lanello, he is carrying on his sacred labor with the Ascended Masters as they make contact with their unascended chelas. And so the Messengers, the "other two, the one on this side of the bank of the river and the other on that side of the bank of the river," as Daniel described his vision of their service, remain the servants of the LORD and of his children in Spirit and in Matter.

Elizabeth Clare Prophet, serving as Mother of the Flame and representative of the World Mother, continues to call "the lost sheep of the house of Israel" to the Coming Revolution in Higher Consciousness. These are the Lightbearers of the ages East and West who came to earth with the Ancient of Days and are coming together to experience God in the Great Synthesis of the Mother Flame.

A Pledge from the Knight Commander

To Those Who Seek Initiation on the Path:

To be a Keeper of the Flame is to be a torchbearer of the age. To be a Keeper of the Flame is to run with the fires of the resurrection, that all life might be regenerated in the flame of Reality.

The crumbling of the old order and the building of the new take place simultaneously. Some identify with the downward spiral and some with the upward spiral. Keepers of the Flame recognize that this is a time for the gathering of the sheaves of consciousness. This is a time when men must reap the sowings of the past. This is a time when the foundation of a golden age must be built.

The crosscurrents of world karma with individual reckoning of the Law of Life must be reconciled with the oncoming tide of cosmic light that spirals from the central sun of a cosmos throughout all galaxies evolving from the center of the Creative Mind. The Great White Brotherhood summons devotees of the Law of Being—those who recognize that this is an hour when souls and worlds are crying out for salvation. This is an hour when those who have the vision to see the end from the beginning must leave their nets and their lesser causes for the one cause that counts—the cause of freedom.

The four sacred freedoms enshrined in the heart of America—freedom of religion, freedom of speech, freedom of the press, and freedom to assemble—are still the bulwarks of liberty secured by sons and daughters of God who saw the wilderness as the place to be prepared for the coming of the Divine Mother and her seed. As we dedicated this land to be the land of opportunity for the proving of Christhood, so now we come to dedicate the human heart as the threshing floor of the Almighty, as the place where the flame of Life must be forged and won by each individual soul desiring to merge with the fountainhead of Life that is God.

Hierarchy stands as the mediator between Creator and creation. Hierarchy comes forth in this age with a special dispensation of light and opportunity, presenting the gift of the sacred Teachings of the ages to all who will respond with the fervor and the joy, the dedication and the self-discipline which are necessary if this planet, this people, and this civilization are to endure beyond the twentieth century.

It is time for men and women mature in judgment, capable in leadership, humble before God, and possessed with a profound

Keepers of the Flame receive through the Mother of the Flame anointing, baptism, teaching, blessings with the Emerald Matrix, initiations, Holy Communion, and the laying on of hands as she serves as the instrument for the healing Christ.

vision of the consequences of mankind's turning from their God, to make the decision to come together in the communion of the flame under the aegis of the Great White Brotherhood to sponsor the revolution of the ages—the revolution of Light, Love, and the Victory of the Flame. Keepers of the Flame and those who would be, accept the challenge! For it is nothing less than the reversing of the tide of sin, disease, and death and the arresting of the spirals of disintegration and decay now outpicturing in the mass consciousness of the world.

This is a time when men and women must face their responsibilities or face the consequences. It is a time to accept the challenge of individual karma, to meet every crisis, personal and planetary, with the determination that the flame of freedom and the fires of the Holy Ghost can and shall consume all error and all misuse of the Law of Life. This is a time to pursue the dharma of a planet and a people with a passionate devotion to the blueprint of Life and to the divine plan for all.

I am come as the Master of the Aquarian age. And I summon lovers of freedom, devotees of the Ascended Masters, and all who are born with a will to bring to fruition the seeds that God has planted within the soul—seeds of virtue and invention, seeds of creativity and individuality, seeds of humility and righteousness. I come to marshall the spirits of those who are already aligned with hierarchy at inner levels and who now come before the altar of the Divine Mother to make their energies count in manifestation in Matter on behalf of the youth and the incoming souls, on behalf of all who have ever lived to defend the flame of freedom.

As I look upon the saints in heaven who form a phalanx of the armies of the LORD, as I look at the souls who have given their lives for the cause of righteousness, I remember the words of the sixteenth president of the United States ". . . that these dead shall not have died in vain." And I say that all who have ever lived for the cause of the Great White Brotherhood shall not have lived in vain. I pledge my all, my causal body, my entire momentum of freedom, for the victory of the sons and daughters of God in this age. And I summon, with the love of my heart, all who will give their all to that cause.

"Come now, and let us reason together, saith the LORD." Let us join together in a fraternity of Lightbearers "as Above, so below"—one with the Masters ascended, one with the chelas unascended—to forge a union of the Spirit that shall not be broken, a union that will drive back the astral hordes and secure this planet for the Light for all time and space. And I say, if you are willing, sons and daughters of Liberty, we can still win in the fight for freedom and for the ascension in the Light of every soul, and bring forth an age of peace and enlightenment for all. Let us find strength in our Union. Let us win by the conviction of our souls and the merging of the souls of all in the fire of the I AM Presence.

In memory of all who have overcome the world, all who have set their feet on the path of initiation, I, Saint Germain, stand in this age to receive the Lightbearers as my own.

Will you receive me as your own?

I AM and I remain the Knight Commander of the Keepers of the Flame,

Saint Germain

You who would keep the flame of Life are encouraged to make your vote count for Saint Germain and for world freedom—as a votive flame. The flame in the heart of the Keeper of the Flame is the sign of his vigil for Life, for Light, for Liberty and Victory to all.

For more information on the Fraternity, membership policies, and how to apply, write Box A, Malibu, CA 90265. After February 15, 1987, Box A, Livingston, MT 59047.

THE KEEPER OF THE FLAME

YOUR DIVINE SELF

Chart of Your Divine Self

There are three figures represented in the Chart, which we will refer to as the upper figure, the middle figure, and the lower figure.

The upper figure is the I AM Presence, the I AM THAT I AM, the individualization of God's presence for every son and daughter of the Most High.

The Divine Monad consists of the I AM Presence surrounded by the spheres (color rings) of light which comprise the causal body. This is the body of First Cause that contains within it man's "treasure laid up in heaven"—words and works, thoughts and feelings of virtue, attainment, and light—pure energies of love that have risen from the plane of action in time and space as the result of man's judicious exercise of free will and his harmonious qualification of the stream of life that issues forth from the heart of the Presence and descends to the level of the Christ Self, thence to invigorate and enliven the embodied soul.

The middle figure in the Chart is the Mediator between God and man, called the Holy Christ Self, the Real Self, or the Christ consciousness. It has also been referred to as the Higher Mental Body or one's Higher Consciousness.

This Inner Teacher overshadows the lower self, which consists of the soul evolving through the four planes of Matter using the vehicles of the four lower bodies (the etheric, or memory, body; the mental body; the emotional, or desire, body; and the physical body) to balance karma and fulfill the divine plan.

The three figures of the Chart correspond to the Trinity of Father (the upper figure), Son (the middle figure), and Holy Spirit (the lower figure). The latter is the intended temple of the Holy Spirit, whose sacred fire is indicated in the enfolding violet flame. The lower figure corresponds to you as a disciple on the Path. Your soul is the nonpermanent aspect of being which is made permanent through the ritual of the ascension. The ascension is the process whereby the soul, having balanced her karma and fulfilled her divine plan, merges first with the Christ consciousness and then with the living Presence of the I AM THAT I AM. Once the ascension has taken place, the soul, the nonpermanent aspect of being, becomes the Incorruptible One, a permanent atom in the Body of God. The Chart of Your Divine Self is therefore a diagram of yourself—past, present, and future.

The lower figure represents the son of man or child of the Light evolving beneath his own 'Tree of Life'. This is how you should visualize yourself standing in the violet flame, which you invoke daily in the name of the I AM Presence and your Holy Christ Self in order to purify your four lower bodies in preparation for the ritual of the alchemical marriage—your soul's union with the Beloved, your Holy Christ Self.

The lower figure is surrounded by a tube of light, which is projected from the heart of the I AM Presence in answer to your call. It is a cylinder of white light which sustains a forcefield of protection 24 hours a day, so long as you guard it in harmony. It is also invoked daily with the "Heart, Head, and Hand Decrees" and may be reinforced as needed.

The threefold flame of Life is the divine spark sent from the I AM Presence as the gift of life, consciousness, and free will. It is sealed in the secret chamber of the heart that through the Love, Wisdom and Power of the Godhead anchored therein the soul may fulfill her reason for being in the physical plane. Also called the Christ flame and the liberty flame, or fleur-de-lis, it is the spark of a man's Divinity, his potential for Christhood.

The silver (or crystal) cord is the stream of life, or "lifestream," that descends from the heart of the I AM Presence to the Holy Christ Self to nourish and sustain (through the chakras) the soul and its vehicles of expression in time and space. It is over this 'umbilical' cord that the energy of the Presence flows, entering the being of man at the crown and giving impetus for the pulsation of the threefold flame as well as the physical heartbeat. When a round of the soul's incarnation in Matter-form is finished, the I AM Presence withdraws the silver cord, whereupon the threefold flame returns to the level of the Christ, and the soul clothed in the etheric garment gravitates to the highest level of her attainment where she is schooled between embodiments, until her final incarnation when the great law decrees she shall go out no more.

The dove of the Holy Spirit descending from the heart of the Father is shown just above the head of the Christ. When the son of man puts on and becomes the Christ consciousness as Jesus did, he merges with the Holy Christ Self. The Holy Spirit is upon him and the words of the Father, the beloved I AM Presence, are spoken, "This is my beloved Son in whom I AM well pleased" (Matt. 3:17).

A more detailed explanation of the Chart of Your Divine Self is given in *The Lost Teachings of Jesus* and *Climb the Highest Mountain* by the Prophets.

30

SUMMIT UNIVERSITY
AT THE ROYAL TETON RANCH

An Inner Retreat Experience
at Maitreya's Mystery School
"The Place of Great Encounters"

In every age there have been some, the few, who have pursued an understanding of God and of selfhood that transcends the current traditions of doctrine and dogma. Compelled by a faith that knows the freedom To Be, they have sought to expand their awareness of God by probing and proving the infinite expressions of his Law. Through the true science of religion, they have penetrated the mysteries of both Spirit and Matter and come to experience God as the All-in-all.

Having discovered the key to Reality, these sons and daughters of God have gathered disciples who desired to pursue the disciplines of universal Law and the inner teachings of the mystery schools. Thus Jesus chose his apostles, Bodhidharma his monks, and Pythagoras his initiates at Crotona. Gautama Buddha called his disciples to form the *sangha* (community) and King Arthur summoned his knights of the Round Table to the quest for the Holy Grail.

Summit University is Maitreya's Mystery School for men and women of the twentieth century who are searching for the great synthesis—the gnosis of Truth which the teachings of the Ascended Masters afford. These adepts are counted among the few who have overcome in every age to join the immortals as our elder brothers and sisters on the Path.

Gautama Buddha and Lord Maitreya sponsor Summit University with the World Teachers Jesus and Kuthumi, the Lords of the Seven Rays, the Divine Mother, the beloved Archangels and the

"numberless numbers" of "saints robed in white" who have grad-
uated from earth's schoolroom and are known collectively as the
Great White Brotherhood. To this university of the Spirit they lend
their flame, their counsel and the momentum of their attainment,
even as they fully give the living Teaching to us who would follow in
their footsteps to the Source of that reality which they have become.

   Founded in 1971 under the direction of the Messengers Mark L.
Prophet and Elizabeth Clare Prophet, Summit University holds three
twelve-week retreats each year—fall, winter, and spring quarters—
as well as two-week summer and weekend seminars, and five-day
quarterly conferences. Each course is based on the development of the
threefold flame and the unfoldment of the inner potential of the
Christ, the Buddha, and the Mother flame. Through the teachings of
the Ascended Masters dictated to the Messengers, students at Summit
University pursue the disciplines on the path of the ascension for the
soul's ultimate reunion with the Spirit of the living God.

   This includes the study of the sacred scriptures of East and
West taught by Jesus and Gautama, John the Beloved and other
adepts of the Sacred Heart; exercises in the self-mastery of the

chakras and the aura under Kuthumi and Djwal Kul; beginning and intermediate studies in alchemy under the Ascended Master Saint Germain; the Cosmic Clock—a new-age astrology for charting the cycles of personal psychology, karma, and initiation diagramed by Mother Mary; the science of the spoken Word combining prayer, meditation, dynamic decrees and visualization—all vital keys to the soul's liberation in the Aquarian age.

In addition to weekend services including lectures and dictations from the Masters delivered through the Messengers (in person or on videotape), a midweek healing service—"Be Thou Made Whole!"—is held in the Chapel of the Holy Grail at which the Messenger or ministers offer invocations for the infirm and the healing of the nations. "Watch with Me" Jesus' Vigil of the Hours is also kept with violet-flame decrees for world transmutation.

Students are taught by professionals in the medical and health fields to put into practice some of the lost arts of healing, including prayer and scientific fasting, realignment through balanced nutrition, and natural alternatives to achieve wholeness on a path whose goal is the return to the Law of the One through the soul's

reintegration with the inner blueprint. The psychology of the family, marriage, and meditations for the conception of new-age children are discussed and counseling for service in the world community is available.

Teachings and meditations of the Buddha taught by Lord Gautama, Lord Maitreya, Lanello, and the bodhisattvas of East and West are a highlight of Summit University experience. The violet-flame and bija mantras with those of Buddha and Kuan Yin enhance the raising of the Kundalini under the sponsorship of Saint Germain. Classes in Hatha Yoga convene daily, while spiritual initiations as a transfer of Light from the Ascended Masters through the Messengers are given to each student at healing services and at the conclusion of the quarter.

Summit University is a twelve-week spiral that begins with you as self-awareness and ends with you as God Self-awareness. As you traverse the spiral, light intensifies, darkness is transmuted. Energies are aligned, chakras are cleared, and the soul is poised for the victorious fulfillment of the individual divine plan. And you are experiencing the rebirth day by day as, in the words of the apostle Paul, you "put off the old man" being "renewed in the spirit of your mind" and "put on the new man which after God is created in righteousness and true holiness." (Eph. 4:22–24)

In addition to preparing the student to enter into the Guru/chela relationship with the Ascended Masters and the path of initiation outlined in their retreats, the academic standards of Summit University, with emphasis on the basic skills of both oral and written communication, prepare students to enroll in undergraduate and graduate programs in accredited schools and to pursue careers as constructive members of the international community. A high school diploma (or its equivalent) is required, a working knowledge of the English language, and a willingness to become the disciplined one—the disciple of the Great God Self of all.

Summit University is a college of religion, science and culture, qualifying students of any religious affiliation to deliver the Lost Teachings of Jesus and his prophecy for these troubled times. Advanced levels prepare students for ordination as ministers (ministering servants) in Church Universal and Triumphant. Taking its sponsorship and authority from the Holy Spirit, the saints and God's calling upon the Messengers, Summit University has neither sought nor received regional or national accreditation.

Summit University is a way of life that is an integral part of Camelot—an Aquarian-age community located in the Paradise Valley on the 33,000-acre Royal Teton Ranch in southwest Montana adjacent to Yellowstone Park. Here ancient truths become the joy of everyday living in a circle of fellowship of kindred souls drawn together for the fulfillment of their mission in the Universal Christ through the oneness of the Holy Spirit. The Summit University Service/Study Program offers apprenticeship training in all phases of organic farming and ranching, construction, and related community services as well as publishing—from the spoken to the written Word.

Montessori International is the place prepared at the Royal Teton Ranch for the tutoring of the souls of younger seekers on the Path. A private school for infants through twelfth grade, Montessori International was founded in 1970 by Mark and Elizabeth Prophet. Dedicated to the educational principles set forth by Dr. Maria Montessori, its faculty strives to maintain standards of academic excellence and the true education of the heart for the child's unfoldment of his Inner Self.

For those aspiring to become teachers of children through age seven, Summit University Level II in conjunction with the

Pan-American Montessori Society offers, under the capable direction of Dr. Elisabeth Caspari or her personally trained Master Teachers, an in-depth study of the Montessori method and its application at home and in the classroom. This six-month program includes an examination of one's personal psychology, tracing behavioral characteristics from birth through childhood and adolescence to the present, taking into consideration the sequences of karma and reincarnation as well as hereditary and environmental influences in child development. Following their successful completion of this information course, students may apply for acceptance into the one- or two-year internship programs, which upon graduation lead to teacher certification from the Pan-American Montessori Society.

For information on Summit University and related programs or how to contact the center nearest you for group meetings and study materials, including a library of publications and audio- and videocassettes of the teachings of the Ascended Masters, call or write Camelot at the Royal Teton Ranch, Box A, Livingston, MT 59047 (406) 222-8300.

NOTES

For an alphabetical listing of many of the philosophical and hierarchical terms used in *The Great White Brotherhood,* see the comprehensive glossary, "The Alchemy of the Word: Stones for the Wise Masterbuilders," in *Saint Germain On Alchemy.*

Introduction
1. John 14:12.
2. Deut. 14:2.
3. John 5:17.
4. Exod. 13:21.

Chapter 1
1. Ps. 19:1–4.
2. Exod. 3:2.
3. Exod. 3:13, 14.
4. Jer. 31:33.
5. Matt. 3:3.
6. Jer. 13:23.
7. This song and all other decrees and songs given in this book are contained in *Prayers, Meditations, and Dynamic Decrees for the Coming Revolution in Higher Consciousness,* sections I, II, and III, $2.95 each, and *The Summit Lighthouse Book of Songs,* $8.50.

Chapter 2
1. William Shakespeare, *The Tempest,* act 4, sc. 1, lines 156–57.
2. Mark 4:39.
3. El Morya, *The Chela and the Path,* quality paperback, p. 77, $4.95.
4. Lanello, December 31, 1974, "The Crown of the World Mother for 1975," audiocassette B7509, $6.50, on *New Beginnings in the Flame of the Holy Spirit,* 8-cassette album, A7502, $50.00.
5. Hercules, March 16, 1975, "Scaling the Mountain of Hierarchy," audiocassette B7636, $6.50, on *The Seven Elohim in the Power of the Spoken Word,* 4-cassette album, A7636, $26.00.
6. Ibid.
7. Ibid.

Chapter 3
1. Gen. 1:28.
2. John 8:58.
3. Dan. 7:9.

4. For information on the Keepers of the Flame Fraternity, see Chapter 29.
5. Saint Germain, October 14, 1972, "Won't You Be Free?" audiocassette B7648, $6.50, on *Saint Germain, Chohan of the Seventh Ray,* 2-cassette album, A7648, $12.95.
6. Rev. 2:17.

Chapter 4
1. Gen. 6:5.
2. Gen. 5; Ps. 90:10.
3. *Climb the Highest Mountain,* pp. 276–77, hardback, $21.95; quality paperback, $16.95.
4. James 4:8.
5. Matt. 6:9.
6. Ezek. 20:47.
7. Heb. 12:29.
8. Ezek. 1:4.
9. Ezek. 18:4, 20.
10. Acts 7:48, 17:24.
11. Hab. 1:13.
12. John 1:14.
13. I Cor. 11:24.
14. *The Science of the Spoken Word,* quality paperback, $7.95.
15. Isa. 45:11.
16. John 14:2.
17. I Cor. 15:41.
18. James 4:3.
19. Djwal Kul, *Intermediate Studies of the Human Aura,* quality paperback, p. 16, $7.95.
20. I Cor. 6:19.
21. Isa. 1:18.
22. Rev. 2:11; 20:6, 14; 21:8.
23. Matt. 28:18.
24. See *Climb the Highest Mountain,* p. 33.
25. Luke 22:42.
26. Gal. 6:7.
27. El Morya, *The Chela and the Path.*
28. Luke 3:16.

Chapter 5

1. El Morya, *The Chela and the Path*, p. 122.
2. I Kings 4:25; Mic. 4:4; Zech. 3:10.
3. Gen. 2:9.
4. Acts 2:2.
5. Luke 24:13–35.
6. Manly Palmer Hall, *The Secret Destiny of America* (Los Angeles: Philosophical Research Society, 1944), pp. 136–45.
7. Ps. 8:1, 3, 4.

Chapter 6

1. Matt. 24:30, 31.
2. Rev. 21:16.
3. Jer. 31:33.
4. Exod. 20; John 13:34.

Chapter 7

1. Rev. 1:8.
2. Rev. 4:8.
3. Gen. 1:3.
4. Job 38:7.
5. John 1:14.
6. John 5:30; 14:10; 5:17.
7. Matt. 13:24–30, 36–43.
8. Henry Wadsworth Longfellow, "The Builders," stanza 5.
9. El Morya, *The Chela and the Path*, p. 60.
10. John 3:30.
11. Matt. 25:40.
12. Matt. 10:41.
13. I John 2:18.
14. James 3:11.
15. Matt. 7:15, 20.
16. I John 4:1.
17. Gen. 28:12.
18. Matt. 11:12.
19. Matt. 8:12; 24:51.

Chapter 8

1. Prov. 29:18.
2. Luke 12:3.
3. John 8:32.
4. Matt. 26:41.
5. Rev. 3:11.

Chapter 9

1. El Morya, "The Ownership of God's Will," in *Kuthumi On Selfhood*

(1969 *Pearls of Wisdom*, vol. 12, no. 11), p. 48, $17.95; *The Sacred Adventure*, clothbound, pocket edition, p. 59, $7.95.
2. Matt. 10:8; 25:35; 25:40.
3. El Morya, *A White Paper from the Darjeeling Council Table*, pp. 7–10, $.50.
4. William Jennings Bryan, ed., *The World's Famous Orations*, 10 vols. (New York: Funk and Wagnalls Co., 1906), 8:81.
5. Henry Van Dyke, *The Americanism of Washington* (New York: Harper & Brothers Publishers, 1906), pp. 6–7.
6. Cooper and Fenton, *American Politics*, 1884.
7. Henry Wadsworth Longfellow, "Santa Filomena," stanza 10.
8. Exod. 14:19–22.
9. *Encylopaedia Britannica*, 1963, s.v. "Lincoln, Abraham."
10. Marion Mills Miller, ed., *Life and Works of Abraham Lincoln*, Centenary Edition, 9 vols. (New York: Current Literature Publishing Co., 1907), 3:36.
11. Sister Joan Mary, *Mother Cabrini* (Derby, N.Y.: Daughters of St. Paul, Apostolate of the Press, 1955), p. 63.
12. Harriet Beecher Stowe, *Uncle Tom's Cabin* (New York: Airmont Publishing Co., 1967), pp. 413–14.
13. Percy H. Epler, *The Life of Clara Barton* (New York: Macmillan Co., 1915), pp. 402–3.
14. Matt. 10:28.
15. Ronald W. Clark, *Einstein: The Life and Times* (New York: World Publishing, Times Mirror, 1971), p. 200.
16. Albert Einstein et al., *Living Philosophies* (New York: Simon and Schuster, 1931), p. 6.
17. Matt. 16:25.
18. John 15:13.
19. Bryan, *The World's Famous Orations*, pp. 62–63.
20. Ibid., pp. 66–67.
21. B. F. Tefft, ed., *The Speeches of Daniel Webster, and His Masterpieces* (Philadelphia: Porter and Coates, 1854), p. 349.
22. Ibid., p. 411.

Chapter 10
1. Rev. 13:1, 11.
2. Rev. 19:11.
3. Num. 21:8, 9.
4. John 8:44.
5. Matt. 5:18.

Chapter 11
1. Prov. 29:18.
2. Matt. 25:13.
3. Heb. 12:6.

Chapter 12
1. Matt. 13:24–30.
2. Josh. 24:15.
3. Matt. 25:29.
4. Dan. 7:9.
5. Gen. 6.
6. Gen. 18, 19.
7. Mount Shasta is also the focus of Gabriel the Archangel and his divine complement, the Archeia Hope.
8. Matt. 22:1–14.
9. John 1:5.
10. John 8:32.

Chapter 13
1. Matt. 7:21.

Chapter 14
1. Mary's Scriptural Rosary for the New Age, dictated by Mother Mary to Elizabeth Clare Prophet, is published in the cassette album A8048 and in the book *My Soul Doth Magnify the Lord!* quality paperback, $7.95. *A Child's Rosary to Mother Mary* is published in the 3-cassette albums A7864, A7905, A7934, and A8045, $9.95 each, and *The Fourteenth Rosary: The Mystery of Surrender* in 2-cassette album V7538, $12.95.

Chapter 15
1. John 14:18, 26.
2. William Shakespeare, *Hamlet,* act 3, sc. 1, line 67.
3. Gen. 3:21.
4. *Studies in Alchemy,* quality paperback, $3.95; *Saint Germain On Alchemy,* pocketbook, pp. 1–99, $5.95.
5. Acts 2:3.
6. See *Liberty Proclaims,* dictations by the Goddess of Liberty.
7. Ezek. 20:47.

8. The following paperback books on the Montessori system are available through The Summit Lighthouse: *Maria Montessori: Her Life and Work* by E. M. Standing; *The Secret of Childhood* by Maria Montessori; *The Discovery of the Child* by Maria Montessori; *The Child in the Family* by Maria Montessori; *The Absorbent Mind* by Maria Montessori; and *Childhood Education* by Maria Montessori.
9. Luke 2:49.
10. For further information on the cycles of the moon, see 1976 *Pearls of Wisdom,* vol. 19, IX to XI of Kuthumi's series "An Exposé of False Teachings."

Chapter 18
1. El Morya, *The Chela and the Path,* pp. 59, 60.
2. John 3:8.
3. *Climb the Highest Mountain,* pp. 50–51.

Chapter 19
1. Rev. 13:16, 17.
2. Rev. 2:11; 20:6, 14; 21:8; Isa. 14:12.
3. On April 16, 1975, Lucifer was bound by Archangel Michael and taken to the Court of the Sacred Fire on Sirius, where he stood trial before the Four and Twenty Elders over a period of ten days. The testimony of many souls of light in embodiment on Terra and other planets and systems in the galaxy were heard, together with that of the ascended masters, archangels, and Elohim. On April 26, 1975, he was found guilty of total rebellion against Almighty God by the unanimous vote of the Twenty Four and sentenced to the second death. As he stood on the disc of the sacred fire before the court, the flame of Alpha and Omega rose as a spiral of intense white light, canceling out an identity and a consciousness that had influenced the fall of one third of the angels of the galaxy and countless lifewaves evolving in this and other systems of worlds.
4. Matt. 13:24–30, 36–43.

Chapter 20

1. I John 2:18; Rev. 11–20.
2. Isa. 14:12.
3. Rev. 12:4, 7–9.
4. Rev. 12:12.
5. Gen. 3:3, 4.
6. Rev. 2:11, 20:6, 14; 21:8.
7. Matt. 22:12.
8. Exod. 3:14.
9. Gen. 7:14–16.
10. Rev. 20:12, 13.
11. Rev. 20:14, 15.
12. Rev. 12:10.
13. Rev. 16:14, 16.
14. Rev. 11:3–13.
15. Rev. 12:1.
16. Rev. 12:5.
17. Rev. 22:18, 19.
18. Ezek.; Dan. 7–12.
19. Rev. 13:1, 11.
20. Gal. 5:7.
21. II Tim. 2:15.
22. John 5:17, 30; 14:10.
23. Prov. 4:5–9.
24. Purity and Astrea, May 25, 1975, "Releasing the Light of the Mother within You," audiocassette B7533, $6.50, on *The Buddha and the Mother*, 6-cassette album, A7532, $37.50.
25. John 14:26.
26. Acts 2:2.
27. Matt. 7:20.

Chapter 21

1. Matt. 27:40.

Chapter 23

1. Rev. 13:1, 11.
2. Rev. 21:2.
3. Rev. 12:5.
4. See *Tenets of Church Universal and Triumphant*.

5. See *Vows of Sons and Daughters of the Dominion of the Water Element*.

Chapter 24

1. Luke 12:32.
2. Acts 1:11.
3. Matt. 19:14.
4. Ps. 23:5.
5. Job 19:26.
6. Ps. 19:14.
7. John 12:3–8.

Chapter 25

1. I Pet. 2:5.
2. The vows of the Franciscans and the Poor Clares are poverty, chastity, and obedience; however, in the esoteric sense purity is the flame of Mother Poverty, whom the devotees of this order espouse.

Chapter 26

1. Matt. 13:30.

Chapter 27

1. Heb. 13:2. Although this statement is not attributed to Jesus in the four Gospels, it is believed that the writer of Hebrews was quoting a statement of Jesus that was traditionally ascribed to the Master.
2. John 21:16, 17.
3. I Thess. 5:17.

Chapter 28

1. John 21:15–17.
2. John 5:17.
3. John F. Kennedy, First Inaugural Address.
4. Luke 16:8.
5. John 15:12.
6. John 15:13–21.
7. Luke 24:13–35.
8. Matt. 3:8.
9. Isa. 55:11.

Unless otherwise noted, all publications and audiocassettes are Summit University Press (Box A, Livingston, MT 59047), released under the Messengership of Mark L. Prophet and Elizabeth Clare Prophet. **Postage Rates.** For books $5.95 and under, please add $.50 for the first book, $.25 each additional book; for books $7.95 through $15.95, add $1.00 for the first, $.50 each additional; for books $16.95 and over, add $1.50 for the first, $.75 each additional. For single audiocassettes, please add $.50 for the first cassette and $.30 for up to 4 additional cassettes; for 2- or 3-cassette albums, add $.90 for the first album, $.30 for each additional album; for 4-cassette albums, add $1.15 for the first, $.25 for each additional album; for 6–8 cassette albums, add $1.30 for the first, $1.15 for each additional album.

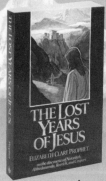
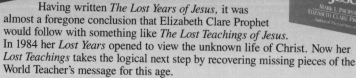

Welcome to the Heart
of the Inner Retreat
where people of every nation
gather to study and apply
the Lost Teachings of Jesus
in a celebration of Life

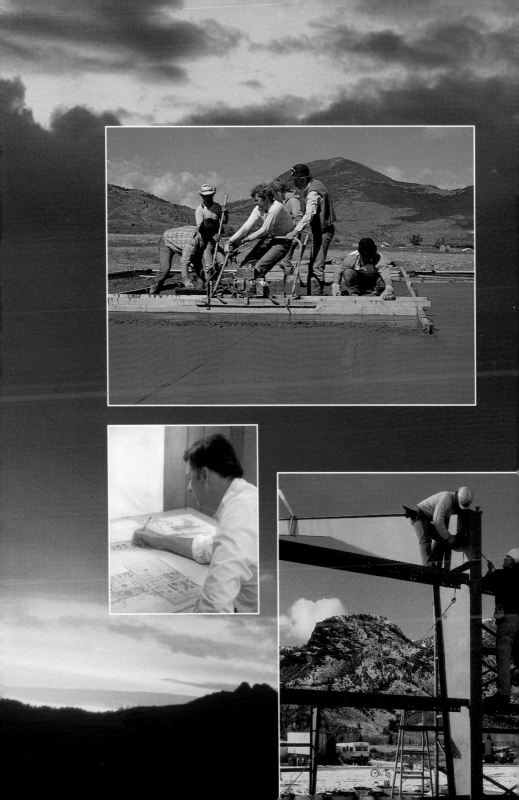

Welcome to the Heart
of the Inner Retreat
The Place of Great Encounters